THE YORK CORPUS CHRISTI PLAY
SELECTED PAGEANTS

THE YORK CORPUS CHRISTI PLAY
SELECTED PAGEANTS

a *Broadview Anthology of Medieval Drama* edition

Contributing Editor,
The York Corpus Christi Play: Selected Pageants
Christina M. Fitzgerald, University of Toledo

Contributing Editor, *The Nativity* and *The Shepherds*: Robert W. Barrett Jr.
Contributing Editor, *The Slaughter of the Innocents*: Jane Tolmie

General Editors,
The Broadview Anthology of Medieval Drama:
Christina M. Fitzgerald, University of Toledo
John T. Sebastian, Loyola Marymount University

broadview press

Broadview Press – www.broadviewpress.com
Peterborough, Ontario, Canada

Founded in 1985, Broadview Press remains a wholly independent publishing house. Broadview's focus is on academic publishing: our titles are accessible to university and college students as well as scholars and general readers. With over 600 titles in print, Broadview has become a leading international publisher in the humanities, with world-wide distribution. Broadview is committed to environmentally responsible publishing and fair business practices.

The interior of this book is printed on 100% recycled paper.

How to cite this book: Broadview Anthology editions are stand-alone volumes presenting material that is also available within the stated anthology. Taken as a whole, each of these anthologies is typically the result of a highly collaborative editorial process. Where a contributing editor for a stand-alone volume is identified, however, that individual has taken primary responsibilitiy for editing the particular volume, and should be named in any citation of that volume. (For example, this book should be cited as "edited by Christina M. Fitzgerald"; in citing this volume there is no need to reference the general editors of *The Broadview Anthology of Medieval Drama*.)

Library and Archives Canada Cataloguing in Publication

York plays
    The York Corpus Christi play / contributing editor, The York Corpus Christi play: selected pageants, Christina M. Fitzgerald (University of Toledo) ; contributing editor, The nativity and The shepherds: Robert W. Barrett, Jr. ; contributing editor, The slaughter of the innocents: Jane Tolmie ; general editors, the Broadview anthology of medieval drama: Christina M. Fitzgerald (University of Toledo), John T. Sebastian (Loyola Marymount University). — A Broadview anthology of medieval drama edition.

ISBN 978-1-55481-429-9 (softcover)

    1. Mysteries and miracle-plays, English—England—York. 2. Christian drama, English (Middle)—England—York. 3. English drama—To 1500. 4. Bible plays, French. I. Fitzgerald, Christina Marie, editor II. Title.

PR1261.Y67Y67 2018   822'.051608942843   C2018-902696-0

Broadview Press handles its own distribution in North America:
PO Box 1243, Peterborough, Ontario, K9J 7H5, Canada
555 Riverwalk Parkway, Tonawanda, NY 14150, USA
Tel: (705) 743-8990; Fax: (705) 743-8353
email: customerservice@broadviewpress.com

Distribution is handled by Eurospan Group in the UK, Europe, Central Asia, Middle East, Africa, India, Southeast Asia, Central America, and the Caribbean. Distribution is handled by Footprint Books in Australia and New Zealand.

Broadview Press acknowledges the financial support of the Government of Canada for our publishing activities.

Canada

Developmental Editor: Jennifer McCue
Cover Designer: Lisa Brawn
Typesetter: Alexandria Stuart

PRINTED IN CANADA

Contents

Introduction

The York *Corpus Christi Play* began its life in the late fourteenth century when the city, the seat of the Archbishop of York, was second only to London in prominence and population. At the same time the *Corpus Christi Play* was getting its start, Geoffrey Chaucer was writing *Troilus and Criseyde* and *The Canterbury Tales* in London, William Langland was creating *Piers Plowman* in the West Midlands, and the Gawain Poet was writing *Gawain and the Green Knight* and *Pearl* in the northwest of England. The play continued to be performed and to evolve through the prosperous fifteenth century and well into the sixteenth century, overlapping with the life of William Shakespeare and the reign of Elizabeth I. The *Corpus Christi Play* was, by any measure, a massively successful and significant cultural event for many generations; it is therefore not only medieval but also early modern drama, and it speaks to the continuity of culture across these supposedly disparate periods.

Significantly, however, the very last days of The York *Corpus Christi Play* pre-date the building of the first dedicated theaters in England, and so to read, study, and understand this play is to grapple with a phenomenon for which there is no real modern analogue. Like all early English drama before the rise of the theater, the *Corpus Christi Play* is embedded in its place and community, and its sponsors and audience alike are woven into the fabric of the play itself. The play subtly references present time and place, and makes frequent and pointed use of anachronism to break any sense that its play world is separate from the audience's world. The porous boundaries between the play and its audience, between ancient and medieval (and even future) time, between the biblical world and the world of late medieval York, are functions of both the devotional meaning of the play—its audience is implicated in the story it tells—and the aesthetic practices of a drama that is not bound to a fixed, purpose-built location, but instead transforms the everyday world into the sacred and the marvelous.

The York *Corpus Christi Play* as we know it consists of 47 surviving individual plays or "pageants," including the ones reproduced here. References to three additional pageants appear in York's records, but no play text survives for them. (For the sake of variety, this edition alternates between the terms "pageant," "play," and "episode" in discussing individual parts of the whole. The whole is always referred to in the singular, following the usage of medieval York itself.) Together the 47 pageants comprise a narrative concerning the Christian history of the world from the Creation to Judgment Day, with an emphasis on humankind's implication in and redemption through the Passion and resurrection of Christ. This cycle of plays was produced by the York civic government and its occupational guilds—called "crafts"—and performed annually for nearly 200 years on Corpus Christi day, a mid-summer feast with a movable date that could fall between May 23 and June 24. The York *Corpus Christi Play* is the only extant and complete cycle of plays performed on Corpus Christi day in England throughout the play's life.[1] The earliest record we have of the York play is from 1376; the last performance until the twentieth century was in 1569, although a failed attempt was made in 1580. Twenty-seven pageants are presented here; together these plays represent the core narrative of creation, fall, and salvation.

The Feast of Corpus Christi (Latin: Body of Christ) is a religious holiday celebrating the sacrament of the Eucharist—the consecration and sharing of bread and wine during the Mass in imitation and commemoration of Jesus during the Last Supper. Pope Urban IV established the feast for celebration throughout the universal Church in 1264. It served as an occasion for giving physical expression to belief in transubstantiation: that the consecrated bread and wine become, in reality (and not merely symbolically), the body and blood of Jesus Christ, a point of doctrine clarified by the Fourth Lateran Council in 1215. In other words, the Feast of Corpus Christi celebrates the mystery of Christ's "real presence" in the Eucharist. The feast day was widely observed in England by the second quarter of the fourteenth century, and the most common form of celebration was through a mass followed by a Church-organized procession in which a priest held aloft the Eucharist wafer in a "monstrance" (a decorative vessel used to display a sacred object) and the parishioners or citizens (in a city-wide event) processed behind him. York had such a procession in which the most prominent crafts and civic office-holders, as well as the Corpus Christi guild (a devotional organization), played a significant role as torch-bearers. Both the procession and the play were held on the feast day until the late fifteenth century, when the procession was moved to the day after Corpus Christi day, seemingly

---

1   The Chester cycle of plays began its life associated with Corpus Christi day, but moved to a three-day performance in Whitsun week; the plays have come down to us in that form. Only two plays of Coventry's ten-play Corpus Christi cycle survive. Two other collections of seeming Creation-to-Judgment-Day "cycles," the N-Town plays and the Towneley plays, are now largely understood to be collections of plays from various sources, and neither is associated with Corpus Christi day.

giving the city's lay-controlled play pride of place over the Church-sponsored procession.

A spectacular and logistically complex event with over 300 speaking parts and more than 14,000 lines of dialogue, The York *Corpus Christi Play* required the participation of a large number of York's citizens. That organizational feat was accomplished by enlisting the city's crafts, who were themselves socially significant organizations. Not only did they regulate the manufacture and trade of goods and train new craftsmen and merchants through apprenticeship, but they also organized the social and even spiritual lives of their members, families, and neighbors. Guildsmen tended to live in the same areas of the city as members of their own craft, and thus attended the same parish church; what is more, guilds often served spiritual and devotional as well as practical purposes. Craft masters were also the enfranchised citizens who elected the city's government. Thus, in calling on the crafts to organize the play, the civic council was calling on its most prominent citizens. Each craft, or sometimes a group of crafts, was assigned a pageant for which it would be responsible every year (though those assignments sometimes changed over the years). Individual pageants were performed on wagons (called "pageants" in York records, but "pageant wagons" in modern scholarship), movable stages custom-built for and possibly by the sponsoring craft or crafts. Great care was taken of these wagons, which were costly in and of themselves, and could be lavish in design. It is perhaps no surprise that the first surviving record of the play concerns wagon storage. In the Mercers' Indenture itemizing the wagon and materials of their *Last Judgment* pageant (included in the contextual materials in this volume), one can see how elaborate the wagons and props could be.

Each pageant played multiple times on Corpus Christi day at designated stopping places, or "stations," on a pre-determined route through the city's center, thus emphasizing the important economic, social, and religious spaces of the city. Although the stations might change from year to year, the culturally significant route never did. (See the map following this introduction for one arrangement of the stations.) The play served both civic and religious purposes, but was the direct product of the city and of lay devotion, not of the Church in any official capacity (although individual churchmen were almost certainly involved throughout). The York *Corpus Christi Play* signifies the growing participation of lay people in devotional culture and spiritual life, and of the urban middle classes in literary culture.

The late Middle Ages witnessed an increase in lay involvement in spiritual matters and devotional practices, and a growth in literacy, especially in the urban middle class, along with a greater investment of the urban middle classes in literary and artistic culture. These phenomena are interdependent as well as complex in their origins, effects, and manifestations, and so will only be briefly touched upon here, but they are important; together they made the York *Corpus Christi Play* possible. It is often erroneously imagined that medieval religious practice was monolithically controlled by the Church, while a cowed and illiterate lay populace blindly followed along. In fact, the lay population, especially in urban centers, was deeply involved in the life of their local church and other religious foundations, and through them, in the Church as an institution. Lay people raised money for parishes and religious houses, donated time, contributed to their upkeep and economies, and shaped their aesthetic and cultural programs. Lay people provided patronage, audience, and readership for vernacular works such as sermons, devotional guides, religious lyrics and, obviously, drama, as well as religious works in the visual and material arts, all of which then shaped tastes and culture in the late Middle Ages.

One local, York example will serve to show the interconnectedness of these phenomena: the *"Prick of Conscience* Window," a stained glass window at the parish Church of All Saints, North Street, made in the fifteenth century. (A simple Google image search will allow you to view this window.) The *Prick of Conscience* was a long (over 9,000 lines) and very popular fourteenth-century Middle English poem—it survives in more manuscripts than any other work of Middle English verse—that served as a guide to religious knowledge, natural history, and penitential practice, and guided readers to an understanding of their relationship with God. Like the York *Corpus Christi Play*, its narrative moves from fall to redemption and emphasizes humankind's responsibility for their sins. The *Prick of Conscience* Window illustrates a small part of this text: the fifteen signs foretelling the Day of Judgment and the end of the world. Significantly, the images are accompanied by excerpts from the poem, in English, rather than inscriptions in Latin, as would be conventional in stained glass at this time. The window also depicts its donors (a common aspect of late medieval public art), members of the intermarried Henryson and Hessle families, elite citizens of the city. Lay devotion, patronage of public art, civic prominence, literacy and literary interests among the urban elite: all these are displayed by the *Prick of Conscience* Window, and all helped to make the York *Corpus Christi Play* possible.

What survives of the complete play is contained in one manuscript, copied sometime between 1463 and 1477 by a city official. This manuscript was the official "Register" of the complete cycle, kept by the

York civic authorities. Each guild also had a copy of its own individual pageant, called the "Original"; all but one of these Originals have now been lost. Since the cycle was performed annually over two centuries, the surviving Register can best be seen as a kind of snapshot of the performance at a point in time. In fact, other records from the city and its crafts—such as the *Ordo Paginarum*, included in the contextual materials in this volume—tell us that the play changed over time. As a living celebration, performance, and annual event, the York *Corpus Christi Play* was subject to revision and alteration, growing and changing with the city and citizens that gave it its life.

Scholars don't know for certain who wrote any of the individual pageants in the cycle, although linguistic and stylistic evidence suggests that a number of them were written or at least revised by a single author, who has been dubbed "The York Realist" by scholars for the playwright's interest in psychologically motivated characters and realistic details. Eight plays are conventionally assigned to this author, who wrote in a long alliterative line that was popular in the North and West of England from the end of the fourteenth century (it is also found in such works as *Sir Gawain and the Green Knight* and *Piers Plowman*). The eight plays assigned to the Realist are: Pageant 26: *The Conspiracy*; 28: *The Agony in the Garden and the Betrayal*; 29: *The Trial Before Caiaphas and Annas*; 30: *The First Trial Before Pilate (The Dream of Pilate's Wife)*; 31: *The Trial Before Herod*; 32: *The Remorse of Judas*; 33: *The Second Trial Before Pilate (The Judgment)*; and 36: *The Death of Christ*. Of course, this attribution is based on stylistic analysis alone, and both the attribution and the name "The York Realist" are the product of critical convention rather than verifiable fact.

More recent scholarship has been less interested in literary authorship of the plays than in the corporate sponsorship of the city and its guilds, and in the communal and cultural meaning of the cycle. Scholars have pointed to various thematic unities, or at least continuities, across pageants—including pageants attributed to "the Realist" and pageants that "the Realist" had no hand in. The themes, images, and language of work, labor, manufacture, and craft culture persist throughout. Given the sponsorship of the crafts, none of this is surprising; though the crafts or the civic government may have hired clergy or established poets to write the play, the craftsmen underwrote and authorized it, and may have influenced its final shape on the page as well as on the stage.

The association between sponsoring craft and the content of the play did not necessarily have any literal or straightforward significance. Although some associations seem obvious—for example, the Shipwrights' sponsorship of the *Building of the Ark* play—and others potentially allowed the sponsoring craft to advertise its wares or skills (for example, the Vintners' sponsorship of the now lost *Marriage at Cana* play, where water is turned into wine), others are more broadly metaphoric, adding to the general theme of labor, its uses, and its abuses. See, for example, the discussion of the Pinners' sponsorship of the *Crucifixion* play in its headnote. Still other craft assignments may have met merely practical needs and had no real symbolic value at all. A glance at the complete play and its sponsors will show this variety of associations. At the time the Register was created, the play consisted of the following pageants and sponsors. The plays included in this volume are marked with an asterisk (*). The pageants that have been lost but which are attested in records appear in parentheses.

*	The Barkers	Pageant 1	*The Creation of the Angels and the Fall of Lucifer*
*	The Plasterers	Pageant 2	*The Creation*
	The Cardmakers	Pageant 3	*The Creation of Adam and Eve*
	The Fullers	Pageant 4	*Adam and Eve in Eden*
*	The Coopers	Pageant 5	*The Fall of Adam and Eve*
	The Armorers	Pageant 6	*The Expulsion from Eden*
	The Glovers	Pageant 7	*Cain and Abel*
*	The Shipwrights	Pageant 8	*The Building of the Ark*
*	The Fishers and Mariners	Pageant 9	*The Flood*
*	The Parchmentmakers and Bookbinders	Pageant 10	*Abraham and Isaac*
*	The Hosiers	Pageant 11	*Moses and Pharaoh*
*	The Spicers	Pageant 12	*The Annunciation and Visitation*
*	The Pewterers and Founders	Pageant 13	*Joseph's Troubles About Mary*
*	The Tilethatchers	Pageant 14	*The Nativity*
*	The Chandlers	Pageant 15	*The Shepherds*

* The Pinners	Pageant 35	*The Crucifixion*
* The Butchers	Pageant 36	*The Death of Christ*
* The Saddlers	Pageant 37	*The Harrowing of Hell*
* The Carpenters	Pageant 38	*The Resurrection*
* The Winedrawers	Pageant 39	*Christ's Appearance to Mary Magdalene*
The Woolpackers and Woolbrokers	Pageant 40	*The Supper at Emmaus*
The Scriveners	Pageant 41	*The Incredulity of Thomas*
The Tailors	Pageant 42	*The Ascension*
The Potters	Pageant 43	*Pentecost*
* The Drapers	Pageant 44	*The Death of Mary*
(The Linenweavers	Pageant 44A	*The Funeral of Mary*)
* The Weavers	Pageant 45	*The Assumption of Mary*
The Hostelers	Pageant 46	*The Coronation of Mary*
* The Mercers	Pageant 47	*The Last Judgment*

Looking at the list of all the pageants, one might notice some patterns: there are three times as many New Testament episodes as Old Testament ones; the Old Testament narratives come mainly from Genesis, with one from Exodus; the New Testament episodes are focused largely on the birth and then the Passion and resurrection of Christ, with little coverage of his life and ministry; and there is also significant attention paid to the Virgin Mary, particularly through episodes centering on Christ's infancy and then Mary's own death, assumption, and coronation as Queen of Heaven. Much of this makes sense in context of the Feast of Corpus Christi with which the plays are associated. The fact that the episodes of Chester's Whitsun week cycle display a similar emphasis, though, suggests that the Corpus Christi feast day is not the sole determining factor.

The play as a whole focuses on a narrative of fall and redemption—hence its zeroing in on the Genesis story of the fall of humankind (spread out over multiple pageants), the Gospel accounts of the coming of the savior (the infancy episodes), and the suffering, death, and resurrection of Christ, through which redemption comes. Mary, commonly recognized during the Middle Ages as "co-redemptrix" of humanity alongside Jesus, also figures in this story. The Noah, Abraham and Isaac, and Moses pageants also participate in the general pattern of fall and redemption through the method of interpretation of sacred texts known as "typology." Medieval Christians were encouraged through their religious instruction and practices to see everything in the Old Testament as prefiguring the events and persons of the New, or to see later episodes as recapitulating earlier ones. Some moments can look both backwards and forwards. For instance, take the Noah story. The destruction of the sinful world looks back to the original sin of Adam and Eve and their expulsion from Eden, and also forward to the Last Judgment and the end of the world. Noah, meanwhile, is a figure for or "type" of Christ, and the ark prefigures the Church as the means of salvation. The rebellious character of Noah's Wife might be read as a type of Eve, while the obedient Mary is the anti-type of both. (That said, see the headnote for the *Noah's Flood* pageant for alternative interpretations; notably, Noah's Wife may also stand for the ordinary person.)

This way of reading Christian sacred history was central to a great deal of medieval Christian story-telling, whether through drama, through art, or through devotional literature. Some of the literary works that have been identified as direct sources for the York Play also follow such narrative logic, including the fourteenth-century narrative poem *Cursor Mundi*, which likewise tells a Creation-to-Judgment history of the world with a theme of fall and redemption, and an emphasis on Christ's Passion. Of course, the cycle of worship in the Church also follows such patterns, especially congregating around the two major holy seasons, Lent through Easter and the Advent-Christmas season. It is from the patterns of liturgy (the program of worship in the Church) and the art and literature inspired by it that the structure of the York play derived. While not a Church-sponsored event, it is nevertheless one that reflects lay devotional practices and ways of understanding their faith.

Although unified by the narrative arc to which they contribute, the pageants included here show a remarkable range in poetic structure, tone, and rhetorical style. Multiple verse and stanza forms are used throughout the cycle, varying in length of both line and stanza, and in complexity of rhyme schemes. Some plays make use of alliterative meter, with an emphasis on four strong beats per line, aligned with the alliteration, while others use meters based on syllable count and alternating stresses. The cycle repeats some poetic forms, as well, since they are flexible enough to be put to multiple rhetorical and tonal uses. The most tonally and structurally formal of the plays are often those that stand outside of human time and are dominated by divine and supernatural characters, such as the Plasterers' *Creation* and the Mercers' *Last Judgment*. In the *Creation*, God is the only speaking character, although modern performances have made use of actors dressed as Angels to enact the work of the creation as celestial prop-masters. God speaks in dignified, regular, and predictable 12-line stanzas rhyming abababcbcb; though this may seem stiff and repetitive on the page, an accomplished actor can project God's pleasure, energy, and joy in his creation, while the everyday, ordinary level of the diction suggests an intimate God, and the regularity projects his constancy. Contrast this with the *Crucifixion* play, which puts a very similar 12-line stanza form to different use and effect. Only Jesus is given full stanzas; the soldiers share stanzas as well as lines between them, and sometimes their dialogue stretches across stanza boundaries. This obscures the regularity of the poetic structure, producing a more informal, naturalistic rhythm. The play also makes use of everyday language, but often of a much coarser variety than the *Creation* play, lending a much darker tone to the *Crucifixion*.

That darkness of tone, which can be found throughout the pageants, is often directed at Jews, as well as other non-Christian characters; there is no getting around the inherent prejudices at work here. Christianity saw itself as superseding Judaism, and so to remain a Jew in the face of Christ's message that he was the promised savior was, in the view of all too many Christians, to deny God himself. Such refusals to see Judaism as legitimate then led to more widespread anti-Semitism. York itself played a role in one of the most horrific moments in the history of anti-Semitism (arguably, one of the most horrific moments in the history of England itself), about two hundred years before the development of the *Corpus Christi Play*. In the late twelfth century, anti-Semitic feeling and acts of terror against Jews were on the rise across Europe, including in England. In York, this fomenting of hatred manifested itself in a wave of riots that culminated in the massacre of about 150 Jews—York's entire Jewish community—who had taken refuge in a castle where Clifford's Tower now stands. On March 16, 1190, as they found themselves surrounded by a mob calling for Jewish blood, the refugees chose suicide as the only way out; those few who did not kill themselves died as the castle burned or were killed by the rioters.

Over the course of the thirteenth century, laws increasingly restricted Jews' rights until, in 1290, King Edward I ordered all Jews expelled from England. Jews would not be officially allowed to return until the mid-seventeenth century; thus, during the entire life of the York *Corpus Christi Play*, there were no Jews in England (or at least no Jews who openly identified as such). And yet, despite that absence, the kind of scapegoating and anti-Semitism that drove the twelfth-century riots and massacres can still be seen in the plays. Old Testament patriarchs and Christ's own Jewish family and followers are not portrayed in anti-Semitic terms, because of the practice of reading them as types of Christ or as the first Christians. The Pharisees, on the other hand, are portrayed as Jews who refuse to see the light, who accuse Jesus of breaking their Jewish law instead of accepting the new law he offers them.

If anti-Semitism is a strong presence in the York play, however, it is not an entirely consistent one. Compare, for example, the way in which Christ's crucifiers are depicted in the different pageants. In *Christ's Appearance to Mary Magdalene*, Mary Magdalene identifies the Jews as "the false Jews [who] slew" Jesus and who "him nailed until a tree"; identification of Jesus' crucifiers as Jews—and thereby defining Jews as "Christ killers" and setting them up as targets of hate—is one of the more common anti-Semitic tropes of the Middle Ages (and beyond). But significantly, York's own crucifixion play does not make such an identification. Instead, each of its crucifiers is labeled "Miles" (Latin: soldier) in the manuscript speech headings, and they behave and speak as ordinary fifteenth-century York workmen, inviting audience identification with them and suggesting the audience's own complicity, through their sins, in the crucifixion. The difference between the depiction of the crucifixion and the words of Mary Magdalene about the crucifixion in the very same cycle of plays reminds us that the play is the product of a communal effort, and that multiple voices of many generations were involved in its production. It also speaks to the difference of attitudes one can find even in a single city in late medieval England.

The *Crucifixion* pageant's identification of the soldiers as ordinary York workmen is one instance of a pattern that recurs frequently in the York *Corpus Christi Play*; the contemporary world of York and its guilds lends the play rich layers of social, political, and theological meaning. The wealth, power, and influence suggested by the 1433 document called The York Mercers' Indenture is a case in point. That document (included with the contextual documents in this volume) details the construction of the Mercers' *Last Judgment* pageant. While the prominent and wealthy Mercers could no doubt have afforded a more lavish pageant than most crafts, the details of this pageant nevertheless suggest the possibility for spectacle in the rest of the cycle. As a whole the York *Corpus Christi Play* was an extraordinary and long-lived public event of vast proportions, requiring serious annual commitment—financial, organizational, social, and spiritual—from the citizens of the city, a commitment that signaled their status and prestige as much as their piety and devotion.

The level of that commitment is made clear in the longevity of the play; it was performed for almost 200 years, at least from the first record (1376) to the last performance (1569). But with the rise of Protestantism and of the Church of England in the sixteenth century, and with increasing state control over theater and performance in the Elizabethan age—including blasphemy laws that prohibited any depiction of the deity on stage—the continuing tradition of the York *Corpus Christi Play* was doomed. The play would not be performed again in any significant form until 1951. That performance, an abridged version of the cycle performed in the ruins of York's St. Mary's Abbey on a stationary stage, was produced as part of the Festival of Britain; the play's history and antiquity allowed it to be part of a celebration of pride in Britain's past and of its hope for the future after World War II. Similar fixed-stage productions were mounted in the same location roughly every three to four years through the 1980s and again in 2012, and there have been performances in other locations in York, including the York Minster. Wagon plays have also been produced in York, beginning with individual plays in concert with the productions in the abbey ruins, and expanding to abbreviated cycles in the city streets in the 1990s, some even involving modern descendants of the medieval guilds. The "York Mystery Plays Supporters Trust" now intends to mount productions every two years, alternating between performances on wagons and on a fixed stage. It seems that the York *Corpus Christi Play* is once again a significant cultural institution; according to the Supporters Trust, over 32,000 people came to see the 2012 fixed-stage production over the course of its summer run.

Large-scale, academic-led productions, in Leeds, England, and in Toronto, Canada have also been mounted for research purposes. In the first of these, at the University of Leeds in 1975, various amateur academic groups stood in for individual guilds and performed the entire cycle on wagons over three days. This was the first performance of the entire cycle and also the first performance on wagons since the sixteenth century. The University of Toronto productions, inspired by Leeds, mounted full cycles—again with the help of many independent groups of players standing in for the guilds—this time on a single day, first in 1977 and then again in 1998. Toronto custom-built wagons for the purpose, and performed the play at three stations in 1977 and four stations in 1998.[1] Each performance sought to answer through performance questions that could not be answered on the page of the text or in the archives, and each has contributed to scholarly knowledge and audience appreciation of the plays. Given the interest in the play in York as a prominent cultural institution, and the academic interest in it, it seems possible that the York *Corpus Christi Play's* second life will last as long as its first life.

About This Edition

The editorial procedures and conventions followed here are the same as those followed in *The Broadview Anthology of Medieval Drama*, edited by Christina M. Fitzgerald and John T. Sebastian. With three exceptions, the pageants included in this volume, as well as the "In Context" materials, have been edited by Fitzgerald; the exceptions are *The Nativity* and *The Shepherds* (edited by Robert W. Barrett, Jr.) and *The Slaughter of the Innocents* (edited by Jane Tolmie). Their contributions are gratefully acknowledged.

Throughout The York *Corpus Christi Play*, the most important core principle has been to provide an accessible text, with a sufficient amount of information provided in the headnotes and annotations to enable students at all levels to read, perform, and interpret the plays on their own. Those plays and contextual materials which previously appeared in *The Broadview Anthology of Medieval Drama* have been re-edited for this volume.

TEXT: The base text for the pageants newly edited for this volume is Richard Beadle's first edition of *The York Plays* (London: Edward Arnold, 1982), available in electronic form in the Corpus of Middle English Prose and Verse in the Middle English Compendium, hosted online at the University of Michigan. Also consulted were Beadle's subsequent edition of *The York Plays* in two volumes for the Early English Text Society, S. S. 23 and S. S. 24 (Oxford University Press, 2009 and 2013), as well as Clifford Davidson's *The York Corpus Christi Plays* (Kalamazoo: Medieval

---

1   Photos of the performances in Toronto in 1977 and 1998 can be found on the Flickr gallery operated by the Poculi Ludique Societas, the historical performance group at the University of Toronto that sponsored both productions: https://www.flickr.com/photos/plspls/sets/.

Institute Publications, 2011), Richard Beadle and Pamela King's *York Mystery Plays* (Oxford University Press, 1995, reissued 2009), and the facsimile of British Library MS Additional 35290 published by the University of Leeds in 1983.

The selected pageants presented here are presented in modernized spelling, with archaic and difficult words and passages glossed or footnoted. The aim is to preserve the character of the original while presenting as readable and accessible a text as possible for students of both literature and theater, so that they may grapple with the complex and sometimes difficult concepts, themes, and worldviews of these texts with fewer linguistic barriers. Similarly, documents in the "In Context" section that were originally written in English have been presented in modernized spelling; those written in Latin or French have been translated. Latin rubrications and stage directions through the pageants and ancillary materials have also been translated, except where they note the opening words of a Latin hymn, in which case the original language has been retained and translated in a footnote. Likewise, the occasional use of Latin or French within the dialogue of the pageants has been retained and noted.

Since the text of the York *Corpus Christi Play* dates from the mid-fifteenth century, and many historical linguists would count that period as the beginning of Early Modern English, this volume applies the conventions and standards for the editing of early modern drama in the presentation of the text here. Wherever possible, words are given their present-day spelling. In cases of obsolete words, we rely on the first headword spelling of the *Oxford English Dictionary*, on the principle that that is the lexical reference work most students would turn to after the glosses and footnotes that have been provided. Where the word is so archaic or rare that even the *OED* provides no entry for it, we retain the original spelling and gloss it. Modernization inevitably affects rhyme, but in most cases where spelling changes rhyme, some sense of partial rhyme often remains; meter is (perhaps surprisingly) less affected than rhyme. In cases where modernization would so disrupt rhyme or meter that it might obscure it entirely, or where the original spelling provides a pun, play on words, or other significant meaning that modernization would defeat, the original spelling has been retained.

ANNOTATION: The aims of the annotation in this volume are similar to those of the modernization: to provide students access to, and understanding of, the denotative meaning of the text and to give context where necessary. Since it is assumed that instructors may not assign every pageant presented here, we do not expect students to have previously encountered any given word, even a very common one, and therefore gloss frequently. As in *The Broadview Anthology of Medieval Drama*, the policy has been to annotate wherever it is considered likely that many undergraduate students would have difficulty understanding.

Stage directions are also sometimes added where the dialogue suggests that an action takes place, but the text does not provide its own directions. The York *Corpus Christi Play* provides few directions of its own; when it does, they are in Latin, which is here translated. Directions that are original to the text are presented in parentheses; editorially provided stage directions are always distinguished by square brackets. As with annotations, the aim is to adhere to a purely denotative, literal mode, leaving ideas about different possible interpretations and competing staging possibilities to the reader, while occasionally noting points of critical debate about such issues.

Finally, all Latin character names have been translated, and a list of speaking characters has been included with each pageant, even though such lists do not appear in the fifteenth-century text.

Map of Medieval York and the Route of the *York* Corpus Christi Play

The York *Corpus Christi Play* was a processional play, performed on custom-built, movable, wheeled stages that scholars refer to as "pageant wagons." (See the introduction for more details.) After playing at the first stopping place, Station 1, an individual pageant (an episode of the whole *Corpus Christi Play*) would then move on to Station 2, while the next pageant would be wheeled into position at Station 1, and so on, until the entire city was filled with simultaneous performance. The map on the opposite page shows the route and the most common arrangement of the playing stations during the life of the York *Corpus Christi Play*. The route never changed, always beginning on Micklegate just inside Micklegate Bar. (Confusingly, "gate" here means street—it derives from the Old Norse "gata"—so Micklegate is "Great Street." The word "bar," meanwhile, means what we think of as a gate; Micklegate Bar is the main gate to the walled medieval city, and means "Great Street Gate.") Performances began in front of Holy Trinity Priory, where the first station was positioned; then pageants proceeded to additional stations on Micklegate and crossed the River Ouse, where the route then traveled clockwise around the city center, tracing main streets, playing in front of the Minster (the cathedral and seat of the Archbishop of York), and ending in the area known as the Pavement, the city's commercial center. The stations were variable in number and location over time, except for the first and the final stations, which remained fixed throughout the play's life. A "Virtual Tour" of some of the stations can be found on *Broadview Anthology of Medieval Drama* website, where one can get a sense of the three dimensional space of the play route, since much of York's late medieval streetscape still survives.

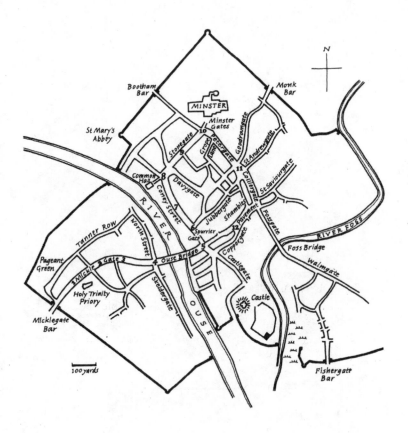

MAP   25

The York Corpus Christi Play:
The Creation of the Angels and the Fall of Lucifer

The York *Creation of the Angels and Fall of Lucifer*, which would have opened the cycle at dawn on Corpus Christi Day, was produced and performed by the Barkers, also known as the Tanners, who tanned hide into leather. A wealthy guild, they were well-suited to creating what must have been a spectacular opening pageant, with its nine orders of angels, showy costumes, and depictions of both heaven and hell, the latter possibly represented by a monstrous mouth intended to symbolize the entrance to the underworld (see a manuscript illustration of such a hellmouth in the "In Context" section). They would also have been able to provide hell with its notorious smells, as tanning was an especially odiferous and noxious trade.

That the cycle begins with a story of rebellion that disrupts group harmony, followed by the reestablishment of order, seems pointedly appropriate for a guild-produced, civic event. The story of the fall of Lucifer and his fellow rebellious angels is not narrated directly in the Bible, but comes from the Church Fathers' interpretations of key passages throughout both the Old and New Testaments. Especially important are Isaiah 14.12–15 ("How art thou fallen from heaven, O Lucifer, who didst rise in the morning? how art thou fallen to the earth, that didst wound the nations? / And thou saidst in thy heart: I will ascend into heaven, I will exalt my throne above the stars of God, I will sit in the mountain of the covenant, in the sides of the north. / I will ascend above the height of the clouds, I will be like the most High. / But yet thou shalt be brought down to hell, into the depth of the pit," Douay-Rheims translation) and Luke 10.18 ("And he said to them: I saw Satan like lightning falling from heaven," Douay-Rheims translation). The events of the rebellion and fall are traditionally assumed to take place before the rest of creation, which begins at the end of this play and continues in Pageant 2: *The Creation*, effecting a new beginning for God and his creation.

The Creation of the Angels and the Fall of Lucifer establishes many of the larger themes of the cycle—good vs. evil, obedience vs. disobedience, harmony vs. discord—and employs figurative motifs and stylistic, formal, and dramatic techniques that the pageants will return to again and again. Harmony is conveyed through the angels' singing, and discord through the shouting and frantic emoting of the devils. The very language and poetic form of the play participates in these patterns of order and chaos: God and good angels speak only in whole stanzas (here, eight-line stanzas rhyming ababcddc), while Lucifer and Devil 2 share stanzas from the moment of their fall and share lines as they bicker. Even Lucifer's alliteration seems more excessive and cacophonous than those of God and the other angels. Motifs of light and dark, high and low, beauty and ugliness run through this pageant and recur throughout the cycle. Finally, this pageant establishes a symbolic use of space and movement that is characteristic of the cycle's theatrical style. Lucifer seeks to be "like unto to him that is highest on height" and attempts to sit on God's throne ("There shall I set myself"). Following the spatial hierarchies of medieval art and the real-world practices of royal courts, God's throne would have been higher than other planes of the performance, likely on a dais, or perhaps even on a second level of the pageant wagon, as suggested by the Mercers' Indenture for their *Last Judgment* pageant. In the moment that Lucifer over-reaches, he immediately falls into hell, a level lower than heaven, perhaps on the ground level of York's streets—spatial symbolism that then would remind the audience of their own potential to fall into sin.

Pageant 1 of the York Corpus Christi Play:
The Creation of the Angels and the Fall of Lucifer

CHARACTERS

God
Seraphim→messengers
Lucifer
Cherubim
Angel 2 / Devil 2

GOD. *Ego sum Alpha et Omega;*
Vita, via, veritas, primus et novissimus.[1]

I am gracious and great, God without beginning,
I am maker unmade, all might is in me;

---

1 *Ego sum ... novissimus* Latin: I am the Alpha and the Omega; the life, the way, the truth, beginning and end. See Revelation 22.13 ("I am the Alpha and Omega, the first and the last, the beginning and the end") and John 14.6 ("I am the way, and the truth, and the life: no one cometh unto the Father, but by me"); *Alpha* The first letter of the Greek alphabet; *Omega* The last letter of the Greek alphabet. These lines are extra-metrical and may not be intended to be spoken.

I am life and way unto wealth-winning,[1]
I am foremost and first, as I bid shall it be.
My blessing of blee° shall be blending,°   *(my) countenance / dazzling* 5
And hielding,° from harm to be hiding,°   *pouring forth / protecting*
My body in bliss ay° abiding,   *always*
Unending,° without any ending.[2]   *eternal*

Since I am maker unmade and most is of might,
And ay° shall be endless, and naught° is but I,   *forever / nothing* 10
Unto my dignity dear shall duly be dight°   *created*
A place full of plenty to my pleasing at ply;[3]
And therewith° also will I have wrought   *in addition*
Many diverse doings bedene,°   *immediately*
Which work shall meekly contain,°   *continue* 15
And all shall be made even of° naught.   *out of*

But only the worthly° work of my will   *worthy*
In my spirit shall inspire the might of me;[4]
And in the first, faithly,° my thought to fulfill,   *certainly*
Bainly° in my blessing I bid at here be   *readily* 20
A bliss all-bielding° about me,   *all-protecting*
In the which bliss I bid at be here
Nine orders of angels[5] full clear,
In lofing° ay-lasting°   *praise / ever-lasting*
   at lout° me.   *show reverence to*

(*Then the angels sing, "Te Deum laudamus, te Dominum confitemur."*)[6]

---

1   *wealth-winning* Attainment of salvation.
2   *My blessing ... ending* The blessing of my countenance shall be dazzling and pouring forth, protecting (all) from harm, my body always abiding in bliss, eternally, without any ending.
3   *at ply* Fit, in good condition.
4   *But only ... might of me* But my power shall inspire by means of my spirit only the worthy work of my will.
5   *Nine orders of angels* In medieval Christian tradition, the nine orders of angels were seraphim, cherubim, thrones, dominions, virtues, powers, principalities, archangels, and angels. Although only seraphim, cherubim, and angels have speaking parts here, presumably the other orders are represented as well.
6   *Te Deum ... confitemur* Latin We praise thee, God; we acknowledge thee to be Lord. The *Te Deum* was the conventional hymn of Matins, the morning service, and also frequently used on ceremonial occasions.

25	Here underneath me now a nexile[1] I neven,°	*name (and create)*
	Which ile° shall be earth. Now all be at once	*isle or aisle*
	Earth wholly, and hell, this highest be heaven,	
	And that wealth° shall wield°	*well-being / enjoy*
	shall won° in this wones.[2]	*dwell*
	This grant I you, ministers mine,	
30	To-whiles° ye° are stable in thought—	*as long as / you (pl.)*
	And also to[3] them that are not,°	*not (stable)*
	Be put to my prison at pine.°	*pain*

	Of all the mights I have made, most next after me	
	I make thee° as master and mirror of my might.	*you (sg.), i.e., Lucifer*
35	I bield° thee here, bainly° in bliss for to be;	*shelter, protect / obediently*
	I name thee for Lucifer, as bearer of light.	
	Nothing here shall thee be dering;°	*harming*
	In this bliss shall be your bielding,°	*protection*
	And have all wealth° in your wielding,	*well-being*
40	Ay-whiles° ye[4] are buxomly° bearing.°	*as long as / obediently / behaving*

(*Then the angels sing,* "Sanctus, sanctus, sanctus, Dominus Deus Sabaoth.")[5]

	SERAPHIM.[6] Ah, merciful maker, full mickle° is thy might,	*great*
	That all this work at a word worthily has wrought.	
	Ay lovèd° be that lovely Lord of° his light,	*worshipped / for*
	That us thus mighty has made, that now°	*until now*
	was right° naught,°	*totally / nothing*
45	In bliss for to bide° in his blessing.	*dwell*
	Ay-lasting° in lof° let us lout° him,	*ever-lasting / praise / worship*

---

1   *nexile*   A detached portion of the created universe (a figurative use of "isle" plus the prefix "nex(t)". Some editors gloss this as a wing of a building (again figurative), i.e., an offshoot of heaven (from "aisle," rather than "isle"). See "ile" in the next line.

2   *And that wealth ... in this wones*   And those who enjoy well-being shall dwell in this place.

3   *And also to*   And also [I grant] to.

4   *ye*   You, plural. God is now addressing all of the angels, beginning at "In this bliss shall be your bielding." "Ye" and "you" are also formal, but he addresses Lucifer familiarly as "thee" three lines above, so the "your" and "ye" usage signifies plurality here.

5   *Sanctus ... Sabaoth*   Latin: Holy, holy, holy, Lord God of Hosts. The fifth verse of the *Te Deum* hymn, and also a regular part of the Latin Mass.

6   SERAPHIM   In the manuscript, Seraphim is called "I Angelus, Seraphyn," or "1st Angel, Seraphin," and Cherubim is labeled "Angelus Cheraphyn." Both character names are simplified here. See more below regarding other character designations.

At bield us[1] thus bainly° about him,   *willingly*
Of mirth nevermore to have missing.

• Alliteration

LUCIFER.[2] All the mirth that is made is marked in me!
The beams of my brighthood° are burning so bright,   *brightness*   50
And I so seemly in sight myself now I see,
For like a lord am I left to lend° in this light.   *dwell*
More fairer by far than my feres,°   *companions*
In me is no point that may pair;°   *deteriorate*
I feel° me° featous° and fair,   *perceive / myself / handsome*   55
My power is passing my peers.

Arrogant → Better than everyone else

CHERUBIM. Lord, with a lasting lof° we love thee alone,   *praise*
Thou mightful maker that marked us and made us,
And wrought us thus worthily to wone° in this wone,°   *dwell / abode*
There° never feeling of filth may foul° us nor fade us.   *where / befoul*   60
All bliss is here bielding° about us;   *dwelling*
To-whiles° we are stable in thought   *as long as*
In the worship of him that us wrought,
Of dere° never thar° us   *harm / will be necessary*
    more doubt° us.[3]   *worry*

ANGEL 2.[4] O, what° I am featous° and fair   *how / handsome*   65
    and figured° full fit!°   *made / attractive*
The form of all fairhood° upon me is fest,°   *beauty / fixed*
All wealth° in my wield° is,   *well-being / possession*
    I wot° by my wit;°   *know / intelligence*
The beams of my brighthood are bigged with the best.[5]

Reflection of Lucifer

My showing° is shimmering and shining,   *appearance*
So bigly° to bliss am I brought;   *firmly*   70

---

1 *At bield us* So that we flourish.
2 *LUCIFER* In the manuscript, Lucifer is identified first as "I Angelus Deficiens, Lucifer" ("First Deficient or Failing Angel, Lucifer"), and then later, after his fall as "Lucifer in Inferno" ("Lucifer in Hell").
3 *Of dere … doubt us* It will never be necessary for us to worry ourselves about harm.
4 *ANGEL 2* In the manuscript, this Angel is first identified as "II Angelus Deficiens," or "2nd Deficient or Failing Angel." Then, after his fall with Lucifer, he is identified as "II Diabolus," or "2nd Devil." Here he is simply designated "Angel 2" and then "Devil 2." It seems likely that there are other "deficient" angels who fall with Lucifer, as he later addresses them in the plural (see more below).
5 *are bigged with the best* Remain among the best, most beautiful.

Me needs for to noy° me right not,[1]   *concern*
Here shall never pain me be pining.°   *tormenting*

SERAPHIM. With all the wit that we wield, we worship thy will,
    Thou glorious God that is ground of all grace;
75 Ay° with steadfast steven° let us stand still,   *forever / voice*
    Lord, to be fed with the food of thy fair face.
    In life that is leally° ay-lasting,°   *truly / ever-lasting*
    Thy dole,° Lord, is ay daintily°   *gift, grace / delightfully*
      dealing,°   *bestowing*
    And whoso° that food may be feeling—   *whoever*
80 To see thy fair face—is not fasting.

LUCIFER. Oh, certes,° what° I am   *certainly / how*
    worthily wrought with worship, iwis!°   *truly*
For in a glorious glee° my glittering it gleams.   *radiance*
I am so mightily made, my mirth may not miss°—   *fail*
    Ay° shall I bide° in this bliss   *forever / dwell*
      through brightness of beams.
85 Me needs not of noy° for to neven,°   *harm / speak*
    All wealth[2] in my wield° have I wielding;°   *power / control*
    Above yet shall I be bielding,°   *dwelling*
    On height in the highest of heaven.

There° shall I set myself full seemly to sight,   *i.e., in God's throne*
90 To receive my reverence through right of renown;
I shall be like unto him that is <u>highest on height.</u>
    Oh, what I am dearworth° and deft°—   *worthy / noble*
      Oh! Deus! All goes down![3]
    My might and my main° is all marrand°—   *power / deteriorating*
    Help, fellows! In faith I am falland.°   *falling*
95 ANGEL 2. From heaven are we hielding° on all hand,[4]   *sinking*
    To woe are we wending,° I warrand.°   *going / warrant*

---

1 *Me needs ... not* I need not be concerned in the least.

2 *wealth* Here, just as Lucifer is about to usurp God's throne, the meaning of "wealth" starts
   to slip from "well-being" to the more material meaning of wealth, just as "wield" in the same
   line begins to shade into "power" and "control" rather than merely "possession."

3 *All goes down!* This and "I am falland" are likely both cues for the moment of the fall and
   therefore of Lucifer's and the Angel's descent from the wagon stage to a place on the ground
   representing hell. After this stanza, Lucifer is identified as "Lucifer, Diabolous in Inferno"
   in the manuscript.

4 *on all hand* In all directions.

Plunging into hell

LUCIFER. Out! Out! Harrow![1] Helpless, slike hot at is here;[2]
   This is a dungeon of dole° that I am to° dight.°   _misery / into / thrust_
   Where is my kind become,[3] so comely and clear?
   Now am I loathest,° alas, that ere° was light.   _most loathsome / before_ 100
   My brightness is blackest and blo° now,   _leaden-colored_
   My bale° is ay beeting° and burning—   _misery / kindling_
   That gares° one go gowling° and grinning.° _makes / wailing / grimacing_
   Out! Ay wellaway![4] I well° even in woe now.   _boil_

DEVIL 2. Out! Out! I go wood° for woe,   _insane_ 105
   my wit is all went° now,   _gone_
   All our food is but filth we find us beforn.[5]
   We that were bielded° in bliss,   _sheltered_
   in bale° are we burnt now—   _sorrow_
   Out on thee Lucifer, lurdan,°   _scoundrel_
   our light has thou lorn.°   _lost_
   Thy deeds to this dole now has dight us,
   To spill° us thou was our speeder,°   _destroy / instigator_ 110
   For thou was our light and our leader,
   The highest of heaven had thou hight° us.   _promised_

LUCIFER. Wellaway! Woe is me now; now is it worse than it was.
   Unthrivingly° threap° ye[6]— I said but a thought. _unprofitably / chide_
DEVIL 2. We![7] lurdan,° thou lost us.   _scoundrel_
LUCIFER.   Ye lie! Out, alas!   115
   I wist° not this woe should be wrought.   _knew_
   Out on you, lurdans, ye smore° me in smoke.   _smother_
DEVIL 2. This woe has thou wrought us.
LUCIFER.   Ye lie, ye lie!
DEVIL 2. Thou lies, and that shall thou buy.°   _pay for_
LUCIFER. We, lurdans, have at you, let look![8]   120

---

1 _Out! Out! Harrow!_ Conventional cry of distress.
2 _Helpless … here_ (I am) helpless, such heat there is here.
3 _Where is my kind become_ What has become of my nature.
4 _wellaway_ An exclamation of sorrow, lamentation. Literally, well-being (is gone) away.
5 _us beforn_ Before us.
6 _ye_ You, plural. This usage provides evidence that Lucifer has more companions on stage than only Angel-2-turned-Devil-2 with a speaking role. Although "ye" and "you" are also used as formal variants of the singular, the Devil addresses Lucifer using the familiar singular form "thou," so it seems unlikely that Lucifer would use a formal form of address in return.
7 _We!_ An interjection of consternation or indignation.
8 _have at you, let look!_ Fighting words meaning "let me have a go at you, see here!"

CHERUBIM. Ah, Lord, lovèd° be thy name   *praised*
    that us this light lent,°   *gave*
Since Lucifer our leader is lighted° so low,   *alighted, descended*
For his unbuxomness° in bale°   *disobedience / hell-fire*
    to be brent°—   *burnt*
Thy rightwiseness° to reward on row[1]   *righteousness*
125 Ilka° work after is wrought.[2]   *each*
Through grace of thy merciful might
The cause I see it in sight,
Wherefore° to bale° he is brought.   *for which reason / torment*

GOD. Those fools for° their fairhead°   *because of / beauty*
    in fantasies fell,
130 And had moan° of my might that marked them   *complaint*
    and made them.
Forthy° after° their works were,   *therefore / according as*
    in woe shall they well,°   *suffer*
For some are fallen into filth that evermore
    shall fade° them,   *corrupt*
And never shall have grace for to girth° them.   *protect*
So passing° of power them thought them,   *surpassing*
135 They would not me worship that wrought them;
Forthy shall my wrath ever go with them.

And all that me worship shall wone° here, iwis;°   *dwell / certainly*
Forthy more forth[3] of my work, work now I will.
Since than[4] their might is for-marred°   *destroyed*
    that meant° all amiss,   *intended*
140 Even to mine own figure° this bliss to fulfill,° *image / fill up, complete*
Mankind of mould° will I make.   *earth*
But first will I form him before[5]
All thing° that shall him restore,°   *things / sustain*
To which that his talent will take.[6]

---

1 *on row*   Duly, properly.
2 *Thy rightwiseness ... is wrought*   (It is) thy righteousness to duly reward each work according to its merits.
3 *more forth*   Even more.
4 *Since than*   Since.
5 *him before*   Before him. It is not unusual for Middle English poetry to reverse prepositional phrases.
6 *his talent will take*   His inclination or ability will lend itself.

And in my first making, to muster° my might,   _display_ 145
Since earth is vain° and void and mirkness°   _empty / darkness_
  amell,°   _amid_
I bid in my blessing ye angels give light
To the earth, for it faded when the fiends fell.
In hell shall never mirkness be missing,°   _lacking_
The mirkness thus name I for night;   150
The day, that call I this light—
My after°-works shall they be wissing.°   _later / known_

And now in my blessing I twin° them in two,   _divide_
The night even from the day, so that they meet never,
But either in a kind° course their gates° for to go.   _natural / ways_ 155
Both the night and the day, do duly your dever,°   _duty_
To all I shall work by ye wissing.°   _guiding_
This day work is done ilka° deal,[1]   _every_
And all this work likes° me right well,   _pleases_
And bainly° I give it my blessing.   _willingly_ 160

*God summarizes
What happened → Displays
everlasting
power*

---

1 *ilka deal* In every respect.

The York Corpus Christi Play: The Creation

The York *Creation* play, produced and performed by the Plasterers' craft, covers the creation of the world to the fifth day (thus excluding the creation of humans), as depicted in Genesis 1. It is the second play in the York *Corpus Christi Play* cycle, following the *Creation of the Angels and the Fall of Lucifer*, the events of which God mentions in lines 8–20. This play, then, presents a new beginning of order and harmony after the chaos of Lucifer's rebellion. At a mere 172 lines long, it is one of the shorter plays in the cycle; however, beginning with the fourth stanza, God's words are also acts of creation, necessitating stage time for those actions to be made concrete through scenery, props, special effects, and other stage business. In a performance of the play in Toronto in 1998, the Department of Drama and Theatre Arts of the University of Birmingham (UK) realized this spectacle through a series of painted hangings and backdrops; props included three-dimensional birds, fish, and animals, all unfurled on wooden frames, wires, and other supports as God spoke.

Such stage business also mimics theatrically the patterns of the creation in Genesis 1, in which God often *speaks* forth the world: "And God said: Be light made. And light was made" (Gen. 1.3, Douay-Rheims translation). Moreover, the play celebrates the power of language, literature, and performance to imagine and bring forth a world before our eyes. The poetic form also suggests the power, creative energy, and stability of God. Spoken in stately, twelve-line stanzas rhyming abababbcbcb, God's monologue presents a world emanating entirely and steadily from his words. The continuous pattern of b-rhymes, meanwhile, creates a sense of stability and suggests God's eternal nature as he brings forth a fresh world.

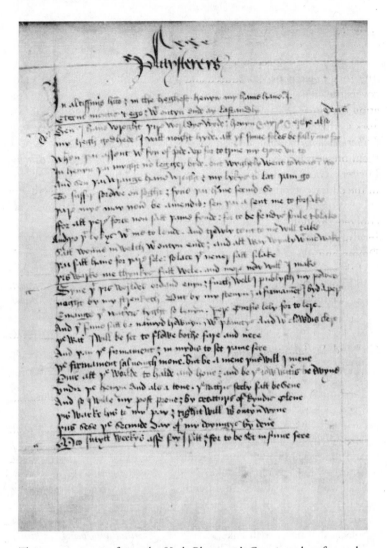

The opening page from the York Plasterers' *Creation* play, from the "Register," or official copy, of the York cycle (York, c. 1463–77), London, British Library MS Add. 35290, f. 7v. The Plasterers' play is a continuous monologue by God in 12-line stanzas rhyming abababcbcb, but the manuscript's scribe has written two poetic lines per line of manuscript, thus giving it the appearance of prose. Since God is the only speaker, he is denoted only on the first page, as Deus, in the right margin.

CHARACTERS

God

GOD. In *altissimis habito*,
In the highest heaven my home have I;
Eterne mentis et ego,[1]
Without end ay-lastingly.°   *ever-lastingly*

5   Since I have wrought these worlds wide,
Heaven and air and earth also,
My high Godhead I will not hide
All-if° some fools be fallen me fro.°   *although / from*
When they assent° with sin of pride   *agreed*
10 Up for to trine° my throne onto,[2]   *step, approach*
In Heaven they might no longer bide°   *remain*
But wightly° went to wone° in woe;   *immediately / dwell*
And since they wrong have wrought
My like° is to let them go,   *preference*
15 To suffer sorrow unsought,
Since they have served so.

Their miss° may never be amend°   *sin / amended*
Since they assent me to forsake;
For° all their force° none shall them fend°   *despite / strength / prevent*
20 For to be fiends foul and black.[3]
And those that like with me to lend,°   *dwell*
And truly tent° to me will take,   *heed*
Shall wone° in wealth° without end   *remain / well-being*
And always winly° with me wake;°   *joyfully / live*
25 They shall have for their sele°   *reward*
Solace° that never shall slake.°   *spiritual well-being / diminish*
This work me thinks full well°   *seems very good to me*
And more now will I make.

---

1   *In altissimis ... et ego*   Latin: I dwell in the highest (place), and I (am) of mind eternal.
2   *When they assent ... my throne onto*   When they agreed, through sin of pride, to step up onto my throne.
3   *For all their force ... foul and black*   No matter their strength, no one will prevent them from being foul, blackened fiends.

Since that this world is ordained° even,°   *ordered / properly*
Forth will I publish° my power: *make known* 30
Not by my strength, but by my steven°   *voice*
A firmament I bid appear,
Among the waters, light so levin,°   *flashing*
Their courses[1] leally° for to lere,°   *precisely / prescribe*
And that same shall be named Heaven,
                                   35
With planets and with clouds° clear.   *skies*
The water I will° be sent   *cause through my will*
To flow both far and near,
And then the firmament
In midst to set° them sere.°[2]   *make / separate* 40

The firmament shall not move,
But be a mean,° thus will I mean,°   *center point / intend*
Over all the world to hold and hove,°   *hover protectively over*
And be those two waters between.[3]
Under the Heaven and also above   45
The waters serely° shall be seen,   *separately, distinctly*
And so I will my poustie° prove   *power*
By creatures of kinds clean.°   *splendid*
This work hies° to my pay°   *succeeds / satisfaction*
Right well, without ween;°   *doubt* 50
Thus cease the second day
Of my doings bedene.°   *immediately*

More subtle works assay° I shall,   *try*
For to be set in service sere:[4]
All the waters great and small   55
That under Heaven ere° ordained° here,   *before / created*
Go together and hold you all,

---

1 *Their courses* I.e., the movement of the planets and the seeming movement of the constellations.
2 *And then ... them sere* And then (I will) set the firmament in the midst to separate them (the waters).
3 *The firmament ... between* What's being described here and above is a pre-Copernican view of the cosmos, in which the "firmament" is a fixed and rigid sphere between the earth's atmosphere and the heavenly waters that it holds back. In this view, the stars and planets are fixed in place in the firmament and the latter rotates around the earth creating the seeming "movement" of the constellations. The firmament "shall not move" in the sense that it will always be there around the earth, holding back the heavenly waters.
4 *For to be set in service sere* To have several functions.

And be a flood° fastened in fere,[1]	*body of water*
So that the earth, both down° and dale,°	*hill / valley*
60 In dryness plainly may appear.	
The dryness 'land' shall be	
Named both far and near,	
And then I name thee 'sea,'	
Gathering of waters clear.	

65 The earth shall foster° and forth bring	*nourish*
Buxomly,° as I will bid,	*obediently*
Herbs° and also other thing,	*plants*
Well° for to wax° and worthy to weed;	*good / grow*
Trees also thereon shall spring	
70 With branches and with boughs on brede,[2]	
With flowers fair on height to hang	
And fruit also to fill and feed.	
And then I will that they	
Of° themselves have the seed	*from*
75 And matter, that they may	
Be lasting forth in lede.[3]	

And all these matters are in mind	
For to be made of° mickle° might,°	*by means of / great / power*
And to be cast° in diverse kind°	*made / natures*
80 So for to bear sere° burgeons° bright.	*various / buds, shoots*
And when their fruit is fully fined°	*finished ripening*
And fairest seeming unto sight,	
Then the weather wet and wind	
Away I will° it wend° full wight;°	*desire / go away / promptly*
85 And of their seed full soon	
New roots shall rise upright.	
The third day thus is done,	
These deeds are duly dight.°	*performed*

Now since the earth thus ordained is,	
90 Measured and made by mine assent—	
Gradely° for to grow with grass	*properly*

---

1 *in fere* Together.
2 *on brede* Far and wide.
3 *in lede* In the land.

And weeds that soon away are went[1]—
Of my goodness now will I guess,°   *ordain, decide to make*
So that my works no harms hent,°   *receive*
Two lights, one more° and one less,°   *greater / lesser* 95
To be fest° in the firmament.   *fastened*
The more light to the day
Fully soothly° shall be sent,   *truly*
The lesser light always
To the night shall take intent.   100

These figures fair that forth are found°   *created*
Thus on sere° sides serve they shall: *separate*
The more light shall be named the sun,
Dimness to waste° by down and by dale. *lay to waste, destroy*
Herbs and trees that are begun   105
All shall he° govern, great and small;   *i.e., the sun*
With cold if they be closed or bound
Through heat of the sun they shall be hale.° *healed, healthy*
As they have honors
In all-kind° wealth° to wale,[2]   *every kind of / well-being* 110
So shall my creatures
Ever bide without bale.°   *misery*

The sun and the moon on fair manner
Now gradely° gang° in your degree;[3]   *properly / go*
As ye have ta'en° your courses clear,   *taken* 115
To serve forth look ye be free,°   *generous*
For ye shall set° the seasons sere,°   *distinguish / separate*
Kindly° to know in ilka° country, *according to your nature / every*
Day from day and year from year
By certain signs soothly° to see.   *truly* 120
The heaven shall be overhead
With stars to stand plenty.
The fourth day is fulfillèd,
This work well likes° me.   *pleases*

Now since these works are wrought with win°   *joy* 125
And founden° forth by firth° and fell,° *created / forest / pasture land*

---

1 *are went* Have gone.
2 *to wale* In abundance.
3 *in your degree* As is fitting to your position.

The sea now will I set within
Whales wightly° for to dwell,   *doughtily, boldly*
And other fish to flit with fin—
130   Some with scale and some with shell,
Of diverse matters more and min°—   *less*
In sere° manner to make and mell;°   *various / mix*
Some shall be mild and meek,
And some both fierce and fell.°   *deadly*
135   This world thus will I eke,°   *improve*
Since I am wit of well.[1]

Also up in the air on height
I bid now that there be ordained
For to be fowls fair and bright,
140   Duly in their degree dwelland,°   *dwelling*
With feathers fair to fraist° their flight   *assist*
From stead° to stead where they will stand,   *place*
And also lightly for to alight
Whereso° them likes in ilka land.   *wherever*
145   Then fish and fowls sere,°   *individually*
Kindly° I you command   *according to your nature*
To meng° in your manner,   *mingle, copulate*
Both by sea and sand.

These matters more yet will I mend,
150   So for to fulfill my forethought,
With diverse beasts in land to lend
To breed and be with° belly° forth brought.   *from / womb*
And with beasts I will° be blend°   *want / blended, mixed*
Serpents to be seen unsought,
155   And worms upon their wombs° shall wend°   *stomachs / go*
To wone° in earth and worth° to naught.°   *dwell / come / nothing*
And so it shall be kenned°   *known*
How all that eme° is ought,°   *attention / owed*
Beginning, midst, and end,
160   I with my word have wrought.[2]

For as I bid, bus° all things be   *must*
And duly done as I will dress:°   *put in order*

---

1   *wit of well*   The well (source) of wisdom.
2   *How all ... wrought*   With the attention it deserves, how I have made beginning, middle,
and end with my word.

Now beasts are set in sere degree
On mold° to move, both more and less;   *earth*
Then fowls in air and fish in sea   165
And beasts on earth of bone and flesh,
I bid ye wax° forth fair plenty   *grow, produce*
And gradely° grow, as I you guess.°   *properly / ordain*
So multiply ye shall
Ay° forth in fair process,°1   *forever / passage of time*   170
My blessing have ye all;
The fifth day ended is.

The York Corpus Christi Play:
The Fall of Adam and Eve

The fifth pageant of the York *Corpus Christi Play* depicts the story from Genesis 3 of the "original sin" of human beings—the root cause, according to Christian theology, of human suffering and death. Produced and performed by the Coopers—who made barrels, casks, buckets, and such—the play leaves behind the divine spectacle of the *Fall of Lucifer* or the *Creation* and instead depicts the world's origins in terms of domestic psychology, turning the narrative focus to ordinary humanity. Even Satan (a name interchangeable with Lucifer in these plays) seems less compelling or charismatic than Pageant 1's rebellious scenery-chewer. Eve and Adam seem the easy marks of a two-bit charlatan, while Adam comes across as childish and petty in immediately blaming Eve. There is still room for theatricality and spectacle, however, as the player performing Satan must transform into "a worm's likeness." (No records or stage directions survive to tell us how this was accomplished.)

In the *Creation* play, what God had "wrought" (made) was all of creation, and it was good. Here, what is "wrought" is the "work" of sin, of doing wrong and making a "bad bargain." Language of "work" (including synonyms such as "travail," "swink," and variations on "wrought," that which is worked or made) begins to appear with more frequency here—a pattern that continues through the rest of the cycle (perhaps not surprising given the guild sponsorship of the plays). This may underscore

---

1   *process*   May also be a pun on plays themselves. Process can mean "play, pageant, performance."

for the York merchants, artisans, and laborers that Adam and Eve's sinful "work" and its "fruits" are their own.

The verse form of this play—11 lines rhyming ababcbcdcdc—is unique among the York plays; like other forms, it shows great flexibility for creating meaning. Although Satan opens the play in monologue, speaking entire stanzas (perhaps underscoring his self-centered jealousy of humankind's favored status), he soon shares stanzas and lines with Eve, emphasizing the sway he holds over her. But she then shares stanzas with Adam, signifying a transfer of influence. Although Adam shares stanzas and lines with God, that occurs only in the moment of his punishment, ironically highlighting the impending distance of humankind from God's presence.

Pageant 5 of the York Corpus Christi Play: The Fall of Adam and Eve

CHARACTERS

Satan
Eve
Adam
God
Angel

(*Satan begins, saying.*)

SATAN. For woe my wit is in a were°	*turmoil*
That moves° me mickle° in my mind;	*distresses / greatly*
The Godhead that I saw so clear,	
And perceived that he should take kind[1]	
5 Of a degree[2]	
That he had wrought,° and I dedigned°	*made / was offended*
That angel kind should it not be;	
And we were fair and bright,	
Therefore me thought that he	
10 The kind of us ta'en might,[3]	
And thereat° dedigned me.	*on account of that*

---

1 *take kind* Take the form, assume the nature.

2 *Of a degree* Of an order (of beings), i.e., humankind. Satan here has foreknowledge of the Incarnation, that is, of God taking humankind's form as Jesus.

3 *The kind of us ta'en might* Might have taken the form of us (angels).

The kind of man he thought to take
And thereat had I great envy,
But he has made to him a make,°   *mate*
And hard° to her I will me hie°   *quickly / go*   15
That ready° way,   *quick*
That purpose proof to put it by,[1]
And fand° to pick° from him that prey.   *try / steal*
My travail° were° well set°   *effort / would be / contrived*
Might I him so betray,   20
His liking° for to let,°   *pleasure / end*
And soon I shall assay.°   *make an attempt*

In a worm's° likeness will I wend,°   *serpent's / go*
And fand to feign° a loud° leasing.°   *fabricate / flagrant / lie*
Eve, Eve.
EVE.   What is there?
SATAN.   I, a friend.   25
And for thy good is the coming
I hither sought.[2]
Of all the fruit that ye see hang
In paradise, why eat ye not?
EVE. We may of them ilkone°   *each one*   30
Take all that us good thought,[3]
Save° a tree out is ta'en,°   *except / taken*
Would do harm to nigh° it aught.°   *approach / at all*

SATAN. And why that tree, that would I wit,°   *know, understand*
Any more than all others by?°   *nearby*   35
EVE. For our Lord God forbids us it,
The fruit thereof, Adam nor I
To nigh it near;
And if we did we both should die,
He said, and cease our solace° sere.°   *pleasure / sundry*   40
SATAN. Yea, Eve, to me take tent;[4]
Take heed and thou shalt hear
What that the matter meant
He moved° on that manner.[5]   *urged*

---

1 *That purpose proof to put it by*   Put that plan to a test, i.e., test Eve's character.
2 *And for thy good ... hither sought*   It is for your benefit that I sought to come here.
3 *us good thought*   Seems good to us.
4 *take tent*   Pay attention.
5 *What that ... on that manner*   What those words meant that he urged in that way.

45	To eat thereof he you defend°	*forbade*
	I know it well, this was his skill:°	*reason*
	Because he would none other kenned°	*knew*
	These great virtues that longs° theretill.°	*belong / to that*
	For will thou see,	
50	Who° eats the fruit of good and ill°	*whoever / evil*
	Shall have knowing as well as he.	
	Eve. Why, whatkin° thing art° thou	*what kind of / are*
	That tells this tale to me?	
	Satan. A worm, that wotteth° well how	*knows*
55	That ye may worshipped° be.	*honored*

	Eve. What worship° should we win thereby?°	*honor / by that*
	To eat thereof us needeth it not,[1]	
	We have lordship to make mastery	
	Of all thing that in earth is wrought.°	*made*
60	Satan. Woman, do way![2]	
	To greater state ye may be brought	
	And° ye will do as I shall say.	*if*
	Eve. To do is us full° loath°	*very / reluctant*
	That should our God mispay.[3]	
65	Satan. Nay, certes° it is no wothe,°	*certainly / danger*
	Eat it safely ye may.	

	For peril right there none in lies,[4]	
	But worship and a great winning,°	*gain*
	For right° as God ye shall be wise	*just*
70	And peer to him in allkin° thing.	*all kinds of*
	Aye,° gods shall ye be,	*yes*
	Of ill° and good to have knowing,	*evil*
	For to be as wise as he.	
	Eve. Is this sooth° that thou says?	*truth*
75	Satan. Yea, why trows° thou not me?	*believe*
	I would by no kins[5] ways	
	Tell not but truth to thee.	

---

1 *To eat ... it not* To eat of it, we have no need.
2 *do way!* Stop!
3 *To do ... God mispay* We are very reluctant to do (anything) that would displease our God.
4 *For peril ... lies* For there is no danger in that.
5 *no kins* No kind of.

EVE. Then will I to thy teaching trast°   *trust*
    And fang° this fruit unto our food.   *take*

(*And then she must take the fruit.*)

SATAN. Bite on boldly, be not abashed,°   *ashamed*   80
    And bear Adam[1] to amend° his mood   *improve*
    And eek° his bliss.°   *also / happiness*

(*Then Satan leaves.*)

EVE. Adam, have here of fruit full good.
ADAM. Alas woman, why took thou this?
    Our Lord commanded us both   85
    To tent° the tree of his.   *take heed*
    Thy work will make him wroth.°   *angry*
    Alas, thou hast done amiss.

EVE. Nay Adam, grieve thee not at it,
    And I shall say the reason why.   90
    A worm has done me for to wit[2]
    We shall be as gods, thou and I,
    If that we eat
    Here of this tree; Adam, forthy,°   *therefore*
    Let not[3] that worship° for to get.   *honor*   95
    For we shall be as wise
    As God that is so great,
    And as mickle° of price;°   *great / worth*
    Forthy, eat of this meat.°   *food*

ADAM. To eat it would I not eschew°   *avoid*   100
    Might I me° sure° in thy saying.[4]   *myself / assure*
EVE. Bite on boldly, for it is true,
    We shall be gods and know all thing.
ADAM. To win that name
    I shall it taste at thy teaching.   105

---

1 *And bear Adam* And carry (some) to Adam.
2 *done me for to wit* Caused me to know, informed me.
3 *Let not* Do not fail.
4 *To eat it … thy saying* I would not avoid eating it, if I might be assured (of the truth) of
   what you're saying.

(And he accepts and eats.)

Alas, what have I done, for shame!
Ill° counsel,° woe worth thee!¹   *evil / counselor*
Ah, Eve, thou art to blame,
To this enticed thou me.
110   Me shames with my licham,²

For I am naked as methink.°   *it seems to me*
EVE. Alas Adam, right° so am I.   *also*
ADAM. And for sorrows sere° why ne° might we sink,   *several / not*
For we have grieved God almighty
115   That° made me man—   *who*
Broken his bidding bitterly.°   *wickedly*
Alas that ever we it began.
This work, Eve, hast thou wrought,
And made this bad bargain.
120 EVE. Nay Adam, wite° me not.   *blame*
ADAM. Do way, lief° Eve, whom then?   *dear*

EVE. The worm to wite well° worthy were,³   *very*
With tales untrue he me betrayed.
ADAM. Alas, that I let at⁴ thy lare°   *lore, teaching*
125   Or trowed° the trifles° that thou me said.⁵   *believed / nonsense*
So may I bid,⁶
For I may ban° that bitter° braid°   *curse / terrible / hasty act*
And dreary° deed, that I it did.   *evil*
Our shape° for dole°   *appearance / sorrow*
    me deaves;°   *stupefies, worries*
130   Wherewith they shall be hid?⁷
EVE. Let us take° there fig leaves,   *place*
Sithen° it is thus betid.⁸   *since*

---

1 *woe worth thee!* May woe be upon you!
2 *Me shames ... licham* My body is shameful to me; I am ashamed of my body.
3 *The worm ... worthy were* The serpent is truly worthy of blame.
4 *let at* Paid attention to, heeded.
5 *Or trowed ... thou me said* Or believed the nonsense you told me.
6 *So may I bid* Thus I must live.
7 *Our shape ... shall be hid?* Our (naked) appearance shocks me with sorrow; with what shall
   they (our bodies) be concealed?
8 *Sithen it is thus betid* Since it has happened thus.

ADAM. Right as thou says so shall it be,
  For we are naked and all bare;
  Full wonder fain[1] I would hide me   135
  From my Lord's sight, and° I wist° where,   *if / knew*
  Where I ne° rought.[2]   *not*
GOD. Adam, Adam.
ADAM.   Lord.
GOD.   Where art thou, yare?°   *quickly*
ADAM. I hear thee, Lord, and see thee not.
GOD. Say, whereon is it long,[3]   140
  This work, why hast thou wrought?°   *done*
ADAM. Lord, Eve gart° me do wrong   *caused*
  And to that brigue° me brought.   *plight*

GOD. Say, Eve, why hast thou gart thy make°   *mate*
  Eat fruit I bade° thee should hang still,[4]   *ordered* 145
  And commanded none of it to take?
EVE. A worm, Lord, enticed me theretill;°   *to that*
  So wellaway,[5]
  That ever I did that deed so dill.°   *foolish*
GOD. Ah, wicked worm, woe worth thee[6] ay,°   *always, forever* 150
  For thou in this manner
  Hast made them swilk° affray;°   *such / trouble*
  My malison° have thou here   *curse*
  With all the might° I may.   *power*

And on thy womb° then shall thou glide,   *belly* 155
  And be ay full of enmity
  To all mankind on ilka° side,[7]   *every*
  And earth it shall thy sustenance be
  To eat and drink.
  Adam and Eve also, ye   160
  In earth then shall ye sweat and swink,°   *work*
  And travail° for your food.   *labor*
ADAM. Alas, when might we sink,

---

1 *Full wonder fain* Most gladly.
2 *ne rought* Would not be troubled.
3 *Say, whereon is it long* Tell me, what is the reason for it (i.e., "this work" in the next line).
4 *should hang still* Should remain hanging.
5 *wellaway* An exclamation of sorrow, lamentation. Literally, well-being (is gone) away.
6 *woe worth thee* May woe come upon you, woe to you.
7 *on ilka side* Everywhere.

We that have all world's good?
165 Full° derfly° may us think.[1]   *most / grievous*

GOD. Now Cherubim, mine angel bright,
    To middle-earth[2] tite° go drive these two.   *quickly*
ANGEL. All ready, Lord, as it is right,
    Since thy will is that it be so,
170 And thy liking.
    Adam and Eve, do you two go,
    For here may ye make no dwelling;
    Go ye forth fast to fare,°   *travel*
    Of sorrow may ye sing.
175 ADAM. Alas, for sorrow and care
    Our hands may we wring.

The York Corpus Christi Play:
The Building of the Ark

The Building of the Ark was produced and performed by the Shipwrights;
it is one of a handful of obvious alignments in the cycle between craft
and pageant subject-matter. (Other such alignments include the next
pageant, *The Flood*, produced by the Fishers and Mariners; the Goldsmiths' taking responsibility for the Magi in the *Herod and the Magi*
combined plays; the Vintners' *Marriage at Cana* pageant, now lost; and
the Bakers' production of *The Last Supper*.) In making this pairing, the
play brings together the sacred story and the everyday world of York
ship-building, much as the play itself depicts the divine intervention of
God in Noah's earthly life.

The parallels between sacred history and present-day York continue
in the very language of the play. Once again, the diction of "work"
and that which is "wrought" permeates the plays, as does the language
of "craft." The technical language of shipbuilding fills the dialogue as
Noah builds the ark before the audience's eyes with God's guidance.
Noah's uncertainty, combined with God's patient insistence that he will
teach Noah, and the intimacy of the two players on stage, all suggest an

---

1   *may us think* It may seem to us.
2   *middle-earth* The world, the earth, as the mid-point between Heaven and Hell.

idealized master-apprentice relationship. Given that the ark is conventionally seen as prefiguring the Church, the play may be taken to suggest that the building of that Church is, literally and figuratively, then and now, the responsibility of humanity, but only possible through God's grace. Indeed, the last lines of the pageant return to the language of "craft" that is "kenned" (taught) by God, who will "wis" (instruct) us.

The events of the building of the ark and the flood take place in Genesis 6–9, and are usually depicted together in medieval drama, although they are sometimes represented separately in art, as in the Bedford Hours illustration of the ark's construction (see this in the "In Context" section). York is unique in separating them in performance. In isolating the building from the flood episode itself, York divides Noah from his family and creates an entirely masculine space for this part of the story. The homosocial intimacy is echoed in the stanza form: the eight-line stanzas rhyme simply ababababab and when Noah and God share stanzas, they thus share interlocking rhymes. The pageant also presents the first depiction in the cycle of elderly men finding renewal through God's divine intervention, a trope to which the cycle will return with the figures of Abraham and Joseph.

Pageant 8 of the York Corpus Christi Play: *The Building of the Ark*

CHARACTERS

God
Noah

GOD. First when I wrought° this world so wide—	*made*
Wood and wind and waters wan°—	*dark*
Heaven and hell was not to hide;[1]	
With herbs° and grass thus I began.	*edible plants*
In endless bliss to be and bide.°	*reside* 5
And° to my likeness made I man,	*then*
Lord and sire° on ilka° side[2]	*ruler / every*
Of all middle-earth[3] I made him then.	
A woman also with him wrought I,	
All in law to lead their life,	10

---

1 *not to hide* Not hidden, plain to see.
2 *on ilka side* Everywhere.
3 *middle-earth* The world, the earth, as the mid-point between Heaven and Hell.

I bad° them wax° and multiply,	*ordered / grow*
To fulfill° this world, without strife.	*fill (i.e., populate)*
Sithen° has man wrought so woefully,	*since then*
And sin is now reigning so rife,°	*abundantly*
15 That me repents and rues° forthy°	*regrets / therefore*
That ever I made either man or wife.°	*woman*
But since° they make me to repent—	*ever since*
My work I wrought so well and true—	
Without cease will not assent,°	*comply, obey*
20 But ever is boun° more bale° to brew.¹	*ready / evil*
But for their sins they shall be shent°	*destroyed*
And fordone° wholly, hide and hue;²	*laid to waste*
Of them shall no more be meant,°	*said*
But work this work I will all new.	
25 All new I will° this world be° wrought	*desire / to be*
And waste away that° wones° therein;°	*who / dwells / in that place*
A flood above° them shall be brought	*over*
To stroy° middle-earth, both more and min.³	*destroy*
But° Noah alone, leave shall it not⁴	*except for*
30 Till all be sunken for their sin;	
He and his sons, thus is my thought,	
And with their wives away shall win.°	*escape*
Noah, my servant sad° and clean,°	*sober, solemn / pure*
For° thou art stable in stead and stall,⁵	*because*
35 I will° thou work, without ween,°	*command / doubt*
A work to save thyself withal.°	*with*
NOAH. Oh, mercy Lord, what may this mean?	
GOD. I am thy God of great and small,	
Is come to tell thee of thy teen,°	*trouble*
40 And what ferly° shall after fall.°	*wonder / befall, happen*

---

1 *But since they … more bale to brew* Ever since they made me repent, my creation, which I wrought so well and true, has been continually disobedient and ever ready to stir up more evil.

2 *hide and hue* Entirely, in every respect.

3 *both more and min* Both great and small, i.e., entirely.

4 *leave shall it not* Nothing shall be spared.

5 *stead and stall* In all places, in every respect.

NOAH. Ah, Lord, I love° thee loud and still°   *praise / continually*
    That unto me, wretch unworthy,
    Thus with thy word, as is thy will,
    Likes° to appear thus properly.°   *is pleased / in person*
GOD. Noah, as I bid thee, do fulfill: 45
    A ship I will° have° wrought in hie;°   *desire / to have / haste*
    All-if° thou can° little skill,   *although / know*
    Take it in hand, for help shall I.

NOAH. Ah, worthy Lord, would thou take heed,
    I am full° old and out of quart,°   *very / condition, fitness*   50
    That me list° do no day's deed°   *would rather / work*
    But if great mister° me gart.[1]   *need*
GOD. Begin my work behooves thee need[2]
    And° thou will pass° from pains smart,°   *if / escape / severe, sharp*
    I shall thee succor° and thee speed°   *aid / assist*   55
    And give thee heal° in head and heart.   *health*

    I see such ire° among mankind   *hostility*
    That of° their works I will take wrake;[3]   *for*
    They shall be sunken° for their sin,   *i.e., drowned*
    Therefore a ship I will° thou make.   *command*   60
    Thou and thy sons shall be therein,
    They shall be saved for thy sake.
    Therefore go boldly and begin
    Thy measures and thy marks to take.

NOAH. Ah, Lord, thy will shall ever be wrought   65
    As counsel° gives of ilka° clerk,[4]   *advice / every*
    But first, of ship-craft can° I right not;[5]   *know*
    Of their making have I no mark.°   *skill*
GOD. Noah, I bid thee heartily have no thought,[6]
    I shall thee wis° in all thy work,   *guide*   70
    And even till it to end be wrought;[7]

---

1   *That me list ... me gart* So that I would rather do no day's work, unless a great need made me.
2   *Begin my work behooves thee need* You must begin my work.
3   *take wrake* Inflict punishment.
4   *As counsel gives of ilka clerk* As every learned person advises.
5   *of ship-craft can I right not* I know nothing about building ships.
6   *have no thought* Don't worry.
7   *And even till it to end be wrought* Until it is finished.

Therefore to me take heed and hark.°   *listen*

Take high trees and hew them clean,°   *neatly*
  All by square and not of squin,[1]
75 Make of° them boards°   *from / planks*
    and wands° between   *thin wood strips, battens*
  Thus thrivingly,° and not over-thin.   *skillfully*
  Look that thy seams° be subtly° seen°   *gaps / carefully / attended to*
  And nailed well that they not twin;°   *come apart*
  Thus I devise° ilka deal[2] bedene,°   *order / immediately*
80 Therefore do forth, and leave thy din.[3]

Three hundred cubits it shall be long,
  And fifty broad, all for thy bliss;
  The height, of thirty cubits strong,
  Look leally° that thou think on this.   *truly*
85 Thus give I thee gradely° ere° I gang° *readily / before / go*
  Thy measures, that thou do not miss.°   *err*
  Look now that thou work not wrong
  Thus witterly° since I thee wis.°   *undoubtedly / guide*

  NOAH. Ah, blissful Lord, that all may bield,°   *protect*
90 I thank thee heartily both ever and ay;°   *always*
  Five hundred winters I am of eld°—   *age*
  Methink° these years as yesterday.   *it seems to me*
  Full weak I was and all unwield,°   *feeble*
  My weariness is went° away,   *gone*
95 To work this work here in this field
  All by myself I will assay.°   *try*

To hew this board I will begin,
  But first I will lay on my line;°   *measuring line*
  Now bud° it be all inlike° thin,   *must / equally*
100 So that it neither twin° nor twine.°   *split / warp*
  Thus shall I join it with a gin°   *tool*
  And sadly° set° it with simmon° fine: *firmly / seal / caulk*
  Thus shall I work it both more and min°   *less*
  Through teaching of God, master mine.

[handwritten annotation: Twisted cutting]

---

1 *by square and not of squin* Squarely and not at a slant.
2 *ilka deal* Every whit, completely.
3 *do forth, and leave thy din* Get to work, and say no more.

More subtly° can no man sew;°   *skillfully / join (seams)* 105
It shall be clinked° everilka deal²   *clenched, fastened*
With nails that are both noble° and new,   *of high quality*
Thus shall I fast° it fast° to feal.°   *fasten / firmly / cover (it)*
Take° here a rivet, and there a rew°   *put / rove, washer*
With these the bow now work I well;   110
This work I warrant° both good and true.   *guarantee*

Full true it is, who will take tent,°   *heed*
But fast my force° begins to fold.°   *strength / fail*
A hundred winters away is went
Since I began this work, full gradely° told,°   *carefully / counted* 115
And in slike° travail° for to be bent°   *such / labor / engaged*
Is hard to him that is thus old.
But he that to me these messages sent
He will be my bield,° thus am I bold.°   *support / emboldened*

GOD. Noah, this work is near an end   120
And wrought right as I warned° thee.   *instructed*
But yet in manner³ it must be mend,°   *improved*
Therefore, this lesson learn at° me: *from*
For diverse beasts therein must lend,°   *dwell*
And fowls also in their degree,°   *ranks* 125
And for° that they shall not sam° blend,°   *so / together / mix*
Diverse stages° must there be.   *levels*

And when that it is ordained° so,   *arranged*
With diverse stalls and stages sere,°   *various*
Of ilka° kind° thou shall take two,   *every / species* 130
Both male and female fare in fere.⁴
Thy wife, thy sons, with thee shall go
And their three wives, without were;°   *doubt*
These eight bodies, without mo,°   *more*
Shall thus be saved in this manner.   135

---

1   ….   A line is missing here in the manuscript.
2   *everilka deal*   In each and every part.
3   *in manner*   In one way, in a certain respect.
4   *fare in fere*   Going in company.

Therefore to my bidding be bain,°   *obedient*
Till all be harbored, haste thee fast;
After the seventh day shall it rain
Till forty days be fully past.
140   Take with thee gear° slike° as may gain°   *provisions / such / be useful*
To man and beast their lives to last.°   *sustain*
I shall thee succor° for certain   *aid*
Till all thy care away be cast.

Noah. Ah, Lord, that° ilka°   *who / every*
        miss° may mend,   *fault, sin*
145   I love° thy lore° both loud   *praise / teaching, counsel*
        and still.°   *continuously*
I thank thee both with heart and hend,°   *hands*
That me will help from angers° ill.°   *tribulations / severe*
About this work now bus me wend,[1]
With beasts and fowls my ship to fill.
150   He that to me this craft has kenned,°   *taught*
He wis° us with his worthy will.°   *instructs / command*

The York Corpus Christi Play: The Flood

The ninth pageant of the York *Corpus Christi Play*, appropriately presented by the Fishers and Mariners, continues the story of Noah, the ark, and the flood; this time the story also involves his wife, his three sons, and his sons' wives. In the biblical account in Genesis 6–9 the unnamed family members are merely mentioned in passing and are given no significant narrative role. Medieval dramatic tradition (as well as other literary and artistic traditions), by contrast, expands all of these roles. Much of the dramatic interest, both in this play and other versions, concerns the rebelliousness of the Wife, and unfolds through tensions between discord and harmony, disobedience and obedience. Many versions of the story also involve broad, physical comedy that often engages in violence, as it does here when the Wife strikes Noah. This extra-biblical story of the stubborn wife derives originally from Eastern legend, but by the late Middle Ages had become conventional in English literature and art.

---

1   *bus me wend*   I must go.

At first glance, the comically recalcitrant Wife character might seem an anti-feminist satire of stereotypical stubborn womanhood, making her a type of Eve. But in this play, especially, the Wife ultimately comes to represent all of humankind; humans are all sinners who need the Church—prefigured by the Ark—for salvation. The play conveys all this in numerous ways. First, it uses space symbolically; the pageant wagon was likely completely filled by the representation of the ark, for in the argument between Noah and his Wife she refuses to leave the "hard land" to "turn up" on the ark, while she also tells Noah that he should "come down." This use of space thus aligns Noah's Wife on the ground level with the audience. What is more, she voices a repeated concern for "town" and her "tools," aligning her with the civic body of York and the craft guilds who produced the plays. Also like the audience, she does not have direct access to God's plan and she chastises Noah for not letting her in on such "lore" so that she may "wit" (know) it. The audience, like her, must also trust what they are told through God's messengers and chosen ones. Meanwhile, her empathy for those who drown offers a more humane response to the flood than does Noah's rigid righteousness; the contrast underscores the difficulty of understanding God's will and the reason for human suffering.

Where York especially differs from other dramatic versions of this story is in its lack of true resolution of the tensions between the Wife's worldview and that of Noah's (and, by extension, those of his obedient Sons and their wives). Other plays generally include a reformed and obedient Wife in the final harmony of their stories, but in York, it is only Noah and his sons who sing in thanksgiving after landing on dry land. The Wife still mourns for the dead and worries about tribulations in the future; Noah's only response is to remind her coldly she will not be alive to see the world end in fire at Doomsday. Though the play ultimately ends with Noah's blessing and God's—delivered now indirectly only through a human—the mournful and troubled note the Wife sounds never fully dissipates. This very human and psychologically-driven play is well-served by its complex fourteen-line stanzas rhyming ababab-cdcccd; they provide flexibility for lively exchanges in shared stanzas and lines, as well as for more formal speeches.

CHARACTERS

Noah
Wife
Son 1
Son 2
Son 3
Daughter 1
Daughter 2
Daughter 3

Less focus on God

NOAH. That Lord that lives ay-lasting° life,		*ever-lasting*
I love° thee ever with heart and hand,		*praise*
That° me would rule,° by reason rife,°		*who / command / abundant*
Six hundred years to live in land.		
5 Three seemly° sons and a worthy wife		*handsome*
I have ever at my steven° to stand;		*voice, call*
But now my cares are keen° as knife,		*sharp*
Because I ken° what is command.°		*know / commanded*
There comes to ilka° country,		*every*
10 Yea, cares both keen and cold.		
For God has warned me		
This world wasted shall be,		
And certes° the sooth° I see,		*certainly / truth*
As forefathers have told.		

15 My father Lamech who, likes to neven,[1]		
Here in this world thus long gan lend,[2]		
Seven hundred years seventy and seven,		
In swilk° a space his time he spend.°		*such / spent*
He prayed to God with stable° steven°		*steady / voice*
20 That he to him a son should send,		
And at the last there come from heaven		
Slike° hetting° that him mickle° amend,[3]		*such / promise / greatly*
And made him grub° and grave°		*dig / delve*
As ordained fast° beforn,°		*firmly / beforehand*
25 For he a son should have,		

---

1 *likes to neven* It is suitable to mention.
2 *long gan lend* Lived a long time.
3 *Slike hetting … amend* Such a promise that greatly improved his situation.

As he gan after crave;[1]
And as God vouchsave°   *granted*
In world then was I born.

When I was born, Noah named he me,
And said these words with mickle° win:°   *great / joy* 30
"Lo," he said, "this ilk° is he   *same*
That shall be comfort to mankin."°   *mankind*
Sirs, by this, well wit° may ye,   *understand*
My father knew both more and min°   *less*
By certain signs he could well see,   35
That all this world should sink for sin;
How God should vengeance take,
As now is seen certain,
And end of mankind make
That° sin would not forsake;   *who* 40
And how that it should slake,°   *end*
And a world wax° again.   *grow*

I would God it wasted° were,   *destroyed*
So that I should° not tent°   *need / attend, pay attention*
  theretill.°   *to it*
My seemly sons and daughters dear,   45
Take ye intent° unto my skill.°   *notice / purpose*
SON 1. Father we are all ready here,
  Your bidding bainly° to fulfill.   *obediently*
NOAH. Go call your mother, and come near,
  And speed us[2] fast that we not spill.°   *die* 50
SON 1. Father, we shall not fine°   *stop*
  To° your bidding be done.   *until*
NOAH. All that lives under line[3]
  Shall, son, sooner pass to pine.°   *torment*
SON 1. Where are ye, mother mine?   55
  Come to my father soon.

WIFE. What says thou son?
SON 1.   Mother, certain,
  My father thinks to flit° full far.   *flee*

Wife doesn't believe

---

1 *gan after crave* Longed for.
2 *speed us* Let us hurry.
3 *under line* In a lineage; in other words, everything that lives.

He bids you haste with all your main°   *strength*
60 Unto him, that° nothing you mar.[1]   *so that*
WIFE. Yea, good son, hie° thee fast again   *hasten*
  And tell him I will come no nar.°   *nearer*
SON 1. Dame, I would do your bidding fain,°   *happily*
  But you bus° wend,° else be it war.°   *must / go / worse*
65 WIFE. War? That would I wit.[2]
  We bourd° all wrong,[3] I ween.°   *jest / think*
SON 1. Mother, I say you yet,
  My father is boun° to flit.°   *prepared / flee*
WIFE. Now certes,° I shall not sit°   *certainly / rest*
70 Ere° I see what he mean.   *before*

SON 1. Father, I have done now as ye command,
  My mother comes to you this day.
NOAH. She is welcome, I well warrand;°   *guarantee*
  This world shall soon be wasted away.
WIFE. Where art thou Noah?
75 NOAH.   Lo, here at hand,
  Come hither fast dame, I thee pray.
WIFE. Trows° thou that I will leave the hard° land   *think / dry*
  And turn° up here in tor° deray°?   *go / excessive / confusion, disarray*
  Nay Noah, I am not boun°   *willing*
80 To fond° now over these fells.°   *set about / hills*
  Do° bairns,° go we and truss° to town.   *come on / children / go*
NOAH. Nay, certes,° soothly° then   *indeed / truly*
  mun° ye drown.   *must*
WIFE. In faith thou were as good[4] come down
  And go do somewhat° else.   *something*

85 NOAH. Dame, forty days are nearhand° past   *nearly*
  And gone since it began to rain,
  On life shall no man longer last
  But we alone, is not to lain.[5]
WIFE. Now Noah, in faith thou fons° full fast,°   *act foolishly / extremely*
90 This fare° will I no longer frayne;°   *matter / inquire into*

---

1 *that nothing you mar* So that nothing harms you.
2 *That would I wit* I would like to know how.
3 *We bourd all wrong* We joke badly; or: this isn't funny. Noah's Wife doesn't believe her son.
4 *thou were as good* You might as well.
5 *is not to lain* Is not to be concealed (i.e., this is clear).

Thou art near° wood,° I am aghast,°   *nearly / insane / afraid*
Farewell, I will go home again.
NOAH. Oh woman, art thou wood?
  Of my works thou not wot;°   *understand*
  All that has bone or blood   95
  Shall be over-flowed with the flood.
WIFE. In faith, thee were as good
  To let me go my gate.°   *way*

  We! Out! Harrow!¹
NOAH.   What now, what cheer?²
WIFE. I will no nar° for no-kins need.³   *nearer*   100
NOAH. Help, my sons, to hold her here,
  For till° her harms° she takes no heed.   *concerning / peril(s)*
SON 2. Be merry mother, and mend your cheer;
  This world be° drowned, without dread.⁴   *will be*
WIFE. Alas, that I this lore° should lere.°   *information / learn*   105
NOAH. Thou spills° us all; ill might thou speed.⁵   *would destroy*
SON 3. Dear mother, won° with us,   *stay*
  There shall no thing you grieve.
WIFE. Nay, needlings° home me bus,⁶   *of necessity*
  For I have tools to truss.°   *gather*   110
NOAH. Woman, why does thou thus?
  To make us more mischieve?°   *mischief, harm*

WIFE. Noah, thou might have let me wit;°   *know*
  Early and late thou went thereout,°   *outside, out and about*
  And ay° at home thou let me sit   *always*   115
  To look° that nowhere were well about.⁷   *see to it*
NOAH. Dame, thou hold me excused of it:
  It was God's will without doubt.
WIFE. What, weens° thou so for to go   *think*
    quit?°   *free of blame or responsibility*

---

1 *We! Out! Harrow!* A conventional cry of distress.
2 *what cheer?* What's the matter?
3 *for no-kins need* On any account.
4 *without dread* Undoubtedly.
5 *ill might thou speed* You may accomplish evil.
6 *Nay, needlings home me bus* No, I must go home.
7 *And ay at home ... were well about* All this time you let me sit at home to make sure all
    was well nowhere. The expression is idiomatic and sarcastic; in other words, he left her in
    ignorance, wasting her time.

120   Nay, by my troth, thou gets a clout.°   *blow*
      [*She hits him.*]
    NOAH. I pray thee dame, be still.
      Thus God would have it wrought.
    WIFE. Thou should have wit° my will,   *found out*
      If I would assent theretill,°   *to it*
125   And Noah, for that same skill,°   *cause*
      This bargain° shall be bought.°   *business / paid for*

      Now at first[1] I find and feel°   *perceive*
      Where thou hast to the forest sought.
      Thou should have told me for our sele°   *happiness*
130   When we were to slike° bargain brought.   *such*
    NOAH. Now dame, thee thar° not dread a deal,[2]   *need*
      For till° account it cost thee naught.°   *to / nothing*
      A hundred winter, I wot° well,   *know*
      Is went since I this work had wrought.
135   And when I made ending,
      God gave me measure fair
      Of every-ilka° thing;   *every single*
      He bad° that I should bring   *commanded*
      Of beasts and fowls young,
140   Of ilka° kind a pair.   *each*

    WIFE. Now certes,° and° we should scape°   *certainly / if / escape*
      from scathe°   *harm*
      And so be saved as ye say here,
      My co-mothers° and my cousins° both,   *godmothers / kin*
      Them would° I went with us[3] in fere.°   *would like / company*
145 NOAH. To wend° in the water it were wothe,°   *go / dangerous*
      Look in and look without were.[4]
    WIFE. Alas, my life me° is full loath,°   *to me / loathsome*
      I live over-long this lore° to lere.°   *knowledge / learn*
    DAUGHTER 1. Dear mother, mend your mood,
150   For we shall wend you with.
    WIFE. My friends that I from yode°   *went*
      Are overflowed with flood.

---

1 *at first* For the first time.
2 *a deal* Any amount, at all.
3 *Them would I went with us* I would like them to go with us.
4 *Look in ... without were* Enter and do it quickly; *without were* Literally, without doubt.

DAUGHTER 2. Now thank we God all good
  That us has granted grith.°   *protection*

DAUGHTER 3. Mother, of this work now would ye not ween,° *believe* 155
  That all should worth° to waters wan.°   *be converted to / dark*
SON 2. Father, what may this marvel mean?
  Whereto° made God middle-earth[1] and man?   *to what end*
DAUGHTER 1. So selcouth° sight was never none seen,   *marvelous*
  Since first that God this world began.   160
NOAH. Wend° and spear° your doors bedene,° *go / shut / immediately*
  For better counsel none I can.°   *know*
  This sorrow is sent for° sin,   *because of*
  Therefore to God we pray
  That he our bale° would blin.°   *trouble / end* 165
SON 3. The king of all mankin°   *mankind*
  Out of this woe us win,
  As thou art Lord, that may.[2]

SON 1. Yea, Lord, as thou let us be born
  In this great bale, some boot° us bid.°   *help / offer* 170
NOAH. My sons, see ye midday and morn
  To these cattle° take good heed;   *livestock animals*
  Keep them well with hay and corn;°   *feed grain*
  And women, fang° these fowls and feed,° *take / feed (them)*
  So that they be not lightly° lorn°   *carelessly / lost* 175
  As long as we this life shall lead.
SON 2. Father, we are full fain°   *happy*
  Your bidding to fulfill.
  Nine months passed are plain°   *fully*
  Since we were put to pain.   180
SON 3. He that is most of main°   *power*
  May mend it when he will.

NOAH. Oh bairns,° it waxes° clear about, *children / grows*
  That may ye see there where ye sit.
SON 1. Ay, lief° father, ye look thereout,   *dear* 185
  If that the water wane° aught° yet. *subsides / at all*
NOAH. That shall I do without doubt,
  Thereby the waning may we wit.°   *know*

---

1 *middle-earth* The world, the earth, as the mid-point between Heaven and Hell.
2 *that may* Who has the power.

Humorous — we would've laughed at Noah's wife (handwritten marginalia)

Ah, Lord, to thee I love° and lout.°   *give praise / worship*

190   The cataracts° I trow°   *floodgates (of heaven) / believe*
       be knit.°   *shut*
    Behold, my sons all three,
    The clouds are waxen° clear.   *grown*
   SON 2. Ah, Lord of mercy free,°   *generous*
    Ay° lovèd° might thou be.   *eternally / praised*
195 NOAH. I shall assay° the sea,   *test*
    How deep that it is here.

   WIFE. Lovèd be that Lord that gives all grace,
    That kindly thus our care would keel.°   *diminish*
   NOAH. I shall cast lead and look the space[1]
200 How deep the water is ilka deal.[2]
    Fifteen cubits of height it has
    Over ilka° hill fully to feal;°   *every / hide*
    But be well comforted in this case,
    It is waning, this wot° I well.   *know*
205 Therefore a fowl of flight
    Full soon shall I forth send,
    To seek if he have sight,
    Some land upon to light;°   *alight*
    Then may we wit° full right   *know*
210 When our mourning shall mend.°   *be alleviated*

    Of all the fowls that men may find
    The raven is wight,° and wise is he.   *strong*
    Thou art full crabbed° and all thy kind,   *disagreeable*
    Wend° forth thy course,° I command thee,   *go / way*
215 And warily° wot,° and hither°   *carefully / discover / here*
       thee wind°   *come back*
    If thou find other land or tree.
    Nine months here have we been pined,°   *afflicted*
    But when God will,° better mun° be.   *wills / must*
   DAUGHTER 1. That Lord that lends us life
220 To lere° his laws in land,   *obey*
    He° made both man and wife,°   *he who / woman*
    He help to stint° our strife.[3]   *end*

---

1   *I shall cast lead and look the space*   I will plumb the water and look for awhile.

2   *ilka deal*   Everywhere.

3   *He help to stint our strife*   May he help to bring our troubles to an end.

DAUGHTER 3. Our cares are keen° as knife,   *sharp*
     God grant us good tidand.°   *tidings, news*

SON 1. Father, this fowl is forth° full long;   *away*   225
     Upon some land I trow° he lend,°   *think / has landed*
     His food there for to find and fang° —   *capture, seize*
     That makes him be a failing friend.
NOAH. Now son, and if he so forth gang,°   *has gone*
     Since he for all our wealth° gan° wend,°   *well-being / did / go* 230
     Then be he for his works wrong
     Evermore waried° without end.   *cursed*
     And certes,° for to see   *certainly*
     When our sorrow shall cease,
     Another fowl full free°   *noble*   235
     Our messenger shall be;
     Thou dove, I command thee,
     Our comfort to increase.

     A faithful fowl to send art thou
     Of° all within these wones wide;[1]   *from among*   240
     Wend° forth I pray° thee, for our prow,°   *go / bid / good*
     And sadly° seek on ilka side[2]   *seriously*
     If the floods be falling now,
     That thou on the earth may bield° and bide;°   *remain / stay*
     Bring us some tokening° that we may trow°   *sign / have trust* 245
     What tidings° shall of us betide.° *events, circumstances / befall, happen*
DAUGHTER 2. Good Lord, on us thou look,
     And cease our sorrow sere,°   *diverse*
     Since we all sin forsook
     And to thy lore° us took.   *teaching*   250
DAUGHTER 3. A twelve-month but° twelve week[3]   *except for*
     Have we be hovering° here.   *waiting*

NOAH. Now bairns, we may be blithe and glad
     And love° our Lord of heavens king;[4]   *praise*
     My bird has done as I him bad:°   *commanded*   255
     An olive branch I see him bring.
     Blessed be thou fowl, that never was fade,°   *hostile, inimical*

---

1   *within these wones wide*   In every place.
2   *on ilka side*   Everywhere.
3   *A twelve-month but twelve week*   Twelve months except for twelve weeks, i.e., nine months.
4   *Lord of heavens king*   Lord, king of the heavens.

	That in thy force° makes no failing;	*strength*
	More joy in heart never ere° I had,	*before*
260	We mun° be saved, now may we sing.	*must*
	Come hither my sons in hie,[1]	
	Our woe away is went,	
	I see here certainly	
	The hills of Armenie.°	*Armenia*
265	SON 1. Lovèd° be that Lord forthy°	*praised / therefore*
	That us our lives has lent.°	*granted*

(*Then Noah and his sons should sing.*)

	WIFE. For° wreaks° now that we may win°	*from / disaster / escape*
	Out of this woe that we in were;[2]	
	But Noah, where are now all our kin	
270	And company we knew before?	
	NOAH. Dame, all are drowned, let be thy din,[3]	
	And soon° they bought° their sins sore.°	*recently / paid for / wicked*
	Good living let us begin,	
	So that we grieve our God no more.	
275	He was grieved in degree[4]	
	And greatly moved° in mind	*troubled*
	For° sin, as men may see:	*because of*
	Dum dixit, "Penitet me." [5]	
	Full sore° forthinking° was he	*sorely, greatly / repentant*
280	That ever he made mankind.	

	That makes us now to toll° and truss;°	*toil / haul*
	But sons, he said—I wot° well when—	*know*
	"Arcum ponam in nubibus."[6]	
	He set his bow clearly to ken°	*make known*
285	As a tokening between him and us,	
	In knowledge till° all Christian men,	*to*
	That from° this world were	*from the moment*
	fined° thus,	*finished, ended*

---

1 *in hie* Quickly.

2 *For wreaks … we in were* From disasters now we are able to escape out of the woe we were in.

3 *let be thy din* Be quiet.

4 *in degree* Duly.

5 *Dum dixit, "Penitet me"* Latin: When he said, "I repent me." From Genesis 6.7: "For it repenteth me that I have made them."

6 *Arcum ponam in nubibus* Latin: I do set my bow in the clouds (Genesis 9.13).

With water would he never waste° it then.[1]   *destroy*
Thus has God most of might
Set his sign full clear   290
Up in the air of height;[2]
. The rainbow it is right,
As men may see in sight
In seasons of the year.

SON 2. Sir, now since God, our sovereign sire,   295
  Has set his sign thus in certain,
  Than may we wit° this world's empire   *know*
  Shall evermore° last, is not to lain.[3]   *forever*
NOAH. Nay son, that shall we not desire,
  For and° we do, we work in vain;   *if* 300
  For it shall once° be waste° with fire,   *one day / destroyed*
  And never worth° to° world again.   *exist / as*
WIFE. Ah, sire, our hearts are sore
  For these saws° that ye say here,   *sayings*
  That mischief° mun° be more.   *harm / must* 305
NOAH. Be not afraid therefore,°   *of that*
  Ye shall not live then yore°   *so long*
  By many hundred year.
SON 1. Father, how shall this life be led

  Since none are in this world but we?   310
NOAH. Sons, with your wives ye shall be stead,°   *settled*
  And multiply your seed shall ye.
  Your bairns shall ilkone° other° wed   *each one / another*
  And worship God in good degree;
  Beasts and fowls shall forth be bred,   315
  And so a world begin to be.
  Now travail° shall ye taste°   *labor / experience*
  To win° you bread and wine,   *earn*
  For all this world is waste;°   *destroyed*
  These beasts must be unbraced,°   *unharnessed* 320
  And wend° we hence in haste,   *go*
  In God's blessing and mine.

---

1 *That from this world ... never waste it then* That from the moment that the world was ended thus (i.e., with the flood), that he would never destroy it in such a way (again).

2 *of height* On high.

3 *is not to lain* It shall not be concealed (i.e., that is true; truly).

The York Corpus Christi Play: Abraham and Isaac

The *Abraham and Isaac* pageant, depicting the events found in Genesis 22 (with some reference to material from earlier chapters), was presented by the Parchment Makers and Bookbinders. In the previous play, Noah's Wife's mourning for those drowned in the flood has dramatized the difficulty of understanding and having faith in God and his plan. Now the *Abraham and Isaac* play dramatizes a terrifying tension between human attachments and human values, and loyalty to God's seemingly cruel commands.

Isaac was conventionally read typologically as prefiguring Christ; such a reading aligns Abraham with God, who willingly sacrificed his son. The York version of the story underscores this association by aging Isaac to "thirty year and more somedeal," analogous to the age conventionally assigned to Jesus at the time of his ministry and subsequent death. Although such a change in age removes the pathos of a young child willingly accepting his death at his mournful father's hands, it brings the story into the contemporary world in new way. Abraham speaks of Isaac as his "bield" or protection, and here Isaac is of an age at which he might establish his own trade as a master, and perhaps care for his aging parents. The adult age of Isaac also underscores his symbolic value as a stand-in for York's adult audience members, who must themselves make difficult choices in remaining faithful to God's command.

The play is written in a twelve-line stanza that rhymes abababab-cdcd—a pattern found frequently in the cycle.

Pageant 10 of the York Corpus Christi Play: Abraham and Isaac

CHARACTERS

Abraham
Angel
Isaac
Servant 1
Servant 2

ABRAHAM. Great God that all this world has wrought,°	*made*
And wisely wot° both good and ill° —	*knows, distinguishes / evil*
I thank him throly° in my thought	*steadfastly*

Of all his love he lends° me till,°   *gives / to*
That thus from barrenhood° has me brought,   *barrenness*   5
A hundred winters° to fulfill[1]—   *years*
Thou grant me might° so that I mought°   *strength / may*
Ordain° my works after° thy will.   *order / according to*
For in this earthly life
Are none to God more bound°   *ready (to obey)*   10
Then is I and my wife,
For friendship° we have found.   *good will, favor (of God)*

Unto me told God on a tide,[2]
Where I was teld° under a tree,   *encamped*
He said my seed should° be multiplied   *would*   15
Like to the gravel° of the sea,   *sand*
And as the stars were strewed° wide,   *spread*
So said he that my seed should be;
And bad° I should° be circumcised   *commanded / must*
To fulfill the law; thus learnèd° he me.   *taught*   20
In world whereso° we won°   *wherever / dwell*
He sends us riches rife;
As far as shines the sun,
He is stinter° of strife.   *ender*

Abram first named was I,   25
And sithen° he set a syllab° ma;°   *then / syllable / more*
And my wife hight° Sarai   *was called*
And sithen was she named Sarah.

But Sarah was uncertain then
That ever our seed should sogate° yield,°   *in this manner / generate*   30
Because herself she was barren
And we were both gone in great eld.°   *age*
But she wrought° as a wise woman: *proceeded*
To have a bairn° us for to bield,°   *child / support, protect*
Her servant privily° she won   *secretly*   35
Unto my bed, my will to wield.[3]

---

1 *A hundred winters to fulfill* A hundred years to complete. The events that Abraham narrates next, and that lead up to the conception of Isaac (and thus the ending of Abraham's and Sarah's *barrenhood*, referred to in the previous line), took place in his hundredth year.

2 *on a tide* Once.

3 *my will to wield* To wield to my will.

	Soon after then befell,°	it happened
	When God our deed would dight,°	determine
	She brought forth Ishmael,	
40	A son seemly° to sight.	handsome

	Then afterward when we waxèd° old,	grew
	My wife she fell in fear for same;[1]	
	Our God needs° tidings° till° us told	necessarily / news / to
	Where we were in our house at hame,°	home (northern dialect)
45	Till° have a son we should be bold,°	to / assured
	And Isaac should be his name,	
	And his seed should spring manifold.°	abundant
	If I were blithe,° who would me blame?	merry
	And for° I trowed° this tiding,	because / believed
50	That God told to me then,	
	The ground° and the beginning	foundation
	Of truth that time[2] began.	

	Now owe° I greatly God to yield,°[3]	ought / make an offering
	That° so would tell me his intent,	who
55	And not gainstanding° our great eld°	withstanding / age
	A seemly° son he has us sent.	fair, fit
	Now he is wight° himself to wield°	strong (enough) / take over
	And from me is all wightness° went,	strength
	Therefore shall he be my bield.°	support, protection
60	I love° him that this loan° has lent,°	praise / gift / given
	For he may stint° our strife	end
	And fend° us from all ill;	defend
	I love him as my life,	
	With all mine heart and will.[4]	

ANGEL. Abraham, Abraham!

65 ABRAHAM.   Lo, I am here.

---

1 *fell in fear for same* I.e., she became fearful once again, for the same reason (their advanced age), that they wouldn't produce the many generations promised.

2 *that time* At that time.

3 *Now owe ... yield* Now I very much ought to make an offering to God.

4 *I love him ... will* The masculine pronouns here are artfully ambiguous. The first "him" must be God, since he has "lent" this "loan." But both Isaac and God may "stint [the] strife" of Abraham and Sarah, and Abraham could love both Isaac and God "as [his] life." Since Isaac is conventionally read as a type of Christ—that is, as prefiguring Christ—the conflation of God and Isaac here in the language makes sense in such a typological scheme.

ANGEL. Now bodeword° unto thee I bring: *message*
    God will assay° thy will and cheer,° *test / behavior*
    If thou will bow till° his bidding; *to*
    Isaac thy son that is thee° dear, *to thee*
    Whom thou loves over all thing,   70
    To the land of vision[1] wend° in fere[2] *go*
    And there of him thou make offering.
    I shall thee show full soon
    The stead° of sacrifice. *place*
    God will° this deed be done, *wills that*   75
    And therefore thee advise.[3]

ABRAHAM. Lord God that lends° ay-lasting° light, *gives / everlasting*
    This is a ferly° fare° *dreadful, astonishing / matter*
      to feel.° *experience*
    Till° have a son seemly to sight, *to*
    Isaac, that I love full well—   80
    He is of eld,° to reckon° right, *age / count*
    Thirty year and more somedeal°— *somewhat*
    And unto death him bus be dight.[4]
    God has said me° so for my sele,° *to me / well-being*
    And bids me wend° on all wise[5] *go*   85
    To the land of vision,
    There to make sacrifice
    Of Isaac that is my son.

    And that is hither° three days' journey *from here*
    The gainest° gate° that I can go; *most direct / way*   90
    And certes,° I shall not say him° nay° *certainly / to him / no*
    If God command myself to slo.° *slay*
    But to my son I will naught° say, *nothing*
    But take him and my servants two,
    And with our ass wend forth our way;   95
    As God has said, it shall be so.

---

1 *land of vision* Moriah, as translated in the Vulgate Latin Bible (*terram visionis*), Genesis 22.2.

2 *in fere* Together.

3 *thee advise* Directs you.

4 *unto death him bus be dight* It behooves him to be put to death; it is necessary to put him to death.

5 *on all wise* By all means.

Isaac, son, I understand
To wilderness now wend will we,[1]
There for to make our offerand,°   *offering*
100   For so has God commanded me.

ISAAC. Father, I am ever at your will,
As worthy is without train;°   *treachery*
God's commandment to fulfill
Owe° all folk for to be fain.°   *ought / glad*
105 ABRAHAM. Son, thou says me full good skill,[2]
But all the sooth° is not to sayn.[3]   *truth*
Go we sen° we shall theretill°—   *then / thereto, to that place*
I pray God send us[4] well again.
ISAAC. Children,[5] lead forth our ass
110   With wood that we shall brin.°   *burn*
Even as God ordained has,
To work we will begin.

SERVANT 1. At your bidding we will be boun°   *prepared*
What way in world that ye will wend.°   *go*
115 SERVANT 2. Why, shall we truss out forth of town[6]
In any uncouth° land to lend?°   *strange / remain*
SERVANT 1. I hope they have in this season
From God of heaven some solace send.°   *sent*
SERVANT 2. To fulfill it° is good reason,   *i.e., Abraham's command*
120   And kindly° keep that° he has kenned.°   *naturally / what / instructed*
SERVANT 1. But what they mean° certain°   *intend / truly*
Have I no knowledge clear.
SERVANT 2. It may not greatly gain°   *be advantageous*
To move° of swilk° matter.   *speak / such*

---

1   *Isaac, ... will we*   In staging, Isaac presumably does not enter or is not close enough to hear his father until these lines, as Abraham has just said he will not tell his son anything.

2   *thou says me full good skill*   You speak to me very reasonably.

3   *all the sooth is not to sayn*   Not all of the truth is to be said; i.e., not everything can be revealed.

4   *send us*   Send us home.

5   *Children*   Servants, helpers. "Child" can be used to address young people in service or apprenticeship, or attendants and helpers of various kinds.

6   *truss out forth of town*   Depart from town; get moving out of town.

ABRAHAM. No, noy you[1] not in no degree[2]   125
  So for to deem° here of our deed,   *judge*
  For as God commanded, so work will we;
  Until° his tales° us bus° take heed.[3]   *to / words / must*
SERVANT 1. All those that will his servants be
  Full specially he will them speed.°   *cause to prosper*   130
ISAAC. Children, with all the might in me
  I love° that Lord of ilka° lede,°   *praise / every / person*
  And worship him certain;
  My will is ever unto.°   *in agreement (with his)*
SERVANT 2. God give you might° and main°   *strength / power*   135
  Right here so for to do.

ABRAHAM. Son, if our Lord God almighty
  Of myself would have his offerand,°   *offering, sacrifice*
  I would be glad for him to die,
  For all our heal° hangs in his hand.   *well-being*   140
ISAAC. Father, forsooth,° right so would I,   *truly*
  Liefer° than longer to live in land.   *rather*
ABRAHAM. Ah, son, thou says full well, forthy°   *therefore*
  God give thee grace gradely° to stand.[4]   *willingly*
  Children, bide° ye here still,   *wait*   145
  No farther shall ye go,
  For yonder I see the hill[5]
  That we shall wend° unto.   *go*

ISAAC. Keep well our ass and all our gear
  To° time we come again you till.[6]   *until*   150
ABRAHAM. My son, this wood behooves thee[7] bear
  Till thou come high upon yon hill.
ISAAC. Father, that may do no dere,°   *harm*

---

1   *noy you*   Trouble yourselves.
2   *in no degree*   To any extent.
3   *us bus take heed*   It is necessary for us to take heed; we must take heed.
4   *Ah, son ... gradely to stand*   It might make sense for Abraham to say these two lines as an
    aside, since he has not yet told Isaac that he is the intended sacrifice. But it is also possible
    to take the lines as being spoken directly to Isaac; in that case, Isaac would presumably
    understand them as referring to some unknown future.
5   *I see the hill*   The "hill" could easily be the pageant wagon, the action of the journey to it
    thus taking place on the ground.
6   *you till*   To you.
7   *behooves thee*   It is necessary that you; you must.

God's commandment to fulfill,
155 For from all wothes° he will us were°   *dangers / protect*
Whereso° we wend to work his will.   *wherever*
ABRAHAM. Ah, son, that was well said.
Lay down that wood even here
Till our altar be graithèd;°   *made ready*
160 And, my son, make good cheer.

ISAAC. Father, I see here wood and fire,
But whereof° shall our offering be?   *of what*
ABRAHAM. Certes° son, good God, our suffering sire,[1]   *certainly*
Shall ordain° it in good degree.°   *arrange / way, manner*
165 For son, and° we do his desire,   *if*
Full good reward therefore get we.
In heaven there mun° we have our hire,°   *shall / reward*
For unto us so hight° has he.   *promised*
Therefore son, let us pray
170 To God, both thou and I,
That we may make this day
Our offering here duly.

Great God that all this world has wrought
And gradely° governs good and ill,°   *worthily / evil*
175 Thou grant me might° so that I mought°   *strength / am able*
Thy commandments to fulfill.
And if my flesh grutch° or grieve ought,°   *complain / at all*
Or certes[2] my soul assent theretill,°   *to that matter*
To burn all that I hither brought
180 I shall not spare if° I should spill.[3]   *even if*
ISAAC. Lord God of great poustie°   *power*
To whom all people prays,
Grant both my father and me
To work thy will always.

185 But father, now would I frayne° full fain°   *inquire / gladly*
Whereof° our offering should be graithed?°   *from where / procured*

---

1 *our suffering sire* I.e., Christ, who suffered on the cross. Medieval biblical drama typically
uses anachronism to point to the ways in which Old Testament stories are read typologically
as prefiguring New Testament ones. References to Christ here underscore Isaac's Christ-like
role as sacrifice.

2 *Or certes* Even though.

3 *if I should spill* Even if I should die (in the process); even if it kills me.

ABRAHAM. Certes son, I may no longer lain:°   *be silent*
   Thyself should bide° that bitter braid.°   *endure / affliction*
ISAAC. Why father, will° God that I be slain?[1]   *desires, wants*
ABRAHAM. Yea, soothly° son, so has he said.   *truly* 190
ISAAC. And I shall not grutch° there° again,   *complain / about it*
   To work his will I am well paid;°   *pleased, satisfied*
   Since it is his desire,
   I shall be bain° to be   *ready, willing*
   Brittened° and burnt in fire,   *dismembered* 195
   And therefore mourn not for me.

ABRAHAM. Nay son, this gates must needs be gone,[2]
   My Lord God will I not gainsay,°   *deny*
   Nor never make mourns nor moan
   To make offering of thee this day.   200
ISAAC. Father, since God our Lord alone
   Vouchsafe° to send, when ye gan° pray,   *graciously granted / did*
   A son to you, when ye had none,
   And now will that he wend° his way,[3]   *go*
   Therefore fand° me to fell°   *endeavor / kill* 205
   Till° offering in this place;   *as*
   But first I shall you tell
   My counsel° in this case.   *advice*

   I know myself by course of kind,°   *nature*
   My flesh for° death will be dreadand.°   *concerning / dreading* 210
   I am feared° that ye shall find   *afraid*
   My force° your forward° to withstand.°   *strength / promise / oppose*
   Therefore is° best that ye me bind   *it is*
   In bands fast,° both foot and hand.   *firmly fixed*
   Now whilst I am in might and mind,   215
   So shall ye safely make offerand,°   *offering*
   For father, when I am bound
   My might° may not avail.°   *strength / be effectual*
   Here shall no fault be found
   To make your foreward° fail.   *covenant* 220

---

1 *Why father, ... slain?*   Why father, does God want me to be slain? ("Why" is an exclamation here.)

2 *this gates must needs be gone*   This way must be taken.

3 *will that he wend his way*   (God) wants that he (Isaac) should go his way (i.e., depart this life, die).

	For ye are old and all unwield,°	*feeble*

For ye are old and all unwield,°   *feeble*
And I am wight° and wild° of thought.   *strong, manly / impetuous*
ABRAHAM. To bind him that° should be my bield!°   *who / protection*
Out-taken° God's will, that would I not.   *except for*
225 But lo, here shall no force° be felt,   *coercion*
So shall God have that° he has sought.   *that which*
Farewell my son, I shall thee yield
Till° him that all this world has wrought.   *to*

Now kiss me heartily, I thee pray.
230 Isaac, I take my leave for ay°—   *ever*
Me bus[1] thee miss.
My blessing have thou entirely,
And I beseech God almighty
He give thee his.

235 Thus are we sam° in assent°   *together / agreement*
After° thy words wise.   *according*
Lord God, to this take tent,[2]
Receive thy sacrifice.

This is to me a peerless° pine,°   *unequaled / pain*
240 To see mine own dear child thus bound.
Me had well liefer° my life to tine°   *lose*
Than see this sight thus of my son.
It is God's will, it shall be mine;
Against his sand° shall I never shun,°   *message, command / hesitate*
245 To God's commandment I shall incline,
That° in me fault none be found.   *so that*
Therefore, my son so dear,
If thou will anything say,
Thy death it draws near,
250 Farewell, for once and ay.°   *always*

ISAAC. Now my dear father, I would you pray,
Hear me three words, grant me my boon°   *request, prayer*
Since I from this° shall pass for ay;°   *this (earth) / always*
I see mine hour is come full soon.
255 In word, in work, or any way

---

1   *Me bus* I must.
2   *take tent* Pay attention, attend to.

That I have trespassed or aught° misdone, *anything*
Forgive me father ere° I die this day, *before*
For his love that made both sun and moon.
Here since we two shall twin° *part*
First God I ask mercy, 260
And you in more and min,° *less*
This day ere ever I die.

ABRAHAM. Now my great God Adonai,[1]
  That all this world has worthily wrought,
  Forgive the son, for his mercy, 265
  In word, in work, in deed and thought.
  Now son, as we are lered,° *instructed*
  Our time may not miscarry.° *go wrong*
ISAAC. Now farewell all middle-earth,[2]
  My flesh waxes ° faint for ferd;° *grows / fear* 270
  Now father, take your sword,
  Methinks° full long ye tarry. *it seems to me*

ABRAHAM. Nay, nay son, nay, I thee behet,° *promise*
  That do I not, without were.° *doubt*
  Thy words make me my wanges° *cheeks* 275
    to wet° *become wet (i.e., with tears)*
  And changes, child, full often my cheer.
  Therefore lie down, hands and feet,
  Now may thou wit° thine hour is near. *know*
ISAAC. Ah, dear father, life is full sweet,
  The dread of death does all my dere.° *suffering* 280
  As I am here your son
  To God I take° me° till,° *entrust / myself / to*
  Now am I laid here boun,° *ready*
  Do with me what ye will.

For father, I ask no more respite,° *delay* 285
  But hear a word what I would mean:° *advise*
  I beseech you ere° that ye smite,° *before / strike*
  Lay down this kerchief on mine eyen,° *eyes*
  Then may your offering be parfite° *perfect*
  If ye will work thus as I ween.° *hope* 290

---

1 *Adonai* Hebrew name for God.
2 *middle-earth* The world, the earth, as the mid-point between Heaven and Hell.

And here to God my soul I wit°   *commend*
And all my body to burn bedene.°   *immediately*
Now father be not missing,¹
But smite fast as ye may.
295 ABRAHAM. Farewell, in God's dear blessing
And mine, forever and ay.°   *always*

That peerless prince I pray
Mine offering heretill° have it,   *hereto, for this purpose*
My sacrifice this day
300 I pray the Lord receive it.

ANGEL. Abraham, Abraham!
ABRAHAM.   Lo, here iwis.°   *truly*
ANGEL. Abraham, abide,° and hold thee still.   *wait*
Slay not thy son; do him no miss.°   *harm*
Take here a sheep thy offering till,²
305 Is° sent thee from the king of bliss   *it is*
That faithful ay° to thee is fon;°   *always / found*
He bids thee make offering of this
Here at this time, and save thy son.

ABRAHAM. I love° that Lord with heart entire   *praise*
310 That of his love this loan° me lent,°   *gift / gave*
To save my son, my darling dear,
And sent this sheep to this intent,
That we shall offer it to thee here;
So shall it be as thou has meant.°   *conveyed*
315 My son, be glad and make good cheer,
God has till° us good comfort sent.   *to*
He will° not thou be dead,   *desire, wants*
But till his laws take keep;°   *care*
And see son, in thy stead°   *place*
320 God has sent us a sheep.

ISAAC. To make our offering at his will
All for our sake he has it sent.
To love° that Lord I hold° great skill°   *praise / consider / reasonableness*
That till° his meinie° thus has meant.°   *to / people / intended*

---

1 *be not missing* Don't fail.
2 *thy offering till* As your offering.

This deed I would have ta'en° me till[1]   *taken* 325
Full gladly Lord, to thine intent.
ABRAHAM. Ah, son, thy blood would he not spill,
Forthy° this sheep thus has he sent;   *therefore*
And son, I am full fain°   *glad*
Of our speed° in this place,   *good fortune* 330
But go we home again
And love° God of his grace.   *praise*

ANGEL. Abraham, Abraham!
ABRAHAM.   Lo, here indeed.
Hark son, some salving° of° our sore.°   *remedy / for / suffering*
ANGEL. God says thou shall have mickle° meed°   *great / reward* 335
For this good will that thou in were.
Since thou for him would do this deed—
To spill° thy son and not to spare—   *kill*
He means° to multiply your seed   *intends*
On sides sere,° as he said ere;°   *several / before* 340
And yet he hight° you this,   *promises*
That of your seed shall rise,
Through help of him and his,
Overhand° of all enemies.   *above*

Look ye him love, this is his list,°   *desire* 345
And leally° live after° his lay,°   *faithfully / according to / law*
For in your seed all mun° be blest   *shall*
That there be born by night or day.
If ye will in him trow° or trust,   *believe*
He will be with you ever and ay.°   *always* 350
ABRAHAM. Full well ware us[2] and we it wist,°   *know*
How we should work his will alway.
ISAAC. Father, that shall we frayne°   *inquire*
At wiser men than we,
And fulfill it full fain,°   *gladly* 355
Indeed, after our degree.°   *station, social status*

ABRAHAM. Now son, since we thus well has speed,°   *good fortune*
That God has granted me thy life,
It is my will that thou be wed

---

1 *ta'en me till* Accepted, taken on.
2 *Full well ware us* Let us be fully mindful.

360	And wield° a woman to thy wife;	*have*
	So shall thy seed spring and be spread	
	In the laws of God by reason rife.°	*abundantly*
	I wot° in what stead she is stead¹	*know*
	That thou shall wed, without strife:	
365	Rebecca that damsel,	
	Her fairer² is none fon,°	*found*
	The daughter of Bethuel	
	That was my brother's son.	

ISAAC. Father, as you like my life to spend,
370   I shall assent unto the same.
   ABRAHAM. One of my servant's sons shall I send
     Unto that bird° to bring her home.°   *lady*

The gainest° gates° now will we wend.°   *quickest / ways / travel*
My bairns,³ ye are not to blame
375 If ye think long that we here lend;°   *linger*
Gather sam° our gear, in God's name,   *together*
And go we home again
Even unto Beersheba.
God that is most of main°   *might*
380 Us wise° and with you be.   *guide*

---

1 *what stead she is stead* What place she lives.
2 *Her fairer* Fairer than her.
3 *bairns* Children; here, figurative, directed at the servants as well as Isaac, and by extension, possibly also the audience.

The York Corpus Christi Play: Moses and Pharaoh

York's *Moses and Pharaoh* play, presented by the Hosiers (makers of stockings and undergarments), is a complex play full of spectacle and special effects. Part of the complexity comes from its multiple settings— Pharaoh's court (in two different time periods), Mt. Sinai, Goshen, and the Red Sea—and the movement between them that is necessary (for Moses especially). Medieval performances of the play almost certainly utilized the ground level for movement of the characters, and perhaps also for some settings. The play also requires multiple special effects and elaborate spectacle. Pharaoh's court is among the more lavish displays of worldly power in the cycle; moreover, the play gives us Moses's marvel of turning his rod into a snake and back again, God speaking to Moses from a burning bush, and the parting of the Red Sea for the Hebrews, followed by the drowning of Pharaoh and the Egyptians. The rod trick (performed by Aaron in Exodus, but here given to Moses himself) is still a basic magic trick today; a search of YouTube for "wand to snake" or "cane to snake" will turn up many variations, and some similar technology was probably used here. Pyrotechnics, a favorite special effect of the medieval stage, were likely involved in the burning bush. Records for the Smith's play in the city of Coventry list a payment for a "half a yard of Red Sea," suggesting that they used cloth to represent the sea in their own play. York might have followed suit, with non-speaking extras manipulating the cloth.

The York *Moses and Pharaoh* play not only makes use of spectacle and special effects; it is also *about* spectacle and wonder, and about the difference between trickery and true miracle, earthly and divine power, and manipulation and truth. It seems also to comment on the power and limits of dramatic representation, as the ten plagues visited on the Egyptians are largely brought forth through dialogue and imagination (although it is possible that the dialogue cues further special effects and props).

In the midst of all this is the dramatic tension inherent in a confrontation between two people. In removing Aaron from the story, the playwright creates a drama in which one man speaks truth to power. In typological terms, the play prefigures the *Harrowing of Hell* episode, where one man, Jesus, frees his people—the Old Testament Jews who died before his salvation—from a ruthless and false power, Satan. To medieval audiences, the play might also have come across as a general, more worldly lesson, about the necessity to resist corrupt power.

The events depicted in the play take place in Exodus 2–14, although they are filtered through generations of artistic, literary, liturgical, and other traditional depictions, as with the rest of the cycle. The verse form, a twelve-line stanza rhyming abababababcdcd, is frequently used throughout the cycle.

Pageant 11 of the York Corpus Christi Play: Moses and Pharaoh

CHARACTERS

Pharaoh
Counselor 1
Counselor 2
Moses
God
Boy 1
Boy 2
Boy 3
Egyptian 1
Egyptian 2

PHARAOH. O peace, I bid that no man pass,
    But keep the course that I command,
    And take good heed to him that has
    Your life all wholly in his hand.
5   King Pharaoh my father was,
    And led the lordship° of this land,   *lords*
    I am his heir, as eld will as,[1]
    Ever in his stead° to stir and stand.[2]   *place*
    All Egypt is mine own
10   To lead after° my law,   *according to*
    I will my might be known
    And honored as it owe.°   *ought*

    Therefore as king I command peace
    To all the people of this empire,
15   That no man put him forth in press[3]
    But that[4] will do as we desire.

---

1 *as eld will as* As age will demand, i.e., now that I have come of age.
2 *to stir and stand* To take action and be steadfast.
3 *put him forth in press* Put himself forth in the crowd, i.e. assert himself.
4 *But that* Unless he.

And of your saws° I rede° you cease,   *talking / advise*
And seise° to me, your sovereign sire,   *endow (the kingdom)*
That most your comfort may increase
And at my list° lose° life and lire.°   *will / destroy / body*   20
COUNSELOR 1. My Lord, if any were
That would not work your will,
And we wist° which they were,   *knew*
Full soon we should them spill.°   *kill*

PHARAOH. Throughout my kingdom would I ken,°   *be aware*   25
And can them thank that could me tell,
If any were so waried° then   *wicked*
That would aught° fand°   *anything / attempt*
  our force° to fell.°   *power / overthrow*
COUNSELOR 2. My Lord, there are a manner° of men   *type*
That muster° great masteries°   *display / deeds*   30
  them amell,°   *among*
The Jews that won° here in Goshen¹   *dwell*
And are named the children of Israel.
They multiply so fast
That soothly° we suppose   *truly*
They are like,° and° they last,°   *likely / if / continue*   35
Your lordship° for to lose.°   *power / destroy*

PHARAOH. Why, devil, what gauds° have they begun?   *tricks*
Are they of might° to make affrays?°   *power / attack*
COUNSELOR 1. Those felon° folk, sir, first was found   *wicked*
In King Pharaoh your father's days.   40
They come of Joseph, Jacob's son,
That° was a prince worthy to praise,   *who*
And sithen° in rest forth are they run,²   *since*
Now are they like to lose° our lays.°   *destroy / laws, customs*
They shall confound° us clean   *defeat*   45
But if³ they sooner cease.
PHARAOH. What devil ever may it mean
That they so fast increase?

---

1   *Goshen* According to the Bible, Goshen is the area of Egypt where the Jews settled from
    the time of Joseph in Genesis to their departure in Exodus.
2   *sithen ... run* Since then they have increased in numbers unchecked.
3   *But if* Unless.

COUNSELOR 2. How they increase full well we ken,°   *know*
50 As our elders before us found,
    They were told° but sixty and ten   *numbered*
    When they entered into this land.
    Sithen° have they sojourned° here in Goshen   *since then / lived*
    Four hundred year, this we warrand,°   *guarantee*
55 Now are they numbered of mighty men
    Well more than three hundred thousand,
    Without wife and child
    And herds° that keep their fee.°   *herdsmen / cattle*
PHARAOH. So might we be beguiled;
60 But certes,° that shall not be,   *certainly*

    For with quantise° we shall them quell,°   *cunning / suppress*
    That they shall no farrer° spread.   *farther*
COUNSELOR 1. Lord, we have heard our fathers tell
    How clerks,° that full well could   *scholars*
        read,°   *interpret (holy) texts*
65 Said a man should wax° them amell°   *grow up / among*
    That should fordo° us and our deed.[1]   *destroy*
PHARAOH. Fie[2] on them, to the devil of hell!
    Swilk° destiny shall we not dread.   *such*
    We shall make midwives to spill° them,   *kill*
70 When our Hebrews are born,
    All that are man-kind° to kill them,[3]   *male*
    So shall they soon be lorn.°   *ruined*

    For of the other have I none° awe.°   *no / fear*
    Swilk bondage shall we to them bid:°   *offer*
75 To dike° and delve, bear° and draw,°   *dig / carry / pull*
    And do all swilk unhonest° deed.°   *unseemly, lowly / tasks*

---

1 *Said a man ... our deed* The prophecy refers to Moses.

2 *Fie* An exclamation expressing contempt, disapproval, or indignation; *Fie on them* I.e., curse them!

3 *All ... kill them* In Exodus 1, the midwives circumvent this order from Pharaoh to kill the male newborns; they claim that the liveliness of Hebrew boys in the womb causes the Hebrew women to give birth before the midwives arrive, and thus they are turned away. Pharaoh then orders that all male newborns be cast into the river. That plan is not carried out explicitly in the narrative; that the threat is real, however, is implied in the opening of Exodus 2, when Moses's mother hides him in a basket among the reeds on the bank of the Nile (Exodus 2.1–3). The threat of infanticide and Moses's escape ties him typologically to the Slaughter of the Innocents and Christ's escape of that fate.

Thus shall the lads° behold° law,   *men of low birth / obey, be held to*
As losels° ever their life to lead.   *wretches*
COUNSELOR 2. Certes° Lord, this is a subtle saw,°   *certainly / speech*
So shall the folk no farrer° spread.   *farther* 80
PHARAOH. Yea, help to hold them down,
That we no faintise° find.   *treachery*
COUNSELOR 1. Lord, we shall ever be boun°   *ready*
In bondage them to bind.

MOSES.[1] Great God that all this ground° began   *world* 85
And governs ever in good degree,°   *order*
That made me, Moses, unto man
And saved me sithen° out of the sea[2]—   *thereafter*
King Pharaoh he commanded then
So that no sons should saved° be,   *spared* 90
Against his will away I won°—   *lived*
Thus has God showed his might in me.
Now am I here to keep,°   *tend*
Set under Sinai's° side,°   *Mt. Sinai's / slope*
The bishop[3] Jethro's sheep, 95
So better boot° to bide.°   *fortune / await*

Ah, mercy God, mickle° is thy might,   *great*
What man may of thy marvels mean!°   *tell*
I see yonder a full selcouth° sight   *amazing*
Whereof before no sign was seen. 100
A bush I see yonder burning bright
And the leaves last ay° alike green;   *always*
If it be work of worldly° wight°   *earthly / person*
I will go wit° without ween.°   *know / doubt*
GOD. Moses, come not too near 105
But still in that stead° dwell,°   *place / remain*
And take heed to me here,
And tent° what I thee tell.   *pay attention*

---

1 *bind ... MOSES* The location changes here. It is possible that some of this action takes place on the ground.

2 *saved ... sea* Sea: Nile River. The reference is to the story told in Exodus 2.1–10, in which Moses is hidden by his mother on the banks of the Nile. Pharaoh's own daughter finds him and saves him, raising him as her own. The play has clearly jumped in time from Pharaoh's plans prior to Moses' birth to Moses' adulthood.

3 *bishop* Religious leader, priest. Medieval texts often use anachronistic Christian titles for religious leaders of other religions and times.

I am thy Lord, without lack,°	*fault*
110 To length° thy life even as me list,[1]	*prolong*
And the same God that sometime° spake°	*once / spoke*
Unto thine elders as they wist;°	*learned*
Both Abraham and Isaac	
And Jacob, said I, should be blist°	*blessed*
115 And multiplying, them to make,°	*prosper*
So that their seed° should not	*offspring*
be missed.°	*allowed to die out*
And now King Pharaoh	
Fouls° their children full fast.°	*oppresses / severely*
If I suffer° him so°	*allow / (to do) so*
120 Their seed should soon be past.	
To make thee message° have I meant	*messenger*
To him that them so harmed has,	
To warn him with words hend°	*polite*
So that he let my people pass,	
125 That they to wilderness may wend°	*go*
And worship me as whilom° was.	*formerly*
And if he longer gar° them lend°	*cause / to remain*
His song full soon shall be 'alas'.	
MOSES. Ah, Lord, since, with thy leave,	
130 That lineage° loves me not,	*people, nation*
Gladly they would me grieve°	*cause harm*
And° I slike° bodeword° brought.	*if / such / message*
Therefore Lord, let some other frast°	*try*
That has more force° them for to fear.°	*power / make afraid*
135 GOD. Moses, be not abashed°	*afraid*
My bidding boldly to bear.	
If they with wrong aught° would thee wrast,°	*in any way / deceive*
Out of all wothes° I shall thee were.°	*dangers / protect*
MOSES. We,[2] Lord, they will not to me trast°	*trust*
140 For all the oaths that I may swear.	
To neven° slike° note° of new[3]	*announce / such / matter*
To folk of wicked will,	
Without token° true,	*sign, proof*
They will not take tent° theretill.°	*heed / of that*

---

1   *as me list* As it pleases me.

2   *We* Interjection. A conventional cry of distress or consternation.

3   *of new* Anew, newly, suddenly.

GOD. And if they will not understand   145
    Ne° take heed how I have thee sent,   *nor*
    Before the king cast down thy wand°   *rod*
    And it shall seem as a serpent.
    Sithen° take the tail in thy hand   *after*
    And hardily° up thou it hent,°   *boldly / take*   150
    In the first state as thou it found,
    So shall it turn by mine intent.°   *will*
    Hide thy hand in thy barm°   *bosom*
    And as a leper it shall be like,
    Sithen° hale° without harm;   *after / healthy*   155
    Thy signs shall be slike.°   *such*

    And if he will not suffer° then   *permit*
    My people for to pass in peace,
    I shall send vengeance nine or ten[1]
    To sue° him sorer,° ere° I cease.   *pursue / more fiercely / before*   160
    But the Jews that won° in Goshen   *dwell*
    Shall not be marked° with that mes,°   *afflicted / calamity*
    As long as they my laws will ken°   *recognize*
    Their comfort shall I ever increase.
MOSES. Ah, Lord, lovèd° be thy will   *praised*   165
    That makes thy folk so free,
    I shall tell them until[2]
    As thou tell unto me.

    But to the king, Lord, when I come
    And° he ask me what is thy name,   *if*   170
    And I stand still then, deaf and dumb,[3]
    How shall I be without blame?°   *censure*
GOD. I say thus *ego sum qui sum*,[4]
    I am he that I am the same,
    And if thou might not move ne mum[5]   175
    I shall thee save from sin and shame.
MOSES. I understand this thing

---

1   *vengeance nine or ten*   Nine or ten vengeances.
2   *them until*   To them.
3   *deaf and dumb*   Because the God of Israel has no proper name (unlike Egyptian gods),
    Moses has nothing he can say, and hence will seem "deaf and dumb." In the Exodus account
    (3.13), it is actually the Israelites that Moses assumes will ask for God's name.
4   *ego sum qui sum*   Latin: I am who am (Exodus 3.14).
5   *move ne mum*   Speak nor whisper.

With all the might in me.

GOD. Be bold in my blessing,
180 Thy bield° ay° shall I be.   *protection / always*

MOSES. Ah, Lord of life, lere° me my lare°   *teach / skill*
That I these tales may truly tell.
Unto my friends now will I fare,°   *go*
The chosen children of Israel,
185 To tell them comfort of their care,[1]
And of their danger that they in dwell.
[*Moses travels to his people and addresses them.*]
God maintain you and me evermore,
And mickle° mirth° be you amell.[2]   *great / joy*
BOY 1. Ah, Moses, master dear,
190 Our mirth is all mourning,
We are hard° holden° here   *securely / held*
As carls° under the king.   *slaves*

BOY 2. Moses, we may mourn and min,°   *ponder*
There is no man us° mirths° mase;°   *to us / joys / makes, brings*
195 And since we come all of a kin,[3]
Ken° us some comfort in this case.   *tell, proclaim*
MOSES. Be of your mourning blin,°   *delivered*
God will defend you of° your fais.°   *from / foes*
Out of this woe he will you win°   *rescue*
200 To please him in more plainer° place.   *open*
I shall carp° to the king   *speak*
And fand° to make you free.   *attempt*
BOY 3. God send us good tiding,
And always with you be.

[*Moses travels to Pharaoh's court.*]

205 MOSES. King Pharaoh, to me take tent.°   *heed*
PHARAOH.[4] Why, what tidings can thou tell?
MOSES. From God of heaven thus am I sent

---

1 *To tell … care* To bring them comfort for their suffering.
2 *you amell* Among you.
3 *all of a kin* From one people.
4 *PHARAOH* This Pharaoh is actually the son of the Pharaoh who opens the play, but the text makes no distinction in speech headings.

To fetch his folk of Israel;
To wilderness he would° they went.   *desires*
PHARAOH. Yea, wend° thou to the devil of hell.   *go* 210
  I make no force[1] how° thou has meant,°   *what / complained about*
  For in my danger° shall they dwell.   *power*
  And faitour,° for thy sake,   *liar*
  They shall be put to pine.°   *punishment*
MOSES. Then will God vengeance take   215
  On thee and on all thine.

PHARAOH. Fie on thee, lad, out of my land!
  Weens thou[2] with wiles° to lose° our lay?°   *trickery / destroy / law*
  Whence° is this warlock° with his wand   *from where / sorcerer*
  That would thus win our folk away?   220
COUNSELOR 2. It is Moses, we well° warrand,°   *fully / assert*
  Against all Egypt is he ay.°   *always*
  Your father great fault in him found,
  Now will he mar° you if he may.   *destroy*
PHARAOH. Nay, nay, that dance° is done,   *business (figuratively)* 225
  That lurdan° lerèd° over-late.°   *scoundrel / learned / too late*
MOSES. God bids thee grant my boon,°   *request*
  And let me go my gate.°   *way*

PHARAOH. Bids God me? False lurdan, thou lies!
  What token told° he, took thou tent?°   *revealed / notice* 230
MOSES. Yea sir, he said thou should despise
  Both me and all his commandment.
  In thy presence cast, on this wise,[3]
  My wand he bad° by his assent,°   *commanded / will*
  And that thou should thee well advise°   *take notice* 235
  How it should turn to a serpent.
  And in his holy name
  Here shall I lay it down:
  Lo sir, see here the same.
  [*The wand turns into a serpent.*]
PHARAOH. Ah! Dog! The devil thee drown!   240

MOSES. He said that I should take the tail
  So for to prove his power plain,

---

1 *I make no force* I don't care.
2 *Weens thou* Do you think.
3 *on this wise* In this manner.

And soon he said it should not fail
For to turn a wand again.
Lo sir, behold.
245 PHARAOH.   Hap ill hail![1]
Now certes this is a subtle° swain,°   *cunning / fellow*
But these boys° shall bide° here in our bail,°   *knaves / stay / custody*
For all their gauds° shall not them gain;°   *tricks*
But worse, both morn and noon,[2]
250 Shall they fare for thy sake.[3]
MOSES. God send some vengeance soon,
And on thy work take wrake.°   *retribution*

[*Enter Egyptian 1 and Egyptian 2.*]

EGYPTIAN 1. Alas, alas, this land is lorn,°   *ruined*
On° life we may no longer lend.°   *in / live*
255 EGYPTIAN 2. So° great mischief° is made   *such / misfortune*
since morn°   *morning*
There may no medicine° us amend.°   *remedy*
COUNSELOR 1. Sir King, we ban° that we were born,   *curse*
Our bliss is all with bales° blend.°   *misfortunes / blended*
PHARAOH. Why cry you so, lads? List°   *want, desire*
you scorn?°   *ridicule*
260 EGYPTIAN 1. Sir King, slike° care was never kenned.° *such / known*
Our water that was ordained°   *intended*
To° men and beasts' food,°   *as / sustenance*
Throughout all Egypt land
Is turned to red blood.

265 Full ugly° and full ill° is it   *horrifying / harmful*
That was full fair and fresh before.
PHARAOH. This is great wonder for to wit°   *know, discover*
Of all the works° that ever were.   *happenings*
EGYPTIAN 2. Nay Lord, there is another yet
270 That suddenly sues° us full sore,   *afflicts*
For° toads and frogs we may not flit,°   *because of / move*
Their venom loses° less and more.[4]   *destroys*

---

1 *Hap ill hail!* May bad luck befall (you)!
2 *both morn and noon* Always, all the time.
3 *for thy sake* Because of you.
4 *less and more* I.e., everything.

EGYPTIAN 1. Lord, great mises° both morn and noon   *gnats*
  Bite us full bitterly,°   *fiercely*
  And we hope° all be done   *believe* 275
  By Moses, our enemy.

COUNSELOR 1. Lord, whilst we with this meinie°   *people*
  move°   *associate*
  Mun° never mirth be us among.   *must*
PHARAOH. Go say we shall no longer grieve°—   *suffer*
  But they shall never the titer° gang.°   *sooner / go, escape* 280
EGYPTIAN 2. Moses, my Lord has granted leave
  At° lead thy folk to liking° land,   *to / promised*
  So that we mend of° our mischief.°   *from / misfortune*
MOSES. I wot° full well their words are wrong;   *know*
  That shall full soon be seen,   285
  For hardily° I him het,°   *confidently / promised*
  And° he of malice mean,°   *if / intends*
  Mo° marvels mun° he met.°   *more / must / endure*

EGYPTIAN 1. Lord, alas, for dole° we die,   *misery*
  We dare not look out at no door.   290
PHARAOH. What devil ails you so to cry?
EGYPTIAN 2. We fare now worse than ever we fore.°   *fared*
  Great lops° over all this land they fly,   *flies*
  That with biting makes° mickle° blore.°   *causes / great / lamentation*
EGYPTIAN 1. Lord, our beasts lie dead and dry°   *shriveled* 295
  As well on midden° as on moor°—   *dung heap / wasteland or marsh*
  Both¹ ox, horse, and ass
  Fall dead down suddenly.
PHARAOH. Thereof° no man harm has   *of that*
  Half so mickle° as I.   *great in degree* 300

COUNSELOR 2. Yes, Lord, poor men has mickle woe
  To see their cattle° be out cast.²   *livestock*
  The Jews in Goshen fare not so,
  They have all liking in to last.³
PHARAOH. Go say we give them leave to go   305
  To° time their perils be over-past°—   *until (such) / ended*

---

1 *Both* Frequently extended to more than two objects in Middle English.
2 *out cast* Destroyed.
3 *They ... last* I.e., they continue to prosper, live happily.

But ere° they flit° over-far us fro°		*before / depart / from*
We shall gar° fast° them four so fast.°¹		*cause / to bind / securely*

EGYPTIAN 2. Moses, my Lord gives leave
310 Thy men for to remove.
MOSES. He mun° have more mischief°   *must / misfortune*
But if² his tales be true.

EGYPTIAN 1. We,³ Lord, we may not lead this life.
PHARAOH. Why, is their grievance° grown again?   *misfortune*
315 EGYPTIAN 2. Swilk° powder,° Lord, upon us   *such / ash*
    drive°   *rains down*
That where it beats° it makes a blain.°   *hits / blister*
EGYPTIAN 1. Like mesels° makes it man and wife.°   *lepers / woman*
Sithen° are they hurt with hail and rain;   *subsequently*
Our vines in mountains may not thrive,
320 So are they thrust° and thunder-slain.⁴   *beaten down*
PHARAOH. How do they⁵ in Goshen,
The Jews, can ye aught° say?   *anything*
EGYPTIAN 2. This care° nothing they ken,°   *sorrow / know of*
They feel no such affray.°   *misfortune*

325 PHARAOH. No! Devil! And sit they so in peace
And we ilka° day in doubt° and dread?   *every / fear*
EGYPTIAN 1. My Lord, this care° will ever increase   *sorrow*
Till Moses have leave them to lead.
COUNSELOR 1. Lord, were they went,° then would it cease,   *gone*
330 So should we save us° and our seed,°   *ourselves / offspring*
Else be we lorn°—this is no lease.°   *destroyed / lie*
PHARAOH. Let him do forth, the devil him speed!⁶
For his folk shall no far°   *farther*
If he go welling wood.⁷
335 COUNSELOR 2. Then will it soon be war,
Yet were better they yode.°   *went*

---

1 *We … fast* We will cause them to be bound four times as securely.
2 *But if* Unless.
3 *We* Interjection. A conventional cry of distress or consternation.
4 *thunder-slain* Destroyed by lightning (here metonymically represented by the thunder that accompanies it).
5 *How do they* I.e., how do they fare, how are they?
6 *the devil him speed!* May the devil cause him to prosper (ironic); i.e., bad luck to him.
7 *welling wood* Raving mad.

EGYPTIAN 2. We, Lord, new harm is come to hand.
PHARAOH. No! Devil! Will it no better be?
EGYPTIAN 1. Wild worms[1] is laid over all this land,
   They leave no fruit ne° flower on tree;   *nor* 340
   Against that storm may nothing stand.
EGYPTIAN 2. Lord, there is more mischief think me,
   And three days has it been durand,°   *continuing*
   So murk° that none° might other° see.   *dark / no one / another*
EGYPTIAN 1. My Lord, great pestilence   345
   Is like° full long to last.   *likely*
PHARAOH. Oh, comes that in our presence?
   Then is our pride all past.

EGYPTIAN 2. My Lord, this vengeance lasts long,
   And mun° till Moses have his boon.°   *must / request* 350
COUNSELOR 1. Lord, let them wend,° else work we wrong, *go away*
   It may not help to hover° ne° hone.°   *hesitate / nor / delay*
PHARAOH. Go say we grant them leave to gang°   *go*
   In the devil way, since it bus° be done,   *must*
   For so may fall[2] we shall them fang°   *seize* 355
   And mar° them ere° tomorn° at noon. *destroy / before / tomorrow*
EGYPTIAN 1. Moses, my Lord has said
   Thou shall have passage plain.°   *full, complete*
MOSES. And to pass° am I paid.°   *go / pleased*
   My friends, be now fain,°   *glad* 360

   For at our will now shall we wend,
   In Land of Liking[3] for to lend.°[4]   *dwell*
BOY 1. King Pharaoh, that felonous° fiend,   *wicked*
   Will have great care° from this be kenned,[5] *consternation, trouble*
   Then will he shape° him° us to shend° *prepare / himself / destroy* 365
   And soon his host after us send.
MOSES. Be not afeared,° God is your friend,   *afraid*
   From all our foes he will us fend.°   *defend*
   Therefore come forth with me,

---

1 *Wild worms* Any insects or crawling, creeping creatures; here, specifically, the biblical
   locusts (grasshoppers).
2 *For so may fall* For it may happen that.
3 *Land of Liking* Promised Land.
4 *shall we wend ... to lend* Moses and the Hebrews begin their journey here, perhaps moving
   off the pageant wagon onto the street level.
5 *from this be kenned* From this being known; i.e., once this is known.

370	Have done[1] and dread you naught.°	*nothing*
	Boy 2. My Lord, lovèd° mote° thou be,	*praised / must*
	That us from bale° has brought.	*evil*

	Boy 3. Swilk° friendship never before we found,	
	But in this fare° defaults° may fall.°	*matter / harms / befall*
375	The Red Sea is right near at hand,	
	There bus us bide[2] to° we be thrall.°	*until / enslaved*
	Moses. I shall make us way with my wand,	
	For God has said he save us shall;	
	On either side the sea shall stand—	
380	Till we be went°—right° as° a wall.[3]	*gone / exactly / like*
	Therefore have ye no dread,	
	But fand° ay° God to please.	*strive / always*
	Boy 1. That Lord to land us lead,°	*will lead*
	Now wend° we all at ease.	*travel*

385	Egyptian 1. King Pharaoh, these folk are gone.	
	Pharaoh. How now, is there any noise of new?[4]	
	Egyptian 2. The Hebrews are went° ilkone.°	*gone / each one*
	Pharaoh. How says thou that?	
	Egyptian 1. These tales are true.	
	Pharaoh. Horses harness tite,° that° they	*quickly / so that*
	be ta'en,°	*taken, captured*
390	This riot° radly° shall them rue.	*disorder / immediately*
	We shall not cease ere° they be slain,	*before*
	For to the sea we shall them sue.°	*pursue*
	Do charge° our chariots swith°	*load / quickly*
	And freckly° follow me.	*eagerly*
395	Egyptian 2. My Lord, we are full blithe°	*glad*
	At your bidding to be.	

	Counselor 2. Lord, to your bidding we are boun°	*ready*
	Our bodies° boldly for to bid,°	*selves / offer*
	We shall not bide,° but ding° them down	*wait / strike*
400	Till all be dead, without dread.	

---

1   *Have done*   Cease, desist; i.e., be silent.
2   *bus us bide*   We must wait.
3   *right as a wall*   Exactly like a wall. How this was represented is unknown.
4   *noise of new*   News.

PHARAOH. Heave up your hearts ay to Mahound,[1]
   He will be near us in our need.[2]
   Out! Ay harrow![3] Devil, I drown!
EGYPTIAN 1. Alas, we die for all our deed.°   *deeds*
BOY 1. Now are we won° from woe   *taken* 405
   And saved out of the sea,
   Cantemus domino,[4]
   To God a song sing we.

The York Corpus Christi Play: The Annunciation and Visitation

The Spicers' *Annunciation and Visitation* play seems simple on the page: a long monologue by the Doctor figure, plus two short dialogues, one between Mary and the Angel Gabriel and another between Mary and Elizabeth. But the text we have does not give us all that transpires in the play. Three stage directions call for Latin songs that would have greatly extended the playing time of the pageant, as well as set its numinous atmosphere. What is more, the moment of the conception of Christ, though not noted explicitly in any original direction, is likely to have been enacted with spectacular stage business and special effects, perhaps in imitation of the conventional iconography of beams of light descending on Mary's womb.

The play breaks down into three separate scenes, each enumerated in the *Ordo Paginarum* and each set off by a separate stanza type. The songs and stage business of the conception also bookend the scenes. The first scene consists of the Doctor's interpretation of the prophecies of the virgin birth. Doctor or "expositor" figures are common in medieval drama, although less common in York than in other cycles and collections. Here, the Doctor's exegesis serves to link the Old Testament

---

1 *Mahound* Muhammad, prophet and founder of Islam (c. 570–632). Medieval English texts often depict all non-Christian characters as worshipping or otherwise calling on Muhammad, as a way to construct their "otherness."
2 Between this line and the next, the waters—however represented—come crashing down on Pharaoh and his men.
3 *Out! Ay harrow!* Interjections expressing distress.
4 *Cantemus domino* Latin: Let us sing to the Lord (Exodus 15.1). As with other plays in the cycle, music is used here to suggest celebration, harmony, and divine order.

episodes, which we have just left behind in the previous *Pharaoh and Moses* pageant, with those of the New Testament, demonstrating the Christian belief that the New Testament is the fulfillment of the Old. The Doctor's monologue is written in a typical York twelve-line stanza rhyming ababababcdcd, with extrametrical Latin lines inserted that do not adhere to the meter or rhyme scheme. Given that the English lines reiterate the Latin quotations, it is possible that the Latin was inserted at some point in the play's development before the official "Register" of the plays was made, providing the Doctor with a truly medieval sense of authority, and underscoring the textual authority for the virgin birth.

The second and third scenes focus on the women and draw on traditional representations of the story narrated in Luke 1. After the Angel enters and sings, the verse form changes to an eight-line stanza rhyming ababababab. The musical interlude and the switch in stanza form demarcate the boundary between the contemporary Doctor and the biblical Mary. Unlike the many York plays that set their stories simultaneously in the past and the present, this play formally sets off Mary's encounter with the divine as separate from the audience's world. To be sure, some connection between Mary's world and that of the audience could be made when she journeys to visit Elizabeth, which might logically require her to leave the pageant wagon and then return to mark the beginning of a different scene.

The new scene is also demarcated by yet another change in stanza. Although the stanzas are still eight lines in length and still rhyme ababababab, each line is a foot shorter, with three beats instead of four. Though Mary and Elizabeth both speak in full stanzas, the briefness of the lines makes their lines seem somewhat more conversational than those in previous sections of the play.

The play ends with Mary singing the "Magnificat"; with that the play completes its move from masculine authority at a remove from events to female experience of those events.

Pageant 12 of the York Corpus Christi Play: *The Annunciation and Visitation*

CHARACTERS

Doctor
Angel
Mary
Elizabeth

DOCTOR. Lord God, great marvel is to mean°   *tell*
 How man was made without miss,°   *sin*
 And set where he should ever° have been   *always*
 Without bale,° biding° in bliss;   *sorrow / dwelling*
 And how he lost that comfort clean,°   *completely*   5
 And was put out from paradise,
 And sithen° what sorrows sore° were seen   *subsequently / bitter*
 Sent unto him and to all his;
 And how they lay long space[1]
 In hell, louken° from light,   *locked, shut out*   10
 Till God granted them grace
 Of help, as he had hight.°   *promised*

 Then is it needful° for to neven°   *necessary / tell*
 How prophets all God's counsels kenned,°   *revealed*
 As prophet Amos in his steven°   *voice*   15
 Lered° while he in his life gan lend:[2]   *taught*
 Deus pater disposuit salutem fieri in medio terre, etc.[3]
 He says thus: God the father in heaven
 Ordained in earth mankind to mend;
 And to graith° it with Godhead even,   *cause to be*   20
 His Son he said that he should send
 To take kind° of mankin,°   *the nature / mankind*
 In a maiden full mild;
 So was many saved of° sin   *from*
 And the foul fiend beguiled.°   *tricked*   25

 And for° the fiend should so be fed   *because*
 By teen,° and to no truth take tent,[4]   *anger*
 God made that maiden to be wed
 Ere° he his Son unto her sent.   *before*
 So was the Godhead closed and clad   30
 In weed° of wedding where   *garment*
   they° went;   *i.e., Mary and Joseph*
 And that° our bliss should so be bred,°   *so that / brought about*
 Full many matters may be meant:

---

1 *long space* For a long time.
2 *gan lend* Was living.
3 *Deus pater ... terre, etc.* Latin: God the Father will grant salvation in the midst of the earth, etc. (The origin of this quotation has not been identified.)
4 *And for ... take tent* And because the fiend is so fed by anger (i.e., blinded by anger), and to no truth pays heed.

Quoniam in semine tuo benedicentur omnes gentes, etc.[1]

35   God himself said this thing
    To Abraham as him list:[2]
    Of° thy seed shall up spring   *from*
    Wherein° folk shall be blest.°   *through which / blessed*

    To prove these prophets ordained ere°—   *before*
40   As° Isaiah, unto old and young,   *such as*
    He moved° our mischiefs° for to mar,°   *spoke of / misfortunes / destroy*
    For thus he prayed God for this thing:
    Rorate, celi, desuper,[3]
    Lord, let thou down° at thy liking°   *descend / pleasure*
45   The dew to fall from heaven so far,
    For then the earth shall spread and spring
    A seed that us shall save,
    That now in bliss are bent.[4]
    Of clerks° whoso will crave°   *scholars / ask*
50   Thus may these gates° be meant:°   *ways (i.e., matters) / spoken of*

    The dew to the good Holy Ghost
    May be remened° in man's mind,   *compared*
    The earth unto the maiden chaste,[5]
    Because she comes of earthly kind.
55   These wise words were not wrought in waste,°   *vain*
    To waft° and wend° away as wind,   *blow / turn*
    For this same prophet soon in haste
    Said furthermore, as folks may find:
    Propter hoc dabit dominus ipse vobis signum, etc.[6]
60   Lo, he says thus: God shall give
    Hereof a sign to see
    Till° all that° leally° live,   *to / who / loyally*
    And this their sign shall be,

---

1   *Quoniam … gentes, etc.*   Latin: Because in thy seed shall all the nations be blessed, etc. (Genesis 22.18).

2   *as him list*   As it pleased him (God).

3   *Rorate, celi, desuper*   Latin: Drop down, dew, from heaven (Isaiah 45.8).

4   *in bliss are bent*   Are inclined toward bliss.

5   *The dew … maiden chaste*   The dew may be compared in man's mind to the good Holy Ghost, the earth (compared) to the chaste maiden.

6   *Propter … signum, etc.*   Latin: Therefore the Lord himself shall give you a sign, etc. (Isaiah 7.14).

Ecce virgo concipiett, et pariet filium, etc.[1]

Lo, he says a maiden mun°	*must*	65
Here on this mould° mankind amell,°	*earth / among*	
Full clear[2] conceive and bear a son,		
And neven° his name Emmanuel.	*name*	
His kingdom that ever is begun		
Shall never cease, but dure° and dwell;	*endure*	70
On David's siege° there shall he won,°	*throne / dwell*	
His dooms° to deem° and truth to tell.	*judgments / pronounce*	

Zelus domini faciet hoc, etc.[3]

He says, love of our Lord		
All this shall ordain° then,	*arrange*	75
That° means° peace and accord	*who / intends*	
To make with earthly man.[4]		

More of this maiden moves me;[5]		
This prophet says for our succor,		
Egredietur virga de Jesse,[6]		80
A wand° shall breed° of Jesse°	*rod / grow / Jesse's*	
bower,°	*chamber (i.e., lineage)*	
And of this same also says he:		
Upon that wand shall spring a flower		
Whereon° the Holy Ghost shall be,	*on which*	
To govern it with great honor.		85
That wand means° until° us	*signifies / to*	
This maiden, even° and morn,	*evening*	
And the flower is Jesus,		
That of that blest° be born.	*blessed one (i.e., the Virgin)*	

---

1 *Ecce virgo ... filium, etc.* Latin: Behold a virgin shall conceive, and bear a son, etc. (Isaiah 7.14).

2 *Full clear* Without guilt.

3 *Zelus domini faciet hoc, etc.* Latin: The zeal of the Lord will perform this, etc. (Isaiah 9.7).

4 *He says ... earthly man* He says: the Lord's love—(the Lord) who intends to make peace and accord with earthly mankind—will arrange all of this.

5 *moves me* I.e., moves me to speak.

6 *Egredietur virga de Jesse* Latin: And there will come forth a rod of Jesse (Isaiah 11.1). This prophecy is the inspiration for the "Jesse tree" of iconography, a genealogical tree representing the human lineage of Mary and Christ, in which the tree or vine bursts forth from Jesse's body and the lineage culminates in Christ.

90	The prophet Joel, a gentle° Jew,	*noble*
	Sometime° has said of the	*in the past*
	same thing,°	*i.e., the conception of Jesus*
	He likens Christ even as he knew	
	Like to the dew in down-coming:°	*descending*
	Ero quasi ros; et virgo Israell germinabit sicut lilium.[1]	
95	The maiden of Israel all new,	
	He says, shall bear one and forth bring	
	As the lily flower, full fair of hew.	
	This means so° to old and young,	*thus*
	That the high Holy Ghost	
100	Come° our mischief° to mend	*will come / misfortune*
	In Mary, maiden chaste,	
	When God his Son would send.	

	This lady is to the lily like,°	*comparable to*
	That is because of her clean° life,	*pure*
105	For in this world was never slike°	*such (as her)*
	One to be maiden, mother, and wife.	
	And her son, king in heaven-riche,°	*the kingdom of heaven*
	As oft° is rede° by reason rife,°	*often / guided / common*
	And her husband, both master and make,°	*companion, partner*
110	In charity to stint° all strife.	*end*
	This passed all worldly wit,°	*knowing*
	How God had ordained them then	
	In her one to be knit,	
	Godhead, maidenhead, and man.	

115	But of this work great witness was	
	With forefathers, all folk may tell.	
	When Jacob blessed his son Judas	
	He told the tale them two amell:[2]	
	Non auferetur septrum de Juda,	
120	*Donec veniat qui mittendus est.*[3]	
	He says the scepter shall not pass	
	From Judah land of Israel,	
	Ere° he come that God ordained has	*before*

---

1 *Ero ... lilium* Latin: I will be as the dew, Israel shall spring as the lily (Hosea 14.6). The attribution to Joel is incorrect.

2 *them two amell* Between the two of them.

3 *Non auferetur ... mittendus est* Latin: The scepter shall not be taken away from Judah till he come that is to be sent (Genesis 49.10).

To be sent fiend's force to fell.° *destroy*

Et ipse erit expectacio gencium.[1] 125

Him shall all folk abide,° *await, expect*

And stand° unto his steven.° *obey / voice*

Their° saws° were signified *i.e., the prophets' / sayings*

To Christ,[2] God's Son in heaven.

For how he was sent, see we more, 130

And how God would his place purvey;° *arrange in advance*

He said, Son, I shall send before

Mine angel to rede° thee thy way: *prepare, guide*

Ecce mitto angelum meum ante faciem tuam,

Qui preparabit viam tuam ante te.[3] 135

Of John Baptist he meaned° there, *signified*

For in earth he was ordained ay° *always*

To warn the folk that wilsome° were *erring, wandering*

Of Christ's coming, and thus gan° say: *did*

Ego quidem baptizo in aqua vos, autem 140

Baptizabimini spiritu sancto.[4]

After me shall come now

A man of mights most,

And shall baptize you

In the high Holy Ghost. 145

Thus of Christ's coming may we see

How Saint Luke speaks in his gospel:

From God in heaven is sent, says he,

An angel is named Gabriel,

To Nazareth in Galilee, 150

Where then a maiden mild gan° dwell, *did*

That° with Joseph should wedded be; *who*

Her name is Mary, thus gan he tell.

How God his grace then graid° *prepared*

To° man° in this manner, *for / humankind* 155

And how the angel said,

Take heed, all that will hear.

---

1   *Et ipse ... gencium*   And he will be the expectation of the nations (Genesis 19.10).

2   *were signified / To Christ*   Predicted Christ.

3   *Ecce mitto ... ante te*   Latin: Behold I send my angel before thy face, who shall prepare the way before thee (Mark 1.2).

4   *Ego quidem ... sancto*   Latin: I indeed baptize you in water, but you will be baptized in the Holy Spirit (Matthew 3.11).

[*Exit Doctor. Enter Angel and Mary.*[1]]

(*Then the Angel shall sing.*)[2]

ANGEL. Hail Mary, full of grace and bliss,
    Our Lord God is with thee
160   And has chosen thee for his,
    Of all women blessed mot° thou be.   *may*
MARY. What manner of halsing° is this   *greeting*
    Thus privily° comes to me?   *privately*
    For in mine heart a thought it is,
165   The tokening° that I here see.   *sign*

(*Then the angel shall sing, "Ne timeas, Maria."*)[3]

ANGEL. Ne dread thee not[4] thou mild Mary,
    For nothing° that may befall,°   *anything / happen*
    For thou has found sovereignly°   *surpassingly*
    At° God a grace over other all.[5]   *from*
170   In chastity of thy body
    Conceive and bear a child thou shall;
    This bodeword° bring I thee, forthy°   *message / for this reason*
    His name Jesu shall thou call.

    Mickle° of might then shall he be,   *great*
175   He shall be God and called God's Son.
    David's siege,° his father° free,°   *throne / forefather / noble*
    Shall God him give to sit upon;
    As king forever reign shall he,
    In Jacob's house ay° for to won,°   *always / dwell*
180   Of his kingdom and dignity
    Shall no man earthly know ne° con.°   *nor / can (know)*

---

1 *Enter Angel and Mary* This stage direction is conjectural. It is possible that Mary is sitting on the wagon stage the entire time the Doctor expounds upon the prophecies of the virgin birth, and that, when the Doctor exits, only the Angel enters.

2 *Then the Angel shall sing* This stage direction was added in the 16th century by John Clerke, assistant clerk to the common clerk of the city, and may signify the singing of the Latin *Ave Maria* chant. Certainly there is a change of scene here, from the Doctor's exegesis of prophecies of the virgin birth to the scene of the Annunciation itself; the music helps mark that change.

3 *Ne timeas, Maria* Latin: Do not fear, Mary.

4 *Ne dread thee not* Do not fear.

5 *over other all* Over all others.

MARY. Thou God's angel, meek and mild,
   How should it be, I thee pray,
   That I should conceive a child
   Of any man by night or day?   185
   I know no man that should have filed°   *defiled*
   My maidenhood, the sooth° to say.   *truth*
   Without will° of° works° wild   *desire / for / deeds*
   In chastity I have been ay.°   *always*

ANGEL. The Holy Ghost in thee shall light,°   *alight* 190
   High virtue shall to thee hold,
   The holy birth of thee so bright
   God's Son he shall be called.
   Lo, Elizabeth thy cousin ne might[1]
   In eld° conceive a child for° eld;   *age / because of* 195
   This is the sixth month full right
   To her that barren has been told.°   *counted*

MARY. Thou angel, blessed messenger,
   Of God's will I hold me paid;°   *rewarded*
   I love my Lord with heart clear,   200
   The grace that he has for me laid.°   *established*
   God's handmaiden, lo, me here
   To his will all ready graid,°   *prepared*
   Be done to me of all manner
   Through thy word as thou hast° said.[2]   *have* 205

[*Exit Angel. Mary visits Elizabeth.*]

Now God that all our hope is in,
Through the might of the Holy Ghost,
Save thee, dame,° from sake° of sin,   *i.e., Elizabeth / guilt*
And wis° thee from all works waste.°   *guide / idle, barren*
Elizabeth mine own cousin,   210
Methought° I covet° always most   *it seems to me / desire*

---

1 *ne might* Could not.

2 *To his will ... said* The moment of the conception was probably staged visually after these lines, once Mary has consented. Conventional iconography called for beams of light descending from God in heaven to Mary; how that would have been represented here is unknown. (The mercantile Spicers would have been able to afford lavish effects.) The next stanza then begins the Visitation episode, so the stage business of the conception would also create a break between the "scenes."

To speak with thee of all my kin,
Therefore I come thus in this haste.

ELIZABETH. Ah, welcome mild Mary,
215   Mine own cousin so dear,
Joyful woman am I
That I now see thee here.
Blessed be thou only°   *exclusively*
Of all women in fere,[1]
220   And the fruit of thy body
Be blessed far and near.

This is joyful tiding°   *event*
That I may now here see,
The mother of my lord king
225   Thus-gate° come to me.   *in this way*
Soon as the voice of thine halsing°   *greeting*
Might mine ears entering be,
The child in my womb so young
Makes great mirth unto thee.

230 MARY. Now, Lord, blessed be thou ay°   *always*
For the grace thou has me lent;°   *given*
Lord, I love° thee, God verray,°   *praise / true*
The sand° thou hast me sent.   *message*
I thank thee night and day,
235   And praise with good intent;
Thou make me to thy pay,°   *liking*
To thee my will is went.

ELIZABETH. Blessed be thou gradely° graid° *quite / readily*
To God through chastity,
240   Thou trowed° and held thee payed° *trusted / satisfied*
At his will for to be.
All that to thee is said
From my Lord so free,°   *noble, gracious*
Swilk° grace is for thee laid°   *such / stored up*
245   Shall be fulfilled in thee.

---

1 *in fere* Together.

MARY. To his grace I will me ta,°   *take*
  With chastity to deal,°   *maintain*
  That made me thus to ga°   *go (Northern form)*
  Among his maidens fele.°   *many*
  My soul shall loving° ma°   *praise / make*   250
  Unto that Lord so leal,°   *true*
  And my ghost° make joy also   *spirit*
  In God that is my heal.°   *well-being*

(*Then she sings "Magnificat."*)[1]

The York Corpus Christi Play: Joseph's Troubles about Mary

Joseph's Troubles about Mary, presented by the Pewterers and Founders, is a comic relief play, based on apocryphal sources, that nevertheless presents important theological and devotional concepts through its humor. Joseph, an impotent old man who suspects he has been cuckolded by his young wife, is a character drawn from farces and fabliaux (short, comic, often bawdy tales), a type that is also found in Geoffrey Chaucer's *Canterbury Tales*—especially in *The Miller's Tale* and *The Merchant's Tale*, the former of which tells a "legend and a life / Both of a carpenter and of his wife."

Joseph is here a comic inversion of Noah and Abraham, the other elderly men of the York cycle. But unlike those inimitable patriarchs, who obey God in seemingly impossible situations, Joseph is a figure of doubt and of the audience's own potential disbelief. He speaks to the contemporary audience directly in soliloquy, forging a bond and an identification with them.

The comedy of the episode also plays with the typological trope of Mary's meek obedience as a reversal of Eve's sinful disobedience, reversing gender stereotypes as it does. Joseph keeps accusing Mary of infidelity, even as we know she is innocent. He suspects other women are in cahoots with her, and uses gendered stereotypes to ironic effect. In other words, he sees her as an Eve type. But it is Joseph who recalls both Eve

---

1 *Magnificat* Latin: "[My soul] doth magnify [the Lord]" (Luke 1.40–55). The "Magnificat" is a Latin hymn, also known as the "Song of Mary," based on the words in Luke. The actor playing Mary—perhaps a boy chorister—would sing this.

and Noah's Wife in his recalcitrance and refusal to heed God's word; even though he knows the prophecies of the virgin birth, he refuses to believe they could apply to Mary. In his wielding of sexist stereotypes—even at the very end of the play—and his refusal to believe women's words, he himself becomes the type of "feminine" disobedience.

A recapitulation of tropes found in the *Fall of Adam and Eve* is also to be found in the language of this play. Once again the diction of a "bad bargain" having been "wrought" or "worked" appears, as does the idea that someone has been "beguiled." Of course, the "bad bargain" here is not Mary's doing, but Joseph's. Mary, in fact, has begun a chain of events that will make possible Christ's purchase of humankind's salvation via his death—a good "bargain" indeed. It is Joseph who, like Eve, has been "beguiled." *Joseph's Troubles about Mary* even partly borrows the verse form of the *Fall of Adam and Eve*—portions of this play are in the same eleven-line stanza rhyming ababcbcdcdc in which the earlier play is written.

Other verse forms in this mixed-stanza play include a unique ten-line stanza rhyming ababccbccb; there are also shorter fragments in other stanza forms, but these may be errors of copying into the Register.

The Pewterers and Founders made domestic utensils, among other metal implements, and so may have been particularly appropriate guilds to assign to this play about domestic matters. Perhaps the "gear" that Joseph gathers at the end of the play included their own wares.

Pageant 13 of the York Corpus Christi Play: *Joseph's Troubles about Mary*

CHARACTERS

Joseph
Maiden 1
Maiden 2
Mary
Angel

JOSEPH. Of great mourning° may I me mean[1]   *grief*
And walk full wearily by this way,[2]

---

1   *may I me mean*   I may speak.
2   *this way*   the action may begin on the ground level with the wagon reserved for Mary's chamber.

For° now° then wend°   *because / by now / thought*
 I best° have been   *most*
At ease and rest,[1] by reason ay.°   *eternal*
For I am of great eld,°   *age* 5
Weak and all unwield,°   *powerless, impotent*
As ilka° man see it may;   *every*
I may neither busk° nor bield° *move easily / remain*
But either in frith° or field.   *woods*
For shame what shall I say,   10

That thus-gates° now in mine old days *in this manner*
Has wedded a young wench° to° my wife, *young woman, maiden / as*
And may not well trine° over two straws? *step*
Now Lord, how long shall I lead this life?
My bones are heavy as lead   15
And may not stand in stead,°   *place*
As kenned° it is full rife.° *known / widespread*
Now Lord, thou me wis° and rede° *advise / guide*
Or soon me drive to dead,[2]
Thou may best stint° this strife.   *end* 20

For bitterly then may I ban°   *curse*
The way I in the Temple went,[3]
It was to me a bad bargain,°   *enterprise*
For ruth° I may it ay° repent. *sorrow / forever*
For therein was ordained   25
Unwedded men should stand,
All sembled° at assent,° *assembled / appointed time and place*
And ilka one a dry° wand°   *dead / stick*
On height[4] held in his hand,
And I ne wist[5] what it meant.   30

Among all others one bore I;
It flourished fair, and flowers on° spread, *on it*

---

1 *For now … At ease and rest* Because by now I thought I would have been most at ease and
 rest.
2 *me drive to dead* Lead me to death.
3 *in the Temple went* Joseph begins to recount the apocryphal story, depicted in other drama,
 literature, and art (but not otherwise dramatized here), in which he is recognized in a ceremony
 in the Temple as the chosen husband of Mary by the sign of a miraculously flowering stick.
4 *On height* Aloft.
5 *ne wist* Did not understand.

And they said to me forthy°   *therefore*
That with a wife I should be wed.
35   The bargain I made there,
That rues me now full sare,¹
So am I straitly stead.²
Now casts it me³ in care,
For well I might evermore
40   Onlepy° life have led.   *solitary*

Her works me works my wanges° to wet;⁴   *cheeks*
I am beguiled—how, wot° I not.   *know*
My young wife is with child full great,
That makes° me now sorrow unsought.   *causes*
45   That reproof° near° has slain me,   *shame / nearly*
Forthy° if any man frayne° me   *therefore / inquire of*
How this thing might be° wrought,°   *have been / accomplished*
To gab° if I would pain me,⁵   *lie*
The law stands hard again° me: *against*
50   To dead° I mun° be brought.⁶   *death / must*

And loath methinketh, on the other side,
My wife with any man to defame,⁷
And whether° of these two⁸ that I bide°   *whichever / endure*
I mun° not scape° without shame.   *may / escape, avoid*
55   The child certes° is not mine;   *certainly*
That reproof does° me pine°   *causes / torment*
And gars° me flee from hame.°   *causes / home (Northern dialect)*
My life if I should tine,⁹

---

1   *That rues me now full sare*   That causes me great regret;   *sare*   Sorely, bitterly.
2   *straitly stead*   Sorely beset, in dire straits.
3   *casts it me*   Puts me in.
4   *Her works ... wanges to wet.*   Her actions cause me to wet my cheeks (i.e., cause me to cry).
5   *To gab if I would pain me*   If I took the trouble to lie (and say it is mine).
6   *To dead I mun be brought*   I must be put to death (for the lie). Joseph thinks that it would
     be obvious he is not the father (since he is old and "unwield," impotent), and if he lied and
     claimed that he was the father, he would be guilty of bearing false witness, punishable by
     death (or so he thinks—his character is prone to over-reaction).
7   *And loath ... to defame*   I am loath, on the other hand, to defame my wife [by accusing her
     of being] with another man.
8   *these two*   I.e., these two possibilities—my death, or divorcing and defaming Mary.
9   *My life if I should tine*   If I should lose my life, i.e., I stake my life on it.

She is a clean° virgin   *pure, unblemished*
For me,[1] without blame.   60

But well I wot° through prophecy   *know*
A maiden° clean should bear a child,   *virgin*
But it is not she, sikerly,°   *truly*
Forthy° I wot I am beguiled.   *therefore*
And why ne would[2] some young man take her?   65
For certes° I think over-go her[3]   *certainly*
Into some woods wild,
Thus think I to steal° from her.   *slip away*
God shield° there wild beasts slay her,   *prevent*
She is so meek and mild.   70

Of my wending° will I none warn,   *departure*
Nevertheless it is mine intent
To ask her who got her that bairn,°   *child*
Yet would I wit° fain° ere° I went.   *know / gladly / before*

[*Joseph approaches Mary and her maidens.*]

All hail, God be herein.[4]   75
MAIDEN 1. Welcome, by God's dear might.
JOSEPH. Where is that young virgin
    Mary, my bird° so bright?   *lady*

MAIDEN 1. Certes Joseph, ye shall understand
    That she is not full far you fro,[5]   80
    She sits at her book full fast prayand[6]
    For you and us, and for all tho°   *those*
    That aught has need.[7]
    But for to tell her will I go
    Of your coming, without dread.°   *doubt*   85
    Have done[8] and rise up, dame,

---

1 *For me* As far as I am concerned.
2 *why ne would* Why wouldn't.
3 *I think over-go her* I think I will pass her by, i.e., abandon her.
4 *All hail, God be herein* Greetings, may God be (with you) here.
5 *not full far you fro* Not very far from you.
6 *full fast prayand* Very earnestly praying.
7 *That aught has need* Who have need of anything.
8 *Have done* Finish what you are doing.

And to me take good heed—
Joseph, he is come hame.°   *home*
MARY. Welcome, as God me speed.[1]

90   Dreadless° to me he is full dear;   *doubtless*
Joseph my spouse, welcome are ye.
  JOSEPH. Gramercy° Mary, say what cheer,[2]   *thank you, great thanks*
Tell me the sooth,° how is't° with thee?   *truth / is it*
Who has been there?
95   Thy womb is waxen° great, think me,   *grown*
Thou art with bairn, alas for care.°   *woe*
Ah, maidens, woe worth you,[3]
That let her lere° swilk° lare.°   *learn / such / conduct*
  MAIDEN 2. Joseph, ye shall not trow°   *believe*
100   In her no feeble° fare.°   *weak-willed / goings-on, behavior*

  JOSEPH. Trow° it not harm?°   *think / wrong, sin*
  Lief° wench, do way![4]   *dear*
Her sides show she is with child.
Whose is't Mary?
  MARY.   Sir, God's and yours.
  JOSEPH.   Nay, nay,
Now wot I well I am beguiled,
105   And reason why?[5]
With me fleshly was thou never filed,°   *defiled*
And I forsake° it° here forthy.°   *reject / i.e., that cause / therefore*
Say maidens, how is this?[6]
Tell me the sooth,° rede° I;   *truth / advise*
110   And but ye do, iwis,°   *truly*
The bargain shall ye abye.[7]

  MAIDEN 2. If° ye threat° as fast as ye can   *even if / threaten*
There is naught° to say theretill,°   *nothing / to this*
For truly here come never no man
115   To wait° the body with none ill°   *harm / evil (deed)*

---

1   *as God me speed* As God cause me to prosper.
2   *what cheer* How are you.
3   *woe worth you* Shame on you.
4   *Trow it … do way!* Do you think it is not a sin? Dear girl, stop!
5   *And reason why?* And for what reason?
6   *how is this?* How did this happen?
7   *And but … abye.* Unless you do, truly, you shall pay the price for this state of affairs.

Of this sweet wight,°   *creature*
For we have dwelt ay° with her still°   *continually / all the time*
And was never from her day nor night.
Her keepers have we been
And she ay° in our sight;   *always* 120
Come here no man between°   *in the meantime*
To touch that bird° so bright.   *lady*

MAIDEN 1. No, here come no man in these wones°   *rooms*
  And that ever witness will we,
  Save° an angel ilka° day ones°   *except for / each / once* 125
  With bodily food her fed has he,
  Other come none.[1]
  Wherefore we ne wot[2] how it should be
  But through the Holy Ghost° alone.   *spirit*
  For truly we trow° this,   *believe* 130
  His grace with her is gone,[3]
  For she wrought never no miss,[4]
  We witness everilkone.°   *each one (of us)*

JOSEPH. Then see I well your meaning is
  The angel has made her with child.   135
  Nay, some man in angel's likeness
  With somekin° gaud° has her beguiled, *some kind of / trick*
  And that trow° I.   *believe*
  Forthy° needs not[5] swilk° words wild° *therefore / such / unbelievable*
  At carp[6] to me deceivingly.   140
  We,[7] why gab° ye me° so   *lie / to me*
  And feign swilk fantasy?
  Alas, me is full woe,
  For dole° why ne° might I die.   *sorrow / not*

  To me this is a careful° case;°   *woeful / situation* 145
  Reckless° I rave, reft° is my rede.° *heedless / taken away / reason*
  I dare look no man in the face,

---

1 *Other come none* No other came.
2 *ne wot* Don't know.
3 *His grace with her is gone* His grace goes with her.
4 *wrought never no miss* Never did amiss.
5 *needs not* It is not necessary.
6 *At carp* To tell.
7 *We* Interjection. Expresses surprise, derision, or distress.

Derfly° for dole° why ne° were I dead;   *wretchedly / sorrow / not*
Me loathes my life.[1]
150 In temple and in other stead°   *place*
Ilka° man till° hething° will me drive.[2]   *every / to / scorn, ridicule*
Was never wight° so woe,°   *creature / woeful*
For ruth° I all to-rive;°   *sorrow / am torn apart*
Alas, why wrought thou so
155 Mary, my wedded wife?

MARY. To my witness great God I call,
That in mind wrought never no miss.[3]
JOSEPH. Whose is the child thou art° withal?°   *are / therewith, with*
MARY. Yours sir, and the king's of bliss.[4]
160 JOSEPH. Yea, and how then?
No, selcouth° tidings° then is this,   *amazing / news*
Excuse them° well these women can.   *themselves*
But Mary, all that see thee
May wit° thy works are wan,°   *understand / wicked*
165 Thy womb always it wrays° thee,   *accuses*
That thou has met with[5] man.

Whose is it, as fair mote thee befall?[6]
MARY. Sir, it is yours and God's will.
JOSEPH. Nay, I ne have naught° ado°   *nothing / to do*
   withal°—   *with (it)*
170 Name it no more to me, be still!
Thou wot° as well as I,   *know*
That we two same° fleshly   *together*
Wrought never swilk° works with ill.   *such*
Look° thou did no folly   *be sure*
175 Before me privily°   *secretly*
Thy fair maidenhead° to spill.°   *virginity / destroy*

But who is the father? Tell me his name.
MARY. None but yourself.
JOSEPH.   Let be, for shame.

---

1 *Me loathes my life* My life is hateful to me.
2 *till hething will me drive* Will hold me up to ridicule.
3 *That in mind wrought never no miss* Who never thought to do any wrong.
4 *king's of bliss* The king-of-bliss's, i.e., God's.
5 *met with* Euphemism: had intercourse with.
6 *as fair mote thee befall* As good may befall you; or, as you hope to prosper.

I did it never; thou dotest,° dame, by books and bells!¹   *speak foolishly*

Full sackless° should I bear this blame after thou tells,²   *without cause*   180

For I wrought never in word nor deed

Thing° that should mar° thy maidenhead,   *i.e., anything / spoil*

To touch me till.³

For of slike° note° were little need,   *such / state of affairs*

Yet° for mine own I would it feed,   *since*   185

Might all be still;⁴

Therefore the father tell me, Mary.

MARY. But° God and you, I know right° none.   *except for / exactly*

JOSEPH. Ah, slike° saws° make me full sorry,   *such / words*

With great mourning to make my moan.   190

Therefore be not so bold,

That no slike tales be told,

But hold thee still⁵ as stone.

Thou art young and I am old,

Slike works if I do would,⁶   195

These games from me are gone.

Therefore, tell me in privity,°   *secrecy*

Whose is the child thou is with now?

Certes,° there shall none° wit° but we,   *truly / no one / know*

I dread the law as well as thou.   200

MARY. Now great God of his might

That all may dress° and dight,°   *ordain / rule*

Meekly to thee I bow.

Rue° on this weary wight,°   *have pity / creature*

That in his heart might light°   *alight*   205

The sooth° to ken° and trow.°   *truth / understand / believe*

JOSEPH. Who had thy maidenhead Mary? Has thou aught°   *any*

    mind?°   *memory*

MARY. Forsooth,° I am a maiden clean.°   *truly / pure*

JOSEPH. Nay, thou speaks now again° kind,°   *against / nature*

---

1 *by books and bells* A mild oath; these were items conventionally used in exorcisms.

2 *Full sackless … thou tells* Completely without cause am I to take the blame you ascribe.

3 *To touch me till* As far as I am concerned.

4 *For of slike note … be still* There would little need for such a state of affairs (i.e., this argument), since I would feed (and care for) the child as my own, if only there were peace.

5 *hold thee still* Keep quiet.

6 *Slike works … would* Even if I wanted to do such things.

210 Slike° thing might never no man of mean.[1]	
A maiden to be with child?	
These works from thee are wild,[2]	
She° is not born, I ween.°	*i.e., a pregnant virgin / believe*
MARY. Joseph, ye are beguiled,	
215 With sin was I never filed,°	*defiled*
God's sand° is on me seen.	*dispensation*

JOSEPH. God's sand? Yea, Mary, God help!	
But certes° that child was never ours two.	*certainly*
But woman-kind if them list[3] help,	
220 Yet would° they no man wist° their woe.	*want / know*
MARY. Certes° it is God's sand°	*truly / word*
….[4]	
That shall I never go° fro.°	*depart, waver / from*
JOSEPH. Yea, Mary, draw thine ande,[5]	
For further yet will I fand,°	*inquire*
225 I trow° not it be so.	*believe*

The sooth from me if that thou lain,°	*conceal*
The child-bearing may thou not hide;	
But sit still here till I come again,	
Me bus[6] an errand here beside.°	*nearby*
230 MARY. Now great God he you wis,°	*lead, guide*
And mend you of your miss°	*mistake*
Of° me, what so betide.°	*about / happens*
As he is king of bliss,	
Send° you some sand° of this,	*may he send / communication*
235 In truth that ye might bide.°	*remain*

[*Joseph leaves Mary.*]

JOSEPH. Now Lord God that all thing may	
At thine own will both do and dress,°	*ordain*
Wis° me now some ready° way	*guide / easy*

---

1   *Slike thing … mean*   No man might ever assert such a thing.
2   *These works … wild*   I.e., the claims you make are perverse.
3   *if them list*   If they want.
4   ….   A line here is missing in the manuscript.
5   *draw thine ande*   Draw thy breath, i.e., stop talking.
6   *Me bus*   I am obligated to (carry out).

To walk here in this wilderness.[1]
But ere° I pass this hill,   *before*   240
Do with me what God will,
Either more or less,
Here bus me[2] bide° full still   *wait*
Till I have slept my fill,
Mine heart so heavy it is.   245

[Joseph sleeps.]

ANGEL. Waken,° Joseph, and take better keep°   *awaken / attention*
    To Mary, that is thy fellow° fast.°   *mate / faithful*
JOSEPH. Ah, I am full weary, lief,° let me sleep,[3]   *dear*
    Forwandered° and walked in this forest.   *weary from wandering*
ANGEL. Rise up, and sleep no more,   250
    Thou makest her heart full sore
    That loves thee alther best.[4]
JOSEPH. We![5] Now is this a ferly° fare°   *marvelous / state of affairs*
    For to be catched° both here and there,   *chased, pursued*
    And nowhere may have rest.   255

    Say, what art thou? Tell me this thing.
ANGEL. I, Gabriel, God's angel full even[6]
    That has ta'en° Mary to my keeping,°   *taken / care*
    And sent is thee° to say with steven°   *to thee / voice*
    In leal° wedlock thou lead° thee.°   *faithful / conduct / yourself*   260
    Leave her not—I forbid thee—
    Ne° sin of° her thou neven,°   *nor / concerning / mention*
    But till° her fast thou speed thee   *to*
    And of her naught° thou dread° thee,   *nothing / doubt*
    It is God's sand° of° heaven.   *message / from*   265

    The child that shall be born of° her,   *from*
    It is conceived of the Holy Ghost.
    All joy and bliss then shall be after,

---

1   *this wilderness*   Here again, the action may take place on the ground level. Certainly, Joseph
    must leave Mary's presence in some way to go into "this wilderness."
2   *bus me*   It is necessary for me.
3   *lief, let me sleep*   Joseph comically thinks the Angel is Mary.
4   *alther best*   Best of all.
5   *We!*   Interjection (expressing surprise, derision, or distress).
6   *full even*   Truly.

And to all mankind now alther most.[1]
270 Jesus his name thou call,
For slike° hap° shall him fall°   *such / fortune / befall*
As thou shall see in haste.[2]
His people save he shall
Of° evils and angrice° all,   *from / tribulations*
275 That° they are now embraced.°   *in which / entangled*

JOSEPH. And is this sooth,° angel, thou says?   *truth*
ANGEL. Yea, and this to° token right: *as a*
Wend° forth to Mary, thy wife always,   *go*
Bring her to Bedlem° this ilk° night.   *Bethlehem / very*
280 There shall a child born be,
God's son of heaven[3] is he
And man ay° most of might.   *always*
JOSEPH. Now, Lord God, full well is me
That ever that I this sight should see,
285 I was never ere° so light.°   *before / light-hearted*

For for° I would have her thus refused,°   *since / condemned*
And sackless° blamed that ay° was clear,°   *innocent one / always / pure*
Me bus° pray her hold me excused,[4]   *must*
As some men does with full good cheer.
290 Say Mary, wife, how fares thou?[5]
MARY. The better sir, for you.
Why stand ye there? Come near.
JOSEPH. My back fain° would I bow   *gladly*
And ask forgiveness now,
295 Wist I[6] thou would me hear.

MARY. Forgiveness sir? Let be, for shame,
Slike° words should all good women lack.°   *such / do without*
JOSEPH. Yea, Mary, I am to blame
For words long ere° I to thee spake.°   *before / spoke*
300 But gather sam° now all our gear,   *together*

---

1   *alther most*   Most of all.
2   *in haste*   Soon.
3   *God's son of heaven*   God-of-heaven's son.
4   *For for ... excused*   Since I would have thus condemned her, and blamed the innocent one who was always pure, I must ask her to forgive me.
5   *how fares thou?*   How are you?
6   *Wist I*   If I thought.

Slike poor weed° as we wear,   *clothes*
And prick° them in a pack.   *fasten*
Till Bedlem bus me[1] it bear,
For little thing will women dere;[2]
Help up now[3] on my back.   305

The York Corpus Christi Play: The Nativity

Modern audiences accustomed to Nativity pageants chock-a-block with
shepherds, angels, magi, and the inevitably upstaging live animal or two
will find the York *Nativity* a stark contrast in its emphasis on brevity of
text, economy of action, and simplicity of staging. Even its verse form is
a simple seven-line stanza rhyming ababcbc. The pageant uses only two
actors (those portraying Mary and Joseph) and relies on only one setting
(the run-down stable in Bethlehem—although Joseph must temporarily
wander away from it to seek fuel). Props are minimal: a doll representing
the Christ child, a swaddling cloth, a manger, and cutouts filling in for
the ox and ass of Isaiah 1.3 ("The ox knoweth his owner, and the ass his
master's crib"). The closest the pageant comes to spectacle is the brilliant
light that accompanies Christ's birth and so astonishes Joseph. Pageant
14 strips away everything but the bare bones of the Nativity story, focus-
ing audience attention on the miraculous birth that forms the hinge of
Christian history. (Later performances appear to have been even more
stripped down than earlier ones: by the time the pageant was written
down in the York Register, c. 1463–77, it had lost the apocryphal *obstet-
rix* or "midwife" listed in the 1415 *Ordo Paginarum* description of the
play.) When Mary reveals the infant Jesus to the audience (most likely
by pulling aside her cloak), she draws a firm line between the cold and
darkness of the fallen past and the light and warmth of the soon-to-be-
redeemed future—a point the play echoes in its deliberate evocation of
these oppositions in its diction and imagery. The Old Testament prophecies that the Holy Couple cite in the play are now no longer potential
truths but divine promises kept: the New Law has entered the world.
    The guildsmen responsible for producing Pageant 14 were the
Tile-thatchers, specialists in roof-building. While critics frequently cite

---

1   *bus me*   It is necessary for me.
2   *For little ... dere*   Because little things will trouble women.
3   *Help up now*   Help me up with it now.

the thatched stable set atop the pageant wagon as evidence for the appropriateness of the guild's assignment, it is nonetheless worth noting along with Joseph that the stable roof is "raved above our head," split open and thus wholly inadequate for the purposes of protecting the stable's occupants from the harsh winter weather that accompanies Christ's Incarnation. (A better advertisement for the Tile-thatchers' mastery of their craft was the roof they built and maintained for the Cenacle, or upper room, set on the Bakers' *Last Supper* pageant wagon.) This "staged deficiency," in John Parker's phrase, speaks directly to the limits of human labor in a fallen world, qualifying mankind's capacity for work even as the cycle as a whole celebrates it.

Pageant 14 of the York Corpus Christi Play: The Nativity

CHARACTERS

Joseph
Mary

JOSEPH. All-wielding° God in Trinity,		*omnipotent*
I pray thee, Lord, for° thy great might,		*on account of*
Unto thy simple servant see,[1]		
Here in this place where we are pight,°		*situated*
5 Ourselves alone.		
Lord, grant us good harbor° this night		*shelter*
Within this wone.°		*dwelling*

For we have sought both up and down,		
Through diverse streets in this city.		
10 So mickle° people is come to town		*many*
That we can nowhere harbored° be,		*lodged*
There is slike press;[2]		
Forsooth,° I can no succor° see,		*truly / assistance*
But bield° us with these beasts.		*shelter*

15 And if we here all night abide		
We shall be stormed in this stead,[3]		
The walls are down on ilka° side,		*every*

---

1 *Unto thy simple servant see* Look after thy humble servant.
2 *slike press* Such a crowd.
3 *stormed in this stead* Exposed to the elements in this place.

The roof is raved° above our head,   *torn*
As have I ro;[1]
Say, Mary, daughter,[2] what is thy rede?°   *counsel*   20
How shall we do?

For in great need now are we stead°   *placed*
As thou thyself the sooth° may see,   *truth*
For here is neither cloth° nor bed,   *bedclothes*
And we are weak and all weary   25
And fain° would rest.   *gladly*
Now gracious God, for thy mercy,
Wis° us the best.   *teach*

MARY. God will us wis, full well wit° ye,   *know*
Therefore, Joseph, be of good cheer,   30
For in this place born will he be
That shall us save from sorrows sere,°   *various*
Both even° and morn.   *evening*
Sir, wit ye well the time is near
He will be born.   35

JOSEPH. Then behooves us[3] bide here still,
Here in this same place all this night.
MARY. Yes, sir, forsooth it is God's will.
JOSEPH. Then would I fain we had some light,
What so befall.[4]   40
It waxes right murk° unto my sight,   *dark*
And cold withal.°   *as well*

I will go get us light forthy,°   *therefore*
And fuel fand° with me to bring.[5]   *try*
[*Joseph exits stable.*]

---

1 *As have I ro* As I hope to have peace.
2 *daughter* Joseph refers to Mary as "daughter" here not as a father but as an older person expressing affection for a younger woman. Christian thinkers stressed Joseph's advanced age as evidence of his inability to have fathered Christ (a necessary corollary to the doctrine of the virgin birth).
3 *behooves us* It is necessary for us to.
4 *What so befall* Whatever happens.
5 *And fuel ... to bring* And try to bring some fuel back with me.

45 MARY. All-wielding God you govern and guy,°   *guide*
    As he is sovereign of all thing,
    For his great might,
    And lend me grace to his lofing°   *praise*
    That I me dight.[1]

50   Now in my soul great joy have I,
    I am all clad in comfort clear,
    Now will be born of my body
    Both God and man together in fere,°   *company*
    Blest mote° he be.   *may*
55   Jesus my son that is so dear,
    Now born is he.[2]

    Hail, my Lord God, hail prince of peace,
    Hail my father, and hail my son;
    Hail, sovereign segge° all sins to cease,[3]   *man*
60   Hail, God and man in earth to won.°   *dwell*
    Hail, through whose might
    All this world was first begun,
    Murkness° and light.   *darkness*

    Son, as I am simple subject of thine,
65   Vouchsafe,° sweet son I pray thee,   *grant*
    That I might thee take in these arms of mine,
    And in this poor weed° to array° thee.   *garment / dress*
    Grant me thy bliss,
    As I am thy mother chosen to be,
70   In soothfastness.°   *truth*

    JOSEPH. Ah, Lord God, what the weather is cold,[4]
    The fellest° freeze that ever I feeled.°   *cruelest / felt*
    I pray God help them that is old,
    And namely them that is unwield,°   *feeble*
75   So may I say.

---

1 *And lend me grace ... I me dight* And grant me grace so that I might devote myself to praising him.
2 *Now born is he* Mary must reveal the newborn Jesus at this moment, perhaps by simply pulling aside her cloak.
3 *Hail ... to cease* Hail, sovereign man who will end all sins.
4 *weather is cold* Joseph is still wandering away from Mary in the stable when he sees the light coming from it.

Now good God thou be my bield,°   *protection*
As thou best may.

Ah, Lord God, what light is this
That comes shining thus suddenly?
I cannot say, as have I bliss.   80
When I come home unto Mary,
Then shall I speer.°   *ask*
Ah, here be God,¹ for now come I.
[*Joseph enters stable.*]
MARY. Ye are welcome, sir.

JOSEPH. Say Mary, daughter, what cheer with thee?   85
MARY. Right good, Joseph, as has been ay.°   *ever*
JOSEPH. Oh Mary, what sweet thing is that on thy knee?
MARY. It is my son, the sooth to say,
    That is so good.
JOSEPH. Well is me I bode° this day   *waited for*   90
    To see this food.²

Me marvels mickle° of this light   *greatly*
That thusgates° shines in this place,   *in this way*
Forsooth, it is a selcouth° sight.   *marvelous*
MARY. This has he ordained of his grace,   95
    My son so young,
    A star to be shining a space°   *for a time*
    At his bearing.

For Balaam told full long before,
How that a star should rise full high,   100
And of a maiden should be born
A son, that shall our saving be

---

1   *here be God*   May God be here. Joseph thinks he is uttering the traditional blessing upon
    entering a house, but he is also unconsciously acknowledging the fact of the incarnate God's
    presence in the stable.
2   *To see this food*   To see this child. In addition to the literal sense of *food* as "one who is fed,"
    the Christ child is also ultimately the bread and wine (i.e., body and blood) consumed by
    Christians in the sacrament of the Eucharist. This play on words occurs frequently through-
    out the cycle.

From cares keen.[1]
Forsooth, it is my son so free°   *noble*

105   By whom Balaam did mean.

JOSEPH. Now welcome, flower fairest of hue,[2]
I shall thee mensk° with main and might.   *honor*
Hail, my maker, hail Christ Jesu,
Hail, royal king, root of all right,[3]
110   Hail, savior.
Hail my Lord, leamer° of light,   *one who radiates*
Hail, blessed flower.

MARY. Now Lord that all this world shall win,
To thee my son is that I say,
115   Here is no bed to lay thee in,
Therefore, my dear son, I thee pray,
Since it is so,
Here in this crib I might thee lay,
Between these beasts two.

120   And I shall hap° thee, mine own dear child,   *cover*
With such clothes as we have here.
JOSEPH. Oh Mary, behold these beasts mild,
They make lofing[4] in their manner
As they were men.[5]
125   Forsooth, it seems well by their cheer
Their Lord they ken.°   *recognize*

MARY. Their Lord they ken, that wot° I well,   *know*
They worship him with might and main;

---

1 *For Balaam ... cares keen* Mary conflates two Messianic prophecies here. The first prophecy, that of the Gentile prophet Balaam, occurs in Numbers 24.17: "A star shall rise out of Jacob and a scepter spring up out of Israel." The second prophecy comes from Isaiah 7.14: "Behold a virgin shall conceive, and bear a son, and his name shall be Emmanuel"; *keen* Sharp.

2 *flower fairest of hue* Joseph's characterization of Jesus as a flower stems from Isaiah 11.1: "And there shall come forth a rod out of the root of Jesse, and a flower shall rise up out of his root." Jesse was father to King David, the central figure in Matthew's genealogy of Christ (Matthew 1.1–17).

3 *root of all right* Foundation of all that is good. Also a second reference to Isaiah's "root of Jesse."

4 *make lofing* Offer praise.

5 *As they were men* As if they were human.

The weather is cold, as ye may feel,
To hold° him warm they are full fain°   *keep / glad*   130
With their warm breath,
And ande° on him, is not to lain,°   *breathe / conceal*
To warm him with.[1]

Oh, now sleeps my son, blest may he be,
And lies full warm these beasts between.   135
JOSEPH. Oh, now is fulfilled, forsooth I see,
That Habacuc in mind did mean
And preached by prophecy.[2]
He said our savior shall be seen,
Between beasts lie,   140

And now I see the same in sight.
MARY. Yea, sir, forsooth the same is he.
JOSEPH. Honor and worship both day and night,
Ay-lasting° Lord, be done to thee   *everlasting*
Always, as is worthy;   145
And, Lord, to thy service I oblige° me   *dedicate*
With all my heart, wholly.

MARY. Thou merciful maker, most mighty,
My God, my Lord, my son so free,
Thy handmaiden forsooth am I,   150
And to thy service I oblige me,
With all mine heart entire.
Thy blessing, beseech° I thee,   *entreat, beg*
Thou grant us all in fere.[3]

---

1 *And ande on him ... warm him with* And breathe on him for the obvious (lit. "not to be
   concealed") purpose of warming him up.
2 *That Habacuc ... by prophecy* Joseph's reference is to a prophecy found in the Septuagint Bible (the Greek translation preceding St. Jerome's Latin Vulgate version). There, in
   Habacuc 3.2, the prophet states that the Messiah "shall be known between the two living
   creatures." While the Septuagint version of the prophecy mistranslates the original Hebrew
   ("between the two living creatures" should read "in the midst of the years"), it nonetheless
   became part of Christian liturgy and tradition for centuries to follow.
3 *in fere* Together.

The York Corpus Christi Play: The Shepherds

The York *Shepherds* pageant certainly suffers by comparison with its more famous Chester and Towneley counterparts. It lacks the sheep-stealing hijinks of the rascal Mak and his wife Gill in Towneley; the over-the-top smorgasbord of the shepherds Hankin, Harvey, and Tudd in Chester; and the topsy-turvy wrestling victories of their servant Trowle. In place of these carnivalesque entertainments, the York pageant substitutes little more than the incongruous presentation of shepherds taught Hebrew prophecy by their rural sires, and the pleasures of two or three merry songs. (Stage directions account for two songs, and Shepherd 3's play-ending exhortation to return "home again" and "make mirth as we gang" suggests a third.) Worst of all, the play's most spectacular moment—the Annunciation to the Shepherds—is cut short before the angels can even utter a syllable of their song: the York Register manuscript of the pageant is missing a page at this point. What Pageant 15 does offer to modern readers is its very conventionality: prophecy-spouting shepherds (*pastores* in Latin) who double as Christian pastors, three-part harmonies that exemplify social accord even as they point to the greater unity of the Trinity, and simple, rural gifts that testify to Christ's deliberate upheaval of earthly hierarchies.

The pageant's producers, the Chandlers, were makers of candles and thus well-positioned to provide the light that accompanies the onset of the Star of Bethlehem and the now-lost appearance of the angels' chorus. Like the Tile-thatchers who produced the preceding *Nativity* pageant, though, the Chandlers are makers of "staged deficiency." Their star is a pale shadow of its biblical predecessor, and the song of their angels (quite possibly performers hired from the choir in York Minster) a dim approximation of the heavenly *Gloria*. The inadequacy of their labors is nevertheless redeemed by the text of the play: just as the generous intent informing three shepherds' humble gifts to the Christ child of brooch with bell, cob-nut bracelet, and horn spoon proves them equal to the rich presents offered by the Magi in Pageant 16, so too do the sputtering candles of the Chandlers testify to the guild's devotion—a sincere desire that transcends the fallen circumstances of its utterance.

The mixed verse form includes three stanzas each at the beginning and the end in a twelve-line form, at first rhyming abababbcbc, and then later rhyming ababababcdcd. In between, the lively dialogue of

the shepherds—which often includes shared stanzas and lines—takes
the form of seven-line stanzas rhyming ababcac, with some fragmen-
tary and irregular stanzas.

Pageant 15 of the York Corpus Christi Play: The Shepherds

CHARACTERS

Shepherd 1
Shepherd 2 (Hudde)
Shepherd 3 (Colle)

SHEPHERD 1. Brother, in haste take heed and hear	
What I will speak and specify;	
Since we walk thus, without were,°	*doubt*
What mings° my mood now move it will I.[1]	*stirs*
Our forefathers, faithful in fere,°	*company* 5
Both Hosea and Isaiah,	
Proved that a prince without peer	
Should descend down in a lady,[2]	
And to make mankind clearly,[3]	
To leech° them that are lorn;°	*heal / lost* 10
And in Bethlehem hereby°	*close by*
Shall that same bairn° be born.	*child*

SHEPHERD 2. Ere° he be born in burgh° hereby,	*before / town*
Balaam, brother, me have heard say	
A star should shine and signify,	15
With lightful leams° like any day;[4]	*gleams*
And as the text it tells clearly,	
By witty° learned men of our lay,	*law*
With his blessed blood he should us buy,	

---

1   *What mings ... will I*   What stirs my mind I will now declare.
2   *Both Hosea ... a lady*   Here Shepherd 1 invokes the Messianic prophecy of Isaiah 7.14:
     "Behold a virgin shall conceive, and bear a son, and his name shall be Emmanuel." The
     reference to Hosea in this context is misleading: while medieval thinkers did read Hosea
     11.1 ("I called my son out of Egypt") as a prophecy of the Holy Family's return from exile
     in Egypt, the passage has nothing to do with the virgin birth.
3   *to make mankind clearly*   To make humanity clear (i.e., free from sin).
4   *Balaam ... day*   Here Hudde recalls the prediction of the Gentile prophet Balaam in
     Numbers 24.17 that "A star shall rise out of Jacob and a scepter spring up out of Israel."

20 He should take here all of a may.[1]
    I heard my sire° say,   *father*
    When he of her was born,
    She should be as clean maid
    As ever she was before.

25 SHEPHERD 3. Ah, merciful maker, mickle° is   *great*
        thy might,
      That thus will to thy servants see,°   *look after*
      Might we once look upon that light,
      Gladder brethren° might no men be.   *brothers*
      I have heard say, by that same light
30   The children of Israel should be made free,
      The force of the fiend to fell° in fight,   *strike down*
      And all his power excluded should be.[2]
      Wherefore, brethren, I rede° that we   *advise*
      Flit° fast over these fells,°   *go / hills*
35   To fraist° to find our fee,°   *try / livestock*
      And talk of somewhat else.

    SHEPHERD 1. Hey, Hudde!
    SHEPHERD 2.   Hey, how?
    SHEPHERD 1.   Hearken to me.
    SHEPHERD 2. Hey, man, thou mads° all out   *act mad*
        of might.[3]
    SHEPHERD 1. Hey, Colle!
    SHEPHERD 3.   What care is come to thee?
40 SHEPHERD 1. Step forth and stand by me right,
      And tell me then
      If thou saw ever swilk° a sight.   *such*
    SHEPHERD 3. I? Nay, certes,° nor never no man.[4]   *certainly*

    SHEPHERD 2. Say fellows, what, find ye any feast,

---

1   *take here all of a may* Take his form here (i.e., on earth) from a maiden. Balaam's prophecy
    in Numbers does not mention the virgin birth; Hudde is clearly conflating Balaam and
    Isaiah at this point in his exegesis.
2   *all his power excluded should be* All his power should be banished.
3   *thou mads all out of might* You're acting extremely crazy.
4   *nor never no man* Not ever any man. In Middle English, multiple negatives do not cancel
    one another. Instead each negative increases the emphasis of a statement. Colle is thus
    stressing that no one has ever seen a sight such as the Star of Bethlehem.

Me falls for to have part,[1] pardie!°   *by God!*   45
SHEPHERD 1. Hey, Hudde, behold into the east,
  A selcouth° sight then shall thou see   *marvelous*
  Upon the sky.
SHEPHERD 2. Hey, tell me, men, among us three,
  What gars° you stare thus sturdily?   *causes*   50

SHEPHERD 3. As long as we have herdsmen been
  And kept this cattle° in this clough,°   *these sheep / valley*
  So selcouth a sight was never none seen.[2]
SHEPHERD 1. Hey, no, Colle. Now comes it new enough
  That may we find   55
  ...[3]

SHEPHERD 3. It means some marvel us among,[4]
  Full hardily I you behight.°   *promise*

SHEPHERD 1. What it should mean that wot°   *know*
    not ye,
  For all that ye can gape and gane.°   *yawn*
  I can sing it as well as he,   60
  And on assay° it shall be soon   *by trial*
  Proved ere° we pass.   *before*
  If ye will help, let see, hold on,°   *keep up*
  For thus it was:

(And then they sing.)[5]

SHEPHERD 2. Ha ha! This was a merry note,   65
  By the death that I shall die,

---

1 *Say fellows ... to have part* Say, fellows, what, if you find any food, I deserve a portion (literally, "a part falls to me").

2 *never none seen* Never ever seen (another multiple negative for the sake of emphasis).

3 ... The text breaks off here as a page has disappeared from the York Register manuscript of the pageant. The missing portion of the play would have featured the angel's appearance to the shepherds and the hymn of the celestial chorus.

4 *It means ... among* The manuscript resumes in the midst of an unidentified shepherd's reaction to the angelic message. Because the shepherds primarily speak in numerical sequence during the pageant, scholars attribute this partial speech to Colle, who, in his capacity as Shepherd 3, would normally speak before Shepherd 1, the first identified speaker of the resumed text.

5 *And then they sing* The first of two Latin stage directions in the play-text.

I have so cracked° in my throat   *sung*
    That my lips are near dry.
SHEPHERD 3. I trow° thou roose,°   *believe / boast*
70 For what it was fain° wit° would I   *gladly / know*
    That to us made this noble noise.[1]

SHEPHERD 1. An angel brought us tidings new
    A babe in Bethlehem should be born,
    Of whom then spoke our prophecy true,
75 And bade us meet him there this morn,
    That mild of mood.[2]
SHEPHERD 2. I would give him both hat and horn,
    If I might find that freely food.[3]

SHEPHERD 3. Him for to find has we no dread,
80 I shall you tell achesoun° why: *the reason*
    Yon star to that lord shall us lead.
SHEPHERD 2. Yea, thou says sooth.° Go   *the truth*
    we, forthy,°   *therefore*
    Him to honor,
    And make mirth and melody,
85 With song to seek our savior.

    (*And then they sing.*)[4]

SHEPHERD 1. Brethren,° be all blithe and glad,   *brothers*
    Here is the burgh° there we should be.   *where*
SHEPHERD 2. In that same stead now are we stead,[5]
    Therefore I will go seek and see.
90 Slike hap of heal[6] never herdsmen had;
    Lo, here is the house, and here is he.

SHEPHERD 3. Yea, forsooth,° this is the same,   *truly*

---

1 *For what ... this noble noise* For I would gladly know what it was that made the noble noise
    we just heard.
2 *That mild of mood* That one gentle in demeanor.
3 *food* Child. In calling the Christ-child food, Hudde speaks truer than he knows: Jesus is
    not only a child in the sense of "one who is fed" but also the food that will feed Christians
    in years to come—the bread and wine (i.e., body and blood) of the Eucharist.
4 *And then they sing* The second of two Latin stage directions in the play-text.
5 *In that ... are we stead* In that same place we are now located.
6 *Slike hap of heal* Such a chance of salvation.

Lo where that lord is laid
Betwixt° two beasts tame,   *between*
Right as the angel said.   95

SHEPHERD 1. The angel said that he should save
    This world and all that wones° therein,   *dwells*
    Therefore if I should aught after crave[1]
    To worship him I will begin:
    Since I am but a simple knave,   100
    Though all[2] I come of courteous kin,
    Lo here slike° harness° as I have—   *such / gear*
    A barren° brooch by° a bell of tin,   *plain / with*
    At your bosom to be;
    And when ye shall wield° all,   *rule* 105
    Good son, forget not me
    If any fordeal fall.[3]

SHEPHERD 2. Thou son that shall save both sea and sand,[4]
    See to me, since I have thee sought;
    I am over-poor° to make present   *too poor* 110
    As my heart would, if I had aught.°   *anything*
    Two cob-nuts° upon a band,   *hazel nuts*
    Lo, little babe, what I have brought;
    And when ye shall be lord in land
    Do good again, forget me not,   115
    For I have heard declared
    Of cunning° clerks and clean,°   *learned / pure*
    That bounty asks reward;[5]
    Now wot° ye what I mean.   *know*

SHEPHERD 3. Now look on me, my lord dear,   120
    Though all I put me not in press,[6]
    Ye are a prince without peer,
    I have no present that you may please.[7]
    But lo, a horn spoon, that have I here—

---

1   *if I should aught after crave* If there's anything I want later on.
2   *Though all* Even though.
3   *If any fordeal fall* If any opportunity arises.
4   *both sea and sand* The whole world.
5   *bounty asks reward* A gift merits a reward.
6   *Though all … in press* Although I don't push myself forward (as eagerly as the others did).
7   *no present that you may please* No gift that may please you.

125	And it will harbor° forty peas—	*hold*
	This will I give you with good cheer;	
	Slike° novelty may not disease.[1]	*such*
	Farewell, thou sweet swain,°	*young man*
	God grant us living long,[2]	
130	And go we home again	
	And make mirth as we gang.°	*go*

The York Corpus Christi Play:
Herod and the Magi; The Offering of the Magi

The Herod and Magi sequence is unusual in the York *Corpus Christi Play*, as it consists of what were originally two pageants (*Herod and the Magi* followed by *The Offering of the Magi*) produced by two guilds (the Masons and the Goldsmiths, respectively). Two pageant wagons were required, one for Herod's Court in Jerusalem and one for the stable in Bethlehem. Connecting the two episodes and locations are the Magi—the three kings—themselves, who appear in both parts of the sequence and travel between locations, just as they do in the much more simple narrative in Matthew 2.1–12. The travel of the kings in the play would have taken place on the ground level between the wagons, perhaps suggesting a thematic identification with the audience: all are spiritual travelers. The journey might also have added to the spectacle of an already complex and extravagant pageant if the kings traveled on horseback, as generally depicted in the visual arts.

The sequence gives us the first of the cycle's series of bombastic earthly tyrants, whose language is full of self-praise and exaggerated claims of power, who demand loyalty from all, and who react with paranoia to any threat to their power. They also tend to speak in long, heavily alliterative lines—a formal style that matches the extravagance of their egotistical behavior. The typical tyrants of cycle drama are Herod the Great, ruler of Judea, who appears here and in the *Slaughter of the Innocents* pageant; his son, Herod Antipas, before whom the adult Christ is brought after his arrest; and Pontius Pilate, the prefect of Roman Judea, who pronounces Christ's final fate. It is the Herods who are best known

---

1 *Slike novelty may not disease* Such novelty may not be displeasing.
2 *living long* Long life.

for their scenery-chewing behavior, remembered perhaps most famously in Hamlet's instructions to his actors not to "out-Herod Herod."

Herod's bombast stands in contrast to the three kings' formal politeness and humility before the Christ child in the second part of the sequence. Indeed, the combining of the two sequences within one play sets up a number of fruitful symbolic contrasts: the noise, spectacle, unruliness, and overweening and illegitimate power of Herod's court and its wagon contrasts with the stillness, simplicity, order, humility, and legitimate might of the nativity scene and its wagon. Even the verse forms employed underscore these contrasts. Much of the play is in the twelve-line stanza rhyming abababababcdcd that we find used many times throughout the cycle, but Herod's ranting and his obsequious court's responses in the Masons' first section of the play uses a mix of stanza forms and employs the heavy alliteration more frequently found in the Passion sequence of the play.

Pageant 16 of the York Corpus Christi Play: Herod and the Magi; The Offering of the Magi

CHARACTERS

Herod
Soldier 1
Soldier 2
Herod's Son
King 1
King 2
King 3
Messenger
Counselor 1
Counselor 2
Handmaid
Mary
Angel

[*The Masons: Herod's Court*]

HEROD. The clouds clapped in clearness° that their   *splendor*
    climates° encloses—   *celestial zones*
  Jupiter and Jove, Mars and Mercury amid—

Raiking° over my royalty on row° me rejoices,[1]   *rushing / in order*
Blundering° their blasts to blow when   *whirling about*
   I bid.°   *command*
5   Saturn, my subject, that subtly is hid,
   Lists° at my liking[2] and lays him° full low.   *takes heed / himself*
   The rack° of° the red sky full raply° I rid;   *cloud bank / from / quickly*
   Thunders° full throly° by   *thunderbolts / furiously, violently*
      thousands I throw
   When me likes.[3]
10   Venus his[4] voice to me owe,°   *owes*
   That° princes to play in him picks.°[5]   *so that / chooses*

   The prince of planets[6] that proudly is pight°   *adorned*
   Shall brace° forth his beams that our   *radiate*
      bield° blithes,°   *happiness / gladden*
   The moon at my might he musters° his might,   *displays*
15   And caesars° in castles great kindness me kithes.°   *rulers / show to*
   Lords and ladies, lo, lovely° me lithes,°   *courteously / attend on*
   For I am fairer of face and fresher on fold°—   *earth*
   The sooth° if I say shall—seven-and-sixty[7] sithes°   *truth / times*
   Than glorious gules° that gayer is than gold   *red decoration*
20   In price.
   How think ye[8] these tales that I told?
   I am worthy, witty, and wise.

SOLDIER 1. All kings to your crown may clearly commend
   Your law and your lordship as lodestar on height;[9]

---

1   *The clouds ... me rejoices*   The clouds, wrapped in a splendor that encompasses their region
   —(with) Jupiter and Jove, Mars and Mercury in their midst—delight me, rushing in order
   over my royalty;   *climate*   Area of the earth ruled over by one of the seven heavenly
   bodies, which each had their own region: Sun, Moon, Mercury, Venus, Mars, Jupiter, and
   Saturn.
2   *Lists at my liking*   Takes heed to my desires.
3   *The rack ... me likes*   Very quickly I rid the cloud bank from the red sky; I throw thunderbolts by the thousands very violently when it pleases me.
4   *his*   Although as a deity Venus is female, apparently the planet is male here.
5   *That princes ... picks*   So that princes choose to play upon him.
6   *prince of planets*   I.e., the sun. In Middle English, "planet" could designate any heavenly
   body, but especially the seven heavenly bodies of Ptolemaic astronomy: (in order from the
   earth) the moon, Mercury, Venus, the sun, Mars, Jupiter, and Saturn.
7   *seven-and-sixty*   Sixty-seven.
8   *How think ye*   What do you think of.
9   *as lodestar on height*   As a guiding star on high.

What traitor untrue that will not attend,   25
Ye shall lay them full low, from leam° and from light.   *brightness*
SOLDIER 2.   What faitour,° in faith, that does you offend,   *traitor*
We shall set him full sore,°   *sorely, harshly*
    that sot,° in your sight.   *fool*
HEROD. In wealth shall I wis° you to wone°   *arrange for / dwell*
    ere° I wend,°   *before / go*
For ye are wights° full worthy,   *men*   30
    both witty and wight.°   *bold, valiant*

But ye know well, sir knights in counsel full cunning,
That my region so royal is ruled here by rest,[1]
For I wot° of no wight in this world that is wonning°   *know / living*
That° in forges[2] any felony,°   *who / crime*
    with force shall be fast.°   *secured*
Arrest ye those ribalds° that   *scoundrels*   35
    unruly are rounding,°   *speaking*
Be they kings or knights, in care° ye them cast,   *suffering*
Yea, and wield° them in woe to wone,°   *cause / dwell*
    in the waning;[3]
What broll° that is brawling°   *brat / squabbling*
    his brain look ye brast,°   *burst*
And ding° ye him down.   *strike*
SOLDIER 1. Sir, what food° in faith will you feeze,°   *person / punish*   40
    That sot° full soon myself shall him seize.   *fool*
SOLDIER 2. We shall not here doubt°   *fear*
    to do him disease,°   *discomfort*
But with countenance full cruel we shall
    crack here his crown.°   *head or crown*

HEROD. My son that is seemly,° how seems   *honorable*
    thee these saws?[4]
How comely° these knights they carp° in this case.   *fittingly / talk*   45
HEROD'S SON. Father, if they like not to listen° your laws,   *heed*
As traitors untrue ye shall teach them a trace,°   *lesson*
For father, unkindness ye kithe° them no cause.[5]   *show*

---

1   *by rest* In peace.
2   *in forges* Plans.
3   *waning* The reference is to the waning of the moon, which was seen as an inauspicious
      time; thus "in the waning" can also mean "under a curse" or "with ill luck."
4   *how seems thee these saws* How do these opinions sound to you?
5   *unkindness ... no cause* You have shown them no reason for unkindness.

HEROD. Fair° fall° thee my fair son,		*good fortune / befall*
so featous° of face.		*handsome*
50	And knights, I command, who to dole° draws,	*evil*
	Those churls,° as chevaliers,°	*base fellows / knights*
	ye chastise° and chase,[1]	*punish*
	And dread ye no doubt.°	*fear*
	HEROD'S SON. Father, I shall fell° them in fight,	*defeat*
	What rink° that reaves° you your right.	*warrior / robs*
55	SOLDIER 1. With dints° to dead be he dight°	*blows / put*
	That list° not your laws for to lout.°	*chooses / submit to*

[*The Goldsmiths: The Magi*]

	KING 1. Ah, Lord that lives, everlasting light,	
	I love° thee ever with heart and hand,	*praise*
	That me has made to see this sight	
60	Which my kindred was covetand.°	*desirous of*
	They said a star with leams° bright	*rays*
	Out of the east should stably° stand,	*firmly*
	And that it should move° mickle° might	*indicate / great*
	Of one that should be lord in land,	
65	That men of° sin should save.	*from*
	And certes° I shall say,	*certainly*
	God grant me hap° to have	*luck*
	Wissing° of ready way.	*guidance*

	KING 2. All-wielding° God that all has wrought,	*almighty*
70	I worship thee as is worthy,	
	That with thy brightness has me brought	
	Out of my realm, rich Arabie.	
	I shall not cease till I have sought°	*found out*
	What selcouth° thing it shall signify,	*marvelous*
75	God grant me hap° so that I might	*good fortune*
	Have grace to get good company,	
	And my comfort increase	
	With thy star shining sheen;°	*brightly*
	For certes,° I shall not cease	*certainly*
80	Till I wit° what it mean.	*know*

	KING 3. Lord God that all good has begun
	And all may end, both good and evil,

---

1   *Those churls … chase*   Like knights, you punish and pursue those churls.

That made for man both moon and sun,
And stead° yon star to stand stone still,   *placed*
Till I the cause may clearly con,°   *know*   85
God wis° me with his worthy will.   *guide*
I hope° I have here fellows fon°   *believe / found*
My yearning faithfully to fulfill.
Sirs, God you save and see,
And were° you ever from woe.   *defend*   90
KING 1. Amen, so might it be,
  And save you sir, also.

KING 3. Sirs, with your will, I would you pray
  To tell me some of your intent,
  Whither° ye wend° forth in this way,   *to what place / go*   95
  And from what country ye are went?
KING 2. Full gladly sir I shall you say.
  A sudden sight was till° us sent,   *to*
  A royal star that rose ere° day   *before*
  Before us on the firmament,   100
  That gart° us fare° from home   *caused / to travel*
  Some point° thereof° to prove.°   *matter / regarding that / find out*
KING 3. Certes, sirs, I saw the same
  That makes us thus to move;

  For sirs, I have heard say certain°   *certainly*   105
  It should° be sign of selcouth° sere,°   *must / marvels / various*
  And further thereof° I would frayne;°   *of that / inquire*
  That makes me move in this manner.
KING 1. Sir, of fellowship are we fain,°   *eager*
  Now shall we wend° forth all in fere,°   *go / company*   110
  God grant us ere° we come again   *before*
  Some good hearting° thereof to hear.   *encouragement*
  Sir, here is Jerusalem
  To wis° us as we go,   *direct*
  And beyond is Bethlehem,   115
  There shall we seek also.

KING 3. Sirs, ye shall well understand,
  For to be wise now were it need;[1]
  Sir Herod is king of this land

---

1 *were it need* It is necessary.

120   And has his laws here for to lead.°   *rule*

    KING 1. Sir, since we nigh° now thus nearhand,°   *come / close*

       Until° his help us must take heed,[1]   *unto*

       For have we[2] his will and his warrant

       Than may we wend° without dread.°   *go / fear*

125 KING 2. To have leave of the lord,

       That is reason and skill.°   *good sense*

    KING 3. And thereto° we all accord,°   *to that / agree*

       Wend° we and wit° his will.   *go / know*

[*The Masons and the Goldsmiths: The Magi at Herod's Court*]

   [*Enter Messenger*]

MESSENGER. My Lord Sir Herod, king with crown!

130 HEROD. Peace dastard,° in the devil's despite.°   *dullard / malice*

    MESSENGER. My Lord, new note° is near this town.   *news*

    HEROD. What, false harlot,° list thee flite?[3]   *base fellow*

       [*To the soldiers*] Go beat yon boy° and   *worthless fellow*

         ding° him down.   *strike*

    SOLDIER 2. Lord, messengers should no man wite,°   *blame*

135 It may be for your own renown.

    HEROD. That would I hear, do tell on tite.°   *quickly*

    MESSENGER. My Lord, I met at morn°   *morning*

       Three kings carping° together   *talking*

       Of a bairn° that is born,   *child*

140 And they hight° to come hither.°   *promised / to here*

    HEROD. Three kings, forsooth?°   *truly*

    MESSENGER.   Sir, so I say,

       For I saw them myself all fere.°   *together*

    COUNSELOR 1. My Lord, appose° him I you pray.   *interrogate*

    HEROD. Say fellow, are they far or near?

145 MESSENGER. My Lord, they will be here this day,

       That wot I well, without were.°   *doubt*

    HEROD. Do rule° us° then   *dress / the royal "we," i.e., me*

       in rich array,°   *clothing*

       And ilka° man make them merry cheer,° *each / countenance, expression*

---

1   *Until ... heed* It is necessary for us to pay attention to his help.

2   *For have we* For if we have.

3   *list thee flite* Do you want to argue? I.e., how dare you argue.

That no semblant° be seen   *appearance*
But friendship fair and still,   150
Till we wit° what they mean,°   *know / intend*
Whether it be good or ill.

[*Enter three kings.*]

KING 1. The Lord that lends° ay-lasting° light   *gives / eternal*
Which has us led out of our land,
Keep thee, sir king and comely° knight   *noble* 155
And all thy folk that we here find.
HEROD. Mahound,[1] my god and most of might,
That has mine heal° all in his hand,   *well-being*
He save you[2] sirs, seemly in sight;
And tell us now some new tidand.°   *tidings, news* 160
KING 2. Some shall we say° you, sir—   *tell*
A star stood us beforn,°   *before, in front of*
That makes us speak and speer°   *inquire*
Of one that is new-born.

HEROD. New-born? That burden° hold I bad;   *birth* 165
And certes,° unwitty° men ye were   *certainly / foolish*
To leap over land to lait° a lad.   *seek*
Say, when lost ye him? Aught° long before?   *at all*
All wise men will ween° ye mad   *think*
And therefore move° this never more.   *refer to* 170
KING 3. Yes certes, swilk° hearting° have we had *such / encouragement*
We will not cease ere° we come there.   *before*
HEROD. This were a wonder-thing.°   *marvel*
Say, what bairn° should that be?   *child*
KING 1. Forsooth,° he shall be king   *truly* 175
Of Jews and of Judea.

HEROD. King? In the devil's name, dogs, fie![3]
Now see I well ye roy° and rave.   *talk nonsense*
By any shimmering of the sky
When° should ye know either king or knave?   *how* 180

---

1 *Mahound* Muhammad, prophet and founder of Islam (c. 570–632). Medieval English
   texts often depict all non-Christian characters as worshipping or otherwise calling on
   Muhammad, as a way to construct their "otherness."
2 *He save you* May he save you.
3 *fie* Interjection. Expresses disgust or indignant reproach.

HEROD'S SON. Nay, he is king and none but he,
    That shall ye ken° if that ye crave,°   *know / desire*
    And he is judge of all Jewry,
    To speak or spill,° to say or save.[1]   *ruin*
185 HEROD. Swilk° gauds° may greatly grieve,°   *such / tricks / offend*
    To witness that° ne'er° was.[2]   *that which / never*
    KING 2. Now Lord, we ask but leave
    By your power to pass.

    HEROD. Whitherward,° in the devil's name?   *to what place*
190   To lait° a lad here in my land?   *seek*
    False harlots,° but° ye hie° you home   *villains / unless / hasten*
    Ye shall be beat° and bound in band.°   *beaten / bonds*
    COUNSELOR 2. My Lord, to fell° this foul defame,° *defeat / disgrace*
    Let all these high° words fall on hand,[3]   *proud*
195   And speer° them sadly° of the same,   *inquire / gravely*
    So shall ye stably° understand   *absolutely*
    Their mind and their meaning,
    And take good tent° thereto.   *heed*
    HEROD. I thank thee of this thing,
200   And certes so shall I do.

    Now kings, to catch° all care away   *chase*
    Since ye are come out of your kith,°   *native land*
    Look not ye ledge° against our lay,°   *allege / law*
    Upon pain to lose both limb and lith.°   *joint*
205   And so that ye the sooth° will say   *truth*
    To come and go I grant you grith,°   *protection*
    And if your points° be to my pay° *subject matter / satisfaction*
    May fall° myself shall wend° you with.[4] *befall, happen / go*
    KING 1. Sir king, we all accord,
210   And say a bairn is born
    That shall be king and lord,
    And leech° them that are lorn.°   *heal / lost*

    KING 2. Sir, ye thar° marvel nothing°   *need / not at all*

---

1 *To speak ... save* To speak up for (in defense) or to ruin, to say against (i.e., condemn) or to save.
2 *To witness that ne'er was* I.e., to bear false witness, to fabricate something.
3 *fall on hand* Be put aside.
4 *May fall ... you with* It may happen that I will go with you.

Of this ilka° note° that thusgates° news,°   *same / matter / thus / arises*
For Balaam[1] said a star should spring   215
Of° Jacob's kind,° and that is Jews.   *from / kindred*
KING 3. Isaiah says a maiden young
Shall bear a bairn among Hebrews,
That of all countries shall be king
And govern all that on earth grows;   220
Emmanuel beth° his name,[2]   *is*
To say,° "God's son of heaven,"   *mean, signify*
And certes° this is the same   *indeed*
That we here to you neven.°   *name*

KING 1. Sir, the provèd° prophet Hosé°   *trustworthy / Hosea* 225
Full truly told in town and tower,
A maiden of Israel, forsooth° said he,   *truly*
Shall bear one like to lily flower.[3]
He means a child conceived shall be
Without seed of man's succor,°   *help* 230
And his mother a maiden free,°   *gracious*
And he both son and savior.
KING 2. That° fathers° told me beforn° *what / forefathers / before*
Has no man might° to mar.°   *power / spoil*
HEROD. Alas, then am I lorn,°   *lost* 235
This wax° ay° war° and war.   *grows / continually / worse*

COUNSELOR 1. My Lord, be ye nothing°   *not at all*
   abast,°   *abashed, disconcerted*
This brigue° till° end shall well be brought.   *conflict / to*
Bid them go forth and friendly° fraist° *helpfully / put to the test*
The sooth° of this that they have sought,   *truth* 240
And tell it you, so shall ye traist°   *feel assured*
Whether their tales be true or not.
Than shall ye wait° them with a wrest° *wait for / evil turn, trick*
And make all waste[4] that they have wrought.°   *created*

---

1 *Balaam* A prophet who prophesied that "a star shall rise out of Jacob and a sceptre shall spring up from Israel" (Numbers 24.17, Douay-Rheims translation).

2 *Isaiah says ... his name* From Isaiah 7.14: "Behold a virgin shall conceive, and bear a son, and his name shall be called Emmanuel" (Douay-Rheims translation).

3 *Hosé ... lily flower* Although Hosea 14.6 was taken as a prophecy of the birth of Christ ("I will be as the dew, Israel shall spring as the lily, and his root shall shoot forth as Libanus," Douay-Rheims translation), it does not explicitly mention a maiden. The lily was interpreted as Mary.

4 *make all waste* Destroy all.

245 HEROD. Now certes,° this is well said,   *indeed*
         This matter makes me fain.°   *happy*
         Sir kings, I hold° me° paid°   *consider / myself / pleased*
         Of all your purpose plain.°   *clear*

         Wend° forth your foreward° to fulfill,   *go / pledge, promise*
250   To Bethlehem is but here at hand;
         And speer° gradely° both good and ill   *ask (of) / plainly*
         Of him that should be lord in land;[1]
         And come again then me until[2]
         And tell me truly your tidand.°   *tidings, news*
255   To worship him then were° my will,°   *would be / desire*
         This shall ye stably° understand.   *firmly*
         KING 2. Certes sir, we shall you say°   *tell*
         The sooth° of that same child,   *truth*
         In all the haste we may.
260 COUNSELOR 2. Farewell—ye be beguiled.[3]

         [*Exit the three kings.*]

         HEROD. Now certes, this is a subtle train.°   *trick*
         Now shall they truly take their trace[4]
         And tell me of that swittering° swain° *wallowing (i.e., helpless) / boy*
         And all their counsel° in this case.°   *plans / matter*
265   If it be sooth, they shall be slain,
         No gold shall get them better grace;°   *favor*
         But go we till they come again
         And play us in some other place.[5]
         This hold° I good counsel,   *consider*
270   Yet would I no man wist;°   *knew*
         For certes, we shall not fail
         To lose° them as us list.[6]   *destroy*

---

1   *And speer … lord in land*   And ask plainly of both good and wicked people who is lord of
    the land.
2   *me until*   To me.
3   *ye be beguiled*   An aside or spoken after the Kings have departed.
4   *take their trace*   Make their way; *trace* Course, path, way.
5   *play us in some other place*   Given the stage direction after this that directs the Herod wagon
    to move on, Herod's line here works as a metatheatrical pun.
6   *as us list*   As it pleases us.

(*The Herod*[1] *passeth, and the three kings come again to make their offerings.*)

[*The Goldsmiths: The Offering of the Magi*]

KING 1. Ah, sirs, for site° what shall I say?   *sorrow*
    Where is our sign? I see it not.
KING 2. No more do I. Now dare I lay°   *bet, wager* 275
    In our wending° some wrong is wrought.[2]   *traveling*
KING 3. Unto that prince I rede° we pray,   *advise*
    That till° us sent his sign unsought,   *to*
    That he wis° us in ready° way   *guide / proper*
    So° friendly° that we find him mought.°   *so that / lovingly / might* 280
KING 1. Ah, sirs, I see it stand
    Above where he is born;
    Lo, here is the house at hand,[3]
    We have not missed° this morn.°   *failed / morning*

[*The three kings approach the stable.*]

HANDMAID. Whom seek ye sirs,[4] by ways wild,   285
    With talking, traveling to and fro?
    Here wones° a woman with her child   *lives*
    And her husband, here are no mo.°   *more*
KING 2. We seek a bairn that° all shall bield,°[5]   *who / protect*
    His certain sign hath said° us so,   *told* 290
    And his mother, a maiden mild,
    Her hope we to find them two.
HANDMAID. Come near good sirs and see,
    Your way° to end is brought.   *journey*

KING 3. Behold here sirs, hear and see   295
    The same that ye have sought.

---

1 *The Herod* The Herod wagon, signifying Herod's court. The Masons are now free to pull their wagon to the next station, while the Goldsmiths take over the remainder of this play on their wagon.
2 *In our wending ... wrought* We have gone wrong somewhere on our journey.
3 *the house at hand* For this portion of the play, the Goldsmiths clearly must use a second wagon to represent the stable containing the Holy Family.
4 *Whom seek ye sirs* This phrasing anticipates the Angel's words to the three Maries at the tomb in the *Resurrection* play.
5 *that all shall bield* Who shall protect all.

	KING 1. Lovèd° be that Lord that lasts ay,°	*praised / forever*
	That us has kid° thus courteously	*shown*
	To wend° by many a wilsome° way,	*go / desolate*
300	And come to this clean° company.	*pure*
	KING 2. Let us make now no more delay,	
	But tite° take forth our treasury	*quickly*
	And ordained° gifts of good array,°	*intended / order, condition*
	To worship him as is worthy.	
305	KING 3. He is worthy to wield	
	All worship, wealth, and win;°	*joy*
	And for honor and eld°	*age*
	Brother, ye shall begin.	

	KING 1. Hail, the fairest of field,[1] folk for to find,°	*support*
310	From the fiend and his feres° faithfully us fend;°	*companions / defend*
	Hail, the best that shall be born to unbind	
	All the bernes° that are born and	*people*
	in bale° bend.°	*torment / bound*
	Hail, thou mark us thy men and make us in mind,[2]	
	Since thy might is on mould° misease° to amend.	*earth / distress*
315	Hail, clean° that is come of a king's kind,°	*pure one / lineage*
	And shall be king of this kith,°	*people*
	all clergy has kenned.°	*made known*
	And since it shall worth° on this wise,[3]	*happen*
	Thyself have I sought soon, I say thee,	
	With gold that is greatest of price;	
320	Be paid° of this present, I pray thee.	*content, pleased*

	KING 2. Hail, food° that thy folk fully may feed,[4]	*child*
	Hail flower fairest, that never shall fade,	
	Hail, son that is sent of this same seed	
	That shall save us of sin that our sires° had.	*forefathers*
325	Hail mild,° for thou met° to mark us	*meek one / chose*
	to meed,°	*reward*
	Of a may° makeless° thy mother thou made;	*maid / matchless*

---

1 *fairest of field* Fairest in the world.
2 *make us in mind* Keep us in mind, remember us.
3 *on this wise* In this manner.
4 *food … feed* In the first instance, "food" means "child" here, but it also puns on "food" as "sustenance" (as the end of the line makes clear), and in doing so also suggests the spiritual sustenance of the Eucharist, the ritual sharing of the body and blood of Christ.

In° that good° through grace of thy Godhead,	*into / good one*
As the gleam in the glass gladly thou glade.°	*glided*
And sithen° thou shall sit to be deeming,°	*since / judging*
To hell or to heaven for to have us,	330
Incense to thy service is seeming.°	*appropriate*
Son, see to thy subjects and save us.	

KING 3. Hail bairn° that is best our *child*
   bales° to bete,°   *woes / put right*
For our boot° shall thou be bound and bet;°   *aid / beaten*
Hail friend faithful, we fall to thy feet,   335
Thy father's folk from the fiend to thee fet.°   *fetch*
Hail, man that is made to thy men meet,°   *equal*
Since thou and thy mother with mirths°   *joys*
   are met;°   *brought together*
Hail duke that drives death under feet,
But when thy deeds are done, to die is thy debt.°   *duty* 340
And since thy body buried shall be,
This myrrh will I give to thy graving.°   *burial*
The gift is not great of degree,
Receive it, and see to our saving.°   *salvation*

MARY. Sir kings, ye travel not in vain.   345
As ye have meant,° here may ye find,   *sought*
For I conceived my son certain°   *certainly*
Without miss° of man in mind,   *sin*
And bore him here without pain,
Where women are wont° to be pined.°   *accustomed / pained* 350
God's angel in his greeting plain
Said he should comfort all mankind,
Therefore doubt you no deal[1]
Here for to have your boon;°   *desire*
I shall witness full well   355
All that is said and done.

KING 1. For solace° sere°   *joy, spiritual comfort / extraordinary*
   now may we sing,
All is performed that we for prayed;
But good bairn, give us thy blessing,
For fair° hap° is before thee laid.   *good / fortune* 360

---

1   *no deal*   Not at all.

KING 2. Wend° we now to Herod the king   *go*
    For of this point° he will be paid,°   *matter / pleased*
    And come himself and make offering
    Unto this same, for so he said.
365 KING 3. I rede° we rest a throw,°   *advise / short time*
    For to maintain° our might,°   *conserve / strength*
    And then do as we owe,°   *ought*
    Both unto king and knight.

[*Enter angel as three kings leave the stable.*]

ANGEL. Now courteous kings, to me take tent°   *heed*
370 And turn betime° ere° ye be teened;°   *promptly / before / harmed*
    From God himself thus am I sent
    To warn you as your faithful friend.
    Herod the king has malice meant°   *planned*
    And shapes° with shame you for to shend,°   *plans / destroy*
375 And for° that ye none° harms should hent,°   *so / no / suffer*
    By other ways God will° ye wend°   *wants / to go*
    Even to your own country.
    And if ye ask him boon,°   *favor*
    Your bield° ay° will he be   *support / always*
380 For this that ye have done.

KING 1. Ah, Lord, I love° thee inwardly.°   *praise / in the soul*
    Sirs, God has goodly° warned us three,   *kindly*
    His angel here now heard have I,
    And how he said.
KING 2.   Sir, so did we.
385 He said Herod is our enemy,
    And makes him° boun° our bale° to be   *himself / ready / destruction*
    With feigned falsehood, and forthy°   *therefore*
    Far from his force° I rede° we flee.   *power / advise*
KING 3. Sirs, fast I rede we flit,°   *escape*
390 Ilkone° till° our country,   *each one / to*
    He that is well° of wit°   *source / knowledge*
    Us wis,° and with you be.   *guide*

The York Corpus Christi Play:
The Slaughter of the Innocents

The Slaughter of the Innocents presents an episode of infanticide by King Herod of Judea deriving from the Gospel of Matthew 2.16–18. The killing of the baby boys of Bethlehem represents a culmination of the York nativity episodes, leaving audience members with chilling pre-figurative images of maternal grief and the death of beloved sons. For the medieval audience the slaughter of the innocents was a traumatic event proleptic of the murder of Christ and imbued with anti-Semitic hatred for, in the phrase of Geoffrey Chaucer's Prioress, the "cursed folk of Herodes al newe." York's Herod has orientalist, syncretic qualities here and in the Magi episode (pageant 16); he is a Jew who worships Moham-med and invokes devils. On his orders many infants are slaughtered yet he is unable to control all outcomes. Jesus escapes to take up his role of true *maistrie* or mastery, the substance of real power that Herod desires for himself. Given that the records we have for the York plays date from 1376 to 1569 (and given that the Jews had been expelled from England in 1290 by Edward I), it is hardly surprising to find strong elements of post-Crusade fantasy built into this character. Readers may also find relevant the so-called "blood libel" (the accusation that Jews murdered Christian children to use their blood in religious rituals), pre-expulsion massacres of Jewish persons at various locations in England, including York, and the representation of Saracens in Middle English texts.

The physical conflict between the knights of Herod and the mothers of the innocents would most likely have taken place close to the audi-ence rather than on the pageant wagon itself. The subject is addressed in five late Middle English plays (Chester, Towneley, York, Digby, and N-Town), all of which integrate discourses of game, play, and gender bending into the horrific violence of the story, though the York play makes far less use of the antic disposition available in the episode than do other Middle English massacre plays. While the soldiers and mothers exchange some blows and some insults, York's dramatic emphases are mainly on the grotesque inappropriateness of the chivalric language attached to the knights and on the mothers' naked grief. Scholars have also emphasized the ways in which the play, in performance, may draw attention to death and pain. It is noteworthy too that York relies on a mode in which women are present mainly as maternal vessels and are depicted primarily in relation to dead sons, male abuses, and mourning (rather than, for example, as able-bodied, resisting subjects). The York Woman 1 mourns having been born a woman at all.

The play is written in a style unique within the York plays: stanzas of eight lines, with three stresses to a line, in the rhyme scheme ababcaac. *The Slaughter of the Innocents* was put on by the guild of the Girdlers and Nailers.

Pageant 19 of the York Corpus Christi Play: *The Slaughter of the Innocents*

CHARACTERS

> Herod
> Counselor 1
> Counselor 2
> Messenger
> Soldier 1
> Soldier 2
> Woman 1
> Woman 2

HEROD. Poor beausires° about,   *fair sirs*
  Pain° of limb and land,   *on pain*
  Stint° of your stevens° stout°   *cease / voices / loud*
  And still as stone you stand,
5 And my carping° record.°   *speaking / take heed of*
  You ought to dare° and doubt,°   *stand in awe / fear*
  And lere° you low to lout°   *teach / crouch down*
  To me,[1] your lovely lord.

  You ought in field and town
10 To bow at my bidding,
  With reverence and renown,
  As falls° for swilk° a king,   *befits / such*
  The lordliest alive.
  Who hereto is not bound,
15 By almighty Mahound,[2]
  To dead° I shall him drive.   *death*

---

1 *And lere ... To me* And teach yourselves to bow down low/humbly to me.

2 *Mahound* Muhammad, prophet and founder of Islam (c. 570–632). Conflation of Islam and Judaism is common in Middle English plays.

So bold look° no man be   *see that*
For to ask help ne° helde°   *nor / favor*
But° of Mahound and me,[1]   *except*
That have this world in wield,°   *power*   20
To maintain us amell,°   *between us*
For well° of wealth are we   *source*
And my chief help is he;
Hereto what can you tell?°   *say*

COUNSELOR 1. Lord, what you likes° to do   *it pleases you* 25
    All folk will be full fain°   *eager*
    To take intent° thereto,[2]   *attention*
    And none grutch° thereagain.°   *complain / against it*
    That full well wit° shall ye°   *know / you*
    And if they would° not so   *wish*   30
    We should soon work them woe.
HEROD. Yes, fair sirs, so should it be.

COUNSELOR 2. Lord, the sooth° to say,   *truth*
    Full well we understand
    Mahound is God verray,°   *truly*   35
    And you are lord of ilka° land.   *every*
    Therefore, so° have I sele,°   *as long as / good fortune*
    I rede° we wait° allway   *counsel / watch*
    What° mirth most mend° you may.[3]   *whatever / cheer*
HEROD. Certes,° you say right well.   *certainly*   40

    But I am noyed°of new,°   *annoyed / at the moment*
    That blithe may I not be,
    For° three kings, as you know,   *because of*
    That come through this country,
    And said they sought a swain.°   *boy-child*   45
COUNSELOR 1. That rule I hope° them rue,[4]   *believe*
    For had their tales been true
    They had come this way again.

---

1   *So bold ... and me*   See that no man be so bold as to ask for help or favor, except from Muhammad and me.
2   *Lord, what ... thereto*   Lord, whatever it pleases you to do, all folk will be eager to pay attention to it.
3   *I rede ... you may*   I counsel that we watch in every way to whatever mirth may cheer you most.
4   *That rule ... rue*   I believe they will repent that deed.

COUNSELOR 2. We heard how they you hight,°   *promised*
50   If they might find that child
      For to have told you right,°   *accordingly*
      But certes they are beguiled.
      Swilk tales are naught to trow,°   *be believed*
      Full well wot° ilka wight,°   *knows / creature*
55   There shall never man have might
      Ne° mastery unto you.[1]   *nor*

COUNSELOR 1. Them shames so,[2] for certain,
      That they dare meet you no more.
HEROD. Wherefore should they be fain
60   To make swilk fare before,[3]
      To say a boy was born
      That° should be most of main?°   *who / power*
      These gadlings° shall again[4]   *fellows*
      If that° the devil had sworn.[5]   *even though*

65   For by well never they wot°   *knew*
      Whether they work well or wrang,°   *wrong*
      To frayne° gart° them thus-gate°   *to seek / prepare / certainly*
      To seek that gadling gang,
      And swilk carping° to kith.°[6]   *talking / make known*
70 COUNSELOR 2. Nay lord, they lered°   *learned*
             over-late°   *too late*
      Your bliss shall never abate,
      And therefore lord, be blithe.

MESSENGER. Mahound without peer,
      My lord, you save and see.[7]
75 HEROD. Messenger, come near,

---

1 *Full well ... you* Each man knows very well that no one shall ever have power or mastery over you.
2 *Them shames so* They are so ashamed.
3 *Wherefore ... before* Why should they be eager to mention such a business in advance.
4 *These gadlings shall again* These fellows shall go [and search] again.
5 *If that ... sworn* Even though the devil had sworn otherwise.
6 *For by ... kith* Their intention was never good, whether they performed well or badly, they certainly sought to prepare themselves and seek the fellow and to make known the talking [about him].   *This passage is corrupt in the manuscript.
7 *you save and see* Preserve and watch over you.

And beausire, well thee be.[1]
What tiding? Tells thou any?
MESSENGER. Yea, lord. Since I was here
I have sought sides° sere,°[2]   *places / many*
And seen marvels full many.   80

HEROD. And of marvels to mene°   *call to mind*
That were most mirth to me.[3]
MESSENGER. Lord, even as I have seen
The sooth° soon shall you see,   *truth*
If you will, here in hie.°   *haste* 85
I met two towns between[4]
Three kings with crowns clean,°   *without flaw*
Riding full royally.

HEROD. Ah, my bliss, boy, thou bourds°   *speak*
   too broad.°   *out of turn*

MESSENGER. Sir, there may no botment° be.   *amendment* 90

HEROD. Oho, by sun and moon,
Then tide us tales tonight.[5]
Hopes° thou they will come soon   *expect*
Hither, as they have hight,°   *promised*
For to tell me tidand?°   *news* 95
MESSENGER. Nay lord, that dance is done.
HEROD. Why, whither are they gone?
MESSENGER. Ilkone° into their own land.   *each one*

HEROD. How says thou, lad? Let be.°   *cease, be silent*
MESSENGER. I say, forth they are passed.   100
HEROD. What, forth away from me?
MESSENGER. Yea lord, in faith full fast,
For I heard and took heed
How that they went all three

---

1 *well thee be* A blessing on you.
2 *I have … sere* I have traveled very widely/sought many and various places.
3 *And of marvels … me* And call to mind the marvels that would please me most.
4 *two towns between* In between two towns.
5 *Then … tonight* Then we will hear news tonight.

105   Into their own country.
    HEROD. Ah, dogs, the devil you speed.[1]

    MESSENGER. Sir, more of their meaning
       Yet well I understood,
       How they had made offering
110   Unto that freely° food°   *noble / child*
       That now of new° is born.   *newly*
       They say he should be king
       And wield° all earthly thing.   *rule*
    HEROD. Alas, then am I lorn.°   *destroyed*

115   Fie° on them, faitours,° fie!   *a curse / imposters*
       Will they beguile° me thus?   *deceive*
    MESSENGER. Lord, by their prophecy
       They named his name Jesus.
    HEROD. Fie on thee lad, thou lies.
120 COUNSELOR 2. Hence tite but thou thee hie,[2]
       With dole° here shall thou die,   *pain*
       That wrays° him in this wise.°   *proclaims / way*

    MESSENGER. Ye wite° me all with wrong,° *blame / unjustly*
       It is thus and well war.°[3]   *worse*
125 HEROD. Thou lies, false traitor strong,°   *bold*
       Look never thou nigh° me near.   *come*
       Upon life and limb
       May I that faitour fang,°   *catch*
       Full high I shall gar° him hang,° *cause / to be hanged*
130   Both thee, harlot,°and him.   *knave*

    MESSENGER. I am not worthy to wite,°   *blame*
       But farewell all the heap.°   *the lot of you*
    COUNSELOR 1. Go, in the devil's despite,
       Or I shall gar thee leap°   *cause you to jump*
135   And dear abye° this brew.°   *pay for / trouble*
    HEROD. Alas for sorrow and site°   *distress*
       My woe no wight° may write;°   *person / record*
       What devil is best to do?

---

1   *the devil ... speed* May the devil help you.
2   *Hence tite ... hie* Unless you go away from here very quickly.
3   *It is ... war* It is as I say, but even worse.

COUNSELOR 2. Lord, amend your cheer°   *mood*
   And take no needless noy,°   *distress*   140
   We shall you leally° lere°   *loyally / instruct*
   That lad for to destroy,
   By counsel if we can.
HEROD. That may you not come near,
   For it is past two year   145
   Since that this bale° began.   *trouble*

COUNSELOR 1. Lord, therefore have no doubt,
   If it were four or five.
   Gar° gather in great route°   *make / crowd*
   Your knights keen° belive,°¹   *ready for action / in haste*   150
   And bid them ding° to dead°   *strike / death*
   All knave° childer° kept in clout,°   *boy / children / swaddling*
   In Bedlem° and all about,   *Bethlehem*
   To lait° in ilka° stead.°   *seek out / every / place*

COUNSELOR 2. Lord, save none, for your sele,°   *happiness*   155
   That are of two year age within,
   Then shall that foundling feel°   *perceive*
   Belive° his bliss shall blin,°   *quickly / cease*
   With bale° when he shall bleed.   *pain*
HEROD. Certes, you say right well,   160
   And as you deem ilka° deal°   *each / thing*
   Shall I gar do indeed.²

   Sir knights, courteous and hend,°   *worthy*
   Though the note° is now all new,³   *matter*
   You shall find me your friend   165
   And° you this time be true.   *if*
SOLDIER 1. What say you, lord? Let see.°   *tell us*
HEROD. To Bethlehem bus° you wend,   *must*
   That shrew° with shame to shend°   *bad creature / destroy*
   That means to master me.   170

---

1 *Gar gather ... belive* Cause to gather together in a great crowd your eager knights, in haste.
2 *And as ... indeed* And whatever thing you decide, I shall indeed try to do.
3 *Though the ... new* Though the matter has arisen suddenly.

And about Bethlehem both
Bus you well speer° and spy,   °enquire
For else° it will be wothe°   °otherwise / °danger
That he loses° this Jewry,°   °destroys / °kingdom of the Jews
175   And certes° that were great shame.   °certainly
    SOLDIER 2. My lord, that were us loath,[1]
    And° he escaped it were scathe°   °if / °harm
    And we well worthy° blame.   °worthy of

    SOLDIER 1. Full soon he shall be sought,
180   That make I mine avow.°   °promise
    COUNSELOR 1. I bid for him you loght,°   °seize
    And let me tell you how
    To work when you come there:
    Because you ken° him not,°   °know / °not
185   To dead° they must be brought,   °death
    Knave-children, less and more.

    HEROD. Yea, all within two year,
    That none for speech° be spared.   °pleading
    SOLDIER 2. Lord, how you us lere°   °instruct
190   Full well we take reward,°   °take heed
    And certes we shall not rest.
    SOLDIER 1. Come forth[2] fellows in fere,°   °a group
    Lo, foundlings find we here
    ....[3]

    [*Enter Woman 1 and Woman 2.*]

    WOMAN 1. Out on you thieves, I cry,
195   You slay my seemly° son.   °handsome
    SOLDIER 2. These brolls° shall dear abye   °brats
    This bale that is begun,
    Therefore lay from thee[4] fast.
    WOMAN 2. Alas for dole,° I die,   °grief
200   To save my son shall I,
    Ay-whiles° my life may last.   °as long as

---

1   *were us loath* Would be hateful to us.
2   *Come forth* The soldiers leave Herod's presence here and perhaps step off of the wagon to
    encounter the women on the ground level.
3   .... A line is missing in the manuscript here.
4   *lay from thee* Let go.

[*Woman 2 strikes at Soldier 1.*]

SOLDIER 1. Ah, dame, the devil thee speed
  And me, but° it be quit.[1]   *unless*
WOMAN 1. To die I have no dread
  I do thee well to wit,°   *know*   205
  To save my son so dear.
SOLDIER 1. Asarmes,° for now is need;   *to arms*
  But if° we do yon deed   *unless*
  These queans° will quell us here.   *shrewish women*

WOMAN 2. Alas, this loathly strife,   210
  No bliss may be my bet,°   *relief*
  The knight upon his knife
  Hath slain my son so swet,°   *sweet*
  And I had but him alone.
WOMAN 1. Alas, I lose my life,   215
  Was never so woeful a wife°   *woman*
  Ne° half so will of wone;[2]   *ever*

  And certes,° me were full loath[3]   *indeed*
  That they thus harmless° yode.° *unharmed / went away*
[*Woman 1 strikes at Soldier 1.*]
SOLDIER 1. The devil might speed you both,   220
  False witches, are you wood?°   *mad*
WOMAN 2. Nay, false lurdans,° you lie.   *scoundrels*
SOLDIER 1. If° you be wood or wroth° *whether / angry*
  You shall not scape° from scathe;° *escape / injury*
  Wend° we us hence in hie.[4]   *go*   225

WOMAN 1. Alas that we were wrought°   *made*
  In world women to be,
  The bairn° that we dear bought°[5] *child / purchased*
  Thus in our sight to see
  Dispiteously° spill.°   *cruelly / killed* 230

---

1 *but it be quit* Unless (we shall) be even. The soldier here strikes a return blow to "even" the
   score.
2 *will of wone* At a loss.
3 *me were full loath* I would not wish.
4 *Wend ... in hie* Let us go away from here in haste.
5 *dear bought* Purchased at a steep price, i.e., through the pains of childbirth.

WOMAN 2. And certes, their note° is
   naught,°
  The same° that they have sought
  Shall they never come till.°

SOLDIER 1. Go we to the king.
235   Of all this conteck° keen°
  I shall not let° for nothing°
  To say as we have seen.
SOLDIER 2. And certes, no more shall I;
  We have done his bidding
240   How so they wrest or wring,[1]
  We shall say soothfastly.°

SOLDIER 1. Mahound, our god of might,
  Save thee, sir Herod the king.
COUNSELOR 1. Lord, take keep° to
   your knight,
245   He will tell you now tiding
  Of bourds° where they have been.
HEROD. Yea, and° they have gone right
  And hold that they us hight,[2]
  Then shall solace° be seen.

250 SOLDIER 2. Lord, as you deemed° us to doon°
  In countries where we came—
HEROD. Sir, by sun and moon,
  You are welcome home
  And worthy to have reward.
255   Have you got us this gome?°
SOLDIER 1. Where we found fele° or fone°
  Witness we will that there was none.°

SOLDIER 2. Lord, they are dead ilkone,°
  What would you we did more?
260 HEROD. I ask but after one
  The kings told of before,
  That should make great mastery;
  Tell us if he be ta'en.°

Glosses (right margin):
- note° — task
- naught,° — fruitless
- same° — same one
- till.° — to
- conteck° — fighting
- keen° — fierce
- let° — forbear
- nothing° — on any account
- soothfastly.° — truthfully
- keep° — pay heed
- bourds° — sport
- and° — if
- solace° — rejoicing
- deemed° — ordered
- doon° — do
- gome?° — child
- fele° — many
- fone° — few
- none.° — none spared
- ilkone,° — every one
- ta'en.° — taken

---

1 *How so … wring* However they may twist or wring their hands.
2 *and they … hight* If they have done well and kept to what they promised us.

SOLDIER 1. Lord, tokening° had we none   *sign*
  To know that brothel° by.   *wretch*   265

SOLDIER 2. In bale we have them brought
  About all Bethlehem town.
HEROD. You lie, your note° is naught,°   *task / fruitless*
  The devils of hell you drown.
  So may that boy be fled,   270
  For in waste have you wrought.[1]
  Ere° that same lad be sought°   *before / found*
  Shall I never bide° in bed.[2]   *stay*

COUNSELOR 1. We will wend° with you then,   *go*
  To ding° that dastard° down.   *strike / dullard*   275
HEROD. Asarme° every-ilka° man   *at arms / each and every*
  That holds° of° Mahound.   *believes / in*
  Were they a thousand score
  This bargain shall they ban.°[3]   *curse*
  Come after as you can,   280
  For we will wend before.°   *ahead*

The York Corpus Christi Play: The Woman Taken in Adultery and the Raising of Lazarus

Like the *Herod/Magi* pageant, this two-act pageant has a complicated history. In the *Ordo Paginarum*, it is listed as two separate episodes, with *The Woman Taken in Adultery* brought forth by the Plumbers (lead workers) and Pattenmakers (wooden shoe makers), and *Lazarus* presented by the Capmakers, Pouchmakers, and Bottlers. By the time the Register was created, it had become one play, sponsored by the Capmakers alone (although the Hatmakers joined them in the sixteenth century).

    Whereas the *Herod/Magi* pageant requires more than one wagon setting, one wagon could have been used for both settings here.

---

1 *For in … wrought* For you have wasted your time.
2 *bide in bed* I.e., sleep.
3 *This bargain … ban* They will curse this state of events.

Alternatively, Lazarus's tomb could have been set on the ground level, aligning it with earthly mortality—the death that Christ's own resurrection will ultimately defeat, but which audience members will nevertheless experience. Thus Lazarus may be taken not only to prefigure the resurrection of Christ, but also to point to the universal condition of humankind. Similarly, the adulterous Woman's story signifies sin in general, to which all humanity is susceptible, but also the forgiveness which is equally available to all.

Although the two episodes take place in separate chapters of the Gospel of John (8.3–11 and 11.1–44, respectively), the play links them fluidly by having Jesus called away from the first event to Bethany. The verse form, a twelve-line stanza common in the cycle, rhyming abababab-cdcd, also unites the episodes.

Other than the *Transfiguration* pageant and the miracles recounted in the *Entry into Jerusalem* episode, the two stories presented here are the only representation of Christ's ministry in the extant cycle. (The *Ordo* describes a *Marriage at Cana* pageant and a *Feast at Simon's House* pageant, but neither of these was copied into the Register, and neither survives independently.)

The *Woman Taken in Adultery/Lazarus* pageant is significant not least of all for its focus on women in Christ's community—not only the adulteress, but also Mary and Martha, whose mourning instigates Christ's miracle. Overall, the play is positive in its representations of women, and singles out Jesus' forgiving treatment of the sexual sins for which blame is more often assigned to women than to men.

Much less positively, the adulteress episode also draws exaggerated distinctions between Jewish "old law" and Christian "new law." The former is depicted as unbending in its literalism and emphasis on punishment, in contrast to the spirit of forgiveness that Christ brings. Such elaborations, however doctrinal, helped underwrite medieval anti-Semitism.

Pageant 24 of the York Corpus Christi Play:
The Woman Taken in Adultery and the Raising of Lazarus

CHARACTERS

Jew 1
Jew 2
Jew 3
Jew 4
Jesus

Woman
Apostle 1
Apostle 2
Messenger
Mary of Bethany
Martha of Bethany
Lazarus of Bethany

[*Enter Jew 1 and Jew 2 with Woman.*]

JEW 1. Step forth, let us no longer stand,°   *i.e., delay*
    But smartly° that° our gear   *promptly / (see) that*
        were graid;°   *prepared*
    This fellow° that we with folly found,   *socially inferior person*
    Let haste° us fast that° she were flayed.°   *hurry / so that / beaten*
JEW 2. We will bear witness and warrand°   *warrant, give proof*   5
    How we her raised° all unarrayed,°   *roused from bed / undressed*
    Against the laws here of our land,
    Where she was with her lemman° laid.   *lover*
JEW 1. Yea, and he a wedded man—
    That was a wicked sin.   10
JEW 2. That bargain° shall she ban°   *undertaking / curse*
    With bale° now ere° we blin.°   *woe / before / cease*

JEW 1. Ah, false stud-mare°   *promiscuous woman*
    and stinking stry,°   *hag*
    How dare thou steal so still away
    To do so villains° adultery   *wicked*   15
    That is so great against our lay°?   *law*
JEW 2. Her bawdry° shall she dear° abye,°   *unchastity / dearly / pay for*
    For as we saw so shall we say,
    And also her working° is worthy°   *action / deserving*
    She shall be deemed° to death[1] this day.   *judged, sentenced*   20
JEW 1. The masters of the law
    Are here even at our hand.
JEW 2. Go we rehearse by row[2]
    Her faults as we them found.

[*Jew 1 and Jew 2 take the Woman to the masters, Jew 3 and Jew 4.*]

---

1 *her working ... to death* Her actions merit that she be sentenced to death.
2 *by row* In order, one after another.

25 JEW 1. God save you masters, mickle° of main,°   *great / power*
    That great clergy° and counsel° can.°[1]   *learning / wisdom / know*
JEW 3. Welcome friends, but I would frayne°   *ask*
    How fare ye[2] with that fair woman?
JEW 2. Ah, sirs, we shall you say,° certain,°   *tell / certainly*
30   Of mickle sorrow since she began.
    We have her taken with putery° plain,   *promiscuity*
    Herself may not gainsay° it then.   *deny*
JEW 4. What, hath she done folly
    In fornication and sin?
35 JEW 1. Nay, nay, in adultery
    Full bold, and will not blin.°   *cease*

JEW 3. Adultery? Nemn° it not for shame!   *name*
    It is so foul, openly I it fie.[3]
    Is it sooth° that they say thee,° dame?   *truth / of thee*
40 JEW 2. What, sir, she may it not deny.
    We were then worthy for to blame
    To grieve° her but° she were guilty.   *harass / unless*
JEW 4. Now certes,° this is a foul defame°   *certainly / disgrace*
    And mickle bale° must be thereby.°   *woe / because of that*
45 JEW 3. Yea, sir, ye say well there,
    By law and rightwise° rede,°   *correct / advice*
    There falls naught° else therefore   *nothing*
    But to be stoned to dead.°   *death*

JEW 1. Sirs, since ye tell the law this tide[4]
50   And know the course in this country,
    Deem° her on height,[5] no longer hide,[6]   *judge*
    And after your words work shall we.
JEW 4. Be not so breme,° beausires,° abide,°   *fierce / fair sirs / wait*
    A new matter now moves me
    ....
    ....

---

1   *God save … can*   God save you, powerful masters, who know great learning and wisdom.
2   *How fare ye*   What are you doing?
3   *I it fie*   I say "fie!" to it. ("Fie" is here an expression of disgust.)
4   *this tide*   At this time.
5   *on height*   Out loud.
6   *no longer hide*   I.e., don't keep it to yourself.

JEW 3. He shows my misdeeds more° and min,°   *great / small*   55
  I leve° you here, let him alone.   *grant permission to*
JEW 4. Oh, here will new gauds° begin;   *tricks*
  Yea, greet all well, say that I am gone.
JEW 1. And since ye are not bold,
  No longer bide° will I.   *stay*   60
JEW 2. Peace, let no tales be told,
  But pass forth privily.°   *stealthily*

[Exit Jew 1 and Jew 2.]

JESUS. Woman, where are those wight° men went   *eager*
  That keenly here accused thee?
  Who has thee damned, took thou intent?°   *heed*   65
WOMAN. Lord, no man has damned me.
JESUS. And for me shall thou not be shent.°   *hurt*
  Of all thy miss° I make thee free,   *sin*
  Look thou no more to sin assent.
WOMAN. Ah, Lord, ay° lovèd° mot° thou be.   *forever / praised / may*   70
  All earthly folk in fere°   *companionship*
  Loves° him and his high name,   *praises*
  That me on° this manner   *in*
  Hath saved from sin and shame.²

APOSTLE 1. Ah, Lord, we love thee inwardly   75
  And all thy lore,° both loud° and still,°   *teaching / out loud / silently*
  That° grants thy grace to the guilty   *who*
  And spares them that° the folk would spill.°   *whom / kill*
JESUS. I shall you say encheason° why: *reason*
  I wot° it is my father's will,   *know*   80

---

1   .... A leaf of the manuscript is missing here. The missing passages would have included the accusation against the woman, the suggestion of stoning as the appropriate punishment, the initiation of Jesus' involvement as a way of entrapping him, and his entrance with his apostles. Also missing are Jesus' writing in the sand and his well-known words from John 8.6–7: "He that is without sin among you, let him first cast a stone at her." Analogous plays, such as the one in the Chester cycle, include all of this. The unintentional effect of this gap is to highlight the contrast between the Jews' desire to openly accuse the Woman and their later desire to hide themselves.

2   *Hath saved from sin and shame* The Woman may exit after this line—or possibly she exits when Jesus and the Apostles leave to travel to Bethany, below.

And for to make them ware° thereby   aware
To know themselves have° done more ill.[1]   to have
And evermore of this same
Example shall be seen,
85   Whoso shall other blame
Look first themselves be clean.°   pure, without sin

APOSTLE 2. Ah, master, here may men see also
   How meekness° may full mickle° amend,   humility / greatly
   To forgive gladly where we go
90   All folk that hath us aught° offend.   in any way
JESUS. He that will not forgive his foe
   And use meekness with heart and hand,
   The kingdom may he not come to
   That ordained is without end.
95   And more soon shall we see
   Here ere° ye farther fare,°   before / go
   How that my father free
   Will muster mights more.

Lazare mortus.[2]

[*Enter Messenger.*]

MESSENGER. Jesu, that is prophet verray,°   true
100   My ladies Martha and Mary,
   If thou vouchsafe,° they would thee pray°   are willing / ask
   For to come unto Bethany.
   He whom thou loves full well alway°   always
   Is sick, and like,° Lord, for to die.   likely
105   If thou would come, amend° him thou may   cure
   And comfort all that company.
JESUS. I say you that sickness
   Is not unto the dead,°   death
   But joy of God's goodness
110   Shall be showed in that stead.°   place

---

1   *And for ... more ill*   I.e., to make them conscious of their own sins.
2   *Lazare mortus*   Latin: Death of Lazarus. This is not a stage direction, but a heading indicating the subject matter of the rest of the play.

And God's son shall be glorified
By that sickness and signs sere;° *various*
Therefore brother no longer bide,° *remain*
Two days fully have we been here.
We will go sojourn here beside 115
In the Jewry° with friends in fere.[1] *i.e., Judea*
APOSTLE 1. Ah, Lord, thou wot° well ilka° tide° *know / every / time*
The Jews they lait° thee far and near, *look for*
To stone thee unto dead° *death*
Or put to peerless° pain, *unparalleled* 120
And thou to that same stead° *place*
Covet° to gang° again? *want / go*

JESUS. Ye wot° by course well for to cast,[2] *know*
The day is now of twelve hours long,
And while light of the day may last 125
It is good that we gradely° gang.° *readily / go*
For when daylight is plainly past
Full soon then may ye wend° all wrong,[3] *go*
Therefore take heed and travail° fast *labor*
While light of life is you among.[4] 130
And to you say I more,
How that Lazar our friend
Sleeps now, and I therefore
With you to him will wend.

APOSTLE 2. We will be ruled after thy rede,° *advice* 135
But and[5] he sleep he shall be save.° *saved*
JESUS. I say to you, Lazar is dead,
And for you all great joy I have.
Ye wot° I was not in that stead° *know / place*
What time that he was graved° in grave. *buried* 140
His sisters pray with buxom° bead° *humble / prayer*
And for comfort they call and crave,
Therefore go we together
To make there mirths° more. *joys*

---

1 *in fere* Together.
2 *by course* Of course; *for to cast* How to compute.
3 *wend all wrong* Go astray.
4 *you among* Among you.
5 *But and* If.

145 APOSTLE 1. Since he will need wend° thither,　　　　　　　　　　*go*
　　　　Go we and die with him there.

[Jesus and Apostles travel to Mary and Martha while Mary and Martha lament.][1]

MARY. Alas, out-taken° God's will alone　　　　　　　　　　*except*
　　　　That I should sit to see this sight.
　　　　For I may mourn and make my moan,
150　　So woe° in world was never wight.°　　　　　　*woeful / creature*
　　　　That° I loved most is from me gone,　　　　　*the one whom*
　　　　My dear brother that Lazar hight,°　　　　　　*was called*
　　　　And I durst° say I would be slone°　　　　　*dare / slain*
　　　　For now me fails both mind and might.[2]
155　　My wealth° is went forever,　　　　　　　　　*happiness*
　　　　No medicine mend me may.
　　　　Ah, death, thou do thy dever°　　　　　　　　　　*duty*
　　　　And have me hence away.

MARTHA. Alas, for ruth° now may I rave　　　　　　　*sorrow*
160　　And feebly fare° by frith° and field.[3]　　*exist / woods*
　　　　Would God that I were graithed° in grave,[4]　　*prepared*
　　　　That° death had taken me under teld,°　　*so that / cover*
　　　　For heal in heart mun° I never have　　　　　　*shall*
　　　　But if he° help that° all may wield.[5]　　*i.e., Jesus / who*
165　　Of Christ I will some comfort crave
　　　　For he may be my boot° and bield.°　　　*helper / support*
　　　　To seek I shall not cease
　　　　Till I my sovereign see.

[Jesus arrives with the Apostles.]

1　*Jesus and Apostles ... lament* Given various cues in the dialogue from the messenger's speech to this point, it seems clear that Jesus and Apostles travel to Bethany to Mary and Martha but do not arrive until the end of the sisters' laments, when Martha greets him with "Hail, peerless prince..." This dramatic structure might have given the Capmakers (and later the Hatmakers) time to set up Lazarus's tomb on the pageant wagon—if it was not already set up on the ground level. (It would not have been part of the *Woman Taken in Adultery* episode.)

2　*now me fails both mind and might* Now both my mind and strength fail.

3　*by frith and field* I.e., anywhere.

4　*graithed in grave* I.e., given burial, buried.

5　*that all may wield* Who governs everything.

Hail, peerless prince of peace,
Jesu, my master so free.°   *noble* 170

JESUS. Martha, what means thou to make such cheer?°   *expression*
....
....
....[1]
This stone we shall full soon
Remove and set on side.

Father, that is in heaven on height,   175
I thank thee ever over all thing
That hendly° hears me day and night,   *graciously*
And takes heed unto mine asking.
Wherefore° vouchsafe° of thy great might   *therefore / bestow*
So that this people, old and young,
That stands and bides° to see that sight°   *waits / marvel* 180
May truly trow° and have knowing   *believe*
This time here ere° I pass   *before*
How that thou has me sent.
Lazar, *veni foras*,[2]
Come from thy monument.   185

[*Lazarus rises from his tomb.*]

LAZARUS. Ah, peerless prince, full of pity,
Worshipped be thou in world alway
That° thus has showed thy might in me,   *who*
Both dead and dolven,° this is the fourth day.   *buried*
By certain signs here may men see   190
How that thou art God's son verray.°   *true*
All those that truly trust in thee
Shall never die, this dare I say.
Therefore ye folk in fere,°   *company*
Mensk° him with main and might,[3]   *honor* 195
His laws look° that ye lere,°   *see to it / learn*
Then will he lead you to his light.

---

1   .... Another leaf of the manuscript is missing here. It is not certain to whom the following
     two lines belong, but most editors assign them to Jesus.
2   *veni foras* Latin: come forth.
3   *with main and might* With all one's might.

MARY. Here may men find a faithful friend
    That thus has covered° us of our care.   *relieved*
200 MARTHA. Jesu, my Lord and master hend,°   *courteous*
    Of this we thank thee evermore.
JESUS. Sisters, I may no longer lend,°   *remain*
    To other folk now bus me[1] fare,°   *travel*
    And to Jerusalem will I wend
205   For things that must be fulfilled there.
    Therefore rede° I you right,   *advise*
    My men, to wend with me.
    Ye that have seen this sight
    My blessing with you be.

The York Corpus Christi Play: The Entry into Jerusalem

The Skinners' *Entry into Jerusalem* is the most obviously meta-theatrical of the pageants, and serves as the cornerstone of the artistic, theatrical, devotional, and civic complexities of the cycle. The play layers time and place by mixing the biblical story with medieval customs such as the use of "common" domestic animals and medieval figures and places such as "burgesses," a town porter (gatekeeper), and castles (walled towns). Through that layering, Christ's entry into Jerusalem becomes a contemporary Palm Sunday procession, as well as his entry into York itself. Through that layering as well, the formal procession at the end of the play of the citizens—themselves reflections of the guildsmen who made up the civic council of York and produced the Corpus Christi Play—may connect to the practices of the "royal entry," the formal welcoming of a temporal king into a city in his kingdom. Of course, the Entry episode also initiates the events of the Passion, so that the citizens/guildsmen of Jerusalem/York are welcoming Jesus to his death; but since his death is the salvation of all, as the contemporary York audience knows, the welcome remains paradoxically positive. Ironies abound.

    The *Entry into Jerusalem* is also one of the longest and most dramaturgically complex of the pageants, which speaks to its central importance within the cycle. The structure of the pageant creates multiple, intertwining

---

1 *bus me* I must.

"scenes" taking place in different settings, linked by the Porter (the play-wright's invention) and, of course, by Jesus and his apostles. We first see Jesus, Peter, and Philip on the road; then Peter and Philip procuring the ass from the Porter in a village outside of the city; after that, the Porter reporting the encounter to the chief citizens of Jerusalem; then Peter and Philip bringing the ass to Jesus so he may ride into the city; then Christ's miracles and forgiveness on the way; and finally the citizens welcoming Christ as king, prophet, and savior. Such a structure certainly necessi-tated the use of both the pageant wagon and the street, and must have also contributed to a sense of the folding together of time and space. It is likely that the actor playing Jesus rode a real donkey through the street, while the citizens awaited him on the pageant wagon, turning the crowd gathered to see the *Entry into Jerusalem* pageant into the crowd in Jerusalem, as well. If the interactions between Jesus and the Blind Man, Lame Man, and Zacheus the tax collector also took place on the ground level, emerging from the audience, then those three supplicants might connect symbolically with the audience, with their fallen state, and with their need for Christ's spiritual healing. Certainly the motif of Christ as "salver" and "medicine" is repeated throughout the pageant, not only in the miraculous cures, and the necessity of such healing is a major theme of the play.

The sources of this complex play include not only the Gospels (in multiple places), but also traditional elaborations of the biblical material in devotional practices, art, and literature. The verse form—a seven-line stanza rhyming ababcbc—is the same one used in the *Nativity*; it thereby links two significant moments of Christ's arrival in this world. Both plays also make use of formal "Hail" speeches, as does the *Offering of the Magi* episode; the welcome given to Christ by king and commoner alike, uniting a Christian community, is underscored.

The Skinners, who presented this play, worked in animal skin and fur, including the types of fur-lined clothing worn by elites as a sign of status. The civic council of York would have worn such garments, and so the "gaily dight" (well dressed) citizens of the pageant would likely have been costumed in similar ways, again drawing together biblical past and York's present, as well as advertising the Skinners' wares.

Pageant 25 of the York Corpus Christi Play:
The Entry into Jerusalem

CHARACTERS

Jesus
Peter
Philip
Porter
Citizen 1
Citizen 2
Citizen 3
Citizen 4
Citizen 5
Citizen 6
Citizen 7
Citizen 8
Blind Man
Poor Man
Lame Man
Zacheus

JESUS. To me take tent[1] and give good heed
    My dear disciples that been° here,[2]   *are*
    I shall you tell that° shall be indeed.   *what*
    My time to pass hence it draweth near,
5   And by this skill:[3]
    Man's soul to save from sorrows sere°   *many*
    That° lost was ill.°   *i.e., man's soul / evilly*

    From heaven to earth when I descend°   *descended*
    Ransom to make I made promise,
10   The prophecy now draws to end;
    My father's will forsooth° it is   *truly*
    That sent me hither.
    Peter, Philip, I shall you bless,
    And go together

---

1 *take tent* Pay attention.
2 *disciples that been here* Only Peter and Philip have speaking roles, but other apostles may be represented. The *Ordo Paginarum* lists "twelve Apostles," but the play may have changed between the *Ordo*'s writing in 1415 and the creation of the Register c. 1463–77.
3 *by this skill* For this reason.

Unto yon° castle° that is you again,[1]   *yonder / village*   15
Go with good heart and tarry not,
My commandment to do be ye bain.°   *obedient*
Also I you charge° look° it be wrought:°   *instruct / see to / done*
That shall ye find
An ass this feast°[2] as ye had sought.   *feast day*   20
Ye her unbind

With her foal, and to me them bring,
That I on her may sit a space,°   *short time*
So the prophecy's clear meaning
May be fulfilled here in this place: 25
"Daughter Sion,
Lo, thy Lord comes riding an ass
Thee to upon."[3]

If any man will you gainsay,°   *oppose*
Say that your Lord has need of them   30
And shall restore them this same day
Unto what man will them claim;
Do thus this thing.
Go forth ye both and be ay° bain°   *always / obedient*
In my blessing.   35

PETER. Jesus, master, even at thy will
And at thy list° us likes[4] to do.   *pleasure*
Yon beast which thou desires thee till[5]
Even at thy will° shall come thee to,[6]   *desire*
Unto thine ease.[7]   40
Certes,° Lord, we will thither all go,   *certainly*
Thee for to please.

---

1   *you again* In front of you; *yon castle* That village over there. This is an embedded stage
    direction or cue suggesting that Christ and his disciples are still outside of Jerusalem.
2   *feast* I.e., Palm Sunday. Anachronism is embraced in these plays; here, the present-day
    streets of York become the streets of Jerusalem, as the "citizens" of both welcome Christ into
    their midst, past, present, and future.
3   *Daughter Sion … Thee to upon* The passage paraphrases Matthew 21.5, which itself quotes
    Zechariah 9.9. "Daughter Sion" here means Jerusalem and its people; *Thee to upon* To
    thee upon (it).
4   *us likes* We are willing.
5   *thou desires thee till* You want for yourself.
6   *thee to* To you.
7   *Unto thine ease* At your convenience.

PHILIP. Lord, thee to please we are full bain°   *eager*
    Both night and day to do thy will.
45 Go we, brother, with all our main°   *strength*
    My Lord's desire for to fulfill,
    For prophecy
    Us bus° it do to him by skill°   *must / reason*
    Thererto duly.[1]

50 PETER. Yea, brother Philip, behold gradely,°   *plainly*
    For as he said we should soon find,
    Methinks° yon beasts before mine eye   *it seems to me*
    They are the same we should unbind.
    Therefore freely°   *willingly*
55 Go we to him that them gan° bind,   *did*
    And ask meekly.°   *humbly*

PHILIP. The beasts are common,[2] well I know,
    Therefore us needs to ask less leave;[3]
    And° our master keeps the law,   *if*
60 We may them take titer,° I prove.°   *more readily / declare*
    For naught° we let,°   *nothing / refrain*
    For well I wot° our time is brief,   *know*
    Go we them fetch.

PORTER. Say, what° are ye that make here mastery,[4]   *who*
65 To loose these beasts without livery?°   *authorization*
    You seem too bold, since naught° that ye   *nothing*
    Has here to do;[5] therefore rede° I   *advise*
    Such things cease,
    Or else ye may fall in folly
70 And great disease.°   *trouble*

PETER. Sir, with thy leave, heartily we pray
    This beast that we might have.
PORTER. To what intent, first shall ye say,

---

1 *For prophecy … duly* Because of the prophecy, it is necessary for us to duly oblige him in a reasonable way.
2 *common* For common use.
3 *us needs to ask less leave* It is less necessary for us to ask permission.
4 *that make here mastery* Who behave so authoritatively.
5 *since … to do* Since nothing here is to do with you.

And then I grant what ye will crave
By good reason.[1]   75
PHILIP. Our master sir, that all may save,
Asks by chesoun.[2]

PORTER. What man is that ye master call
Swilk° privilege dare to him claim?   *such*
PETER. Jesus, of Jews king and ay° be shall,   *forever*   80
Of Nazareth prophet the same.
This same is he,
Both God and man without blame,°   *fault*
This trust well we.

PORTER. Sirs, of that prophet heard I have,   85
But tell me first plainly, where is he?
PHILIP. He comes at hand, so God me save,
That Lord we left at Bethpagé,
He bides° us there.   *awaits*
PORTER. Sir, take this beast with heart full free,[3]   90
And forth ye fare.°   *go*

And if you think it be to done,[4]
I shall declare plainly his coming
To the chief of the Jews, that° they may soon   *so that*
Assemble sam° to his meeting.[5]   *together*   95
What is your rede?°   *advice*
PETER. Thou says full well in thy meaning.
Do forth thy deed,

And soon this beast we shall thee bring
And it restore as reason will.   100
PORTER. This tiding° shall have no laining,°   *news / concealment*
But be the citizens declared till
Of this city.[6]
I suppose fully that they will
Come meet that free.°   *noble one*   105

---

1 *By good reason*   (If it is) for a good reason.
2 *by chesoun*   For a proper reason.
3 *with heart full free*   I.e., by all means, please.
4 *to done*   Necessary.
5 *to his meeting*   To meet him.
6 *But be ... city*   But be made known to the citizens of this city.

And since I will° they warned be,　　　　　　　　　*wish that*
Both young and old in ilka° state,°　　*every / degree, status*
For° his coming I will them meet　　　　　　　　　　*before*
To let them wit,° without debate.°　　　　　*know / doubt*
110　Lo, where they stand,[1]
The citizens chief, without debate,
Of all this land.

He that is ruler of all right
And freely° shaped° both sand and sea,　*graciously / created*
115　He save you, lordings° gaily dight,°　　　*lords / dressed*
And keep you in your seemlity°　　　　*proper condition*
And all honor.
CITIZEN 1.[2] Welcome porter, what novelty?°　　　*news*
Tell us this hour.

120　PORTER. Sirs, novelty I can you tell
And trust them fully as for true:
Here comes of kind° of Israel　　　　　　*race, people*
At hand the prophet called Jesu,°　*Jesus (Latin variant)*
Lo, this same day,
125　Riding on an ass. This tiding new
Conceive° ye may.　　　　　　　　　　　　　*comprehend*

CITIZEN 2. And is that prophet Jesus near?
Of him I have heard great ferlies° told.　　　　　*wonders*
He does great wonders in countries sere,°　　　　*various*
130　He heals the sick, both young and old,
And the blind gives them their sight.
Both dumb and deaf, as himself would,[3]
He cures them right.°　　　　　　　　　　　　*completely*

CITIZEN 3. Yea, five thousand men with loaves five
135　He fed, and ilkone° had enough.　　　　　　　　*each one*
Water to wine he turned rife,°　　　　　　*abundantly*

1　*Lo, where they stand*　Another embedded stage direction or cue. The Porter and apostles may be on the ground, gesturing and looking towards the citizens on the wagon. Alternatively, they may be at one end of the wagon, while the citizens are at the other.

2　*CITIZEN 1*　The text provides speaking parts for eight citizens, who seem undifferentiated from each other. (By contrast, see the *Ordo Paginarum*, which specifies "six Rich Men and six Poor Men.")

3　*as himself would*　As he wishes.

He gart° corn° grow without plough   *caused / grain*
Where ere° was none.   *before*
To dead men also he gave life;
Lazar was one.   140

CITIZEN 4. In our temple if he preached
  Against the people that lived wrong,
  And also new laws if he teached°   *taught*
  Against our laws we used so long,[1]
  And said plainly   145
  The old shall waste,° the new shall gang,°   *decline / advance*
  That we shall see.

CITIZEN 5. Yea, Moses' law he could° ilka° deal[2]   *knew / every*
  And all the prophets on a row;[3]
  He tells° them so that ilka man may feel°   *expounds / understand*   150
  And what they say entirely know
  If they° were dim.°   *i.e., the prophets / obscure*
  What the prophets said in their saw,°   *sayings*
  All longs° to him.   *pertains*

CITIZEN 6. Emmanuel also by right   155
  They call that prophet by this skill;[4]
  He is the same that ere° was hight°   *before / promised*
  By Isaiah before us till,[5]
  Thus said full clear:[6]
  Lo, a maiden that knew never ill°   *sin*   160
  A child should bear.

CITIZEN 7. David spoke of him, I ween,°   *know*
  And left witness, ye know ilkone;°   *everyone*
  He said the fruit° of his corse° clean°   *offspring / body / pure*
  Should royally reign upon his throne;   165
  And therefore, he

---

1 *Against ... long* Against old, accustomed laws.
2 *ilka deal* In every way.
3 *on a row* In order.
4 *by this skill* For this reason.
5 *us till* To us.
6 *He is ... full clear* He is the same one that was promised to us before by Isaiah, who thus said full clearly.

Of David's kin, and other none,[1]
Our king shall be.

CITIZEN 8. Sirs, methinketh ye say right well
170 And good examples forth ye bring,
  And since we thus this matter feel,°   *understand*
  Go we him meet as our own king,
  And king him call.
  What is your counsel in this thing?°   *matter*
175 Now say ye all.

CITIZEN 1. Against reason I will not plead,
  For well I wot° our king he is.   *know*
  Whoso° against his king list° threat°   *whoever / desires / to offend*
  He is not wise, he does amiss.
180 Porter, come near.
  What knowledge hast thou of his coming?
  Tell us all here,

  And then we will go meet that free,°   *noble one*
  And him honor as we well owe°   *ought*
185 Worthily till° our city,   *to*
  And for our sovereign lord him know,°   *acknowledge*
  In whom we trust.
PORTER. Sirs, I shall tell you all on row[2]
  And ye will list.°   *listen*

190 Of his disciples, two this day,
  Where that I stood, they fair° me gret,°   *politely / greeted*
  And on their master's half° gan° pray°   *behalf / did / ask*
  Our common ass that they might get
  But for a while,
195 Whereon their master soft° might sit   *comfortably*
  Space° of a mile.   *for the distance*

  And all this matter they me told
  Right wholly as I say to you;
  And the ass they have right as they would°   *intended*
200 And soon will bring again, I trow,°   *believe*

---

1 *other none* Of no other.
2 *on row* In order.

So they behest.°   *promised*
What ye will do advise° you now,   *consider*
Thus think me best.[1]

CITIZEN 2. Truly, as for me I say,
 I rede° we make us ready boun°   *advise / prepared* 205
 Him to meet goodly° this day   *in a seemly manner*
 And him receive with great renown
 As worthy is.
 And therefore sirs, in field and town
 Ye fulfill this.[2]   210

PORTER. Yea, and your children with you take,[3]
 Though all[4] in age that they be young,
 Ye may fare the better for their sake
 Through the blessing of so good a king,
 This is no doubt.   215
CITIZEN 3. I can° thee thank for thy saying,° *do / suggestion*
 We will him lout.°   *worship*

 And him to meet I am right bain°   *willing*
 On° the best manner that I can,   *in*
 For I desire to see him fain°   *eagerly* 220
 And him honor as his own man,[5]
 Since the sooth° I see.   *truth*
 King of Jews we call him then,
 Our king is he.

CITIZEN 4. Our king is he—that is no lease°— *lie* 225
 Our own law to it cords° well,   *accords, agrees*
 The prophets all bore full witness
 Which of him secret° gan° tell, *mysterious thing / did*
 And thus would say:
 "Among yourself shall come great sele°   *joy* 230
 Through God verray."°   *true*

---

1 *Thus think me best* So I think is best.
2 *Ye fulfill this* Make this so.
3 *your children with you take* The children do not have speaking parts, but they sing in the procession that forms. The *Ordo Paginarum* specifies "eight Boys with palm branches."
4 *Though all* Even though.
5 *as his own man* As his subject.

CITIZEN 5. This same is he, there is none other,
 Was us° behest° full long before,   *to us / promised*
 For Moses said as our own brother
235 A new prophet God should restore.
  Therefore look° ye   *consider*
 What ye will do, without more,¹
  Our king is he.

CITIZEN 6. Of Judah comes our king so gent,°   *worthy*
240 Of Jesse, David, Solomon;
 Also by° his mother's kin take tent,°   *to / heed*
 The genealogy bears witness on,°   *to it*
  This is right plain.
 Him to honor right as I can
245 I am full bain.°   *willing*

CITIZEN 7. Of your clean° wit° and   *pure / thought*
  your conceit°   *intention*
 I am full glad in heart and thought,
 And him to meet without let°   *delay*
 I am ready, and feign° will not,   *hesitate*
250 But with you sam°   *together*
 Go him again us° bliss° hath brought,²   *to us / joy*
  With mirth and game.°   *rejoicing*

CITIZEN 8. Your arguments they are so clear
 I cannot say but grant you till,³
255 For when I of that counsel hear
 I covet° him with fervent will   *yearn for*
  Once for to see;
 I trow° from thence I shall   *believe*
  Better man be.

260 CITIZEN 1. Go we then with procession
 To meet that comely° as us owe,°   *gracious one / ought*
 With branches, flowers and unison.° *monophonic singing*
 With mightful° songs here on a row⁴   *loud*

---

1 *without more* Without further ado.
2 *Go ... brought* Go in the presence of him who has brought us joy.
3 *I cannot ... you till* I cannot but grant it to you.
4 *on a row* In (proper) order.

Our children shall
Go sing¹ before,° that men may know.   *in front*   265
CITIZEN 2. To this grant° we all.²   *agree*

PETER. Jesu, Lord and master free,°   *worthy*
As thou command° so have we done.   *commanded*
This ass here we have brought to thee,
What is thy will thou show us soon   270
And tarry° not,   *linger*
And then shall we without hone°   *delay*
Fulfill thy thought.°   *will*

JESUS. I thank you, brothers, mild of mood.
Do on this ass your clothes ye lay,   275
And lift me up with hearts good
That I on her may sit this day
In my blessing.
PHILIP. Lord, thy will to do alway,
We grant° this thing.   *agree to do*   280

JESUS. Now my brothers, with good cheer
Give good intent,° for ride I will   *attention*
Unto yon city³ ye see so near.
Ye shall me follow sam and still⁴
As I ere° said.   *before*   285
PHILIP. Lord, as thee list,° we grant thee till,⁵   *wish*
And hold° us paid.°   *consider / rewarded*

(*They all sing*.)⁶

---

1   *Our children … sing* The *Ordo Paginarum* describes "eight Boys with palm branches
    singing *Benedictus*, etc." The word *Benedictus*—Latin: blessed be—likely signifies the litur-
    gical song of thanksgiving based on Luke 1.68–79.
2   *To this grant we all* The procession may start here, but the singing likely begins with the
    stage direction below, after Peter and Philip rejoin Jesus and they ride off towards "yon city."
    Alternatively, the citizens may exit the wagon here to reappear in procession below, at the
    stage direction.
3   *yon city* Like "yon castle" earlier, this cue may signify that Jesus and his disciples are not on
    the pageant wagon, which represents "yon city."
4   *sam and still* All together.
5   *thee till* To thee.
6   *They all sing* I.e., the citizens and their children sing.

BLIND MAN. Ah, Lord, that all this world has made,
 Both sun and moon, night and day,
290 What noise is this that makes me glad?
 From whence it should come I cannot say,
 Or what it mean.
 If any man walk in this way
 Tell him me bedene.[1]

295 POOR MAN. Man, what ails° thee to cry°?   *causes / cry out*
 Where would thou be?[2] Thou say me here.[3]
 BLIND MAN. Ah, sir, a blind man am I
 And ay° has been of° tender° year   *always / from / young*
 Since I was born.
300 I heard a voice with noble° cheer°   *splendid / mood, spirit*
 Here me beforn.[4]

 POOR MAN. Man, will° thou aught° that I can do?[5] *desire / anything*
 BLIND MAN. Yea sir, gladly would I wit°   *know*
 If thou could aught° declare° me to   *in any way / explain*
305 This mirth I heard, what mean may it
 Or understand?°   *signify*
 POOR MAN. Jesu, the prophet full of grace,
 Comes here at hand,

 And all the citizens they are boun°   *ready*
310 Go° him° to meet with melody,   *to go / to him*
 With the fairest procession
 That ever was seen in this Jewry;
 He is right near.
 BLIND MAN. Sir, help me to the street hastily,
315 That I may hear

 That noise, and also that I might through grace
 My sight of° him to crave° I would.   *from / ask*
 POOR MAN. Lo, he is here at this same place.
 Cry fast° on° him, look thou be bold,   *vigorously / to*

---

1 *Tell him me bedene* Let him tell me quickly.
2 *Where would thou be?* Where do you want to be; i.e., what do you want?
3 *say me here* Tell me immediately.
4 *Here me beforn* Here in front of me.
5 *Man, … do?* Man, is there anything I can do?

With voice right high.°   *loud*   320
BLIND MAN. Jesus, the son of David called,
  Thou have mercy.

Alas, I cry, he hears me not,
  He has no ruth° of my misfare.°   *pity / misfortune*
  He turns his ear; where is his thought?[1]   325
POOR MAN. Cry somewhat louder, look thou not spare,°   *hold back*
  So may thou spy.°   *see*
BLIND MAN. Jesus, the salver of all sore,
  To me give good eye.

PHILIP. Cease man and cry not so,   330
  The voice of the people goes thee by.[2]
  Thee owe° sit still and tent° give to,   *ought / attention*
  Here passes the prophet of mercy—
  Thou does amiss.
BLIND MAN. Ah, David's son, to thee I cry,   335
  The king of bliss.

PETER. Lord, have mercy and let him go,
  He cannot cease of his crying.
  He follows us both to and fro,
  Grant him his boon° and his asking°   *request / plea*   340
  And let him wend.°   *go*
  We get no rest ere° that this thing   *before*
  Be brought to end.

JESUS. What would thou, man, I to thee did
  In this present?[3] Tell openly.   345
BLIND MAN. Lord, my sight is from me hid,
  Thou grant me it, I cry mercy,
  This would I have.
JESUS. Look up now with cheer blithely,°   *happily*
  Thy faith shall thee save.   350

BLIND MAN. Worship and honor ay° to thee   *always*

---

1 *He turns ... thought* I.e., he ignores me; what is he thinking?
2 *goes thee by* Overtakes (i.e., drowns out) yours.
3 *What would ... this present* What would you like me to do for you, man, in front of these
  people?

With all the service that can be done,
The king of bliss, lovèd° mote° he be   *praised / may*
That thus my sight hath sent so soon,
355 And by great skill.
I was ere° blind as any stone: *previously*
I see at will.

LAME MAN. Ah, well were them that ever had life,
Old or young whether it were,
360 Might wield their limbs without strife,
Go with this mirth that I see here
And continue;[1]
For I am set in sorrows sere°   *many*
That ay° are new.°   *always / renewed*

365 Thou Lord that shaped° both night and day,   *created*
For thy mercy have mind on me[2]
And help me, Lord, as thou well may
….[3]
I may not gang,°   *walk*
For I am lame as men may see
370 And have been long.

For well I wot,° as known is rife,°   *know / widely*
Both dumb and deaf thou grantest them grace,
And also the dead that thou havest given life;
Therefore grant me, Lord, in this place
375 My limbs to wield.
JESUS. My man, rise and cast° thy crutches   *throw*
    good space°   *distance*
Here in the field,

And look in truth thou steadfast° be,   *unshaken*
And follow me forth with good meaning.°   *intention*
380 LAME MAN. Lord, lo my crutches, where they flee
As far as I may let them fling

---

1 *Ah, well … continue* Ah, good for those that live, whether they be old or young, who can
wield their limbs without difficulty, (and) go with this celebration that I see here and follow
(it).

2 *have mind on me* Attend to me.

3 …. A line is missing in the manuscript here.

With both my hend.°   *hands*
That ever we[1] have meeting
Now I defend,°   *forbid*

For I was halt° of° limb and lame   *crippled / in*   385
And I suffered teen° and sorrows enough.   *torment*
Ay-lasting° Lord, lovèd° be thy name,   *everlasting / praised*
I am as light as bird on bough.
Ay° be thou blest,   *forever*
Such grace hast thou showed to me   390
Lord, as thee list.°   *pleased*

ZACHEUS. Since first this world was made of°   *from*
   naught°   *nothing*
And all thing set in equity,°   *rectitude, righteousness*
Such ferly° thing was never none wrought[2]   *marvelous*
As men this time may see with eye.   395
What it may mean—
I cannot say what it may be,
Comfort or teen.°   *misfortune*

And chiefly of a prophet new,
That mickle° is profit,° and that of late,   *great / spiritual benefit* 400
Both day and night they him asue,°   *follow*
Our people sam° through street and gate.[3]   *together*
....[4]
Our old laws as now they hate
And his keep yare.°   *willingly*

Men from death to life he raise,°   *raises*   405
The blind and dumb give speech and sight,
Greatly therefore our folk him praise
And follow him both day and night
From town to town.
They call him prophet by right   410
As of renown.

---

1 *we* I.e., his crutches and he.
2 *was never none wrought* Has never (before) been brought about.
3 *And chiefly ... and gate* And chiefly (the marvelous thing is) concerning a new prophet,
   from whom comes great spiritual benefit, and whom lately our people together follow both
   day and night through street and road.
4 .... A line is missing in the manuscript here.

And yet I marvel of that thing.
Of publicans° since prince° am I   *tax-collectors / chief*
Of° him I could have no knowing,°   *with / acquaintance*
415   If all[1] I would have come him° nigh,°   *to him / near*
Early and late,[2]
For I am low,° and of men high°   *short / tall*
Full is the gate.°   *street*

But since no better may befall[3]
420   I think what best is for to do,
I am short ye know well all,
Therefore yon tree I will go to
And in it climb.
Whether he come or pass me fro[4]
425   I shall see him.

Ah, noble tree, thou sycamore,
I bless him that thee on the earth brought.
Now may I see both here and there
That under me hid may be naught.[5]
430   Therefore in thee
Will I bide° in heart and thought   *await*
Till I him see.

Unto° the prophet come to town   *until*
Here will I bide, what so befall.°   *happens*
435 JESUS. Do, Zacheus, do fast come down.
   ZACHEUS. Lord, even at thy will hastily I shall,
And tarry not.
To thee on knees Lord here I fall
For sin I wrought.°   *did*

440   And welcome, prophet traist° and true,   *trusted*
With all the people that to thee long.°   *belong (i.e., accompany you)*
  JESUS. Zacheus, thy service new
Shall make thee clean of all the wrong

---

1 *If all* Even though.
2 *If all … late* Even though I would have been near him frequently.
3 *no better may befall* There's no better way.
4 *pass me fro* Go away from me.
5 *hid may be naught* Nothing can be hidden.

That thou hast done.
ZACHEUS. Lord, I let° not for° this throng°   *hesitate / in spite of / crowd* 445
    Here to say soon°   *readily*

    Me shames[1] with sin but ought to mend.
    My sin forsake therefore I will,
    Half my good I have unspend°   *unspent*
    Poor folk to give it till,°   *to* 450
    This will° I fain.°   *will do / happily*
    Whom° I beguiled,° to him I will   *whomever / cheated*
    Make asith° again.   *restitution*

JESUS. Thy clear confession shall thee cleanse,
    Thou may be sure of lasting° life.   *eternal* 455
    Unto thy house, without offense,
    Is granted peace without strife.
    Farewell, Zaché.
ZACHEUS. Lord, thee lout° ay°   *praise / always*
    man and wife,°[2]   *woman*
    Blessed might° thou be.   *may* 460

JESUS. My dear disciples, behold and see,
    Unto Jerusalem we shall ascend,[3]
    Man's son shall there betrayed be
    And given into his enemies' hend°   *hands*
    With great despite.°   *malice* 465
    Their spitting on him there shall they spend° *discharge*
    And smartly° smite.   *violently*

    Peter, take this ass me fro[4]
    And lead it where thou ere° it took.   *previously*
    I mourn, I sigh, I weep also,   470
    Jerusalem on thee to look.
    And so may thou rue°   *regret*
    That ever thou thy king forsook
    And was untrue.

---

1 *Me shames* I am ashamed of myself.
2 *Lord ... wife* Lord, may man and woman (i.e., everyone) praise you always.
3 *ascend* Another embedded cue, suggesting that the wagon represents Jerusalem while Jesus travels to it on the ground level.
4 *me fro* From me.

475 For stone on stone shall none be left
But down to the ground all shall be cast,
Thy game,° thy glee,° all from thee reft,°   *joy / mirth / taken away*
And all for sin that thou done hast.
Thou art unkind;
480 Again° thy king thou hast trespassed,   *against*
Have this in mind.

PETER. Porter, take here thine ass again,
At hand¹ my Lord comes on his feet.
PORTER. Behold where all the burgesses° bain°   *citizens / willing*
485 Come with worship him to meet.
Therefore I will
Let him abide° here in this street²   *remain*
And lout him till.³

CITIZEN 1. Hail, prophet proved without peer,°   *equal*
490 Hail, prince of peace shall ever endure,
Hail, king comely,° courteous, and clear,°   *noble / pure*
Hail, sovereign seemly,° to sinful sure;°   *worthy / a sure help*
To thee all bows.⁴
Hail, Lord lovely, our cares may cure,°   *remedy*
495 Hail, king of Jews.

CITIZEN 2. Hail, flourishing flower that never shall fade,
Hail, violet vernant° with sweet odor,   *blooming*
Hail, mark° of mirth° our medicine° made,   *object / joy / salvation*
Hail, blossom bright, hail, our succor,°   *aid*
500 Hail, king comely.
Hail, menskful° man, we thee honor   *exalted*
With heart freely.

CITIZEN 3. Hail, David's son, doughty° in deed,   *courageous*
Hail, rose ruddy,° hail, beryl clear,   *red*
505 Hail, well° of wealth° may make us meed,⁵   *source / well-being*

---

1 *At hand*   Nearby.
2 *this street*   Again, this language suggests that Jesus, the apostles, and the Porter are on the street level—with the burgesses on the wagon.
3 *lout him till*   Pay homage to him.
4 *To thee all bows*   Everyone bows to you.
5 *well … meed*   Source of well-being who may provide us with reward.

Hail, salver° of our sores sere,°   *healer / various*
We worship thee.
Hail, hendful,° with solace° sere°   *worthy one / joy / abundant*
Welcome thou be.

CITIZEN 4. Hail, blissful babe, in Bethlehem born,   510
  Hail, boot° of all our bitter bales,°   *help / miseries*
  Hail, segge° that shaped° both even° and morn,   *man / made / evening*
  Hail, talker tristful° of true tales,   *trustworthy*
  Hail, comely knight,
  Hail, of mood° that most prevails   *disposition* 515
  To save the tight.°   *imprisoned*

CITIZEN 5. Hail, diamond with druery° dight,°   *jewels / arrayed*
  Hail, jasper gentle of Jewry,
  Hail, lily lofsome,° leamed° with light,   *worthy of praise / gleaming*
  Hail, balm° of boot,° moist and dry   *ointment / aid* 520
  To all has need.
  Hail, bairn° most blessed of mild Mary,   *child*
  Hail, all our meed.°   *reward*

CITIZEN 6. Hail, conqueror, hail, most of might,
  Hail, ransomer of sinful all,[1]   525
  Hail, pitiful,° hail, lovely light,   *one full of pity*
  Hail, to us welcome be shall,
  Hail, king of Jews.
  Hail, comely corse° that we thee call   *person*
  With mirth that news.°   *renews* 530

CITIZEN 7. Hail, sun ay° shining with bright beams,   *always*
  Hail, lamp of life shall never waste,°   *go out*
  Hail, liking° lantern, lovely leams,°   *fair / beams*
  Hail, text° of truth, the true to taste.°   *very word / perceive*
  Hail, king and sire,   535
  Hail, maiden's child that mensked° her most,   *honored*
  We thee desire.

---

1 *sinful all* All sinners.

Citizen 8. . Hail, doomsman° dreadful,°   *judge / stern*
    that all shall deem,[1]
    Hail, that° all quick° and dead shall lout,°   *whom / living / worship*
540   Hail, whom worship most will seem,°   *befit*
    Hail, whom all thing shall dread and doubt.°   *fear*
    We welcome thee,
    Hail, and welcome of all about[2]
    To our city.[3]

    (*They all sing.*)

The York Corpus Christi Play:
The Trial Before Caiaphas and Annas

The Trial Before Caiaphas and Annas, presented by the Bowers and Fletchers (makers of bows and arrows), is one of eight plays conventionally attributed to a presumed single author or reviser whom mid-twentieth-century critic J.W. Robinson dubbed "The York Realist" (see the introduction to this volume). Both the attribution and the name "The York Realist" are the product of critical convention rather than verifiable fact. More recent scholarship has been less interested in literary authorship of the plays than in the corporate sponsorship of the city and its guilds and in the communal and cultural meaning of the cycle.

    Between the *Entry into Jerusalem* (Pageant 25) and this pageant, Judas has conspired with the Pharisees Caiaphas and Annas to betray Jesus (Pageant 26); the Last Supper has taken place (Pageant 27); and Judas has fulfilled his betrayal in the Garden of Gethsemane with a kiss identifying Jesus to the Roman soldiers (Pageant 28), who then take him to the Pharisees. The present pageant picks up the narrative at this point and also makes some reference to the events that led up to this moment.

    This pageant then begins a sequence of "trial" plays, in which Jesus is brought before various authority figures—Jewish religious authorities (the Pharisees here) as well as Roman imperial authorities (Herod and

---

1   *that all shall deem* Who shall judge everyone. This final stanza speaks of the Christ of the second coming, who will be a stern judge whom everyone should fear.

2   *welcome of all about* Welcome from everyone around.

3   *our city* Simultaneously Jerusalem and York.

Pilate in subsequent plays)—and interrogated throughout a single night. In each play an authority figure is asleep or goes to bed, signifying the temporal setting of the play, but also setting up thematic and figurative contrasts. One of these is between those who "sleep" in ignorance and the all-knowing, fully "awake" Son of God; another is between the forces of darkness and those of light. This play also begins a recurring contrast between Christ's relative or complete silence and the garrulous bombast of his interlocutors. Here and in the subsequent trial plays, Christ's accusers are all talk, while he simply is. Finally, the trial plays present a recurring interest in the abuse of power and the law, and a contrast between concepts of law: the "old law" of the Old Testament versus Christ's "new law," and temporal, worldly law versus God's eternal law. That interest is underscored not only through settings in legal chambers and courts but also through a recurrent language of law, lore, and teaching through this play and the following trial plays.

This particular play also introduces a gruesome trope of "play and game" being brought to extreme, violent levels—a pattern that will repeat in other trial plays and later parts of the cycle. First Annas, Caiaphas, and their soldiers speak of Jesus as some kind of showman who works marvelous wonders; in the *Trial Before Herod*, Herod will consistently demand entertainment from Jesus. By the end of this pageant, the four soldiers treat the beating of Christ as a game of "pops," similar to blind man's buff, where a blindfolded player is supposed to guess who gave him the most recent push or "buff." Paradoxically, though Jesus seems to be losing the "game" at this moment, the contemporary audience knows that he will ultimately win, lending dramatic irony to the disturbing violence. Thus the cruel cry from Soldier 1 of "Wassail! Wassail!" (generally a festive interjection meaning "good health!"), read proleptically, takes on shades of its true, festive, and triumphant meaning. At the same time, the soldiers' cruel game suggests what we might today call a "toxic masculinity" of dominance, cruelty, and competition, explicitly contrasted by Jesus' meek silence and refusal to "play" along.

The play uses two main stanza forms, suggesting that the "York Realist" may have revised a pre-existing play. The first part of the play largely consists of alliterative quatrains rhyming abab, with some variations. Beginning with the moment when the soldiers bring Jesus to Caiaphas, the play uses twelve-line stanzas in a long alliterative line, rhyming abababababcdcd. Rather than a meter based on alternating stresses, each alliterative line has four strong beats, three or four of which alliterate.

Pageant 29 of the York Corpus Christi Play: The Trial Before Caiaphas and Annas

CHARACTERS

Caiaphas
Annas
Jesus
Soldier 1
Soldier 2
Soldier 3
Soldier 4
Woman
Peter
Malcus

[*Enter Caiaphas, Annas, Soldier 1, and Soldier 2.*]

CAIAPHAS. Peace beausires°, I bid no jangling° ye make,[1] *fair sirs / noise*
 And cease soon of your saws° and see what I say, *sayings, i.e., talking*
 And true tent° unto me this time that ye take, *attention*
 For I am a lord, learned leally° in your lay.° *truly / law*

5 By cunning° of clergy and casting of wit[2] *skill, knowledge*
 Full wisely my words I wield at my will,
 So seemly in seat me seems for[3] to sit
 And the law for to learn° you and lead° it by skill, *teach / expound*
 Right soon.

10 What wight° so will aught with me,[4] *person*
 Full friendly, in faith,[5] am I found;
 Come off,[6] do tite° let me see *quickly*
 How graciously I shall grant him his boon.° *request*

---

1 *Peace ... ye make* Each of the trial pageants begins with one of the main figures of worldly authority (elsewhere Pilate or Herod) calling for silence—a command that implicates the audience in the action.

2 *By cunning ... wit* By knowledge of learning and application of intelligence.

3 *me seems for* It is appropriate for me.

4 *What wight ... with me* Whoever deals with me.

5 *in faith* Truly.

6 *Come off* Come along.

There is neither lord nor lady learned in the law
Nor bishop nor prelate that proved is for price,[1]   15
Nor clerk° in the court that   *learned man*
   cunning° will know,   *expertise*
With wisdom may were° him,° in world is so wise.[2]   *defend / himself*

I have the reign and the rule of all the royalty,°   *kingdom*
To rule it by right as reason° it is.   *reasonable*
All doomsmen° on dais owe° for to doubt° me   *judges / ought / fear*   20
That has them in bandon° in bale°   *bondage, control / woe*
   or in bliss;°   *joy*
Wherefore take tent° to my tales,°   *heed / words*
   and lout° unto me.   *give reverence*

And therefore, sir knights—

(*They all shall say: "Lord."*)

I charge you challenge° your rights,   *lay claim to*
To wait° both by day and by nights   *keep watch*   25
Of the bringing of a boy into bale.°   *misery*

SOLDIER 1. Yes Lord, we shall wait°   *keep watch*
   if any wonders walk,°   *are happening*
And frayne° how your folks fare   *question*
   that are forth run.°   *run out*
SOLDIER 2. We shall be bain° at your bidding and   *obedient*
   it not to-balk°   *shirk*
If they present you that boy in a band° bound.   *shackle*   30

ANNAS. Why sir, and is there a boy that will not
   lout° to your bidding?   *bow, submit*
CAIAPHAS. Yea sir, and of the curiousness°   *cleverness*
   of that carl there is carping,°   *talking*
But I have sent for that segge° half for hething.°   *man / mockery, jest*
ANNAS. What wonderful°   *extraordinary*
   works° works that wight?   *deeds*

------

1 *that proved is for price* Who is so highly regarded.
2 *With wisdom … so wise* (Who) may defend himself with wisdom, (nor who) in (this)
   world is so wise (as I am).

35 CAIAPHAS. Sick men and sorry° he sends   *distressed*
    sicker° healing,   *certain, sure*
  And to lame men, and blind he sends their sight.

  Of crooked cripples that we know
  It is to hear great wondering,[1]
  How that he heals them all on row,[2]
40   And all through his false happening.°   *luck, chance*

  I am sorry of a sight
  That eggs me to ire,
  Our law he breaks with all his might,
  That is most his desire.

45   Our Sabbath day he will not save°   *observe*
  But is about° to bring it down,   *concerned with*
  And therefore sorrow must him have
  May he be catched° in field or town,   *caught*
  For his false steven,°   *voice*
50   He defames foully the Godhead
  And calls himself God's son of heaven.

  ANNAS. I have good knowledge of that knave:
  Mary me means[3] his mother hight,°   *is called*
  And Joseph his father, as God me save,
55   Was kid° and known well for a wright.°   *recognized / carpenter*

  But one thing me marvels° mickle° over all,   *amazes / greatly*
  Of diverse° deeds that he has done—   *different*
CAIAPHAS. With witchcraft he fares° withal°   *meddles, deals / as well*
  Sir, that shall ye see full soon.

60   Our knights they are forth went
  To take him with a tray,°   *trick*
  By this I hold him shent,°   *defeated*
  He can not wend° away.   *go, get*

  ANNAS. Would ye, sir, take your rest—

---

1 *It is ... wondering* It is truly astonishing to hear.
2 *all on row* One after another.
3 *me means* I believe.

This day is come on hand[1]—   65
And with wine slake your thirst?
Then durst° I well warrand°   *dare / promise*

Ye should have tidings soon
Of the knights that are gone,
And how that they have done   70
To take him by a train.°   *trick*

And put all thought away
And let your matters rest.
CAIAPHAS. I will do as ye say,
Do get us wine of the best.   75

SOLDIER 1. My Lord, here is wine that will make you to wink,°   *sleep*
It is liquor full delicious my Lord, and° you like.   *if*
Wherefore I rede° dreely° a draught that ye drink,   *advise / strongly*
For in this country, that we know, iwis°   *truly*
    there is none slike,°   *such (i.e., so good)*
Wherefore we counsel you this cup savorly° for to kiss.   *with relish* 80

CAIAPHAS. Do on daintily° and dress° me on dais   *graciously / put*
And hendly° hill° on me happing,°   *kindly / cover / bedclothes*
And warn all wights° to be in peace   *persons*
For I am late° laid° unto napping.[2]   *lately, recently / taken*
ANNAS. My Lord, with your leave, and°   *if* 85
    it like° you, I pass.°   *please / go*
CAIAPHAS. Adieu be unt'e,° as the manner° is.   *unto ye / custom*

[*Caiaphas sleeps. Exit Annas. Enter Woman, Soldiers 3 and 4 with Jesus
in fetters, and Peter, following.*]

WOMAN. Sir knights, do keep this boy° in band,°   *(i.e., Jesus) / bonds*
For I will go wit what it may mean,
Why that yon wight° was him followand°   *man (i.e., Peter) / following*
Early and late, morn and e'en.°   *evening* 90

He will come near, he will not let,°   *stop*
He is a spy, I warrant, full bold.

---

1   *come on hand* At its end, almost over.
2   *late laid unto napping* I.e., ready to go to bed.

SOLDIER 3. It seems by his semblant°   *demeanor*
      he had liever° be set°   *rather / seated*
      By the fervent° fire to fleme° him from cold.   *warm / escape*

95 WOMAN. Yea, but and° ye wist° as well as I   *if / knew*
      What wonders that this wight has wrought,
      And through his master sorcery,
      Full derfly° should his death be bought.   *cruelly*

SOLDIER 4. Dame, we have him now at will
100   That we have long time sought,
      If other go by us still
      Therefore we have no thought.[1]

WOMAN. It were great scorn° that he should scape°   *scandal / escape*
      Without he had reason and skill,°   *cause*
105   He looks lurking,° like an ape,   *cowering, furtive*
      I hope I shall haste me him till.[2]

      Thou caitiff,° what moves° thee stand   *wicked one / makes*
      So stable and still in thy thought?
      Thou hast wrought mickle° wrong in land   *great*
110   And wonderful° works hast thou wrought.   *magical, unnatural*

      A lorel,° a leader° of law,   *fool / (false) expositor*
      To set° him° and   *accompany / (i.e., Jesus)*
        sue° has thou sought.   *follow*
      Stand forth and thrust° in yon thrave,°   *join / group*
      Thy mastery° thou bring unto naught.   *great deeds*

115   Wait now, he looks like a brock°   *badger*
      Were he in a band for to bait,[3]
      Or else like an owl in a stock°   *stump*
      Full privily° his prey for to wait.   *secretly*

PETER. Woman, thy words and thy wind° thou not waste,   *breath*
120   Of his company never ere° I was kenned.°   *before / known*
      Thou hast thee mismarked,° truly be traist,°   *mistaken / assured*

---

1 *If other ... no thought* If others evade us, we're not concerned.
2 *I hope ... him till* I believe I will hasten toward him.
3 *Were he ... bait* As if he were tied up to be baited (i.e., with dogs in badger-baiting sport).

Wherefore of thy miss° thou thee amend.°　　　　*mistake / correct*

WOMAN. Then gainsays° thou here the　　　　　　*contradict*
　　saws° that thou said,　　　　　　　　　　　　*sayings*
How he should claim to be called God's son,
And with the works that he wrought whilst he walked,　　　125
Bainly° at our bidding always to be bound.°　　*willingly / loyal*

PETER. I will consent to your saws, what should I say more?
　　For women are crabbed°—that comes　　　　*ill-tempered*
　　　them° of° kind.°　　　　　　　　　　*to them / by / nature*
But I say as I first said: I saw him never ere,
But as a friend of your fellowship shall ye me ay° find.　　*always*　130

MALCUS. Hark, knights that are known in this country
　　as we ken,°　　　　　　　　　　　　　　　*believe*
How yon boy with his boast has brewed mickle° bale.°　*great / misery*
He has forsaken his master before yon women,
But I shall prove° to you pertly°　　　　*demonstrate / openly*
　　and tell you my tale.

I was present with people when press° was full prest[1]　　*crowd*　135
To meet with his master with main° and with might,　　*strength*
And hurled° him hardly°　　　　　　　*dragged / violently*
　　and hastily him arrest,°　　　　　　　　　　*arrested*
And in bands° full bitterly bound him　　　　　　*ropes*
　　sore° all that night.　　　　　　　　　　　*securely*

And of tokening of truth shall I tell you
How yon boy with a brand° brayed° me full near—　*sword / chopped*　140
Do move° of these matters amell° you—　　　*speak / among*
For swiftly he swapped° off mine ear.　　　　　*struck*

His master with his might healed me all whole,
That by no sign I could see,
　　no man could it witten,°　　　　*understand (how it was done)*
And then bad° him bear peace　　　　　　　*commanded*　145
　　in every-ilka° bale,°　　　　　*each and every / difficulty*
For he that strikes with a sword with a sword shall be smitten.°　*struck*

1　*when press was full prest*　When the crowd was at its thickest.

Let see whether grantest thou guilt:[1]
Do speak on and spare not to tell us
Or full fast I shall fond thee flit,[2]
150 The sooth° but° thou say here amell° us.   *truth / unless / among*

Come off, do tite° let me see now,   *quickly*
In saving of thyself from shame
….[3]
Yea, and also for bearing of blame.

PETER. I was never with him in work that he wrought,
155 In word nor in work, in will nor in deed.
I know no corse° that ye have hither brought,   *person*
In no court of this kith,° if I should right read.°   *region / understand*

MALCUS. Hear sirs how he says, and has forsaken
His master to this woman here twice,
160 And newly° our law has he taken—   *readily*
Thus hath he denied him thrice.

JESUS. Peter, Peter, thus said I ere°   *before*
When thou said thou would abide° with me   *stay*
In weal° and woe, in sorrow and care,   *prosperity*
165 Whilst I should thrice forsaken be.

PETER. Alas the while° that I come here,   *time*
That ever I denied my Lord in quart,[4]
The look of his fair face so clear
With full sad sorrow shears° my heart.   *cuts*

[*Exit Peter; Soldier 3 and Soldier 4 approach Caiaphas's chamber with Jesus.*]

170 SOLDIER 3. Sir knights, take keep° of this carl°   *care / base fellow*
    and be connand;°   *clever*
Because of Sir Caiaphas, we know well his thought.
He will reward us full well, that dare I well warrant,

---

1 *whether grantest thou guilt* Whether you admit your guilt.
2 *fond thee flit* Force you to retreat.
3 …. A line is missing in the manuscript here.
4 *Lord in quart* Living lord.

When he wit° of our works how well we have wrought.   *knows*
SOLDIER 4. Sir, this is Caiaphas' hall[1] here at hand,
  Go we boldly with this boy that we have here brought.   175
SOLDIER 3. Nay sirs, us must stalk° to that   *move stealthily*
    stead° and full still stand,   *place*
  For it is noon of the night,[2] if they nap aught.°   *at all*
  Say, who is here?
SOLDIER 1.   Say, who is here?
SOLDIER 3.   I, a friend,
  Well known in this country for a knight.
SOLDIER 2. Go forth, on your ways may ye wend,   180
  For we have harbored° enough for tonight.   *taken in*

SOLDIER 1. Go aback° beausires, ye both are to blame   *away*
  To bourd° when our bishop is boun° to his bed.   *jest / gone*
SOLDIER 4. Why sir, it were worthy to welcome us home,
  We have gone for this warlock° and we have well sped.[3]   *scoundrel* 185
SOLDIER 2. Why, who is that?
SOLDIER 3.   The Jews' king, Jesus by name.
SOLDIER 1. Ah, ye be welcome, that dare I well wed,°   *wager*
  My Lord has sent for to seek him.
SOLDIER 4.   Lo, see here the same.
SOLDIER 2. Abide° as I bid and be not adread.°   *wait / afraid*
  My Lord, my Lord, my Lord,[4] here is lake°   *sport* 190
    and° you list.°   *if / wish, desire*
CAIAPHAS. Peace, losels°! List ye be nice?°   *wastrels, losers / foolish*
SOLDIER 1. My Lord, it is well and° ye wist.°   *if / knew*
CAIAPHAS. What, nemn° us no more, for it is twice.   *call*

  Thou takes none heed to the haste°   *urgency*
    that we have here on hand,
  Go frayne° how our folk fare that are forth run.   *ask* 195
SOLDIER 2. My Lord, your knights have caired°   *proceeded*
    as ye them command°   *commanded*

---

1 *Caiaphas' hall* The preceding actions might have taken place on the ground level, with the
    wagon signifying Caiaphas' hall, or else, two ends of the wagon might serve the purpose for
    inside and outside the hall.
2 *noon of the night* Midnight.
3 *have well sped* Have had good luck.
4 *My Lord, my Lord, my Lord* Presumably here Soldier 2, with Soldier 1, wakes Caiaphas
    while the other two wait "outside."

And they have fallen full fair.[1]

CAIAPHAS.   Why, and is the fool found?

SOLDIER 1. Yea Lord, they have brought a boy in a band bound.

CAIAPHAS. Where now [is] Sir Annas, that is one and able to be near?

200 ANNAS. My Lord, with your leave, me behooves[2] to be here.

CAIAPHAS. Ah, sir, come near and sit we both in fere.[3]

ANNAS. Do sir bid them bring in that boy that is bound.

CAIAPHAS. Peace now sir Annas, be still and let him stand,

And let us grope° if this game be gradely° begun.   *inquire / properly*

205 ANNAS. Sir, this game is begun of the best,

Now had he no force for to flee them.

CAIAPHAS. Now in faith I am fain° he is fast,°   *glad / captured*

Do lead in that lad, let me see then.

SOLDIER 2. [*To Soldier 3*] Lo sir, we have said°   *spoken*

to our sovereign;

210 Go now and sue° to himself° for the same thing.   *proceed / him*

SOLDIER 3. [*To Caiaphas*] My Lord, to your bidding

we have been buxom° and bain,°   *humble / obedient*

Lo, here is the beausire brought that ye bad° bring.   *commanded*

SOLDIER 4. My Lord, fand° now to fear° him.   *seek / frighten*

CAIAPHAS.   Now I am fain,

And fellows, fair mot° ye fall[4] for your finding.   *may*

215 ANNAS. Sir, and ye trow° they be true   *believe*

without any train,°   *deception*

Bid them tell you the time° of the taking.   *circumstances*

CAIAPHAS. Say fellows, how went ye so nimbly by night?

SOLDIER 3. My Lord, was there no man to mar° us   *prevent*

ne mend° us.   *hinder*

SOLDIER 4. My Lord, we had lanterns and light

220 And some of his company kenned° us.   *directed*

ANNAS. But say, how did he, Judas?

SOLDIER 3.   Ah, sir, full wisely and well,

He marked° us his master among all his men   *picked out*

And kissed him full kindly his comfort to keel,°.   *cool, put an end to*

---

1 *fallen full fair* Had good luck.

2 *me behooves* It behooves me; I am obligated.

3 *in fere* Together.

4 *fair mot ye fall* May good (things) befall you; may blessings befall you.

By cause° of a countenance° that carl for to ken.°   *means / sign / know*
CAIAPHAS. And thus did he his dever?°   *duty*
SOLDIER 4.   Yea Lord, every-ilka deal,[1]   225
  He taught us to take him the time after ten.
ANNAS. Now be my faith, a faint° friend   *weak*
  might he there feel.°   *perceive*
SOLDIER 3. Sire, ye might so have said had ye him seen then.
SOLDIER 4. He set° us to the same that he sold us   *directed*
  And feigned to be his friend as a faitour,°   *imposter*   230
  This was the tokening° before that he told us.   *sign*
CAIAPHAS. Now truly, this was a trant° of a traitor.   *trick*

ANNAS. Yea, be he traitor or true give we never tale,[2]
  But take tent° at this time and hear what he tells.   *heed*
CAIAPHAS. Now see that our household be holden°   *held*   235
  here whole,°   *together*
  So that none carp° in case°   *speak / (this) matter*
  but that in court dwells.
SOLDIER 3. Ah, Lord, this brethel° hath brewed   *wretch*
  much bale.°   *sorrow*
CAIAPHAS. Therefore shall we speed us to speer°   *inquire*
  of his spells.°   *sayings*
  Sir Annas, take heed now and hear him.
ANNAS. [*To Jesus*] Say lad, list thee not[3] lout° to a lord?   *bow down*   240
SOLDIER 4. No sir, with your leave we shall lere° him.   *teach*

CAIAPHAS. Nay sir, not so, no haste,
  It is no bourd° to beat beasts that are bound.   *sport*
  And therefore with fairness first we will him fraist°   *question*
  And sithen° further him forth[4] as we have found.   *then*   245
  And tell us some tales truly to traist.°   *trust, have confidence in*
ANNAS. Sir, we might as well talk till°   *to*
  a tome° tun.°   *empty / barrel*
  I warrant him witless, or else he is wrong wraist,°   *distracted in mind*
  Or else he waits to work as he was ere° wone.°   *previously / accustomed*
SOLDIER 3. His wone° was to work mickle° woe   *custom / great*   250
  And make many masteries° amell° us.   *powerful deeds / among*

---

1   *every-ilka deal*   Each and every whit, entirely.
2   *give we never tale*   We never give a thought; it is of no concern to us.
3   *list thee not*   Do you not want to.
4   *further him forth*   Proceed with him further.

CAIAPHAS. And some shall he grant° ere he go,   *admit to*
  Or must you tent° him and tell us.   *attend to*

SOLDIER 4. My Lord, to wit° the wonders   *fully comprehend*
    that he has wrought,
255 For to tell you the tenth it would our tongues tear.
CAIAPHAS. Since the boy for his boast is into bale° brought   *misery*
  We will wit° ere he wend° how his works were.   *understand / goes*
SOLDIER 3. Our Sabbath day, we say, saves° he right not,   *observes*
  That he should hallow° and   *keep holy*
    hold full digne° and full dear.   *worthy*
260 SOLDIER 4. No sir, in the same feast as we the sot° sought   *fool*
  He salved° them of sickness on many sides sere.[1]   *healed*
CAIAPHAS. What then, makes he them gradely°   *truly*
    to gang?°   *go, walk*
SOLDIER 3. Yea Lord, even forth in every-ilka° town   *each and every*
  He them leeches to life after long.[2]
265 CAIAPHAS. Ah, this makes he by the mights of Mahound.[3]

SOLDIER 4. Sir, our stiff° temple that made is of stone,   *strong*
  That passes° any palace of price for to praise,   *surpasses*
  And° it were down to the earth and to the ground gone   *if*
  This ribald° he rouses° him it   *scoundrel / boasts*
    rathely° to raise.[4]   *quickly*
270 SOLDIER 3. Yea Lord, and other wonders he works great wone,[5]
  And with his loud leasings° he loses°   *lies / undermines*
    our lays.°   *laws*
CAIAPHAS. Go loose° him, and leave then and let me alone,   *unshackle*
  For myself shall search° him and hear what he says.   *interrogate*
ANNAS. Hark, Jesus of Jews, we will have joy

---

1 *on many sides sere* On every side.
2 *He them leeches … long* He heals (and brings) them to life after (being) long (dead). Medieval physicians were often metonymically called "leeches" in English, after their common practice of using leeches to drain blood. Thus, "to leech" also means "to heal."
3 *Mahound* Muhammad, prophet and founder of Islam (c. 570–632). Medieval English texts often depict all non-Christian characters as worshipping or otherwise calling on Muhammad, as a way to construct their "otherness."
4 *And it were … raise* If it were torn down and demolished, this scoundrel boasts that he would quickly rebuild it. These lines refer to Jesus' prophecy of the destruction of the Temple and his claim that he will raise it up again in three days, interpreted by the Church as a metaphor for Jesus' own death and resurrection. The Pharisees take it literally. See Matthew 26.61 and Mark 14.58.
5 *great wone* In great quantity.

To spill° all thy sport° for thy spells.°   *mar / pleasure / words* 275

CAIAPHAS. Do move,° fellow, of thy friends°   *i.e., to speak / kin*
    that fed thee beforn,°   *before*
And sithen,° fellow, of thy fare°   *then / business*
    further will I frayne;°   *inquire*
Do neven° us lightly.° His language is lorn![1]   *tell / quickly*
SOLDIER 3. My Lord, with your leave, him likes for to lain,[2]
    But and he should scape° scatheless°   *escape / unscathed* 280
    it were a full° scorn,   *great*
For he has mustered° among us full mickle of his main.[3]   *displayed*
SOLDIER 4. Malcus your man, Lord, that had his ear shorn,
This harlot° full hastily healed it again.   *scoundrel*
CAIAPHAS. What, and list him[4] be nice°   *foolish*
    for the nones,°   *occasion*
And hear how we haste° to rehete° him.   *hasten / rebuke* 285
ANNAS. Now by Belial's[5] blood and his bones,
    I hold it best to go beat him.

CAIAPHAS. Nay sir, none haste, we shall have game ere° we go.   *before*
    Boy, be not aghast° if we seem gay.°   *afraid / richly appareled*
I conjure° thee kindly and command thee also,   *urge* 290
By great God that is living and last shall ay,°   *forever*
If thou be Christ, God's son, tell till° us two.   *to*
JESUS. Sir, thou says it thyself, and soothly° I say   *truly*
    That I shall go to my Father that I come fro°   *from*
And dwell with him winly° in wealth° alway.   *worthily / bliss* 295
CAIAPHAS. Why, fie° on the faitour° untrue,   *curse / imposter*
    Thy Father hast thou foully defamed.
Now needs us no notes° of new,   *evidence*
    Himself with his saws has he shamed.

ANNAS. Now needs neither witness ne°   *nor* 300
    counsel° to call,   *lawyer, legal advisor*

---

1 *His language is lorn* He has lost the ability to speak.
2 *him likes for to lain* He prefers to remain silent.
3 *full mickle of his main* A great deal of his power.
4 *and list him* If it pleases him.
5 *Belial* Belial is a personal name in the Bible, a personification of evil and worthlessness; the name was commonly used as a synonym for Satan in the Middle Ages, but sometimes also denoted a distinct minor demon and fallen angel. Here the distinction is irrelevant— Annas clearly swears by the power of a demonic being.

But take his saws° as he sayeth in the same stead.[1]   *words*
He slanders the Godhead and grieves° us all,   *offends*
Wherefore he is well worthy to be dead.
And therefore sir, say him the sooth.°   *truth*
CAIAPHAS.   Certes° so I shall.   *certainly*

305   Hears thou not, harlot?°   *scoundrel*
          Ill° hap° on thy head!   *bad / luck*
       Answer here gradely° to great and to small[2]   *fittingly*
       And reach us out[3] rathely° some reason, I rede.°   *quickly / advise*
JESUS. My reasons are not to rehearse,°   *recite*
       Nor they that might help me are not here now.

310 ANNAS. Say lad, list thee[4] make verse?
       Do tell on belive,° let us hear now.   *quickly*

JESUS. Sir, if I say thee sooth thou shall not assent,
       But hinder° or haste me to hang.   *slander*
       I preached where people was most in present,[5]
315   And no point in privity[6] to old ne young.
       And also in your temple I told mine intent;
       Ye might have ta'en° me that time for my telling   *taken*
       Well better than bring me with brands unbrent,[7]
       And thus to noy° me by night, and also for nothing.   *harass*
320 CAIAPHAS. For nothing, losel?° Thou lies!   *rogue*
       Thy words and works will have a wreaking.°   *punishment*
JESUS. Sire, since thou with wrong so me wries,°   *denounce*
       Go speer° them that heard of my speaking.   *inquire of*

CAIAPHAS. Ah, this traitor has teened° me   *angered*
          with tales that he has told,
325   Yet had I never such hething° of°   *mockery / from*
          a harlot° as he.   *scoundrel*
SOLDIER 1. What, fie on thee, beggar, who made thee so bold
       To bourd° with our bishop? Thy bane° shall I be.   *jest / slayer*
JESUS. Sir, if my words be wrong or worse than thou would,
       A wrong° witness I wot° now are ye;   *false / know*

---

1   *in the same stead*   In this very place.
2   *to great and to small*   To everyone.
3   *reach us out*   Give out to us.
4   *list thee*   Do you wish to.
5   *was most in present*   Were most numerous.
6   *no point in privity*   Never in secret.
7   *brands unbrent*   Literally, unburnt torches; figuratively, swords.

And if my saws be sooth° they mun° be sore sold,[1]   *true / must*   330
Wherefore thou bourds too broad[2] for to beat me.
SOLDIER 2. My Lord, will ye hear? For Mahound,
  No more now for to neven° that it needs.°   *say / is needed*
CAIAPHAS. Go dress° you and ding° him down,   *make ready / beat*
  And deaf° us no more with his deeds.   *deafen*   335

ANNAS. Nay sir, then blemish° ye   *dishonor*
    prelates'° estate,°   *high priests' / authority*
  Ye owe° to deem° no man to dead° for to ding.[3]   *ought / judge / death*
CAIAPHAS. Why sir? So were better[4] than be in debate,°   *difficulty*
  Ye see the boy will not bow for our bidding.
ANNAS. Now sir, ye must present this boy unto Sir Pilate,   340
  For he is doomsman° near and next to the king,   *judge*
  And let him hear all the whole, how ye him hate,
  And whether he will help him or haste him to hang.
SOLDIER 1. My Lord, let men lead him by night,
  So shall ye best scape out of scorning.[5]   345
SOLDIER 2. My Lord, it is now in the night,
  I rede° ye abide° till the morning.   *advise / wait*

CAIAPHAS. Beausire,° thou says the best and so shall it be—   *good sir*
  But learn° yon boy better to bend and bow.   *teach*
SOLDIER 1. We shall learn yon lad, by my lewty,°   *faith*   350
  For to lout° unto ilka° lord like unto you.   *bow / each*
CAIAPHAS. Yea, and fellows, wait° that he be   *watch*
    ay° waking.°   *always / awake*
SOLDIER 2.   Yes Lord, that warrant° will we,   *guarantee*
  It were a full needless note° to bid° us   *piece of advice / command*
  nap° now.   *to sleep*
SOLDIER 3. Certes,° will ye sit and soon shall ye see   *indeed*
  How we shall play pops[6] for the page's° prow.°   *wretch's / benefit* 355
SOLDIER 4. Let see, who starts° for a stool?   *goes*
  For I have here a hater° to hide° him.   *piece of cloth / blindfold*
SOLDIER 1. Lo, here is one full fit for a fool,

---

1 *be sore sold* Be paid for dearly.
2 *bourds too broad* Joke too unreservedly.
3 *Ye owe ... for to ding* You ought to judge no man to death by beating.
4 *So were better* It would be better.
5 *scape out of scorning* Escape scorn; avoid scandal.
6 *pops* A game similar to blind man's buff, in which the blindfolded "it" must guess who hit him.

Go get it and set thee beside him.

360 SOLDIER 2. Nay, I shall set it myself and frush° him also.   *beat*
    Lo here a shroud° for a shrew,° and of   *garment / evildoer*
      sheen° shape.   *fine*
    [*They blindfold Jesus.*]
SOLDIER 3. Play fair in fere,[1] and there is one and there is two;
    I shall fand° to fast it[2] with a fair° flap°—   *attempt / good / blow*
    And there is three; and there is four.[3]
365   Say now with an evil hap,°   *luck*
    Who nigheth° thee now? Not one word, no!   *comes near*
SOLDIER 4. Do noddle° on him with   *hit*
    nieves° that he not nap.   *fists*
SOLDIER 1. Nay, now to nap is no need,
    Wassail! Wassail![4] I warrant him waking.[5]
370 SOLDIER 2. Yea, and but he better bourds° can bid[6]   *sport, amusement*
    Such buffetts° shall he be taking.°   *blows / receiving*

SOLDIER 3. Prophet, I say, to be out of debate,°   *difficulty*
    Quis te percussit,[7] man? Read,° if thou may.   *prophesy*
SOLDIER 4. Those words are in waste,
    what weens° thou he wot?°   *think / understands*
375 It seems by his working° his wits were away.   *behavior*
SOLDIER 1. Now let him stand as° he stood   *as if*
    in a fool's state,°   *ceremony*
    For he likes not this lake,° my life dare I lay.°   *game / wager*
SOLDIER 2. Sirs, us must present this page to Sir Pilate,
    But go we first to our sovereign and see what he say.
380 SOLDIER 3. My Lord, we have bourded° with this boy   *sported*
    And holden° him full hot° amell° us.   *held / vigorously / among*
CAIAPHAS. Then heard ye some japes° of joy?   *jokes*
SOLDIER 4. The devil have the word, Lord, he would tell us.

---

1 *in fere* Together.
2 *to fast it* To lay it on.
3 *there is one ... there is four* With each count, the corresponding soldier hits Jesus.
4 *Wassail! Wassail!* A festive expression, usually used in drinking to a person's health; here used ironically and menacingly.
5 *I warrant him waking* I believe he's awake.
6 *Yea, and ... can bid* Yes, but unless he can offer better sport.
7 *Quis te percussit* Latin: Who hit you? From the Gospel accounts of the buffeting in Matthew 26.68 and Luke 22.64.

ANNAS. Sir, bid belive° they go and bind him again,   *quickly*
   So that he scape° not, for that were a scorn.°   *escape / shame* 385
CAIAPHAS. Do tell to Sir Pilate our plaints°   *grievances*
   all plain,°   *clearly*
   And say this lad with his leasings°   *lies*
     has our laws lorn.°   *failed to maintain*
   And say this same day must he be slain
   Because of Sabbath day that shall be tomorn,°   *tomorrow*
   And say that we come ourselves for certain,   390
   And for to further° this fare,°   *advance / matter*
   fare° ye beforn.[1]   *went*
SOLDIER 1. My Lord, with your leave, us must wend,°   *go*
   Our message to make° as we may.   *deliver*
CAIAPHAS. Sir, your fair fellowship we betake° to the fiend,   *entrust*
   Go on now, and dance forth in the devil's way.   395

The York Corpus Christi Play: The First Trial Before Pilate (The Dream of Pilate's Wife)

The First Trial Before Pilate (The Dream of Pilate's Wife), presented by the Tapiters (makers of tapestries and other hangings) and Couchers (produ-cers of bedding), is another play assigned to the so-called "York Realist." This particular play seems to have been edited and added to over time, since the *Ordo Paginarum*'s description of the Tapiters' and Couchers' contribution does not mention Pilate's Wife, Procula, or her dream. What is more, approximately the first fifth of the play is written in a nine-line stanza rhyming ababbcbbc, while the rest is in a differently rhymed nine-line stanza (rhyming ababbcddc, with occasional irregularities).

The Procula episode derives from one verse in the Gospel of Matthew (27.19) and its elaboration in the apocryphal (that is, non-canonical and unofficial) *Gospel of Nicodemus*, which was a popular source of art and literature in the Middle Ages. But in *Nicodemus*, the source of Procula's dream is undetermined. Here, in turning her dream into a temptation from Satan, the play makes Procula into a type of Eve. That said, her

---

1 *And for ... beforn* And to advance this matter, you came on ahead.

temptation is morally complex and paradoxical: she is tempted to do the right thing (save an innocent man) for the wrong reason (because Satan wants to keep his right over human souls). Her empathy for Jesus suggests something like character growth and personal redemption, since she has entered the play as a vain and superficial woman, boasting of her husband's lineage; yet, her pleas, if answered, would prevent the true Redemption that Christ intends with his death. Satan's claims, meanwhile, teeter between the emotional—he suffers at the thought of his losses—and the quasi-legalistic: he wants to maintain his rights. This complex mix of motivations looks forward to the *Harrowing of Hell*, but also mirrors the multiple motivations and responses of the men judging Christ in this play.

Like his wife, Pilate is a figure of paradox. He is equally vain and egotistical, and shown here as getting so drunk that he needs help getting to bed. But he is also a reasonable man, an upholder of the rule of law. At the same time, he is not above cruelty, ordering the soldiers to beat Jesus as they take him to Herod. This host of contradictions reflects his position in doctrine: he is both an enemy of Christ, for his role in ordering the crucifixion, and also a necessary player in making Christ's redemption of humanity possible.

Like the other trial plays, this one takes place in the middle of the night; the temporal setting is doubly emphasized by two sleeping figures in two beds or couches: Procula and Pilate. It seems especially appropriate that the Tapiters and Couchers produced this play, as they would have been able to present splendidly rich and sumptuous bedding and décor to signify the wealth and comfort of Pilate's household—in contrast to the nightmarish discomfort that Jesus suffers, shackled, abused, and shuttled from court to court. Also in concert with the sequence of trial plays, Jesus remains largely silent in the play, speaking only four lines out of over five hundred, in contrast to the verbose debate and quarreling of Pilate with the Pharisees. The play also contrasts Christ's immanent spiritual power—through his positive influence over the Beadle—with the weakness of temporal power that can only manifest itself through bullying and violence.

CHARACTERS

Pilate →Judge
Pilate's Wife (Procula)
Beadle
Maid
Boy
Devil
Annas
Caiaphas
First Soldier
Second Soldier
Jesus

PILATE. Ye cursed creatures that cruelly are crying,		
Restrain you from striving for° strength°	*for fear of / force*	
of my strakes;°	*strokes*	
Your plaints° in my presence	*complaints*	
use platly° applying,[1]	*plainly, openly*	
Or else this brand° in your brains soon bursts and breaks.	*sword*	
This brand in his bones breaks,		5
What° brawl° that with brawling	*whatever / bully*	
me° brews,°	*for me / makes trouble*	
That wretch may not wry° from my wreaks,°	*escape / vengeance*	
Nor his sleights° not slyly him slakes;°	*cunning / release*	
Let that traitor not trust in my truce.[2]		
For Sir Caesar was my sire° and I soothly° his son,[3]	*father / truly*	10
That excellent emperor exalted in height		
Which all this wild world with wights° had won,°	*men / conquered*	

---

1 *Your plaints ... applying* Present your complaints in my presence honestly.

2 *What brawl ... my truce* Whatever bully makes trouble for me, that wretch will not be able to escape my vengeance, nor will he release himself slyly (by) his cunning; that traitor should not trust in my good faith.

3 *his son* The idea that Pilate is the illegitimate son of a Caesar is apocryphal. Which Caesar is not specified, though the references to conquest suggest Augustus (53 BCE–14 CE, reigned 27 BCE–14 CE). The association may be unique to this play, although other literary sources create equally fanciful royal lineages for him.

And my mother hight° Pila that
    proud was of plight;°   *was called / bearing*
Of Pila that proud,° Atus her father he hight.   *proud one*
15 This 'Pila' was had° into 'Atus'—   *added*
    Now rinks,° read ye it right?[1]   *men*
    For thus shortly I have showed you in sight
    How I am proudly proved 'Pilatus.'

    Lo, Pilate I am, proved a prince of great pride.
20 I was put into Pontus the people to press,°   *repress*
    And sithen° Caesar himself with senators by his side   *after that*
    Remit° me to their realms the rinks° to redress.°   *sent / people / reform*
    And yet am I granted on ground, as I guess,°   *think, suppose*
    To justify° and judge all the Jews.   *grant justice*
    [*Enter Pilate's Wife.*]
25 Ah, love, here lady? No less?
    Lo, sirs, my worthy wife, that she is,
    So seemly,° lo, certain° she shows.°   *lovely / certainly / appears*

PILATE'S WIFE. Was never judge in this Jewry of so
    jocund° generation,°   *happy / lineage*
    Nor of so joyful genealogy to gentrice°   *noble descent*
    enjoined°   *connected*
30 As ye, my duke doughty,° deemer° of damnation   *resolute / judge*
    To princes and prelates that your precepts°   *commands*
    purloined.°   *put aside*
    Who that your precepts pertly° purloined,   *boldly*
    With dread into death shall ye drive him;
    By my troth,[2] he untruly° is throned   *falsely*
35 That against your behests has honed;°   *tarried (in carrying out)*
    All to rags shall ye rent° him and rive° him.   *pull apart / tear*

    I am dame precious Procula, of princes the prize,
    Wife to Sir Pilate here, prince without peer.°   *equal*
    All well° of all womanhood I am, witty and wise,   *source*
40 Conceive° now my countenance°   *perceive / appearance*
    so comely and clear.°   *fair*
    The color of my corse° is full clear,°   *body / bright*
    And in richesse° of robes I am rayed,°   *wealth / arrayed*

---

1 *read ye it right?* Do you get it?
2 *By my troth* Literally, by my faith; an idiom expressing strong affirmation or assertion.

There is no lord in this land, as I lere,[1]
In faith, that hath a friendlier fere°   *companion*
Than ye my Lord, myself though I say it.   45

PILATE. Now say it may ye safely, for I will certify the same.
PILATE'S WIFE. Gracious Lord, gramercy,°   *many thanks*
    your good word is gain.°   *pleasing*
PILATE. Yet for to comfort my corse° me must kiss you, madam.   *body*
PILATE'S WIFE. To fulfill your foreward,° my fair Lord,   *promise*
    I am fain.°   *glad*
PILATE. Ho, ho, fellows! Now, in faith, I am fain   50
    Of these lips so lovely are lapped.[2]
    [*Aside*] In bed [she] is full buxom° and bain.°   *willing / ready*
PILATE'S WIFE. Yea sir, it needeth not to lain,[3]
    All ladies we covet then both to be kissed and clapped.°   *embraced*

BEADLE. My liberal° Lord, oh leader of laws,   *generous* 55
    Oh shining show° that all shames eschews,°   *spectacle / shuns*
    I beseech you, my sovereign, assent° to my saws,°   *approve of / words*
    As ye are gentle judger and justice of Jews.
PILATE'S WIFE. Do hark how yon javel°   *worthless fellow*
    jangles° of Jews.   *babbles*
    Why, go bet,[4] whoreson boy, when I bid thee.   60
BEADLE. Madam, I do but that due is.[5]
PILATE'S WIFE. But if° thou rest° of   *unless / stop*
    thy reason° thou rues,°   *talk / will be sorry*
    For as a cursed° carl°   *doomed / man of low birth*
    has thou kid° thee!   *shown*

PILATE. Do mend° you, madam, and your mood be amending,   *cheer*
    For me seems it were° sitting°   *would be / appropriate* 65
    to see what he says.
PILATE'S WIFE. My Lord, he told never tale that to me
    was tending,°   *complimentary*
    But with wrenks° and with wiles°   *twists / deceptions*
    to wend° me my ways.[6]   *turn, change*

---

1 *as I lere* As far as I know, as I understand.
2 *Now ... lapped* Now, truly, I am happy to be kissed by these lips so lovely.
3 *it needeth not to lain* It needn't be concealed.
4 *go bet* Go away.
5 *that due is* What is due, called for.
6 *to wend me my ways* To change my ways.

BEADLE. Iwis,° of your ways to be wending   *indeed*
    it longs° to our laws.   *belongs, accords with*
PILATE'S WIFE. Lo, Lord, this lad with his laws!
70   How, think ye it profits well his preaching to praise?
PILATE. Yea love, he knows all our custom,
    I know well …[1]

BEADLE. My seignior,° will ye see now the sun in your sight,   *lord*
    For his stately strength he stems° in his streams?   *diminishes*
75   Behold over your head how he hields° from height   *descends*
    And glides to the ground with his glittering gleams.
    To the ground he goes with his beams
    And the night is nighing° anon.°[2]   *approaching / at once*
    Ye may deem° after no dreams,   *judge*
80   But let my lady here with all her light leams°   *brightness*
    Wightly° go wend° till° her wone;°   *quickly / go / to / dwelling*

    For ye must sit,° sir, this same night,   *sit in judgment*
    of° life and of limb.   *over*
    It is not leeful° for my lady by the law of this land[3]   *permissible*
    In doom° for to dwell,   *(place of) judgment*
    for the day wax° aught° dim,   *grows / somewhat*
85   For she may stacker° in the street   *stumble*
    but° she stalworthly° stand.   *unless / strongly*
    ….[4]
    Let her take her leave while that light is.[5]
PILATE. Now wife, then ye blithely° be buskand.°   *readily / going*
PILATE'S WIFE. I am here sir, hendly° at hand.   *courteously*
PILATE. Lo, this rink° has us rede° as right is.   *man / advised*

90 PILATE'S WIFE. Your commandment to keep to cair° forth   *go*
    I cast° me.   *prepare*
    My Lord, with your leave, no longer I let° you.   *hinder*

---

1 … The manuscript is corrupt here and the line breaks off.
2 *My seignior … nighing anon* The Beadle's point, delivered in rather flowery language, is that the sun is setting and it is getting late.
3 *not leeful … law of this land* It is not entirely clear whether the Beadle is saying that it is not lawful for Procula to be there during court business, or that it is not lawful for her to be out after curfew and thus she cannot delay her departure, or possibly both.
4 …. A line is missing in the manuscript here.
5 *while that light is* While it is still light.

PILATE. It were a reproof° to my person   *rebuke*
   that privily° ye passed° me,   *secretly / left*
  Or ye went from this wones° ere°   *place / before*
   with wine ye had wet° you.   *refreshed*
  Ye shall wend° forth with win° when that ye have wet you.   *go / joy*
  Get drink! What does thou? Have done![1]   95
  Come seemly,° beside me, and sit you.   *lovely one*
  Look, now it is even here that I ere behet° you,   *promised*
  Yea, say° it now sadly° and soon.°   *try, taste / earnestly / right away*

PILATE'S WIFE. It would glad me, my Lord,
   if ye goodly° begin.   *properly*
PILATE. Now I assent to your counsel so comely°   *proper, decorous* 100
   and clear.°   *certain*
  Now drink madam—to death all this din.
PILATE'S WIFE. If it like° you, mine own Lord, I am not to lere;[2] *please*
  This lore° I am not to lere.°   *teaching / learn*
PILATE. Yet eft° to your   *likewise (i.e., offer some)*
   damsel,° madam.   *lady-in-waiting*
PILATE'S WIFE. [*To Maid*] In thy hand, hold now and have here.   105
MAID. Gramercy,° my lady so dear.   *thank you*
PILATE. Now farewell, and walk on your way.

    . . . .
    . . . .[3]
PILATE'S WIFE. Now farewell the friendliest, your foemen°   *enemies*
   to fend.°   *fight*
PILATE. Now farewell the fairest figure that ever did food feed,°   *eat*
  And farewell ye damsel, indeed.   110
MAID. My Lord, I commend me to your royalty.
PILATE. Fair lady, here is shall you lead.[4]
  Sir, go with this worthy° indeed,   *worthy one*
  And what she bids you do, look that buxom° you be.   *obedient*

BOY. I am proud and prest° to pass° on apace,   *ready / proceed* 115
  To go with this gracious,° her goodly° to guide.   *gracious one / properly*

---

1 *Have done!* Expression of impatience. This line might be directed to the Beadle or a super-numerary servant rather than to Procula. If it is read as directed towards Procula, followed by the next, more loving line, it could reveal Pilate's instability of temper.

2 *I am not to lere* I do not need to learn.

3 . . . . Two lines are missing in the manuscript.

4 *here is shall you lead* Here is (someone who) shall guide you.

PILATE. Take tent° to my tale,°   heed / words, command
        thou turn on no trace,[1]
    Come tite° and tell me if any   quickly
        tidings° betide.°   events / happen
BOY. If any tidings my lady betide,
120   I shall full soon, sir, wit you to say.[2]
    This seemly shall I show by her side
    Belive,° sir, no longer we bide.°   quickly / abide, stay
PILATE. Now farewell, and walk on your way.

[*Exit Pilate's Wife with Boy and Maid.*]

    Now went° is my wife, if° it were not her will,   gone / though
125   And she raiks° till° her rest as of nothing she rought.° goes / to / cared
    Time is, I tell thee, thou tent me until;[3]
    And busk° thee belive,°   hasten / quickly
        belamy,° to bed that I were brought   good friend
        ....[4]
    And look° I be richly arrayed.   see that
BEADLE. As your servant I have sadly it sought,
130   And this night, sir, noy shall ye naught,[5]
    I dare lay,° fro° ye lovely° be laid.   wager / when / properly

PILATE. I command thee to come near,
        for I will cair° to my couch.   go
    Have in thy hands hendly°   graciously
        and heave me from hyne,°   hence
    But look that thou teen° me not with thy   anger
        tasting,° but tenderly me touch.[6]   handling
BEADLE. Ah, sir, ye weigh well.
135 PILATE.   Yea, I have wet me with wine
        ....[7]
    Yet hield° down and lap° me even here,   bend / cover

---

1   *turn on no trace*   Don't deviate.
2   *wit you to say*   Inform you, make them known to you.
3   *thou tent me until*   You paid attention to me.
4   ....   A line is missing in the manuscript here.
5   *noy shall ye naught*   Nothing shall annoy you.
6   *Have in thy hands ... touch.*   Use your hands graciously and move me from hence, and see
    to it that you don't anger me with your handling, but touch me gently. (Pilate is drunk and
    thus needs the Beadle to help maneuver him into bed.)
7   ....   Another line is missing in the manuscript.

For I will slyly° sleep unto syne.° *surreptitiously / later*
Look that no man nor no myron° of mine *servant*
With no noise be nighing° me near. *approaching*

BEADLE. Sir, what warlock° you wakens *wicked person* 140
    with words full wild,
That boy for his brawling° were better be unborn. *misbehavior*
PILATE. Yea, who chatters, him chastise, be he churl or child,[1]
    For and° he scape° scatheless° *if / escape / unharmed*
      it were to us a great scorn°— *shame*
    If scatheless he scape it were a scorn.
    What ribald° that readily will roar, *rascal* 145
    I shall meet with that myron tomorn° *tomorrow*
    And for his lither° lewdness° *harmful / misbehavior*
      him learn to be lorn.[2]
BEADLE. We![3] So sir, sleep ye, and say no more.

[Pilate sleeps. Exit Beadle. Enter Pilate's Wife with Boy and Maid, now at her home.][4]

PILATE'S WIFE. Now are we at home. Do help if ye may,
    For I will make me ready and raik° to my rest. *go* 150
MAID. Ye are weary madam, forwent° of° *exhausted / from*
    your way,° *journey*
    Do boun° you to bed, for that hold I best. *make ready (to go)*
BOY. Here is a bed arrayed of the best.
PILATE'S WIFE. Do hap° me, and fast hence° *cover / from here*
    ye hie.° *go*
MAID. Madam, anon° all duly is dressed.° *right away / prepared* 155
BOY. With no stalking° nor no *sneaking around*
    strife° be ye stressed. *commotion*
PILATE'S WIFE. Now be ye in peace, both your carping° *talking*
    and cry.° *shouting*

---

1 *churl or child* Low born man or knight.
2 *And for ... lorn* And for his harmful misbehavior show him how to die.
3 *We!* Interjection. Used to demand attention, give emphasis (as here), or to express surprise, derision, or distress.
4 It is clear the scene changes here and below, but there is no textual or external evidence of how this was done. It is possible that two ends of the pageant wagon were used for the two locations; that approach would emphasize the parallel between the two sleeping figures of Pilate and his wife, and underscore the nighttime secrecy of Jesus' trials.

[*Pilate's Wife and Boy sleep. Enter Devil.*]

DEVIL. Out! Out! Harrow![1] Into bale° am I brought, *misery*
    this bargain° may I ban,° *matter / curse*
  But if° I work some wile,° *unless / trick*
    in woe mun° I won.° *must / dwell*
160 This gentleman, Jesus, of cursedness° *maliciousness*
    he can,° *is capable*
  By any sign that I see this same is God's son.
  And° he be slain our solace° will cease, *if / comfort*
  He will save man's soul from our sound° *safe-keeping*
  And reave° us the realms that are round.° *deprive / around*
165 I will° on stiffly° in this stound° *will (go) / firmly / moment*
  Unto Sir Pilate's wife, pertly,° and put me in press.[2] *boldly*

  Oh woman, be wise and ware,° and won° in thy wit[3] *aware / remain*
  There shall a gentleman, Jesus, unjustly be judged
  Before thy husband in haste, and with° harlots° *by / scoundrels*
    be hit,° *beaten*
170 And that doughty° today to death *good man*
    thus be dighted.° *condemned*
  Sir Pilate, for° his preaching,° and thou, *because of / talk (against Jesus)*
  With need° shall ye namely be noyed.° *deprivation / afflicted*
  Your strife° and your strength shall be stroyed,° *efforts / destroyed*
  Your richesse° shall be reft° you *wealth / taken from*
    that is rude,° *great*
175 With vengeance, and that dare I avow.° *promise*

PILATE'S WIFE. Ah, I am dretched° with a dream *tormented*
    full dreadfully to doubt.° *fear*
  Say child, rise up radly° and rest for no ro,° *quickly / peace*
  Thou must lance° to my lord and *rush*
    lowly him° lout,° *to him / bow*
  Commend me to his reverence, as right will I do.
180 BOY. Oh, what, shall I travail° thus timely° *work / early*
    this tide?° *time*
  Madam, for the dretching° of heaven, *tormenting*
  Slike° note° is noisome° to neven° *such / matter / troubling / mention*

---

1 *Out! Out! Harrow!* Cries of distress. The phrase is extrametrical, making the line unusually long.

2 *put me in press* Exert myself, endeavor.

3 *won in thy wit* Have your wits about you.

And it nighs° unto midnight full even.[1]   *nears*

PILATE'S WIFE. Go bet° boy, I bid no longer   *quickly*
   thou bide,°   *remain*

And say to my sovereign, this same is sooth° that I send him: *true*   185
All naked this night as I napped
With teen° and with train° was I trapped,°   *trouble / guile / ensnared*
With a sweven° that swiftly me swapped°   *dream / struck*
Of one Jesus, the just man the Jews will undo.

She prays tent° to that true man,   *attention*   190
   with teen° be not trapped,[2]   *affliction*
But as a doomsman° duly to be dressing,°   *judge / endeavoring*
And leally° deliver° that lede.°   *in good faith / acquit / man*
BOY. Madam, I am dressed° to° that deed—   *prepared / to (do)*
But first will I nap in this need,
For he has mister° of a   *need*   195
   morn°-sleep that midnight is missing.[3]   *morning*

[*Boy and Pilate's Wife return to sleep. Enter Annas, Caiaphas, Soldiers,
and Jesus as captive, outside Pilate's court.*]

ANNAS. Sir Caiaphas, ye ken° well this caitiff°   *know / wretch*
   we have catched°   *caught*
That oft-times in our temple has teached° untruly.   *taught*
Our meinie° with might at midnight him matched°   *retinue / set upon*
And has driven him till° his deeming°   *to / judgment*
   for his deeds unduly;°   *wicked*
Wherefore I counsel that kindly° we cair°   *by custom / go*   200
Unto Sir Pilate our prince, and pray him
That he for our right will array° him—   *provide for*
This faitour°—for his falsehood to flay him;   *deceiver*
For fro° we say him the sooth: he shall sit him full sore.[4]   *comfort*

CAIAPHAS. Sir Annas, this sport have ye speedily espied,   205
As I am pontifical° prince of all priests.   *high priestly*
We will press to Sir Pilate, and present him with pride

---

1 *full even* Almost.
2 *She prays ... not trapped* (Tell him that) she (i.e., Procula herself) asks for attention to be
   paid to that true man, (so that he will) not be entrapped with affliction.
3 *For he has ... missing* For he who is missing sleep at midnight needs it in the morning.
4 *For fro ... full sore* Regarding (his) comfort, we tell him the truth: things will go badly for
   him.

With this harlot° that has hewed°　　　　　　　*scoundrel / torn*
　　our hearts from our breasts
Through talking of tales untrue.
And therefore sir, knights—
210　SOLDIERS.　　　　　　　Lord.
　CAIAPHAS.　Sir knights that are courteous and kind,
　　We charge you that churl° be well chained.　　*low born man*
　　Do busk° you and gradely° him bind,　　*make ready / immediately*
　　And rug° him in ropes his race°　　*pull violently / conduct*
　　　till he rue.°　　　　　　　　　　　　　　　*regret*

215　FIRST SOLDIER.　Sir, your saws° shall be　　　　*words*
　　　served° shortly and soon.　　　　　　　　　*obeyed*
　　Yea, do fellow, by thy faith; let us fast°　　*fasten*
　　　this faitour full fast.°　　　　　　　　　　*firmly*
　SECOND SOLDIER.　I am doughty° to this deed,　*capable*
　　　deliver,° have done;[1]　　　　　　　　　　*make haste*
　　Let us pull on with pride till his power be past.
　FIRST SOLDIER.　Do have fast and hold at his hands.
220　SECOND SOLDIER.　For this same is he that lightly°　*readily*
　　　avaunted,°　　　　　　　　　　　　　　　　*boasted*
　　And God's son he gradely° him°　　　*boldly / himself*
　　　granted.°　　　　　　　　　　　　　*claimed (to be)*
　FIRST SOLDIER.　He be hurled° for the highness°　*dragged / high status*
　　　he haunted°—　　　　　　　　　　　　　　*claimed*
　　Lo, he stonies° for° us,　　*is stupefied with fear / because of*
　　　he stares where he stands.

　SECOND SOLDIER.　Now is the brothel° bound　*worthless one*
　　　for all the boast that he blew,
225　And the Last Day he let° no lordings°　*believed / rulers*
　　　might law° him.　　　　　　　　　　　*overthrow*
　ANNAS.　Yea, he weened° this world had been wholly his own.　*believed*
　　As ye are doughtiest today till°　　　　　　　*to*
　　　his deeming° ye draw him,　　　　　　　　*judgment*
　　And then shall we ken° how that he can excuse him.°　*know / himself*
　FIRST SOLDIER.　Here, ye gomes,° go a-room,[2]　*men*
　　　give us gate,°　　　　　　　　　　　　　*way*

1　*have done*　Make an end (of it).
2　*go a-room*　Stand aside. This command and the rest of the line may be directed at the
　audience, and may suggest that Annas, Caiaphas, the soldiers, and Jesus are on the ground
　level.

We must step to yon star° of estate.°   *i.e., Pilate / high status*   230
SECOND SOLDIER. We must yaply° wend° in at this gate,   *nimbly / go*
    For he that comes to court, to courtesy must use°   *accustom*
    him.°   *himself*

FIRST SOLDIER. Do rap° on,   *knock*
    the rinks° that we may raise with our rolling.[1]   *men*
    [*To Jesus*] Come forth, sir coward, why cower ye behind?
    [*The soldiers knock on the gate to Pilate's court.*]
BEADLE. O, what javels° are ye that jape°   *brawlers / joke around*   235
    with gowling?°   *shouting*
FIRST SOLDIER. Ah, good sir, be not wroth,°   *angry*
    for words are as the wind.
BEADLE. I say, gadlings,° go back with   *worthless fellows*
    your gauds.°   *tricks*
SECOND SOLDIER. Be suffering,° I beseech you,   *patient*
    And more of this matter ye meek you.[2]
BEADLE. Why, uncunning° knaves, and°   *stupid / if*   240
    I cleek° you,   *catch*
    I shall fell° you, by my faith, for all your false frauds.   *knock down*

PILATE. Say child,° ill cheve you![3] What churls are so clattering?   *fellow*
BEADLE. My Lord, uncunning knaves they cry and they call.
PILATE. Go boldly belive° and those brothels   *quickly*
    be battering,°   *beating*
    And put them in prison upon pain that may fall.   245
    Yea, speedily speer° them if any sport°   *inquire / amusement*
    can they spell,°   *speak of*
    Yea, and look° what lordings they be.[4]   *find out*
BEADLE. My Lord, that is lofful° in lee,°   *praiseworthy / tranquility*
    I am buxom° and blithe°   *obedient / happy*
    to your blee.°   *countenance*
PILATE. And if they talk any tidings come tite° and me tell.   *quickly*   250
BEADLE. Can ye talk any tidings, by your faith, my fellows?
FIRST SOLDIER. Yea sir, sir Caiaphas and Annas are come both together
    To Sir Pilate of Pontus and prince of our laws;

---

1   *Do rap ... rolling*   Do knock on (the gate) so that we may awaken the men with our agitating.
2   *ye meek you*   Be meek and pay attention to.
3   *ill cheve you*   May you get on poorly.
4   *look what lordings they be*   Find out who they are.

And they have latched° a lorel° that is   *caught / wretch*
    lawless and lither.°   *wicked*

BEADLE. [*To Pilate*] My Lord, my Lord!

255 PILATE.   How?

BEADLE. My Lord, unlap° you   *uncover (i.e., get up)*
    belive° where ye lie.   *quickly*

Sir Caiaphas to your court is carried,°   *come*

And sir Annas, but a traitor them tarried.

Many a wight° of that warlock°   *person / wicked person*
    has waried,°   *cursed*

260 They have brought him in a band° his   *rope*
    bales° to buy.°   *misdeeds / pay for*

PILATE. But are these saws° certain in sooth°   *words / truth*
    that thou says?

BEADLE. Yea, Lord, the states° yonder stand,   *magnates*
    for strife are they stunned.

PILATE. Now then am I light as a roe,° and eath° *roe deer / ready*
    for to raise.°   *rise*

Go bid them come in both, and the boy they have bound.

265 BEADLE. [*To Caiaphas and Annas*] Sirs, my lord gives leave in for to
    come.

[*Caiaphas and Annas enter Pilate's court.*]

CAIAPHAS. Hail, prince that is peerless in price,
    Ye are leader of laws in this land,
    Your help is full hendly° at hand.   *graciously*

ANNAS. Hail, strong in your state° for to stand, *estate, status*

270 All this doom° must be dressed° *judgment / addressed*
    at your duly° device.°   *lawful / deposition*

PILATE. Who is there? My prelates?

CAIAPHAS.   Yea, Lord.

PILATE.   Now be ye welcome,
    iwis.°   *indeed*

CAIAPHAS. Gramercy,° my sovereign.   *thank you*
    But we beseech you all sam°   *together*

Because of waking you unwarely°   *unexpectedly*
    be not wroth° with this,   *angry*

For we have brought here a lorel°—he looks like a lamb. *rogue*

275 PILATE. Come in, you both, and to the bench° *judge's seat*
    braid° you.   *hasten*

CAIAPHAS. Nay, good sir, lower is leeful° for us.[1]   *appropriate*
PILATE. Ah, sir Caiaphas, be courteous ye bus.°   *must*
ANNAS. Nay, good Lord, it may not be thus.
PILATE. Say no more, but come sit you beside me in sorrow[2] as I said
   you.

[*Enter Boy.*]

BOY. Hail, the seemliest segge° under sun sought,°   *man / found* 280
   Hail, the dearest duke and doughtiest in deed.
PILATE. Now bienvenue beausire,[3]
   what bodeword° hast thou brought?   *message*
Has any languor° my lady new latched°   *illness / caught*
   in this lede?°   *place*
BOY. Sir, that comely° commends her you to,   *lovely one*
   And says, all naked this night as she napped   285
   With teen° and with tray° was she trapped,   *trouble / deception*
   With a sweven° that swiftly her swapped°   *dream / struck, came to*
   Of one Jesus, the just man the Jews will undo.

   She beseeches you as her sovereign that simple° to save,   *innocent one*
   Deem° him not to death for dread of vengeance.   *judge* 290
PILATE. What, I hope° this be he that   *believe*
   hither harled° ye have.   *dragged*
CAIAPHAS. Yea sir, the same and the self—
   but this is but a skaunce;°   *joke*
   He with witchcraft this wile° has he wrought.   *trick*
   Some fiend of his sand[4] has he sent
   And warned° your wife ere° he went.   *informed / before* 295
PILATE. Yow![5] That shalk° should not   *man*
   shamely° be shent,°   *unjustly / destroyed*
   This is siker° in certain,   *secure*
   and° sooth° should be sought.   *if / truth*

---

1 *to the bench … leeful for us* Pilate beckons Caiaphas and Annas to his "bench," that is, the
   judge's seat, as in a modern courtroom. Caiaphas and Annas refuse on the ground that it is
   not appropriate for them as religious leaders to enter a secular court. It would, in fact, be a
   violation of English law for prelates to be involved in a capital case. Pilate continues to insist
   but since the Boy interrupts, we hear no more on the subject.
2 *in sorrow* Humbly.
3 *bienvenue beausire* French: welcome, good sir.
4 *of his sand* As his messenger.
5 *Yow!* Exclamation used to attract attention.

ANNAS. Yea, through his phantom° and falsehood   *guile*
     and fiend's-craft
   He has wrought many wonder where he walked full wide,
300   Wherefore, my Lord, it were leeful° his life   *fitting*
     were him raft.°   *taken from*
  PILATE. Be ye never so breme,° ye both bus° abide[1]   *angry / must*
   But if° the traitor be taught° for untruth,   *unless / exposed*
   And therefore sermon° you no more.
   I will sikerly° send himself for,[2]   *certainly*
305   And see what he says to° thee sore.°   *in answer to / urgently*
   Beadle, go bring him, for of that rink° have I ruth.°   *man / pity*

[*Beadle brings Jesus to Pilate, accompanied by Soldiers.*]

  BEADLE. This foreward° to fulfill   *agreement*
     am I fain° moved in mine heart.   *eagerly*
   Say, Jesus, the judges and the Jews have me enjoined
   To bring thee before them even bound as thou art.
310   Yon lordings to lose° thee full long   *destroy*
     have they hoined,°   *waited*
   But first shall I worship thee with wit° and with will.   *knowledge*
   This reverence I do thee forthy,°   *therefore*
   For wights° that were wiser than I,   *people*
   They worshipped thee full wholly° on high   *devoutly*
315   And with solemnity sang 'Hosanna' till.°   *to (you)*

  FIRST SOLDIER. My Lord, that is leader of laws in this land,
   All beadles to your bidding should be buxom°   *obedient*
     and bain,°   *willing*
   And yet this boy here before you full boldly was bowand°   *bowing*
   To worship this warlock.
     Methinks° we work all in vain.   *it seems to me*
320 SECOND SOLDIER. Yea, and in your presence he prayed him of peace,
   In kneeling on knees to this knave
   He besought° him his servant to save.   *begged*
  CAIAPHAS. Lo, Lord, such error among them they have
   It is great sorrow to see, no segge° may it cease.   *man*

---

1   *Be ye ... abide*   However angry you are, you both must wait.
2   *I will ... himself for*   I will certainly send for him.

It is no mensk° to your manhood,   *honor* 325
    that mickle° is of might,   *great*
To forbear° such forfeits°   *tolerate / offenses*
    that falsely are feigned,°   *fabricated*
Such spites° in especial would° be   *insults / ought to be*
    eschewed° in your sight.   *avoided*
PILATE. Sirs, move you not in this matter
    but be mildly demeaned,°   *mannered*
For yon courtesy I ken° had some cause.   *know*
ANNAS. In your sight, sir, the sooth shall I say;   330
    As ye are prince, take heed I you pray:
Such a lurdan° unleal,° dare I lay,° *wretch / disloyal / wager*
Many lords of our lands might lead from our laws.

PILATE. Say, losel,° who gave thee leave so for   *knave*
    to lout° to yon lad°   *bow / fellow*
And solace° him in my sight   *give comfort* 335
    so seemly° that I saw?   *in a seemly manner*
BEADLE. Ah, gracious Lord, grieve you not,
    for good case° I had.   *reason*
Ye commanded me to cair,° as ye ken well and know,   *go*
To Jerusalem on a journey, with sele;°   *good fortune*
And then this seemly° on an ass was set *worthy one (i.e., Jesus)*
And many men mildly him met,   340
As a God in that ground° they him gret,°   *place / greeted*
Well psalming° him in way[1]   *singing psalms to*
    with worship leal.°   *faithful*

'Hosanna' they sang, 'the son of David,'
Rich men with their robes they ran to his feet,
And poor folk fetched flowers of° the frith° *from / meadow* 345
And made mirth and melody this man for to meet.[2]
PILATE. Now good sir, by thy faith, what is 'Hosanna' to say?[3]
BEADLE. Sir, construe° it we may by language of this land, *translate*
    as I leve,°   *believe*

---

1 *in way* Along the way.
2 *Ah, gracious Lord ... for to meet* The events the Beadle recounts in this speech are dramatized in the *Entry into Jerusalem* play.
3 *what is 'Hosanna' to say?* What does 'Hosanna' mean?

It is as much to me for to move[1]—
350 Your prelates in this place can it prove°—   *explain*
  As, 'our savior and sovereign thou save us, we pray.'

PILATE. Lo, seigniors,° how seems you?[2]   *lords*
  The sooth° I you said.   *truth*
CAIAPHAS. Yea, Lord, this lad is full lither,° by this light.   *wicked*
  If his saws° were searched°   *words / examined*
  and sadly° assayed,°   *seriously / tested*
355 Save your reverence, his reasons they reckon°   *conform*
  not with right.
  This caitiff° thus cursedly can construe° us.   *wretch / expound (to)*
BEADLE. Sirs, truly the truth I have told
  Of this wight ye have wrapped in wold.[3]
ANNAS. I say, harlot,° thy tongue should thou hold,   *hooligan*
360 And not against thy masters to move thus.

PILATE. Do cease of your saying, and I shall
  examine full sore.°   *carefully*
ANNAS. Sir, deem° him to death or do him away.   *condemn*
PILATE. Sir, have ye said?
ANNAS.   Yea, Lord.
PILATE.   Now go sit you with sorrow and care,
  For I will lose no lede° that is leal° to our lay.°   *man / loyal / law*
365 But step forth and stand up on height°   *high*
  And busk° to my bidding, thou boy,   *make (yourself) ready*
  And for the nonce° that thou   *occasion*
  neven° us an 'oy.'°   *proclaim / 'oyez' (hear ye)*
BEADLE. I am here at your hand to hallo° a 'hoy,'°   *shout / 'oyez'*
  Do move of your master,[4] for I shall mell° it with might.   *speak*

PILATE. Cry 'Oyez.'
BEADLE.   Oyez.
PILATE.   Yet eft,° by thy faith.   *again*
370 BEADLE.   Oyez!
PILATE. Yet louder, that ilka° lede°   *every / man*
  may lithe°—   *pay attention*

---

1 *It is … to move* As far as I can tell.
2 *how seems you* What do you think?
3 *wrapped in wold* Arrested.
4 *Do move of your master* Act from your authority.

Cry peace in this press,° upon pain thereupon,   *crowd*
Bid them swage° of their sweying°   *stop / noise*
  both swiftly and swith°   *quickly*
And stint° of their striving° and stand still as a stone. *stop / unruliness*
Call Jesus, the gentle°   *i.e., gentleman* 375
  of° Jacob, the Jew.   *descended from*
Come prest° and appear,   *quickly*
To the bar[1] draw thee near,
To thy judgment here,
To be deemed° for his deeds undue.°   *judged / illegal*

FIRST SOLDIER. We![2] Hark how this harlot he hields out of harre,[3]   380
  This lotterel° list° not, my Lord, to lout.°   *scoundrel / cares / bow*
SECOND SOLDIER. Say beggar, why brawlest thou?[4]
  Go boun° thee° to the bar.   *take / yourself*
FIRST SOLDIER. Step on thy
  standing° so stern and so stout.   *accused's place of standing*
SECOND SOLDIER. Step on thy standing so still.
FIRST SOLDIER. Sir coward, to court must ye cair°—   *go* 385
SECOND SOLDIER. A lesson to learn of our lore.°   *doctrine, ordinances*
FIRST SOLDIER. Flit° forth, foul° might thou fare.[5]   *move / foully*

SECOND SOLDIER. Say warlock,° thou   *wicked person*
  wantest° of thy will.[6]   *lack*

BOY. Oh Jesus ungentle,° thy joy is in japes,° *unmannerly / tricks, deceit*
  Thou cannot be courteous, thou caitiff° I call thee,   *wretch* 390
  No ruth° were it to rug° thee   *pity / tug*
    and rive° thee in ropes.   *tear apart*
  Why falls thou not flat here, foul° fall° thee,   *wickedness / befall*
  For fear of my father so free?°   *noble*
  Thou wot° not his wisdom, iwis;°   *know / truly*

---

1 *bar* The barrier between the judge and the court. Like "bench" above, this is another
   English legal term with both literal and figurative meaning; both terms remain in use today.
2 *We!* Interjection. Used to demand attention (as here), or to express surprise, derision, or
   distress.
3 *hields out of harre* Behaves in a disorderly way, is out of order. Here the words must be
   meant ironically; Jesus speaks only four of the play's over 500 lines.
4 *why brawlest thou?* Why do you quarrel? Again, ironic.
5 *Flit forth, foul might thou fare* Move forward, and may you fare poorly.
6 *thou wantest of thy will* You have lost your mind.

395 All thine help in his hand that it is,
    How soon he might save thee from this.
    Obey him, brothel,° I bid thee.   *worthless person*

PILATE. Now Jesus, thou art welcome iwis, as I ween;°   *think*
    Be not abashed° but boldly boun°   *afraid / take*
        thee° to the bar.   *yourself*
400 What seignior° will sue for thee sore,[1] I have seen.   *lord*
    To work on this warlock, his wit is in were.[2]
    Come prest,° of a pain,[3] and appear,   *quickly*
    And sir prelates, your points be proving.
    What cause can ye cast° of accusing?   *put forward*
405 This matter ye mark° to be moving,   *undertake*
    And hendly° in haste let us hear.   *quickly*

CAIAPHAS. Sir Pilate of Pontus and prince of great price,
    We trust ye will trow° our tales they be true,   *believe*
    To death for to deem° him   *condemn*
        with duly° device.°   *lawful / deposition*
410 For cursedness° yon knave has in case,[4] if ye knew,   *(the) evil*
    In heart would ye hate him in high.[5]
    For if it ne were so,
    We meant not to misdo;°   *offend*
    Trust, sir, shall ye thereto,°   *to that*
415 We had not him taken to thee.[6]

PILATE. Sir, your tales would I trow, but they touch none intent.[7]
    What cause can ye find now this freke° for to fell?° *man / cast down*
ANNAS. Our Sabbath he saves° not,   *observes*
    but sadly° assent°   *solemnly / is willing*
    To work full unwisely, this wot° I right well,   *know*
    ....[8]
420 He works when he will, well I wot,
    And therefore in heart we him hate.

---

1 *sue for thee sore* Argue against you fervently.
2 *his wit is in were* His wits are lost.
3 *of a pain* Under threat of a punishment.
4 *has in case* Is devising.
5 *in high* Greatly.
6 *We had ... to thee* We would not have taken him to you.
7 *touch none intent* Are not to the point.
8 .... A line is missing in the manuscript.

It sits° you, to strength° your estate,°   *suits / strengthen / position*
Yon losel° to lose° for his lay.°   *knave / put to death / customs*

PILATE. Ilka° lede° for to lose for his lay is not leal.° *every / man / lawful*
   Your law is leeful,° but to your laws longs° it   *lawful / belongs* 425
   This faitour° to feeze° well   *traitor / punish*
     with flaps° full fele,°   *blows / many*
   And woe may ye work him by law, for he wrongs it.
   Therefore take unto you full tite,°   *quickly*
   And like as your laws will you lead,
   Ye deem him to death for his deed.   430
CAIAPHAS. Nay, nay sir, that doom must us dread;
   ....[1]

   It longs° not till° us no lede for to lose.   *is permissible / to*
PILATE. What would ye I did then? The devil mot you draw![2]
   Full few are his friends but fele° are his foes.   *many*
   His life for to lose there longs° no law,   *pertains* 435
   Nor no cause can I kindly° contrive°   *properly / fabricate*
   That why he should lose thus his life.
ANNAS. Ah, good sir, it° raiks°   *i.e., trouble / happens*
     full rife°   *everywhere*
   In steads° where he has stirred mickle° strife   *places / great*
   Of° ledes° that is leal° to your life.   *among / men / loyal* 440

CAIAPHAS. Sir, halt° men and hurt he healed in haste,   *lame*
   The deaf and the dumb he delivered from dole°   *sorrow*
   By witchcraft, I warrant—his wits shall waste°—   *decline*
   For the ferlies° that he fareth° with,   *wonders / deals*
     lo, how they follow yon fool,
   Our folk so thus he frays° in fere.[3]   *frightens* 445
ANNAS. The dead he raises anon—
   This Lazarus that low lay alone
   He grant° him his gates° for to gone,°   *allowed / way / go*
   And pertly° thus proved he his power.   *cleverly*
PILATE. Now good sirs, I say, what would ye seem?°   *have* 450

---

1 .... Another line is missing in the manuscript.
2 *The devil mot you draw* May the devil draw you (i.e., behind a horse, as in the punishment
   for high treason)!
3 *in fere* Altogether.

CAIAPHAS. Sir, to death for to do him or do him adawe.[1]

PILATE. Yea, for he does well his death for to deem?
    Go lake° you sir, lightly; where learned ye such law?   *play the fool*
    This touches no treason, I tell you.

455   Ye prelates that proved are for price,
    Ye should be both witty and wise
    And ledge° our law where it lies,[2]   *allege, expound*
    Our matters ye move thus amell° you.   *amongst*

ANNAS. Misplease° not your person,   *be displeased*
    ye prince without peer,

460   It touches to treason this tale I shall tell:
    Yon briber,° full bainly°   *vagabond / readily*
    he bad° to forbear°   *commanded / withhold*
    The tribute° to the emperor, thus would he compel   *tax*
    Our people thus his points° to apply.   *teachings*

CAIAPHAS. The people he says he shall save,
465   And Christ gars° he call him,[3] yon knave,   *makes*
    And says he will the high kingdom have—
    Look whether he deserves to die.

PILATE. To die he deserves if he do thus indeed,
    But I will see myself what he says.
470   Speak, Jesus, and spend° now thy space°   *use / time*
    for to speed.°   *succeed*
    These lordings they ledge° thee thou list°   *allege / rather*
    not leve on[4] our lays,°   *laws*
    They accuse thee cruelly and keen;
    And therefore as a chieftain I charge thee,
    If thou be Christ, that thou tell me,
475   And God's son thou grudge not to grant thee,[5]
    For this is the matter that I mean.

JESUS. Thou sayest so thyself, I am soothly° the same,   *truly*
    Here woning° in world to work all thy will.   *dwelling*
    My father is faithful to fell° all thy fame;   *cast down*

---

1 *do him adawe* Have him put to death (i.e., by someone else).
2 *where it lies* I.e., as it stands.
3 *Christ gars he call him* He makes (people) call him Christ.
4 *leve on* Believe in, live by.
5 *And God's son … grant thee* And do not hesitate to claim that you are God's son.

Without trespass° or teen° am I   *offence / harm inflicted* 480
    taken thee till.°   *to*
PILATE. Lo, bishops, why blame ye this boy?
Me seems[1] that it is sooth° that he says.   *true*
Ye move all the malice ye may
With your wrenches° and wiles   *cunning tricks*
    to writhe° him away,   *twist (fig.)*
Unjustly to judge him from joy.   485

CAIAPHAS. Not so, sir, his saying is full soothly sooth,[2]
    It brings our bairns° in bale° for to bind.   *people / sorrow*
ANNAS. Sir, doubtless we deem as due° of the death   *deserving*
    This fool that ye favor—great faults can we find
    This day for to deem him to die.   490
PILATE. Say losel,° thou lies by this light!   *knave*
    Nay, thou ribald,° thou reckon° unright.°   *rascal / speak / wrongly*
CAIAPHAS. Advise you sir, with main° and with might,   *power*
    And wreak° not your wrath now forthy.°   *avenge / therefore*

PILATE. Me likes not his language so largely for to lie.[3]   495
CAIAPHAS. Ah, mercy, Lord, meekly, no malice we meant.
PILATE. Now done is it° doubtless, bold be and blithe,   *i.e., his anger*
    Talk on that traitor and tell your intent.
    Yon segge° is subtle ye say;   *man*
    Good sirs, where learned he such lore?   500
CAIAPHAS. In faith, we cannot find where.
PILATE. Yes, his father with some ferlies°   *wonders*
    gan° fare°   *began / to deal*
    And has lered° this lad of his lay.°   *taught / practice*

ANNAS. Nay, nay sir, we wist° that he was   *knew*
    but a wright,°   *carpenter*
    No subtlety he showed that any segge saw.   505
PILATE. Then mean ye of° malice to mar° him   *out of / destroy*
    of° might,   *by*
    Of cursedness convict no cause can ye know.[4]

---

1   *Me seems*   It seems to me.
2   *Not so ... sooth*   It is not so, sir (that) his sayings are truly true.
3   *largely for to lie*   To be so out of bounds.
4   *Of cursedness ... know*   You are unable to find any cause to convict for wickedness.

Me marvels[1] ye malign° amiss.°　　　　　*make false accusations / wrongly*

CAIAPHAS. Sir, from Galilee hither and how°　　　　　*thither*

510　The greatest° against° him gan go,　　*greatest number of (people) / towards*

Yon warlock° to waken° of woe,°　　　　*wicked person / incite / evil*

And of this work bear witness, iwis.°　　　　　*indeed*

PILATE. Why, and has he gone in Galilee, yon gadling°　　　　*base fellow*

ungain?°　　　　*bothersome*

ANNAS. Yea, Lord, there was he born,

yon brothel,° and bred.　　　　*worthless person*

515　PILATE. Now without faging,° my friends,　　　*deception*

in faith I am fain,°　　　　*glad*

For now shall our strife full sternly°　　　*firmly*

be stead.°　　　*fixed (i.e., settled)*

Sir Herod is king there, ye ken,°　　　*know*

His power is proved full prest°　　　*furnished*

To rid° him or reave° him of rest.°　　*free / deprive / peace*

520　And therefore, to go with yon guest°　　　*stranger*

Ye mark us out of[2] the manliest men.

CAIAPHAS. As wit and wisdom your will shall be wrought,

Here is kemps° full keen to the king for to cair.°　*strong warriors / go*

PILATE. Now seigniors, I say you, since sooth shall be sought,

525　But if° he shortly° be sent it may sit us full sore.[3]　*unless / quickly*

And therefore, sir knights—

SOLDIERS.　　　　　　　　　Lord.

PILATE. Sir knights that are cruel and keen,

That warlock ye warrok° and wrest,°　　　*bind / drag away*

And look that he bremely° be brast°　　*vigorously / beaten*

....[4]

530　Do take on that traitor you between.

Till° Herod in haste with that harlot°　　　*to / scoundrel*

ye hie,°　　　*go quickly*

Commend me full meekly unto his most might.

Say the doom° of this boy, to deem him to die,　　*judgment*

Is done° upon him duly, to dress° or to dight°　*made / ordain / do*

1　*Me marvels*　I am surprised.
2　*Ye mark us out of*　Select from us some of.
3　*sit us full sore*　Be the worse for us.
4　....　A line is missing in the manuscript here.

Or life for to leave° at his° list.°   *spare / i.e., Herod's / pleasure* 535
Say aught° I may do him° indeed,   *anything / for him (i.e., Herod)*
His own am I worthily in weed.°   *livery, uniform*
FIRST SOLDIER. My Lord, we shall spring on a-speed.°   *apace, quickly*
Come thence to me, this traitor full trist.°   *certain*

PILATE. Beausires, I bid you ye be not too bold,   540
But take tent° for our tribute full truly to treat.°   *heed / negotiate*
SECOND SOLDIER. My Lord, we shall hie°   *hasten*
    this behest° for to hold   *promise*
And work it full wisely in will and in wit.
PILATE. So, sirs, me seems it is sitting.°   *appropriate*
FIRST SOLDIER. Mahound,[1] sirs, he mensk° you with might.   *favor* 545
SECOND SOLDIER. And save you sir, seemly in sight.
PILATE. Now in the wild vengeance[2] ye walk with that wight,°   *man*
And freshly° ye found° to be flitting.°   *briskly / proceed / departing*

The York Corpus Christi Play: The Trial Before Herod

The Trial Before Herod, presented by the Litsters (dyers of cloth), is another of the eight plays conventionally attributed to the so-called "York Realist." *The Trial Before Herod* comes in the midst of the sequence of trial plays, all of which take place in the middle of the night (established here by Duke 1 encouraging Herod to retire to bed after his nightcap), underscoring the mockery of law and justice that they represent. Jesus remains reticent through each of the trial plays, often only speaking once, briefly, until he goes completely silent here. Although rooted in the biblical narrative as told in Luke 23.6–12, the elaboration and extension of this motif becomes key to the world that the playwright builds in the trial scenes. A reader must work hard to remember Christ's silent presence throughout the play, but an audience would experience a dramatic contrast between the consistent, stable presence of Jesus' "deafening" silence and Herod's chaotic changes of moods and tones, his egotistical bluster, and his pretentious verbosity. Herod rants, raves,

---

1 *Mahound* Muhammad, prophet and founder of Islam (c. 570–632). Medieval English texts often depict all non-Christian characters as worshipping or otherwise calling on Muhammad, as a way to construct their "otherness."

2 *in the wild vengeance* With a vengeance.

cajoles, commands, and prods Jesus until his silence provokes Herod to break down into nonsense. It is actually Herod whose "language is lorn" (lost), as he ironically says of Jesus.

Another contrast with roots in the Gospel narrative that takes on new meaning here involves costume—a contrast to which the Litsters' sponsorship of the play lends additional interest. Herod and his retinue wonder if Christ's silence is due to his awe at their "gay gear"; they wonder if he has been struck dumb by the thought that they are angels. When Jesus continues to refuse to speak, they dub him a fool and dress him in white (an action based on the Latin Vulgate Bible translation of Luke 23.11). To them, this marks him as outcast and other, but for the audience, it contrasts the court's sumptuous excesses with his simplicity and purity, especially since for the medieval audience, a fool's costume was typically motley, or multi-colored. It is Herod and his court who are the true fools.

The mocking of Christ as a fool comes after his refusal to satisfy Herod's desires for some "bourding" (entertainment) and "good game"; Christ is unwilling to make a spectacle of his conjuring tricks (as Herod sees them). These moments engage in the recurring motif of perverse game and play that runs through the cycle. In the context of this pageant's emphasis on costume and speech, the game and play theme speaks to a meta-theatrical concern with the nature and propriety of drama itself, and its engagement with spectacle.

The verbosity and noise of Herod and his court is conveyed mainly in a heavily alliterative fourteen-line stanza which rhymes ababababcdc-ccd. Other verse forms appear in the play as well, and there is much irregularity.

Pageant 31 of the York Corpus Christi Play: The Trial Before Herod

CHARACTERS

King (Herod)
Duke 1
Duke 2
Soldier 1
Soldier 2
Son 1
Son 2
Son 3
Jesus

KING. Peace, ye brothels°   *rogues*
    and brawls° in this broadness embraced,   *brawlers*
And frekes° that are friendly your   *men*
    frekeness° to frayne,[1]   *manliness*
Your tongues from treating° of trifles be trased,°   *speaking / restrained*
Or this brand° that is bright shall burst in your brain.   *sword*
Plead for no places° but plat° you   *positions / prostrate*   5
    to this plain,°   *ground*
And draw to no droving,° but dress° you to dread,[2]   *riot / behave*
    With dashes.°   *blows*
Travail° not as traitors that trust in train,°   *work / deception*
Or by the blood that Mahound[3] bled with this blade shall ye bleed.
Thus shall I britten° all your bones   *hack*   10
    on brede,°   *breadth (i.e., to full extent)*
Yea, and lush° all your limbs with lashes.   *beat*

Dragons that are dreadful shall dark° in their dens   *lurk*
In wrath when we writhe, or in wrothness°   *anger*
    are wapped.°   *consumed*
Against giants ungentle° have we joined°   *violent / i.e., in battle*
    with engines,°   *weapons*
And swans that are swimming to our sweetness[4]   15
    shall be swapped,°   *slaughtered*
And jagged° down their jolliness,   *cut*
    our gentrice° engendering.   *noble qualities*
Whoso reprove° our estate we shall   *should challenge*
    chop° them in chains,   *clap*
All rinks° that are reigning to us shall be revering.°   *men / reverent*
Therefore I bid you cease ere° any bale° be,   *before / trouble*
That no brothel° be so bold boast for to blow.°   *rogue / give vent to*   20
And ye that love your lives, listen to me
As a lord that is learned to lead you by law.

---

1 *Peace … to frayne* Peace, you hooligans and brawlers surrounded in this wide space, and you men who are (so) friendly as to question your manliness. Each of the trial pageants begins with the figure of worldly authority—here Herod; elsewhere Pilate or Caiaphas and Annas—calling for silence, a command that may be interpreted as implicating the audience in the action.

2 *dress you to dread* Behave yourselves in fear.

3 *Mahound* Muhammad, prophet and founder of Islam (c. 570–632). Medieval English texts often depict all non-Christian characters as worshipping or otherwise calling on Muhammad, as a way to construct their "otherness."

4 *to our sweetness* For our pleasure.

And ye that are of my men and of my meinie,°   *company, household*
Since we are come from our kith° as ye well know,   *native land*
25 And semble° all here sam° in this city,   *assemble / together*
    It sits° us in sadness°   *behooves / seriousness*
      to set° all our saws.°   *set forth / sayings*
DUKE 1. My Lord, we shall take keep° to your call   *heed*
    And stir° to no stead° but ye steven° us,   *go / place / command*
    No grievance° too great ne° too small.   *trouble / nor*
30 KING. Yea, but look that no faults° befall.°   *mistakes / happen*
DUKE 2. Leally,° my Lord, so we shall,   *loyally*
    Ye need not no more for to neven° us.   *tell*

DUKE 1. Monseigneur,° demean° you   *my lord (French) / deign*
    to mensk° in mind what I mean   *honor*
    And boun° to your bedward,°   *prepare / towards bed(time)*
      for so hold° I best,   *consider*
35 For all the commons° of° this court   *common people / from*
    been° avoid clean,[1]   *are*
    And ilka° rink,° as reason asks, are gone to their rest;   *every / man*
    Wherefore I counsel, my Lord, ye command you° a drink.   *for yourself*
KING. Now certes,° I assent as thou says.   *certainly*
    See ilka wye° is went on his ways   *man*
40 Lightly,° without any delays.   *quickly*
    Give us wine winly° and let us go wink,°   *pleasantly / sleep*
    And see that no dirdum° be done.   *noise*

(Then the King drinks.)

DUKE 1. My Lord, unlace° you to lie,   *loosen your clothes*
    Here shall none come for to cry.
45 KING. Now speedily look that thou spy°   *look*
    That no noise be nighing° this noon.°   *nearing / midnight*

DUKE 1. My Lord, your bed is new made,
    you needs not for to bide° it.   *wait for*
KING. Yea, but as thou loves me heartily, lay me down softly,
    For thou wot° full well that I am full tenderly hided.[2]   *know*
DUKE 1. How lie ye my good Lord?
50 KING.   Right well, by this light,

---

1 *been avoid clean* Are completely gone.
2 *I am full tenderly hided* I have very sensitive skin.

All wholly at my desire.[1]
Wherefore I pray Sir Satan, our sire,
And Lucifer most lovely of lire,°   *body*
He save you all sirs, and give you good night.

[*Soldiers 1 and 2 enter with Christ bound.*]

SOLDIER 1. Sir knight, ye wot° we are warned°   *know / instructed*   55
    to wend°   *go*
To wit° of° this warlock°   *know / regarding / traitor*
    what is the king's will.
SOLDIER 2. Sir, here is Herod all even here at our hand,
    And all our intent° tite° shall we tell him until.[2] *purpose / immediately*
SOLDIER 1. Who is here?
DUKE 1.   Who is there?
SOLDIER 1.   Sir, we are kenned° *well-known*
    Is come[3] to your counsel this carl° for to kill.   *low-born man*   60
DUKE 1. Sirs, but° your message may   *unless*
    mirths° amend,°   *entertainment / improve*
Stalk° forth by yon streets or stand stone still.   *walk stealthily*
SOLDIER 2. Yes, certes sir, of mirths° we mean,°   *good news / intend*
The king shall have matters to mell° him.   *concern*
We bring here a boy° us between,   *wretch*   65
Wherefore to have worship° we ween.°   *honor / believe*
DUKE 1. Well sirs, so that[4] it turn to no teen,°   *mischief*
Tent° him° and we shall go tell him.°   *attend to / i.e., Jesus / i.e., Herod*

My Lord, yonder is a boy bound that brought is in blame,° *censure*
Haste you in hie,[5] they hove° at your gate.   *wait*   70
KING. What, and shall I rise now, in the devil's name,
To stightle° among strangers in stalls of estate?[6]   *intervene*
But have here my hand, hold now,
And see that my slop° be well sitting.°   *gown / hanging*
DUKE 1. My Lord, with a good will I would° you,   *will see to*   75
No wrong will I wit at my witting.[7]

---

1 *All wholly at my desire* Completely as I wish.
2 *him until* To him.
3 *Is come* Who are come.
4 *so that* As long as.
5 *in hie* Quickly.
6 *stalls of estate* Court.
7 *No wrong ... witting* I will not knowingly allow any fault.

But my Lord, we can tell you of uncouth°   *strange*
    tidand.°   *tidings, news*

KING. Yea, but look ye tell us no tales but true.

DUKE 2. My Lord, they bring you yonder a boy
    bound in a band°   *rope*

80   That bodes° either bourding°   *portends / entertainment*
    or bales° to brew.   *trouble*

KING. Then get we some harrow° full hastily at hand.   *commotion*

DUKE 1. My Lord, there is some note° that is needful   *news*
    to neven° you of new.   *mention to*

KING. Why, hopes° thou they haste him to hang?   *expect*

DUKE 2. We wot° not their will nor their weening,°   *know / intention*

85   But bodeword° full blithely they bring.   *message*

KING. Now, do then,° and let us see of their saying.   *so*

DUKE 2. Lo sirs,° ye shall carp° with the king,   *(to the soldiers) / speak*
    And tell to him manly° your meaning.°   *properly / purpose*

SOLDIER 1. Lord, wealth and worship be with you alway.

KING. What would you?[1]

90 SOLDIER 2.   A word, Lord, and° your will were.[2]   *if*

KING. Well, say on then.

SOLDIER 1.   My Lord, we fare°   *cause*
    fools to flay°   *be punished*
    That to you would forfeit.°   *cause offense*

KING.   We,[3] fair°   *good fortune*
    fall° you therefore.   *befall*

SOLDIER 1. My Lord, fro° ye hear what we say   *when*
    It will heave up your hearts.

KING.   Yea, but say what hind°   *creature*
    have ye there?

95 SOLDIER 2. A present from Pilate, Lord, the prince of our lay.°   *law*

KING. Peace in my presence, and name him no more.

SOLDIER 1. My Lord, he will worship you fain.°   *gladly*

KING. I conceive ye are full foes of him.

SOLDIER 2. My Lord, he would mensk° you   *honor*
    with main,°   *(all his) strength*

100 And therefore he sends you this swain.°   *fellow*

---

1 *What would you?* What do you want?

2 *and your will were* If you would permit it.

3 *We* An interjection to call attention (as here), or to express surprise, derision, or distress.

KING. Go tite° with that gadling° again, *immediately / low-born fellow*
    And say him° a borrowed bean set I not by him.[1] *to him*

DUKE 1. Ah, my Lord, with your leave, they have fared° far, *traveled*
    And for to fraist° of your fare° was no folly. *learn / opinion*
DUKE 2. My Lord, and° this gadling go thus *if* 105
    it will grieve war,° *worse*
    For he gars° grow on this ground° *causes (to) / land*
    great villainy.° *evil*
KING. Why, means thou that that miting° *insignificant one*
    should my mights mar?° *harm*
DUKE 1. Nay, Lord, but he makes on this mould° *earth*
    mickle° mastery.[2] *great*
KING. Go in, and let us see° of the saws° ere,° *examine / claims / soon*
    And but if° they be to our bourding,° *unless / amusement* 110
    they both shall abye.° *pay*
SOLDIER 2. My Lord, we were worthy to blame
    To bring you any message of miss.° *wrong, offense*
KING. Why then, can ye neven° us his name? *tell*
SOLDIER 1. Sir, Christ have we called him at home.
KING. Oh, this is the ilk° self and the same— *very* 115
    Now sirs, ye be welcome, iwis.° *indeed*

    And in faith I am fain° he is fun,° *glad / found*
    His ferlies° to frayne° and to feel;° *marvels / investigate / experience*
    Now these games was gradely° begun. *properly*
SOLDIER 2. Lord, leally° that likes° us well. *truly / pleases* 120

KING. Yea, but dare ye hight° heartily *promise*
    that harlot° is he? *scoundrel*
SOLDIER 1. My Lord, take heed and in haste ye shall hear how.
KING. Yea, but what means° *(does it) mean*
    that this message was made unto me?
SOLDIER 2. My Lord, for it touches to treason, I trow.° *believe*
SOLDIER 1. My Lord, he is culpable kenned[3] in our country 125
    Of many perilous° points,° as Pilate proves now. *dangerous / matters*
SOLDIER 2. My Lord, when Pilate heard
    he° had gone through Galilee, *i.e., Christ*

---

1 *a borrowed bean … him* I don't give a bean about him; I care little about him.
2 *makes … mastery* He performs here great feats.
3 *culpable kenned* Known to be blameworthy.

He learned° us that that lordship°　　　　　*informed / province*
　　longed° to you,　　　　　　　　　　　　　　　　　*belonged*
And ere° he wist° what your wills° were,　*until / knew / wishes*
130　No further would he speak for to spill° him.　*condemn*
King. Then knows he that our mights° are the more?°　*powers / greater*
Soldier 1. Yea, certes° sir, so say we there.　　　*certainly*
King. Now certes, and our friendship therefore
　　We grant him, and no grievance we will° him.　*will (give)*

135　And sirs, ye are welcome, iwis,° as ye well owe,°　*indeed / ought (to be)*
And for to wend° at your will I you warrand,°　　*go / permit*
For I have covet° kindly°　　　　　　　*wished for / naturally*
　　that comely° to know,　　　　　　　　　　*gracious one*
For men carp° that the carl°　　　　　　　　*say / man*
　　should be cunnand.°　　　　　　　　　*cunning, clever*
Soldier 2. My Lord, would he say°　　　　　　*tell*
　　you sooth° of his saw,[1]　　　　　　　　　*truth*
140　Ye saw never slike° selcouth,° by sea nor by sand.　*such / wonder*
King. Now go aback both and let the boy blow,°　*give vent*
　　For I hope we get some harre° hastily at hand.　*important matter*
Soldier 1. Jerusalem and the Jews may have joy
　　And heal° in their heart for to hear him.　　*consolation*
145　King. [*To Jesus*] Say, *bienvenue in bon foi*,[2]
　　Ne please you à parler à moi?[3]
Soldier 2. Nay, my Lord, he can of no
　　bourding,° this boy.　　　　　　*joking, playing around*
King. No sir? With thy leave we shall lere° him.　*teach*

Son 1. My Lord, see these knights that know
　　and are keen,°　　　　　　　　　　*ready for action*
150　How they come to your court without any call.
King. Yea son, and muster° great masteries°—　*perform / deeds*
　　what may this bemean?°　　　　　　　　　*mean*
Duke 1. My Lord, for° your mights are more than their all,[4]　*because*
　　They seek you as sovereign, and certes°　　*certainly*
　　that is seen.°　　　　　　　　　　　　*evident*
King. Now certes, since ye say so, assay° him I shall,　*test*

1　*would he … his saw*　Were he to tell you the truth of his sayings.
2　*bienvenue in bon foi*　French: welcome in good faith.
3　*Ne please you … moi.*　French and English: Does it not please you to speak to me?
4　*their all*　All of theirs.

For I am fainer° of that freke°   *more interested in / man* 155
  then other° fifteen,   *(any) other*
Yea, and him that first found,[1] fair°   *good fortune*
  might him fall.°   *befall*
SOLDIER 1. Lord, leally° we lere° you no lie,   *truly / tell*
  This life that he leads will lose° him.   *ruin*
KING. Well sirs, draw you adrigh,[2]
  And beausires,° bring ye him nigh,°   *fair sirs (French) / near* 160
  For if all[3] that his sleights° be sly   *tricks*
  Yet ere° he pass° we shall appose° him. *before / should leave / question*

Oh, my heart hops for joy
To see now this prophet appear.
We shall have good game with this boy;   165
Take heed, for in haste ye shall hear.

I leve° we shall laugh and have liking°   *believe / pleasure*
To see now this lidderon° here he   *worthless one*
  ledges° our laws.   *expounds*
DUKE 2. Hark, cousin,[4] thou comes to carp° with a king,   *talk*
  Take tent° and be cunning,° and carp as thou knows. *heed / wise* 170
DUKE 1. Yea, and look that thou be not a sot° of° thy saying, *fool / in*
  But sadly° and soon thou set°   *seriously / set forth*
  all thy saws.°   *words*
KING. Him seems full boudish,° that boy that they bring. *sullen*
DUKE 2. My Lord, and of his bourding°   *idle talk*
  great boasting men blows.°   *give vent to*
KING. Why, therefore have I sought him to see.   175
  Look, beausires,° ye be   *fair sirs*
  to our bodes° boun.°   *commands / obedient*
DUKE 1. [*To Jesus*] Kneel down here to the king on thy knee.
DUKE 2. Nay, needlings° it will not be.   *of necessity*
KING. Lo, sirs, he meeks him[5] no more unto me
  Than it were to a man of their own town.   180

DUKE 1. We![6] Go, laumere,° and learn thee to lout°   *fool / bow*

---

1 *him that first found* To him who first tested (Jesus).
2 *draw you adrigh* Stand aside.
3 *For if all* Even if.
4 *cousin* Kinsman; Duke 2 addresses Jesus ironically here.
5 *he meeks him* He makes himself meek, deferential.
6 *We!* Interjection. Used to express surprise, derision (as here), or distress.

Ere° they more blame thee to-bring.[1]   *before*
KING. Nay, dreadless° without any doubt   *surely*
    He knows not the course of a king.

185 And here be[2] in our bail,° bourd°   *custody / entertain (us)*
    ere we blin°—   *conclude*
  Say first at the beginning withal,° where was thou born?   *to begin with*
  Do, fellow, for thy faith, let us fall in.[3]
  First of thy ferlies,° who fed°   *marvels / raised*
    thee beforn?°   *in the first place*
  What, deigns thou not? Lo, sirs, he deafens us with din.
190 Say, where led ye this lidderon?°   *worthless one*
    His language is lorn.°   *lost*
SOLDIER 1. My Lord, his marvels to more and to min,°   *less*
  Ere° musters° among us both midday and morn.   *before now / shows*
SOLDIER 2. My Lord, it were too fele°   *many*
  Of wonders, he worketh° them so wightly.°   *performs / freely*
195 SOLDIER 1. We, man, mumbling may nothing avail,
  Go to the king and tell him from top unto tail.[4]
KING. Do bring us that boy unto bail,°   *close arrest*
  For leally,° we leave° him not lightly.   *truly / let off*

DUKE 1. This mop° means° that   *fool / claims*
  he may mark° men to their meed;°   *assign / reward*
200 He makes many masteries and marvels among.
DUKE 2. Five thousand folk fair gan° he feed   *did*
  With five loaves and two fishes to fang.°   *partake of*
KING. How fele° folk says thou he fed?   *many*
DUKE 2. Five thousand, Lord, that come to his call.
205 KING. Yea, boy? How mickle° bread he them bid?°   *much / offered*
DUKE 1. But five loaves dare I well wed.°   *wager*
KING. Now by the blood that Mahound bled,
  What, this was a wonder at all.°   *certainly*

DUKE 2. Now, Lord, two fishes blessed he eft°   *likewise*
210 And gave them, and there none was forgotten.

---

1 *thee to-bring* Bring on you.
2 *And here be* And since (you) are here.
3 *Do, fellow … fall in* Speak, man, for god's sake, and let's get started.
4 *from top unto tail* From beginning to end.

DUKE 1. Yea, Lord, and twelve leapful°   *baskets full*
 there left°   *remained*
Of relief° when all men had eaten.   *leftovers*

KING. Of such another mangery° no man mean° may.   *feast / speak*
DUKE 2. My Lord, but his masteries°   *accomplishments*
 that° musters° his might.   *(are) what / show*
KING. But say sirs, are these saws° sooth° that they say?   *sayings / true*   215
SOLDIER 2. Yea, Lord, and more selcouth°   *amazing*
 were showed° to our sight.   *Lazarus*
One Lazar,° a lad that in our land lay,   *Lazarus*
Lay locked under lair° from leam° and from light,   *earth / brightness*
And his sister come raking° in   *rushing*
 rueful° array.°   *distressed / state*
And Lord, for° their   *because of*   220
 roaring° he raised him full right,   *wailing*
And from his grave gart° him gang°   *made / go*
Ever forth, without any evil.[1]
KING. We,° such leasings° lasts too long.   *(interjection) / lies*
SOLDIER 1. Why Lord, ween° ye that words be wrong?   *believe*
This same lad lives us among.   225
KING. Why, these hope° I be deeds of the devil.   *believe, expect*

Why should ye haste him to hang
That sought not newly your news?[2]
SOLDIER 2. My Lord, for he calls him a king
And claims to be a king of Jews.   230

KING. But say, is he king in his kith° where he comes fro?°   *region / from*
SOLDIER 1. Nay, Lord, but he calls him a king
 his cares to keel.°   *alleviate*
KING. Then is it little wonder if that he be woe,°   *woeful*
For to be waried° with wrong since he works°   *cursed / performs*
 well;°   *good deeds*
But he shall sit by myself since ye say so.   235
Come near, king, into court. Say, can ye not kneel?
We shall have gauds° full good and games ere° we go.   *sport / before*

---

1 *One Lazar ... any evil* These events are dramatized in Pageant 24: *The Woman Taken in*
 Adultery and the Raising of Lazarus.
2 *That sought ... news* That didn't provoke your anger until recently.

How likes thou?[1] Well, Lord? Say, what, devil, never a deal?[2]
I fault in my reverent *inutile moi*,[3]
240   I am of favor, lo, fairer by far.
Kyte oute yugilment. Uta! Oy! Oy![4]
By any wit that I wot[5] it will wax° it will war.°   *grow / worse*

Servicia primet,[6]
Such losels° and lurdans° as thou, lo,   *louts / rascals*
245   *Respicias timet.*[7]
What the devil and his dame shall I now do?

Do carp on, carl, for I can thee cure.
Say, may thou not hear me? Oy, man, art thou wood?°   *mad, insane*
Now tell me faithfully before how thou fore.°   *fared*
250   Forth,° friend. By my faith, thou art   *(come) forth*
    a fond° food.°   *foolish / person*
DUKE 1. My Lord, it astonies° him, your steven°   *astonishes / voice*
    is so store°   *loud*
Him had liever° have stand[8] stone still there° he stood.   *rather / where*
KING. And whether the boy be abashed° of Herod's   *afraid*
    big blore°   *bluster*
That were a bourd° of the best, by Mahound's blood.   *amusement*
255 DUKE 2. My Lord, I trow your falchion° him flays°   *sword / frightens*
And lets° him.   *hinders*
KING.   Now leally I leve° thee,   *believe*
And therefore shall I wave it away
And softly with a scepter assay.°   *try, test*
Now sir, be pert° I thee pray,   *alert*
260   For none of my grooms° shall grieve thee.   *retainers*
Si loqueris tibi laus,
Pariter quoque prospera dantur;
Si loqueris tibi fraus,

---

1 *How likes thou?* How does this suit you?
2 *never a deal?* Not a word?
3 *I fault ... moi* I am not being honored, (he is) useless (to) me. The seeming French here ("inutile moi") and in the following lines is largely unintelligible gibberish. "Inutile" is largely a guess; the original text reads "in otill moy."
4 This entire line is unintelligible.
5 *By any wit that I wot* By any measure, as far as I can tell.
6 *Servicia primet* Latin: Duty demands.
7 *Respicias timet* Latin: Let him be wary and fear.
8 *Him had ... stand* He would rather have·stood.

Fell, fex, et bella parantur.[1]
My men, ye go mensk° him with main,°   *honor / strength*   265
And look you that it would seem.
DUKE 1. *Dewcus° fayff°* sir and sovereign.   *(unintelligible) / (unintelligible)*
DUKE 2. Sir *udins° amangidre°*   *(unintelligible) / (unintelligible)*
    demain.°   *tomorrow (French)*
KING. Go answer them gradely° again.   *properly*
    What, devil, whether dote we or dream?[2]   270

SOLDIER 1. Nay we get not one word, dare I well wed,°   *wager*
    For he is wrest° of his wit or will of his wone.[3]   *deprived*
KING. Ye say he lacked° your laws as ye that lad led?   *found fault with*
SOLDIER 2. Yea, Lord, and made many gauds°   *jests, tricks*
    as we have gone.
KING. Now since he comes as a knave and as a knave cled,° *clad, dressed*   275
    Whereto° call ye him a king?   *why*
DUKE 1.   Nay, Lord, he is none,
    But an harlot° is he.   *rogue, villain*
KING.   What, devil, I am hard stead,°   *pressed*
    A man might as well stir° a stock° as a stone.   *arouse / tree-stump*
SON 1. My Lord, this faitour° so foully° is afraid,   *deceiver / abjectly*
    He looked never of lord so longly alone.[4]   280
KING. No son, the ribald° sees us so richly arrayed°   *scoundrel / dressed*
    He weens° we be angels every-ilkone.°   *thinks / each and every one*
DUKE 2. My Lord, I hold him aghast[5] of your gay gear.°   *clothing*
KING. Great lords ought to be gay.
    Here shall no man do to thee dere,°   *harm* 285
    And therefore yet nemn° in my ear—   *speak*
    For by the great god, and thou gar° me swear   *make, cause*
    Thou had never dole° ere° this day.   *misery / before*
    Do carp° on tite,°   *chatter / quickly*
      carl,° of thy kin.   *churl, low-born man*
DUKE 1. Nay, needlings° he   *necessarily* 290
    nevens° you with none.[6]   *speaks*
KING. That shall he buy° ere he blin°—   *pay for / concludes*

---

1   *Si loqueris … bella parantur*   Latin: If you praise yourself, likewise success will be granted; if
   you speak fraudulently about yourself, bitterness, drugs, and war will follow.
2   *whether dote we or dream*   Are we out of our minds or do we dream?
3   *will of his wone*   Bewildered.
4   *He looked … alone*   He never looked at a lord alone for so long.
5   *I hold him aghast*   I believe him to be afraid.
6   *nevens … none*   He says nothing to you.

DUKE 2. Ah, leave,° Lord.   *leave (it)*
KING.   Let me alone.

DUKE 1. Now good Lord, and° ye may,   *if*
    move° you no more,[1]   *excite*
  It is not fair to fight with a fond° food,°   *silly / fool*
295 But go to your counsel° and comfort you there.   *advisors*
KING. Thou says sooth.° We shall see if so will be good,   *truth*
  For certes° our sorrows are sad.°   *certainly / solemn, serious*
SON 2. What a devil ails him?
  My Lord, I can gar° you be glad,   *make*
300 For in time our master° is mad.°   *i.e., Jesus (meant ironically) / insane*
  He lurks,° lo, and looks like a lad;   *cowers*
  He is wood,° Lord, or else his wit fails him.   *insane*

SON 3. My Lord, ye have moved you[2] as mickle° as ye may,   *greatly*
  For ye might mensk° him no more were he Mahound;   *honor*
305 And since it seems to be so, let us now assay.°   *try*
KING. Look, beausires,° ye be to our bodes° bound. *fair sirs / commands*
DUKE 1. My Lord, how should he doubt° us?   *fear*
  He dreads not your deray.°   *threats*
KING. Now do forth, the devil might him drown!
  And since he frames° falsehood and   *makes*
    makes foul fray,°   *breach of peace*
310 Roar° on him rudely, and look ye not round.°   *shout / whisper*

SON 1. My Lord, I shall enforce° myself since ye say so.   *attempt (this)*
  Fellow, be not afeared nor feign not[3] therefore,
  But tell us now some trifles between us two,
  And none of our men shall meddle them[4] more.
315 And therefore by reason array° thee,   *prepare*
  Do tell us some point° for thy prow.°   *detail / profit*
  Hear thou not what I say thee?
  Thou mumbling miting,° I may thee   *mite-like, inconsequential thing*
  Help, and turn thee from teen,° as I trow.°   *trouble / believe*

320 SON 2. Look up lad, lightly,° and   *cheerfully*
    lout° to my Lord here,   *bow*

---

1 *and ye may ... no more* If you can help it, don't become any more troubled (about this).
2 *moved you* Put yourself out, tried.
3 *be not afeared nor feign not* Don't be afraid or hold back.
4 *meddle them* Concern themselves.

For from bale unto bliss he may now thee borrow.°   *save*
Carp on, knave, cantly,° and   *boldly*
   cast thee to cord° here,   *agreement*
And say me now somewhat, thou sauterel,° with sorrow.   *wretch*
Why stands thou as still as a stone here?
Spare not, but speak in this place here   325
   Thou gadling,° it may gain thee some grace here. *bastard, lowborn man*
SON 3. My Lord, this faitour° is so feared in your face here   *imposter*
   None answer in this need° he nevens°   *predicament / speaks*
   you° with none here.   *to you*

   Do beausire,° for Belial's[1] blood and his bones,   *fair sir*
   Say somewhat—or it will wax° war.°   *grow / worse*   330
SON 1. Nay, we get not one word in this wones.°   *place*
SON 2. Do cry we all on him at once.
ALL SONS. Oyez! Oyez! Oyez!°   *hear ye*
KING.   O, ye make a foul noise
   for the nonce.°   *purpose*
SON 3. Needling,° my Lord, it is never the nar.° *by necessity / nearer*

SON 1. My Lord, all your muting° amends not a mite,   *disputing* 335
   To meddle with a madman is marvel to me.
   Command your knights to clothe him in white
   And let him cair° as he come to your country.   *go*
KING. Lo sirs, we lead° you no longer a lite,°   *detain / little*
   My son has said sadly° how that it should be—   *seriously* 340
   But such a point° for a page° is too parfite.° *thing / knave / perfect*
DUKE 1. My Lord, fools that are fond°   *unwise*
   they fall such a fee.[2]
KING. What, in a white garment to go,
   Thus gaily gird° in a gown?   *clothed*
DUKE 2. Nay, Lord, but as a fool forced him fro.[3]   345
KING. How say ye sirs, should it be so?
ALL SONS. Yea, Lord.
KING.   We!° Then is there no more,   *(interjection)*
   But boldly bid them be bound.°   *ready*

---

1 *Belial* Belial is a personal name in the Bible, a personification of evil and worthlessness;
   the name is commonly used as a synonym for Satan in the Middle Ages, but sometimes
   also seen as denoting a distinct minor demon and fallen angel. Here the distinction is
   irrelevant—Son 3 clearly swears by the power of a demonic being.
2 *they fall such a fee* To them falls such a reward.
3 *forced him fro* Forced out. Or possibly, forced out of his wits.

Sir knights, we cast° to gar° you be glad, °*try / cause*
350 Our counsel has warned us wisely and well.
White clothes we say falls for[1] a fond lad,
And all his folly, in faith,[2] fully we feel.

DUKE 1. We will with a good will for his weeds° wend,° °*clothes / go*
For we wot° well enough what weeds he shall wear. °*know*
355 DUKE 2. Lo, here is an haterell° here at your hend° °*garment / hands*
All fashioned therefore fools to fere.° °*befit*

SOLDIER 1. Lo here a jupon° of joy, °*tunic*
All such should be good for a boy.
DUKE 1. He shall be rayed° like a roy,° °*arrayed / king (of fools)*
360 And shall be found in his folly.
DUKE 2. We,° thank them, evil mote thou thee![3] °*(interjection)*
SOLDIER 1. Nay, we get not a word, well I warrand.° °*warrant*
SOLDIER 2. Man, muster° some marvel to me. °*show*
DUKE 1. What, wene° ye he be wiser than we? °*think*
365 Leave we[4] and let the king see
How it is forced° and farand.° °*enforced / faring*

My Lord, look if ye be paid,° °*satisfied*
For we have gotten him his gear.
KING. Why, and is this ribald° arrayed? °*good-for-nothing*
370 My blessing, beausires,° ye bear. °*fair sirs*

Go, gar cry[5] in my court and gradely° gar write[6] °*properly*
All the deeds that we have done in this same degree.° °*matter*
And who finds him° grieved,° °*himself / dissatisfied*
let him tell tite,° °*quickly*
And if we find no default him° falls[7] to go free. °*i.e., Jesus*
375 DUKE 1. Oyez!° If any wight with this wretch °*hear ye*
any worse wot°— °*knows*
Works bear witness who so works wrong—

---

1 *falls for* Are appropriate for.
2 *in faith* Truly.
3 *evil mote thou thee!* May you thrive evilly (a curse).
4 *Leave we* Let us leave off.
5 *gar cry* Make cry; proclaim.
6 *gar write* Have written.
7 *him falls* It falls to him.

Busk° boldly to the bar°   *come / i.e., court*
  his bales° to abate,[1]   *grievances*
For my Lord, by my lewty,°   *faith*
  will not be dealing° long.   *sitting in judgment*
My Lord, here appears none to appair° his estate.°   *harm / standing*
KING. Well then, falls him go free.[2]   380
  Sir knights, then graith° you°   *prepare / yourselves*
    goodly° to gang,°   *appropriately / go*
And repair° with your   *return*
    present° and say to Pilate   *present company*
We grant him° our friendship all fully to fang.°   *i.e., Pilate / have*
SOLDIER 1. My Lord, with your leave this way shall we lere,°   *take*
Us likes[3] no longer here to abide.   385
SOLDIER 2. My Lord, and° he worth aught in war,[4]   *if*
We come again with good cheer.
KING. Nay, beausires, ye find us not here;
  Our leave will we take at this tide°   *time*

And rathely° array° us to rest,   *quickly / dress, get ready* 390
For such notes° has noyed° us ere° now.   *matters / annoyed / already*
DUKE 1. Yea, certes° Lord, so hold I best,   *certainly*
For this gadling°   *low-born fellow*
    ungoodly° has grieved you.   *wickedly*
DUKE 2. Look ye bear word as ye wot,°   *know*
How well we have quit° us° this while.   *acquitted / ourselves* 395
SOLDIER 1. We,° wise men will deem it we dote[5]   *(interjection)*
But if° we make end of our note.°   *unless / business*
KING. Wend° forth, the devil in thy throat,   *go*
We find no default him to file.°   *charge (with a crime)*

Wherefore° should we flay° him or   *why / punish* 400
  fleme° him   *condemn*
We find not in rolls of record;[6]
And since that he is dumb, for to deem° him,   *judge*

---

1 *Oyez ... abate* Hear ye! If any man knows something worse about this wretch—[a man's] deeds bear witness to whomever behaves wrongly—[that man] should come boldly before the court to put an end to his (i.e., the plaintiff's) grievances.

2 *falls him go free* It befalls him to go free; he shall go free.

3 *Us likes* It is pleasing to us.

4 *worth aught in war* Becomes in any way worse.

5 *deem it we dote* Judge us foolish.

6 *rolls of record* Medieval parchment rolls of laws and other records.

Were this a good law for a lord?
Nay losels,° good-for-nothings
   unleally° ye learned all too late, disloyally
405 Go lere° thus lordings of your land such lessons to lere.° teach / learn
Repair° with your present° and say to Pilate return / present company
We grant him our power all plain° to appear, fully
And also our grievance forgive we algate° in all respects
And we grant him our grace with a good cheer.
410 As touching° this brothel° concerning / scoundrel
   that brawls° or debate, wrangles
Bid him work as he will, and work not in were.[1]
Go tell him this message from me,
And lead forth that miting,° evil° insignificant one / evilly
   mot he thee.° thrive
SOLDIER 1. My Lord, with your leave, let him be,
415 For all too long led him have we.
SOLDIER 2. What, ye sirs, my Lord, will ye see?[2]

KING. What, fellows? Take ye no tent what I tell you[3]
   And bid you? That yeoman° ye yeme.° underling / look after
SOLDIER 2. My Lord, we shall wage° him an ill way. reward
420 KING. Nay, beausires,° be not so breme.° fair sirs / impatient
Fare° softly,° for so will it seem.° behave / gently / be seemly
SOLDIER 1. Now since we shall do as ye deem,
   Adieu,° sir. goodbye (French)
KING. Dance on, in the devil's way.

The York Corpus Christi Play:
The Second Trial Before Pilate (The Judgment)

Presented by the Tilemakers, and attributed by critics to the so-called "York Realist," *The Second Trial Before Pilate* ends the series of nighttime trials and culminates with the scene of Christ's flagellation and crowning with thorns, and the order for his crucifixion. As in the other trial plays,

---

1 *work not in were* Not act suspiciously.
2 *will ye see?* Will you attend to this?
3 *Take … tell you* Do you pay no attention to what I tell you?

Christ is largely silent; he speaks only one stanza. Here, his reticence and stability strongly suggests a model of masculinity that contrasts with the macho boastfulness and jockeying for power that the other characters display. What is more, his latent power, displayed in the miracle of the banners bowing to him against the wills of the soldiers who hold them, seems only to goad his enemies into greater displays of rage and violence, even against each other. For all that it echoes episodes used for affective devotional purposes and meditation on Christ's suffering—the flagellation and crowning with thorns, especially—the play never loses sight of the irony that those who claim their power most excessively (both here and in the other trial pageants) are the true losers, while the seeming victim will ultimately be the victor.

Though the outline of the events here follows the Gospel accounts, the action is expanded with vignettes from apocryphal and literary sources, including *The Gospel of Nicodemus* and the *Northern Passion*, a Middle English narrative poem. The play is written in a twelve-line alliterative stanza rhyming ababbcbcdccd, found only in this pageant. The cacophony and violence of Christ's enemies, especially the vicious soldiers, is in part created by their sharing of stanzas, sometimes each taking single lines at a time. The effect in performance is a terrifying rapidity to their speech and actions.

Pageant 33 of the York Corpus Christi Play: The Second Trial Before Pilate (The Judgment)

CHARACTERS

Pilate
Annas
Caiaphas
Beadle
Soldier 1
Soldier 2
Soldier 3
Soldier 4
Soldier 5
Soldier 6
Jesus
Barabas

[*Enter Pilate, Annas, Caiaphas, and Beadle, accompanied by four soldiers carrying banners.*][1]

PILATE. Lordings° that are limit°   *gentlemen / bound*
    to the lore° of my liance,°   *law / allegiance*
  Ye shapely° shalks° and sheen° for to show,[2]   *handsome / men / fair*
  I charge you as your chieftain that ye chat° for no chance,[3]   *jabber*
  But look to your lord here and lere° at my law—   *learn*
5 As a duke I may damn you and draw.[4]
  Many bernes° bold are about me,   *knights*
  And what knight or knave I may know°   *discover*
  That list° not as a lord for to lout° me,   *wishes / reverence*
  I shall lere° him   *teach*
10 In the devil's name, that dastard,° to doubt° me.   *wretch / fear*
  Yea, who works any works without me,°   *i.e., my consent*
  I shall charge° him in chains to chare° him.   *put / punish*

  Therefore ye lusty° ledes° within   *hearty / men*
    this length° lapped,°   *space / enclosed*
  Do stint° of your stalking,° and of   *stop / moving about*
    stoutness° be stalling.°   *rebelliousness / stopping*
15 What traitor his tongue with tales has trapped,°   *loaded*
  That fiend for his flattering full foul shall be falling.[5]
  What broll° over-brathly° is brawling   *wretch / noisily*
  Or unsoftly° will say° in these sales,°   *loudly / talk / halls*
  That caitiff° thus carping° and calling°   *scoundrel / talking / shouting*
20 As a boy° shall be brought unto bales.°   *worthless fellow / misery*
  Therefore
  Talk not nor treat° not of tales,   *discourse*
  For that gome° that grins° or gales,°   *man / grimaces / complains*
  I myself shall him hurt full sore.

---

1 The *Ordo Paginarum* specifies "six Soldiers holding poles," as well as "four others leading Jesus from Herod," but the play text gives us only the six soldiers with speaking parts. The stage directions that have been added here for clarity reflect the logic of the play text, but they are by no means definitive.

2 *for to show* In appearance.

3 *for no chance* Under no circumstances.

4 *damn you and draw* Condemn you and draw you; *draw* to punish a person by dragging them behind a horse (usually to the place of their execution), a medieval English practice associated with punishments for treason.

5 *full foul ... falling* Will be falling into great misfortune.

ANNAS. Ye shall sit° him full sore,   *vex*   25
    what segge° will assay° you;   *man / challenge*
If he like not your lordship, that lad,°   *low-born man*
    shall ye lere° him   *teach*
As a peerless prince full prestly° to pay° you,   *quickly / please*
Or as a dearworth° duke with dints°   *worthy / blows*
    shall ye dere° him.   *harm*
CAIAPHAS. Yea, in faith ye have force for to fear° him,   *frighten*
Through your manhood and might be he marred.°   *destroyed*   30
No chivalrous chieftain may cheer° him   *console*
Fro° that churl with charge°   *when / punishment*
    ye have charred°   *chastised*
    ....[1]
In pining° pain be he parred.°   *tormenting / flayed*
ANNAS. Yea, and with scathe° of°   *injury / from*
    skelps° ill scarred   *blows*
From time that your teen° he have tasted.   *anger*   35

PILATE. Now certes,° as me seems,[2] whoso   *indeed*
    sadly° has sought you,   *seriously*
Your praising° is profitable,°   *words of praise / beneficial*
    ye prelates of peace.
Gramercy° your good word,   *many thanks for*
    and ungain shall it not you[3]
That ye will say the sooth° and for no segge° cease.   *truth / man*
CAIAPHAS. Else were it pity we appeared in this press°—   *assembly*   40
But conceive° how your knights are coming.   *perceive*
ANNAS. Yea, my Lord, that leve° ye no lease,°   *believe / lie*
I can tell you, you tides[4] some tiding°   *event, news*
Full sad.°   *serious*
PILATE. See, they bring yon broll° in a band.°   *wretch / rope*   45
We shall hear now hastily at hand
What unhap° before Herod he had.   *misfortune*

[*Enter Soldiers 1 and 2 with Jesus, his hands bound. Soldiers approach Pilate.*]

---

1   ....   A line is missing from the manuscript here.
2   *as me seems*   As it seems to me.
3   *ungain shall it not you*   It shall not be unprofitable for you.
4   *you tides*   You are owed.

SOLDIER 1. Hail, loveliest lord that ever law led°   *expounded*
    yet,°   *until now*
   Hail, seemliest under silk on everilka° side,   *each and every*
50   Hail, stateliest on steed in strength that is stead° yet,   *established*
   Hail, liberal,° hail lusty° to lords allied.[1]   *generous one / bold one*
PILATE. Welcome, what tidings this tide?[2]
   Let no language lightly° now let° you.   *unnecessarily / hinder*
SOLDIER 2. Sir Herod, sir, it is not to hide,
55   As his good friend gradely° he gret° you   *courteously / greets*
   Forever.
   In what° manner° that ever   *whatever / circumstances*
    he met° you,   *should meet*
   By himself full soon will he set you
   And say that ye shall not dissever.°   *part*

60 PILATE. I thank him full throly;° and sir, I say him the same— *sincerely*
   But what marvelous matters
    did this myron° there mell?°   *good-for-nothing / speak*
SOLDIER 1. For all the lord's°   *i.e., Herod's*
   language,° his lips, sir, were lame;   *words*
   For any speerings° in that space no speech   *inquiries*
    would he spell,°   *speak*
   But dumb as a door gan° he dwell.°   *did / remain*
65   Thus no fault in him gan he° find,   *i.e., Herod*
   For his deeds to deem° him to quell,°   *condemn / die*
   Nor in bands° him brathly° to bind;   *ropes / painfully*
   And thus
   He sent him to yourself, and assigned
70   That we, your knights, should be cleanly inclined
   And tite° with him to you to truss.°   *quickly / go*

PILATE. Sirs, harken,° hear ye not what we have upon hand?   *listen*
   Lo, how these knights carp,° that°   *speak / who*
    to the king caired.°   *went*
   Sir Herod, they say, no fault in me found,
75   He fast° me to his friendship, so friendly he fared,° *bound / behaved*

---

1 *Hail, loveliest ... allied* These "Hail" lines parody the "Hail" lyrics to Christ in the *Nativity*, *Magi*, and *Entry into Jerusalem* pageants (Pageants 14, 16, and 25), and look forward to the mocking ones the soldiers will deliver to Jesus near the end of the play.

2 *this tide* (At) this time.

Moreover, sirs, he spake°—and naught° spared—   *spoke / nothing*
Full gently to Jesus, this Jew,
And sithen° to these knights declared   *afterwards*
How faults in him found he but few
To die.   80
He tasted° him, I tell you for true,   *tried, tested*
For to dere° him he deemed° undue,°   *harm / judged / unwarranted*
And sirs, ye° soothly° say I.   *to you / truly*

CAIAPHAS. Sir Pilate, our prince, we prelates now pray you,
  Since Herod fraisted° no further this faitour°   *sought / impostor* 85
    to flay,°   *punish*
  Receive in your sale° these saws° that I say you.   *hall / words*
  Let bring[1] him to bar° and at his beard   *the judicial bar*
    shall we bay.°   *shout*
ANNAS. Yea, for and° he wend° thus by wiles° away   *if / go / trickery*
  I wot° well he work will us wonder.°   *know / mischief*
  Our meinie° he mars° that° he may;   *people / harms / as far as* 90
  With his sayings he sets them in sunder,°   *disarray*
  With sin.
  With his blore° he breeds mickle° blunder.°   *bluster / great / disturbance*
  Whilst ye have him now, hold him under°—   *i.e., under your authority*
  We shall wary° him away if he win.°   *curse / flee* 95

CAIAPHAS. Sir, no time is to tarry this traitor to taste.°   *examine*
  Against Sir Caesar himself he says,° and says   *speaks*
  All the wights° in this world work in waste   *men*
  That take° him any tribute—   *give*
    thus his teaching outrays.°   *goes beyond the limit*
  Yet further he feigns° slike° affrays,°   *contrives / such / outrages* 100
  And says that himself is God's son.
  And sir, our law ledges° and lays°   *affirms / establishes*
  In what faitour° falsehood is found   *imposter*
  Should be slain.
PILATE. For no shame[2] him to shend° will we shun.°   *kill / refuse* 105
ANNAS. Sir, witness of this wones° may be won,°   *matter / discovered*
  That will tell this without any train.°   *deception*

---

1 *Let bring* Let him be brought.
2 *For no shame* I.e., in the absence of guilt.

CAIAPHAS. I can reckon° a rabble°   *call up / crowd*
    of rinks° full right,°   *men / worthy*
  Of pert° men in press° from this place   *clever / the crowd*
    ere° I pass,°   *before / go*
110 That will witness, I warrant, the words of this wight,°   *person*
  How wickedly wrought that this wretch has:
  Simon, Jairus and Judas,
  Dathan and Gamaliel,
  Naphtali, Levi and Lucas,
115 And Amos[1] these matters can mell°   *consider*
  Together.
  These tales for true can they tell
  Of this faitour that false is and fell,°   *evil*
  And in ledging° of laws full lither.°   *expounding / deceitful*

120 PILATE. Yea, tush for your tales, they touch not intent.[2]
  These witnesses I warrant that to witness ye wage,°   *pay (bribe) them*
  Some hatred in their hearts against him have hent[3]
  And purpose° by this process to put down   *intend*
    this page.°   *boy of low status*
  CAIAPHAS. Sir, in faith, us falleth not[4] to fage,°   *deceive*
125 They are trist° men and true, that we tell you.   *honest*
  PILATE. Your swearing, sirs, swiftly ye swage,°   *stop*
  And no more in these matters ye mell° you,   *concern*
  I charge.
  ANNAS. Sir, despise not this speech that we spell you.
130 PILATE. If ye feign° slike° frauds I shall fell° you,   *contrive / such / punish*
  For me likes not your language so large.°   *excessive*

  CAIAPHAS. Our language is too large, but° your lordship   *unless*
    relieve° us.   *assist*
  Yet° we both beseech you let bring him to bar;°   *still / judicial bar*
  What points that we put forth, let your presence approve us—
135 Ye shall hear how this harlot° hields°   *wretch / behaves*
    out of harre.°   *order*
  PILATE. Yea, but be wise, witty,° and ware.°   *thoughtful / alert*

---

1 *Simon ... Amos* This list of witnesses comes from the Middle English version of the apocryphal *Gospel of Nicodemus*.
2 *touch not intent* Do not pertain to the point, are irrelevant.
3 *have hent* (They) have conceived.
4 *us falleth not* It does not occur to us.

ANNAS. Yes sir, dread you not for nothing we doubt° him.¹   *fear*
PILATE. Fetch him, he is not right° far;   *very*
  Do, beadle, busk thee about him.²
BEADLE. I am fain,°   *glad* 140
  My Lord, for to lead him or lout° him.   *reverence*
  Unclothe him, clap° him and clout° him,   *beat / strike*
  If ye bid me, I am buxom° and bain.°   *obedient / willing*

  Knights, ye are commanded with this caitiff° to cair,°   *wretch / go*
  And bring him to bar,° and so my lord bad.° *judicial bar / commanded* 145
SOLDIER 1. Is this thy message?
BEADLE.   Yea, sir.
SOLDIER 1.   Then move° thee no more, *urge*
  For we are light for to leap and lead forth this lad.
  [*Soldiers lead Jesus to the bar.*]
SOLDIER 2. Do step forth; in strife° art thou stad,°   *trouble / placed*
  I uphold° full° evil has   *contend / great*
    thee° happed.°   *to you / occurred*
SOLDIER 1. O man, thy mind is full mad,   150
  In our clutches to be clouted° and clapped°   *struck / beaten*
  And closed.°   *held*
SOLDIER 2. Thou be° lashed, lushed°   *will be / beaten*
  and lapped.°   *surrounded*
SOLDIER 1. Yea, routed,° rushed° and rapped,° *struck / beaten / hit*
  Thus thy name with noy° shall be noised.° *misfortune / spoken of* 155

SOLDIER 2. Lo, this segge° here, my sovereign, that ye for sent.   *man*
  [*Exit Soldier 1 and Soldier 2.*]
PILATE. [*To Jesus*] Well, stir not from that stead,°   *place*
  but stand still there.
  But° he shape° some shrewdness,° with shame *unless / fashion / trick*
  be he shent,°   *disgraced*
  And I will fraist,° in faith, to frayne°   *try / question*
  of his fare.°   *behavior*
  [*Banners held by the remaining soldiers shake and involuntarily lower to the ground.*]

---

1 *dread you ... doubt him* Do not think that we have no reason to fear him.
2 *busk thee about him* Set about (fetching) him.

160 CAIAPHAS. We! Out!¹ Stand may I not,² so I stare.°　　*am astonished*
ANNAS. Yea, harrow,³ of° this traitor with teen.°　　*because of / anger*
PILATE. Say rinks,° what ruth° gars° you roar?　　*men / affliction / causes*
　　Are ye wood° or witless, I ween?°　　*insane / believe*
　　What ails you?
165 CAIAPHAS. Out! Slike° a sight should be seen.　　*such*
ANNAS. Yea, alas, conquered are we clean.°　　*completely*
PILATE. We, are ye fond,° or your force° fails you?　　*insane / strength*

CAIAPHAS. Ah, sir, saw ye not this sight, how that their shafts shook,
　　And these banners to this brothel°　　*worthless fellow*
　　they bowed all on brede?⁴
170 ANNAS. Yea, these cursed knights by craft°　　*cunning*
　　let them crook°　　*bow down*
　　To worship this warlock° unworthy in weed.⁵　　*scoundrel*
PILATE. Was it duly done thus indeed?
CAIAPHAS. Yea, yea sir, ourselves we it saw.
PILATE. We! Spit on them, ill mote° they speed!⁶　　*may*
175　　Say, dastards,° the devil mote you draw,°　　*cowards / drag behind a horse*
　　How dare ye
　　These banners on brede⁷ that here blow
　　Let lout° to this lurdan° so low?　　*bow / vagabond*
　　Oh, faitours,° with falsehood how fare ye?　　*deceivers*

180 SOLDIER 3. We beseech you and those
　　seigniors° beside you sir sit,　　*lords*
　　With none of our governance° to be grievous°　　*behavior / angry*
　　and grill,°　　*furious*
　　For it lay not in our lot° these lances to let,°　　*power / prevent*
　　And this work that we have wrought it was not our will.
PILATE. Thou lies—hearest thou, lurdan?—full ill.°　　*wickedly*
185　　Well thou wot,° if thou witness° it would.　　*know / admit*
SOLDIER 4. Sir, our strength might not stable° them still,　　*keep*
　　They hielded° for aught° we could hold,　　*bowed down / all*
　　Our° unwitting.°　　*(to) our / lack of knowledge*

1　*We! Out!*　Interjections. Expressions of distress.
2　*Stand may I not*　I cannot stand.　Caiaphas—and possibly Annas, too—is miraculously forced into some position of reverence such as a bow or prostration.
3　*harrow*　Interjection. A cry for help.
4　*on brede*　On every side.
5　*unworthy in weed*　Completely unworthy; literally, unworthy in clothing.
6　*ill mote they speed*　Poorly may they prosper. (A curse.)
7　*on brede*　On every side.

SOLDIER 5. For all our force, in faith, did they fold
  As this warlock worship they would—   190
  And us° seemed, forsooth,° it unsitting.°   *to us / truly / unbecoming*

CAIAPHAS. Ah, unfriendly faitours,° full false is your fable,° *liars / story*
  This segge° with his subtlety° to his   *man / cunning*
    set° hath you seized.   *sect*
SOLDIER 6. Ye may say what you seems,[1] sir, but these
  standards° to stable   *banners*
  What freke° him enforces,° full foul   *man / attempts* 195
    shall he be feezed.°   *discomfited*
ANNAS. By the devil's nose, ye are doggedly°   *maliciously*
  diseased°—   *afflicted*
  Ah, hen-hearts,° ill hap° mote you hent.[2] *chickens, cowards / luck*
PILATE. For a whap,[3] so he whined and wheezed,
  And yet no lash to the lurdan was lent.
  Foul° fall° you!   *evil / befall* 200
SOLDIER 3. Sir, iwis,° no wiles° we have went.° *truly / tricks / attempted*
PILATE. Shamefully you sat° to be shent,° *allowed yourselves / overcome*
  Here cumbered° caitiffs° I call you.   *fainthearted / wretches*

SOLDIER 4. Since you likes not, my Lord, our language° *words*
  to leve,°   *believe*
  Let bring the biggest men that abide in this land   205
  Properly in your presence their poustie° to prove;   *strength*
  Behold° that they hield°   *see / bow*
    not from° they have them in hand.   *from that time*
PILATE. Now ye are feardest° that ever I found,   *most fearful*
  Fie[4] on your faint hearts in fere.[5]
  Stir thee, no longer thou stand   210
  Thou beadle, this bodeword° thou bear   *message*
  Through this town,
  The wightest° men unto° were° *most valiant / in the face of / danger*
  And the strongest these standards to steer,°   *handle*
  Hither° blithely° bid them be boun.° *here / eagerly / ready* 215

---

1 *what you seems* What seems to you, how things appear to you.
2 *ill hap mote you hent* May bad luck seize you. (A curse.)
3 *For a whap* As if from a blow.
4 *Fie* Interjection expressing contempt.
5 *in fere* Altogether, the lot of you.

BEADLE. My sovereign, full soon shall be served°   *carried out*
    your saw,°   *words*
    I shall bring to these banners right big men and strong.
    A company of cavels° in this country I know   *brawny men*
    That great are and grill;° to the gomes° will I gang.°   *fierce / men / go*
    [*Exit Beadle to find Soldier 1 and Soldier 2.*]
220 Say, ye ledes° both lusty° and long,°   *men / hearty / tall*
    Ye most pass° to Sir Pilate apace.°   *go / quickly*
SOLDIER 1. If we work not his will it were wrong,
    We are ready to run on a race[1]
    And rake.°   *rush*
225 BEADLE. Then tarry not, but trine on a trace[2]
    And follow me fast to his face.
SOLDIER 2. Do lead us, us likes well this lake.°   *business*

    [*Enter Beadle with Soldier 1 and Soldier 2.*]

BEADLE. Lord, here are the biggest bernes° that   *warriors*
    bield° in this burgh,°   *live / town*
    Most stately° and strong if with strength   *fierce*
    they be strained.°   *assailed*
230 Leve° me, sir, I lie not; to look[3] this land   *believe*
    through,°   *throughout*
    They are mightiest men with manhood demeaned.°   *endowed*
PILATE. Wot° thou well, or else hast   *know*
    thou weened?°   *(merely) believed*
BEADLE. Sir, I wot well without words mo.°   *more*
CAIAPHAS. In thy tale be not tainted° nor teened.°   *suspect / deceptive*
235 BEADLE. We! Nay sir, why should I be so?
PILATE. Well then,
    We shall fraist,° ere they found us far fro,[4]   *find out*
    To what game they begin for to go.[5]
    Sir Caiaphas, declare° them ye can.   *instruct*

240 CAIAPHAS. Ye lusty ledes, now lith° to my lore,°   *listen / instructions*

---

1 *run on a race* I.e., hurry.
2 *trine on a trace* Step lively.
3 *to look* If you were to look.
4 *ere ... fro* Before they go far from us, i.e., before they leave.
5 *To what game ... go* I.e., what they are capable of.

Shape° you to these shafts that so sheenly°   *take up / brightly*
  here shine.
If yon banners bow the breadth of a hair
Platly° ye be put to perpetual pine.°   *immediately / torment*
SOLDIER 1. I shall hold this as even as a line.
ANNAS. Whoso° shakes with shames he shends.° *whoever / is disgraced* 245
SOLDIER 2. I, certain, I say as for mine,
  When it settles° or sadly descends   *sinks*
  Where I stand—
  When it wrings° or wrong it wends,°   *twists / moves*
  Other bursts,° barks,° or bends— *shatters / splinters* 250
  Hardly° let hack off my hand.   *readily, quickly*

PILATE. Sirs, wait° to these wights that   *attend*
  no wiles° be wrought,   *cunning*
  They are burly and broad, their boast have they blown.° *vented*
ANNAS. To neven° of that now, sir, it needs right not,[1] *speak*
  For who cursedly° him° *badly / himself* 255
  quits,° he soon shall be known.   *conducts*
CAIAPHAS. Yea, that dastard° to death shall   *fool*
  be drawn,° *dragged behind a horse*
  Whoso faults,° he foully shall fall.   *fails*
PILATE. Now knights, since the cocks have crown,° *crowed*
  Have him hence with haste from this hall
  His ways.[2]   260
  Do stiffly° step on this stall,[3]   *boldly*
  Make a cry, and cantly° thou call   *loudly*
  Even like as Sir Annas thee says.

  ([*They cry*] *Oyez*.°)   *hear ye*

ANNAS. Oyez. Jesus, thou Jew, of gentle Jacob's kin,
  Thou netherest° of Nazareth, now *lowest* 265
  nevened° is thy name.   *called*
  All creatures thee accuse. We command thee come in° *i.e., to the bench*
  And answer to thine enemies; defend now thy fame.° *reputation*
  (*And the Beadle will recite after Annas, "Let Jesus be judged."*)

---

1 *it needs right not* It isn't necessary.
2 *His ways* On his way.
3 *on this stall* In this place.

CAIAPHAS. We! Out! We are shent all for shame,[1]
    This is wrested° all wrong, as I ween.°   *twisted / think*
270 ANNAS. For all their boasts, yon boys are to blame.
    PILATE. Slike° a sight was never yet seen.   *such*
    Come sit,
    My comfort was caught from me clean°—   *completely*
    I upstrit,° I me° might not abstain°   *rose up / myself / prevent*
275 To worship him in work° and in wit.°   *deed / mind*

CAIAPHAS. Thereof marveled we mickle° what   *greatly*
    moved° you in mind   *troubled*
    In reverence of this ribald° so rudely° to rise.   *scoundrel / suddenly*
    PILATE. I was past all my power though I pained°   *exerted*
    me° and pined,°   *myself / labored*
    I wrought not as I would° in no manner of wise.[2]   *wished*
280 But sirs, my speech well espies:°   *consider*
    Wightly° his ways let him wend,[3]   *quickly*
    Thus my doom° will duly° devise,°   *verdict / properly / prescribe*
    For I am feared him, in faith, to offend
    In sights.[4]
285 ANNAS. Then our law were laught° till° an end   *brought / to*
    To his tales if ye truly attend.
    He enchanted and charmed our knights.

CAIAPHAS. By his sorcery, sir—yourself the sooth saw—
    He charmed our chevaliers° and with   *knights*
    mischief° enchanted.   *evil*
290 To reverence him royally we rose all on row;
    Doubtless° we endure not of° this   *surely / by*
    dastard° be daunted.[5]   *fool*
    PILATE. Why, what harms° has this hathel°   *evil / man*
    here haunted?°   *practiced*
    I ken° to convict him no cause.   *know*
    ANNAS. To all gomes° he God's son him granted[6]   *men*
295 And list° not to leve° on our laws.   *desired / believe, respect*

---

1 *shent all for shame* All utterly disgraced. Once again, the gathered authorities, including
    Pilate himself, find themselves showing acts of deference to Christ against their wills.
2 *I wrought ... wise* I could not do as I wished in any way.
3 *his ways let him wend* Let him go on his way.
4 *For I am feared ... In sights* For I am afraid of offending him publicly.
5 *Doubtless ... daunted* Surely we will not stand to be intimidated by this wretch.
6 *he God's son him granted* He claimed himself to be God's son.

PILATE. Say man,
Conceives° thou not what cumberous°   *understand / serious*
   clause°   *allegation*
That this clergy accusing thee knows?
Speak, and excuse thee if thou can.

JESUS. Every man has a mouth that made is on mould°   *earth*   300
In weal° and in woe to wield at his will;[1]   *well-being*
If he govern it goodly° like as God would,   *well*
For° his spiritual speech him thar not to spill.[2]   *because of*
And what gome so[3] govern it ill,°   *badly*
Full unhendly° and ill° shall he hap;°   *roughly / evilly / fare* 305
Of ilka° tale thou talks, us until   *every*
Thou account shall,[4] thou cannot escape.
PILATE. Sirs mine,
Ye fon,° in faith, all the frap,°   *are insane / crowd*
For in this lede° no lease° can I lap,°   *man / lying / find* 310
Nor no point° to put him to pine.°   *reason / punishment*

CAIAPHAS. Without cause, sir, we come not this
   carl° to accuse him,   *fellow*
And that will° we ye wit° as well is worthy.   *wish / understood*
PILATE. Now I record well the right, ye will no rather refuse him[5]
To° he be driven to his death and deemed° to die; *until / condemned* 315
But take him unto you forthy,°   *therefore*
And like° as your law will you lere,°   *accordingly / instruct*
Deem ye his body to abye.°   *pay the price*
ANNAS. Oh, sir Pilate without any peer,
   Do way,[6]   320
Ye wot° well without any were°   *know / doubt*
Us falls not,[7] nor our fellows° in fere,°   *people / company*
To slay no man—yourself the sooth° say.   *truth*

---

1 *Every man ... his will* Every man created on earth has a mouth to wield at his will, in well-being and in woe.
2 *him thar not to spill* He need not die.
3 *what gome so* Whatever man, whoever.
4 *Of ilka ... shall* Of everything you say, you must account for to us; *us* Jesus refers to himself in the plural as part of the Trinity (God the Father, the Son, and the Holy Spirit).
5 *Now I ... refuse him* Now I understand clearly, (that) you will never release him.
6 *Do way* Say no more (of that).
7 *Us falls not* It does not fall to us, it is not allowed to us.

PILATE. Why should I deem to death, then, without deserving in deed?
325 But I have heard all wholly why in hearts° ye him hate.   *(your) hearts*
He is faultless, in faith, and so God mote me speed,[1]
I grant him my good will to gang° on his gate.°   *go / way*
CAIAPHAS. Not so sir, for well ye it wot,°   *know*
To be king he claimeth, with crown,
330 And whoso stoutly° will step°   *boldly / lay claim*
        to that state°   *status, dignity*
Ye should deem, sir, to be dung° down   *dinged, struck*
And dead.
PILATE. Sir, truly that touched° to treason,   *verged on*
And ere° I remove,° he rue°   *before / leave / repent*
        shall that reason,°   *claim*
335 And ere I stalk° or stir from this stead.   *walk*

Sir knights that are comely,° take this   *well-built*
        caitiff° in keeping,   *wretch*
Skelp° him with scourges and with scathes° him scorn. *strike / injuries*
Wrest° and wring him, too, for woe to° he be weeping,   *twist / until*
And then bring him before us as he was beforn.°   *previously*
340 SOLDIER 1. He may ban° the time he was born;   *curse*
Soon shall he be served as ye said° us.   *commanded*
ANNAS. Do wap° off his weeds° that are worn.   *tear off / clothes*
SOLDIER 2. All ready sir, we have arrayed° us.°   *prepared / ourselves*
Have done,[2]
345 To this broll° let us busk° us and   *worthless person / make ready*
        braid° us   *hasten*
As Sir Pilate has properly° prayed° us.   *personally / instructed*
SOLDIER 3. We shall set to him sadly° soon.   *earnestly*

SOLDIER 4. Let us get off his gear, God give him ill grace.
SOLDIER 1. They are tit° off tite°—lo, take there   *snatched / quickly*
        his trashes.°   *rags*
SOLDIER 3. Now knit° him in this cord.   *bind*
SOLDIER 2.   I am cant°   *eager*
350 in this case.°   *matter*
SOLDIER 4. He is bound fast—now beat on with bitter brashes.° *blows*
SOLDIER 1. Go on, leap, harry,° lordings, with lashes,   *beat (him)*
And enforce° we, this faitour,° to flay him.   *endeavor / deceiver*

---

1 *and so God mote me speed* And so may God help me.
2 *Have done* Enough.

SOLDIER 2. Let us drive° to him derfly°   *move in on / cruelly*
    with dashes,°   *blows*
All red with our routs° we array° him   *blows / adorn*   355
And rent° him.   *tear*
SOLDIER 3. For my part I am prest° for to pay him. *eager*
SOLDIER 4. Yea, send him sorrow, assay° him.   *try*
SOLDIER 1. Take him, that° I have toom° for   *so that / time*
    to tent° him.   *attend to*

SOLDIER 2. Swing to his swire° till swiftly° he sweat.   *neck / freely*   360
SOLDIER 3. Sweat may this swain° for sweight°   *fellows / force*
    of our swaps.°   *blows*
SOLDIER 4. Rush on this ribald° and him   *vagabond*
    rathely° rehete.°   *fiercely / assail*
SOLDIER 1. Rehete him I rede° you with   *advise*
    routs° and raps.°   *strikes / blows*
SOLDIER 2. For all our noy° this niggard° he naps.   *harm / weakling*
SOLDIER 3. We shall waken° him with wind of our whips.   *awaken*   365
SOLDIER 4. Now fling° to° this flatterer with flaps.°   *strike / at / blows*
SOLDIER 1. I shall heartily hit on his hips
    And haunch.
SOLDIER 2. From our skelps° not scatheless°   *blows / unscathed*
    he skips.°   *escapes*
SOLDIER 3. Yet him list not[1] lift up his lips   370
    And pray us to have pity on his paunch.

SOLDIER 4. To have pity of his paunch he proffers no prayer.
SOLDIER 1. Lord, how likes you this lake° and this lore   *game*
    that we lere° you?   *teach*
SOLDIER 2. Lo, I pull at his pilch,° I am   *garment*
    proud payer.°   *inflictor of punishment*
SOLDIER 3. Thus your cloak shall we clout°   *patch*   375
    to cleanse you and clear you.[2]
SOLDIER 4. I am strong in strife for to stir° you.   *rouse*

---

1   *him list not* It pleases him not to; he cares not to.
2   *Thus ... clear you* Thus we will patch your cloak to make you clean and pure. This line is figurative, ironic, and possibly punning: the soldiers "patch" Jesus' "cloak" by bruising and cutting his skin with their blows. Figuratively, to be "patched" is to be marred or marked (often by sin)—the opposite of "clear." Of course, Jesus is without the mark of sin; the soldiers leave only superficial, physical marks. To "clout" can also mean to cuff or strike heavily, so the soldiers strike Jesus' "cloak"—i.e., his skin—to purge and purify him of his supposed crimes.

SOLDIER 1. Thus with chops° this churl shall   *blows*
    we chasty.°   *chasten, punish*
SOLDIER 2. I trow° with this   *think*
    trace° we shall tear you.   *course of action*
SOLDIER 3. All thine untrue teachings thus taste° I,   *test, try*
380   Thou tarand.°   *chameleon-like (changeable) beast*
SOLDIER 4. I hope° I be hardy° and hasty.°   *believe / tough / fierce*
SOLDIER 1. I wot° well my weapon not waste I.   *know*
SOLDIER 2. He swoons or swelts,° I swarand.°   *is overcome / tell you*

SOLDIER 3. Let us loose him lightly,° do lay on your hands.   *quickly*
385 SOLDIER 4. Yea, for and° he die for this deed, undone are we all.   *if*
SOLDIER 1. Now unbound is this broll° and   *wretch*
    unbraced° his bands.   *untied*
SOLDIER 2. Oh, fool, how fares thou now? Foul mote thee fall![1]
SOLDIER 3. Now because he our king gan° him° call   *did / himself*
    We will kindly° him crown with a briar.   *naturally, accordingly*
390 SOLDIER 4. Yea, but first this purpure°   *purple, royal garment*
    and pall°   *robe*
    And this worthy weed° shall he wear,   *garment*
    For scorn.
SOLDIER 1. I am proud at this point to appear.
SOLDIER 2. Let us clothe him in these clothes full clear,°   *fine*
395   As a lord that his lordship has lorn.°   *lost*

SOLDIER 3. Long ere[2] thou meet slike° a   *such*
    meinie° as thou met with this morn.   *company*
SOLDIER 4. Do set him in this seat as a seemly°   *great man*
    in sales.°   *halls (i.e., court)*
SOLDIER 1. Now thring° to him   *thrust*
    throly° with this thick thorn.   *vigorously*
SOLDIER 2. Lo, it hields° to his head that°   *pushes / so that*
    the harns° out hales.°   *brains / pour*
400 SOLDIER 3. Thus we teach him to temper° his tales—   *modify*
    His brain begins for to bleed.
SOLDIER 4. Yea, his blunder° has him brought to   *trouble-making*
    these bales.°   *sorrows*
    Now reach° him and raught° him in a reed   *seize / give*
    So round,

---

1 *Foul mote thee fall!*   May evil befall you!
2 *Long ere*   It will be a long time before.

For his scepter it serves indeed.   405
SOLDIER 1. Yea, it is good enough in this need,
  Let us goodly him greet on this ground.

  Ave,[1] royal roy° and *Rex Judeorum*,[2]   *king*
  Hail,[3] comely king, that no kingdom has kenned.°   *known*
  Hail, undoughty° duke, thy deeds are dumb,°   *weak / useless*   410
  Hail, man unmighty° thy meinie°   *(too) weak / company, people*
    to mend.°   *aid*
SOLDIER 3. Hail, lord without land for to lend,°   *give (to followers)*
  Hail, king, hail knave uncunnand.°   *foolish*
SOLDIER 4. Hail, freke° without force° thee   *man / strength*
    to fend,°   *defend*
  Hail, strang,° that may not well stand   *foreigner*   415
  To strive.°   *fight*
SOLDIER 1. We, harlot!° Heave up thy hand,   *miscreant*
  And us all that thee worship°   *(mock) reverence*
    are workand°   *striving (to do)*
  Thank us, there ill mote thou thrive.[4]

SOLDIER 2. So let lead him belive° and   *quickly*   420
    leng° here no longer,   *linger*
  To Sir Pilate, our prince, our pride will we praise.
SOLDIER 3. Yea, he may sing, ere° he sleep,   *before*
    of sorrow and anger,
  For many derf° deeds he has done in his days.   *evil*
SOLDIER 4. Now wightly° let wend° on our ways,   *briskly / go*
  Let us truss° us, no time is to tarry.   *hasten*   425
SOLDIER 1. My Lord, will ye listen our lays?[5]
  Here this boy is ye bade us go bary°   *beat*
  With bats.°   *blows*
SOLDIER 2. We are cumbered° his   *encumbered*
    corpus° for to carry,   *body (Latin)*
  Many wights on him wonder° and wary.°   *are astonished / curse*   430
  Lo, his flesh all beflapped,° that fat is.   *beaten*

---

1 *Ave* Latin: Hail.
2 *Rex Judeorum* Latin: King of the Jews.
3 *Hail* In mockingly worshipping Jesus, the soldiers parody the "Hail" verses of the *Nativity*,
   Magi, and *Entry into Jerusalem* pageants (Pageants 14, 16, and 25).
4 *there ... thrive* (Or else) may you thrive poorly in that case.
5 *listen our lays* Hear what we have to say.

PILATE. Well, bring him before us as he blushes all blo;°   *livid*
          I suppose of his saying he will cease evermore.
          Sirs, behold upon height and *ecce homo*,[1]
435   Thus bound and beaten and brought you before.
          Me seems that it sues him full sore,[2]
          For his guilt on this ground is he grieved;°   *hurt*
          If you like for to listen my lore.
          In race[3]

          ....[4]

440 [PILATE.] For properly by this process will I prove
          I had no force° from this fellowship this freke° for   *power / man*
               to fend.°   *defend*
          BEADLE. Here is all, sir, that ye for send.
          Will ye wash while the water is hot?
          (*Then he washes his hands.*)
          PILATE. Now this Barabas's bands ye unbend,°   *untie*
445   With grace let him gang° on his gate°   *go / way*
          Where ye will.
          BARABAS. Ye worthy men that I here wot,°   *know*
          God increase all your comely° estate°   *worthy / status*
          For the grace ye have grant° me until.[5]   *granted*

450 PILATE. Hear the judgment of Jesus, all Jews in this stead:° *place*
          Crucify him on a cross and on Calvary him kill.
          I damn him today to die this same death,
          Therefore hang him on height upon that high hill.
          And on either side him I will°   *command*
455   That a harlot° ye hang in this haste.   *reprobate*
          Methinketh it both reason° and skill°   *reasonable / fitting*
          Amidst,° since his malice is most,   *in the middle*
          Ye hang him;

---

1 *ecce homo*   Latin: behold, the man (John 19.5).
2 *Me seems ... sore*   It seems that it (the beating) afflicts him very harshly.
3 *In race*   Uninterpretable. The stanza and the sense here is cut off by the missing manuscript
     page that follows (see next note).
4 ....   An entire leaf is missing in the manuscript here. The actions skipped over likely
     include the Pharisees' demand that Jesus be executed, and the crowd's decision to release
     Barabas. The text picks up with Pilate washing his hands of the whole affair.
5 *me until*   To me.

Then him torment, some teen° for to taste.°   *pain / feel*
More words I will not now waste,   460
But blin° not to death till ye bring him.   *rest*

CAIAPHAS. Sir, us seems in our sight that ye sadly° has said.   *gravely*
  Now knights that are cunning,° with this caitiff°   *wise / wretch*
    ye cair,°   *go*
  The life of this losel° in your list° is it laid.   *scoundrel / pleasure*
SOLDIER 1. Let us alone, my Lord, and lere us no lore.[1]   465
  Sirs, set to him sadly° and sore,°   *resolutely / seriously*
  All in cords his corse° umbecast.°   *body / bind*
SOLDIER 2. Let us bind him in bands all bare.
SOLDIER 3. Here is one, full long will it last.
SOLDIER 4. Lay on hand here.   470
SOLDIER 5. I pull to° my power° is past.   *until / strength*
  Now fast° is he, fellows, full fast;°   *bound / tightly*
  Let us stir us, we may not long stand here.

ANNAS. Draw him fast hence, deliver you, have done.[2]
  Go, do see him to death without longer delay,   475
  For dead bus° him be, needling,° be noon.   *must / necessarily*
  All mirth bus us move[3] tomorn° that we may;   *tomorrow*
  It is soothly our great Sabbath day—
  No dead bodies unburied shall be.
SOLDIER 6. We see well the sooth ye us say.   480
  We shall trail° him tite° to his tree,°   *drag / quickly / i.e., cross*
  Thus talking.
SOLDIER 4. Farewell, now wightly° wend° we.   *briskly / go*
PILATE. Now certes,° ye are a manly meinie,°   *certainly / company*
  Forth in the wild waning° be° walking.   *i.e., of the moon / to be* 485

---

1 *lere us no lore* Give us no instruction.
2 *deliver you, have done* Hurry up, get on with it.
3 *All mirth bus us move* We must be expedient.

The York Corpus Christi Play: The Crucifixion

The *Crucifixion* play was produced by the Pinners' craft, who made pins, needles, and similar items. Even though *The Crucifixion* is not about the Pinners' craft in any literal sense, the theme of work and its consequences still drives this version of the crucifixion narrative, which draws both from the Gospel accounts and from legendary and apocryphal material. The soldiers are simultaneously the Roman men who blindly obeyed orders and also late medieval workmen who seek only to get the day's work over and done with, however shoddily, and regardless of consequences. Such purposeful anachronism is a technique common to late medieval art and literature, especially drama, that seeks to make biblical narratives resonate for late medieval audiences.

Dark humor is also a common trait of medieval drama; even here, in this most violent of sacred episodes, it may be found. Critics have debated the meaning of this cringe-inducing humor. Some have argued that it lulls audience members into unthinking identification with the soldiers until they realize their complicity in the crucifixion in history, through their sin, and also in the play (most of which occurs below a crowded audience's sight-lines until the cross is raised, making them belatedly aware of the target of their laughter). Others insist that the laughter heightens the violence and makes it more terrible; thus the play participates in a form of late medieval devotion known as "affective piety," whereby the audience or reader is meant to come to an understanding of God's love through deep feeling and empathy. Still others see the potential for laughter as both mocking the ignorant soldiers and looking forward to the joy of the resurrection; the cycle as a whole is a comedy in the classical sense, after all, ending triumphantly for Jesus and the faithful.

The York *Crucifixion* is also unusual in its isolation of the crucifixion from other events and characters of the Passion narrative. Although individual crucifixion poems do this also, the York play is the only drama to depict the crucifixion process separately from Jesus' death on the cross, and to depict it without those who mourn for him, who usually include the women in his life. In isolating the crucifixion this way, the York play seems to offer a contrast between competing types of masculinity: the garrulous, social masculinity of the quick-tempered soldiers, concerned with their public reputation and status, versus the stoic, emotionally contained, individual Jesus, set apart from all others.

The *Crucifixion* is written in twelve-line stanzas rhyming ababab-cdcd. Jesus alone speaks in full stanzas. For their part, the soldiers divide stanzas between them, although at times their individual speeches span successive stanzas, masking the play's form and giving their speech a naturalistic effect.

Pageant 35 of the York Corpus Christi Play: *The Crucifixion*

CHARACTERS

Soldier 1
Soldier 2
Soldier 3
Soldier 4
Jesus

[*Enter four Soldiers with Jesus.*]

SOLDIER 1. Sir knights, take heed; hither° in hie!°   *come here / haste*
This deed on dergh° we may not draw.[1]   *aside*
Ye wot° yourself as well as I   *know*
How lords and leaders of our law
Has° given doom° that this dote° shall die.   *have / judgment / fool*   5
SOLDIER 2. Sir, all their counsel well we know.
Since we are come to Calvary[2]
Let ilka° man help now as him owe.[3]   *each*
SOLDIER 3. We are all ready, lo,
That foreward° to fulfill.   *contract, agreement*   10
SOLDIER 4. Let° hear how we shall do,   *let's*
And go we tite° there-til.°   *quickly / to it*

SOLDIER 1. It may not help here for to hone°   *delay*
If we shall any worship° win.   *honor*
SOLDIER 2. He must be dead needling°   *necessarily*   15
by none.°   *canonical hour of nones, i.e., 3 p.m.*
SOLDIER 3. Then is good time that we begin.
SOLDIER 4. Let ding° him down, then is he   *beat*
done.°   *finished, done for*

---

1 *on dergh ... draw* We may not put off.
2 *Calvary* Anglicized Latin name for the place of Jesus' crucifixion. See Luke 23.33: "And when they were come to the place which is called Calvary, they crucified him there."
3 *him owe* He ought to.

He shall not dere° us with his din.   *hurt*
SOLDIER 1. He shall be set and learnèd soon,
20   With care° to him and all his kin.[1]   *sorrow*
SOLDIER 2. The foulest death of all
       Shall he die for his deeds.
SOLDIER 3. That means cross° him we shall.   *crucify*
SOLDIER 4. Behold, so right° he redes.°   *rightly / counsels*

25 SOLDIER 1. Then to this work us must take heed,
       So that our working be not wrong.
SOLDIER 2. None other note° to neven° is need,°   *task / mention / needed*
       But let us haste him for to hang.
SOLDIER 3. And I have gone for gear, good speed,[2]
30   Both hammers and nails large and long.
SOLDIER 4. Then may we boldly do this deed.
       Come on, let kill this traitor strong.°   *villainous*
SOLDIER 1. Fair might ye fall in fere°   *together*
       That has wrought° on this wise.°[3]   *worked / way*
35 SOLDIER 2. Us needs not for to lere[4]
       Such faitours° to chastise.   *deceivers*

SOLDIER 3. Since ilka° thing is right arrayed,°   *every / set in place*
       The wiselier now work may we.
SOLDIER 4. The cross on ground is goodly° graid°   *well / prepared*
40   And bored even as it oweth° to be.   *ought*
SOLDIER 1. Look that the lad on length be laid
       And made° me° then   *secured / for me, i.e., at my command*
       unto this tree.°   *cross*
SOLDIER 2. For all his fare° he shall be flayed,°   *actions / defeated*
       That on assay° soon shall ye see.   *trial*
45 SOLDIER 3. [*To Jesus*] Come forth thou cursèd knave,
       Thy comfort soon shall keel.°   *cool, diminish*
SOLDIER 4. Thine hire° here shall thou have.   *payment, wages*
SOLDIER 1. Walk on! Now work we well.

---

1 *He shall be set ... his kin* He will be set straight and educated soon, with sorrow to him and
   all his kin (as a result).
2 *good speed* With great haste.
3 *Fair might ... on this wise* May good befall you together who have worked in this way.
4 *Us ... lere* It is not necessary for us to be taught how.

JESUS. Almighty God, my father free,°   *noble*
  Let these matters be made in mind:[1]   50
  Thou bade that I should buxom° be   *obedient*
  For Adam's plight for to be pined.°   *pained, punished*
  Here to dead° I oblige° me°   *death / obligate / myself*
  From that sin for to save mankind,
  And sovereignly beseech I thee[2]   55
  That they° for° me may favor find.   *i.e., all humankind / because of*
  And from the fiend them fend,°   *defend*
  So that their souls be safe
  In wealth° without end.   *(spiritual) well-being*
  I keep not else to crave.[3]   60

SOLDIER 1. We,[4] hark° sir knights, for Mahound's[5] blood,   *listen*
  Of Adam-kind° is all his thought.   *Adam's kin, i.e., humankind*
SOLDIER 2. The warlow° waxes° worse   *traitor, felon / grows*
    than wood,°   *insane*
  This doleful° dead° ne dreadeth he not.[6]   *sorrowful / death*
SOLDIER 3. Thou should have mind,° with   *remembrance*   65
    main and mood,[7]
  Of wicked works that thou hast wrought.
SOLDIER 4. I hope° that he had been as good   *think*
  Have ceased of saws° that he up-sought.°[8]   *sayings / made up*
SOLDIER 1. Those saws shall rue him sare[9]
  For all his sauntering° sone.°   *babbling / sound*   70
SOLDIER 2. Ill speed them[10] that° him spare   *who*
  Till he to dead be done.

---

1 *made in mind* Considered.
2 *And ... thee* Principally I beg you.
3 *I ... crave* I desire nothing more.
4 *We* Interjection. Expresses dismay, surprise, or (here) derision.
5 *Mahound* Muhammad (c. 570–632), prophet and founder of Islam. Medieval English texts often depict all non-Christian characters as worshipping or otherwise calling on Muhammad, as a way of constructing their "otherness."
6 *ne dreadeth he not* He does not dread.
7 *with main and mood* Fervently, with determination. Literally, with strength and will.
8 *I hope ... up-sought* I think that he would have been as good (i.e., better off) to have ceased those sayings that he made up.
9 *shall rue him sare* He shall sorely regret.
10 *Ill speed them* Bad luck to them.

SOLDIER 3. Have done belive° boy, and make   *quickly*
    thee boun,°   *ready*
And bend thy back unto this tree.
[*Jesus lies down on the cross.*]
75 SOLDIER 4. Behold, himself has laid him down
    In length and breadth as he should be.
SOLDIER 1. This traitor here tainted° of treason,   *convicted*
    Go fast° and fetter him then ye three; ·   *fasten*
And since he claimeth kingdom with crown,
80 Even as a king here hang shall he.
SOLDIER 2. Now, certes,° I shall not fine°   *certainly / finish*
    Ere° his right hand be fest.°   *before / fastened*
[*Soldier 2 stands at the right hand of the cross.*]
SOLDIER 3. The left hand then is mine—
    Let see who bears him best.

[*Soldier 3 stands at the left hand of the cross.*]

85 SOLDIER 4. His limbs° on length then shall I lead,   *i.e., legs*
    And even unto the bore° them bring.   *nail hole*
[*Soldier 4 stands at the foot of the cross.*]
SOLDIER 1. Unto his head I shall take heed,
    And with mine hand help him to hang.
[*Soldier 1 stands at the head of the cross.*]
SOLDIER 2. Now since we four shall do this deed
90 And meddle with this unthrifty° thing,   *unprofitable*
Let no man spare for special speed[1]
Till that we have made ending.
SOLDIER 3. This foreward° may not fail;   *agreement*
    Now are we right arrayed.°   *prepared*
95 SOLDIER 4. This boy here in our bail°   *custody*
    Shall bide° full bitter braid.°   *experience / blow*

SOLDIER 1. Sir knights, say, how work we now?
SOLDIER 2. Yis,° certes, I hope° I hold this hand,   *indeed / think*
    And to the bore I have it brought
100 Full buxomly° withouten band.°   *obediently / rope*
SOLDIER 1. Strike on then hard, for him thee bought.[2]

---

1 *Let ... speed* Let none of us refrain from all due speed.
2 *for him thee bought* For the sake of him (i.e., Jesus) who redeemed you. Refers anachron-
    istically (and thus ironically) to medieval Christian redemption theology, in which Jesus'
    death on the cross ransomed souls from eternal death.

SOLDIER 2. Yis, here is a stub° will stiffly stand,   *nail*
    Through bones and sinew it shall be sought.°   *found*
    This work is well, I will warrant.°   *guarantee*
    [*Soldier 2 nails Jesus' right hand.*]
SOLDIER 1. Say sir, how do we thore?°   *there (i.e., at left side of cross)* 105
    This bargain° may not blin.°   *business / cease*
SOLDIER 3. It fails° a foot and more,   *falls short*
    The sinews are so gone° in.   *shrunken*

SOLDIER 4. I hope° that mark amiss be bored.   *think*
SOLDIER 2. Than must he bide in bitter bale.°   *misery* 110
SOLDIER 3. In faith, it was over-scantly° scored,°   *inadequately / marked*
    That makes it foully for to fail.
SOLDIER 1. Why carp° ye so? Fast° on a cord   *talk / fasten*
    And tug him to, by top and tail.[1]
    [*Soldier 3 tugs Jesus' left hand to reach the poorly bored nail hole.*]
SOLDIER 3. Ya, thou commands lightly° as a lord;   *easily* 115
    Come help to haul, with ill hail.[2]
SOLDIER 1. Now certes° that shall I do—   *certainly*
    Full snelly as a snail.[3]
SOLDIER 3. And I shall tach° him to,°   *tack, nail / to (the cross)*
    Full nemely° with a nail.   *nimbly* 120

    [*Soldier 3 nails Jesus' left hand to the cross.*]

    This work will hold, that dare I hete,°   *promise*
    For now are fest° fast° both his hend.°   *fastened / firmly / hands*
SOLDIER 4. Go we all four then to his feet,
    So shall our space° be speedily spend.°   *time / spent*
SOLDIER 2. Let see what bourd° his bale might bete;[4]   *jest* 125
    There-to° my back now would I bend.   *to that (task)*
SOLDIER 4. Oh, this work is all unmeet!°   *unworthy*
    This boring° must all be amend.°   *the bore-holes / amended*
SOLDIER 1. Ah, peace man, for Mahound,
    Let no man wot°   *know about* 130
        that wonder.°   *marvel (i.e., poorly bored holes)*

---

1 *And tug ... tail* And tug him to (the holes) from top to bottom.
2 *with ill hail* Bad luck to you! Interjection of displeasure and impatience.
3 *Full snelly as a snail* As quickly as a snail.
4 *Let see ... bete* Let's see what jest can mend his sorrow. The soldiers treat stretching Jesus as
  a game to amuse him, picking up on the perverse game and play motif that runs throughout
  the cycle.

A rope shall rug° him down   *yank*
If° all his sinews go asunder.   *even if*

SOLDIER 2. That cord full kindly° can I   *thoroughly*
    knit,°   *tie*
    The comfort of this carl° to keel.°   *base fellow / diminish*
135 SOLDIER 1. Fast° on then fast° that all be fit,   *fasten / firmly*
    It is no force how fell° he feel.   *terrible*
    [*They pull down on his feet to stretch his body to fit the incorrectly bored*
    holes.]
    SOLDIER 2. Lug on ye both a little yet.
    SOLDIER 3. I shall not cease, as I have sele.°   *bliss*
    SOLDIER 4. And I shall fond° him for to hit.[1]   *test*
    SOLDIER 2. Oh, hail!°   *heave!*
140 SOLDIER 4.   Ho° now, I hold it well.[2]   *hold, stop*
    SOLDIER 1. Have done, drive in that nail,
    So that no fault be found.
    SOLDIER 4. This working would not fail
    If four bulls here were bound.

    [*Soldier 4 nails Jesus' feet to the cross.*]

145 SOLDIER 1. There cords have evil° increased his pains,   *evilly*
    Ere° he were till° the borings brought.   *before / to*
    SOLDIER 2. Yea, asunder are both sinews and veins
    On ilka° side, so have we sought.   *every*
    SOLDIER 3. Now all his gauds° nothing him gains,   *tricks*
150 His sauntering° shall with bale° be bought.   *babbling / woe*
    SOLDIER 4. I will go say to our sovereigns
    Of all this work how we have wrought.
    SOLDIER 1. Nay sirs, another thing
    Falls first to you and me—
155 They bade° we should him hang   *commanded*
    On height that men might see.

    SOLDIER 2. We wot° well so° their words wore,°   *know / such / were*
    But sir, that deed will do us dere!°   *harm*
    SOLDIER 1. It may not mend° for to moot° more,   *help / argue*
160 This harlot° must be hangèd here.   *base fellow, rogue*

---

1 *fond him for to hit* Test him by hitting (him).
2 *I hold it well* I think it (i.e., the task) has been done well.

SOLDIER 2. The mortise° is made   *hole (to hold base of cross)*
 fit therefore.
SOLDIER 3. Fast° on your fingers then, in fere.°   *fasten / together*
 [*They try unsuccessfully to lift the cross.*]
SOLDIER 4. I ween° it will never come thore;° *believe / (up) there*
 We four raise it not right to-year.[1]
SOLDIER 1. Say man, why carps° thou so?   *talk* 165
 Thy lifting was but light.°   *little*
SOLDIER 2. He means there must be mo°   *more (men)*
 To heave him up on height.

SOLDIER 3. Now certes,° I hope° it shall   *indeed / think*
 not need°   *be necessary*
To call to us more company.   170
Methinks° we four should do this deed   *it seems to me*
And bear him to yon° hill[2] on high.   *yonder*
SOLDIER 1. It must be done, withouten dread.
 No more, but look ye be ready,
 And this part° shall I lift and lead.   *i.e., the head* 175
 On length° he shall no longer lie.   *prone*
 Therefore now make you boun;°   *ready*
 Let bear him to yon hill.
SOLDIER 4. Then will I bear here down,°   *i.e., at the feet*
 And tend his toes until.   180

SOLDIER 2. We two° shall see till either side, *i.e., Soldiers 2 and 3*
 For else this work will wry° all wrong.   *go awry*
SOLDIER 3. We are ready.
SOLDIER 4.   Good sirs, abide,°   *wait*
 And let me first his feet up fang.°   *take*
SOLDIER 2. Why tend ye so to tales° this tide?° *talking / time* 185
SOLDIER 1. Lift up!
 [*They try again to lift the cross.*]
SOLDIER 4.   Let see!°   *watch out!*
SOLDIER 2.   Oh, lift along.°   *lengthwise*
SOLDIER 3. From all this harm he should him° hide *himself*
 And° he were God.   *if*
SOLDIER 4.   The devil him hang!

---

1 *We ... to-year* We four will not raise it right in a year.
2 *yon hill* Refers either to the pageant wagon (if the action so far has taken place on the
 ground) or the opposite end of the wagon if the nailing scene is performed on the wagon.

SOLDIER 1. For great harm have I hent°—   *received*
190   My shoulder is in-sunder.°   *asunder*
    SOLDIER 2.   And certes° I am near shent,°   *certainly / disgraced, ruined*
    So long have I borne under.[1]

    SOLDIER 3. This cross and I in two must twin,°   *separate*
    Else breaks my back in-sunder soon.
195 SOLDIER 4. Lay° down again and leave your din,   *set (the cross)*
    This deed for us will never be done.
    [*They put the cross down.*]
    SOLDIER 1. Assay° sirs, let see if any gin°   *try / device*
    May help him up without hone,°   *hesitation*
    For here should wight° men worship° win,   *strong / honor*
200   And not with gauds° all day to gone.   *games*
    SOLDIER 2. More wighter° men than we   *mightier*
    Full few I hope ye find.
    SOLDIER 3. This bargain° will not be,   *business*
    For certes° me wants wind.[2]   *certainly*

205 SOLDIER 4. So wil° of work never we wore.°   *bewildered / were*
    I hope this carl some cautels° cast.   *tricks, spells*
    SOLDIER 2. My burden set me wonder sore;
    Unto the hill I might not last.
    SOLDIER 1. Lift up, and soon he shall be thore;°   *there*
210   Therefore fast on your fingers fast.
    SOLDIER 3. Oh, lift!
    [*They try again to lift the cross.*]
    SOLDIER 1.   We,[3] lo!
    SOLDIER 4.   A little more.
    SOLDIER 2. Hold then!
    SOLDIER 1.   How now?
    SOLDIER 2.   The worst is past.
    SOLDIER 3. He weighs a wicked weight.
    [*They reach the place where the cross will be erected on the "hill."*]
    SOLDIER 2. So may we all four say,
215   Ere° he was heaved on height   *already*
    And raised in this array.°   *manner*

---

1   *borne under*   Borne under the weight of the cross.
2   *me wants wind*   I am lacking breath; i.e., I need to catch my breath.
3   *We*   Interjection. Expresses dismay, surprise, or derision; or, as here, calls for attention.

SOLDIER 4. He made us stand° as any stones,   *motionless*
          So boistous° was he for to bear.   *awkward, huge*
SOLDIER 1. Now raise him nemely° for the nones[1]   *nimbly*
          And set him° by this mortise here,   *i.e., Jesus on the cross* 220
          And let him fall in all at once,
          For certes° that pain shall have no peer.°   *certainly / equal*
SOLDIER 3. Heave up!
          [*They raise the cross.*]
SOLDIER 4.   Let down, so all his bones
          Are asunder now on sides sere.[2]
          [*They drop the cross into the mortise.*]
SOLDIER 1. This falling was more fell°   *wicked, harmful* 225
          Than all the harms he had.
          Now may a man well tell°   *count*
          The least lith° of this lad.   *limb*

SOLDIER 3. Methinketh this cross will not abide°   *hold steady*
          Ne° stand still in this mortise yet.   *nor* 230
SOLDIER 4. At the first time was it made over-wide;
          That makes it° wave, thou may well wit.°   *i.e., the cross / perceive*
SOLDIER 1. It shall be set° on ilka° side   *stabilized / every*
          So that it shall no further flit.°   *move from side to side*
          Good wedges shall we take this tide°   *time* 235
          And fast the foot,° then is all fit.   *i.e., of the cross*
SOLDIER 2. Here are wedges arrayed°   *laid out*
          For that, both great and small.
SOLDIER 3. Where are our hammers laid
          That we should work withal?°   *with* 240

SOLDIER 4. [*Picking up hammer.*] We have them here even at our hand.
SOLDIER 2. [*Picking up wedge.*] Give me this wedge, I shall it in drive.
SOLDIER 4. [*Picking up another wedge.*] Here is another
          yet ordand.°   *ordained, prepared*
SOLDIER 3. Do take° it me° hither belive.°   *give / to me / at once*
SOLDIER 1. Lay on then fast.
SOLDIER 3.   Yis, I warrant.   245
          I thring° them sam,° so mote° I thrive.   *knock / together / must*
          Now will this cross full stably stand,
          All° if he rave they° will not rive.°   *even / i.e., the wedges / split*

---

1 *for the nones* At once.
2 *on sides sere* In many sections.

SOLDIER 1. [*To Jesus*] Say sir, how likes you now,
250 This work that we have wrought?
SOLDIER 4. [*To Jesus*] We pray you say us how
      Ye feel, ere° faint ye ought.°   *before / need to*

JESUS. [*To audience*] All men that walk by way or street,
      Take tent° ye shall no travail tine.[1]   *heed*
255 Behold mine head, mine hands, and my feet,
      And fully feel now, ere ye fine,°   *finish*
      If any mourning may be meet,°   *matched with*
      Or mischief° measured° unto mine.   *misfortune / compared*
      [*He prays.*] My father, that all bales°   *evils, woes*
         may bete,°   *make better, put right*
260 Forgive these men that do me pine.°   *pain*
      What they work wot° they not;[2]   *know*
      Therefore, my father, I crave,
      Let never their sins be sought,°   *examined*
      But see their souls to save.

265 SOLDIER 1. We, hark, he jangles° like a jay.   *chatters*
      SOLDIER 2. Methinks he patters[3] like a pie.°   *magpie*
      SOLDIER 3. He has been doing all this day,
         And made great moving° of mercy.   *prompting*
      SOLDIER 4. Is this the same that gan° us° say   *did / to us*
270 That he was God's son almighty?
      SOLDIER 1. Therefore he feels full fell° affray,°   *cruel / assault*
         And deemèd° this day for to die.   *(is) judged*
      SOLDIER 2. Vah! qui destruis templum![4]
      SOLDIER 3. His saws were so, certain.°   *certainly*
275 SOLDIER 4. And sirs, he said to some
         He might raise it° again.   *i.e., the temple*

---

1 *Take tent ... tine* Take heed you do not lose the work (of my suffering); i.e., do not lose the
   meaning and message of this.
2 *Forgive ... wot they not* See Luke 23.34: "And Jesus said: Father, forgive them, for they
   know not what they do."
3 *patters* Chatters; but also, recites a prayer. Play on the Latin version of the Lord's Prayer,
   which begins "Pater noster." Often used derogatively to mean mumbling prayers indistinctly.
4 *Vah! qui destruis templum!* Latin: Hah! You who destroy the temple! See Mark 15.29:
   "And they that passed by blasphemed him, wagging their heads, and saying: Vah, thou that
   destroyest the temple of God, and in three days buildest it up again." See also Matthew
   27.40.

SOLDIER 1.   To muster that he had no might,
    For all the cautels° that he couth° cast.   *spells / knew how to*
    All if he were in word so wight,°   *strong*
    For° all his force now he is fest.°   *despite / fastened, caught*   280
    As Pilate[1] deemed is done and dight,°   *dealt with*
    Therefore I rede° that we go rest.   *counsel, advise*
SOLDIER 2.   This race° mun° be rehearsed° right, *action / must / reported*
    Through the world both east and west.
SOLDIER 3.   Yea, let him hang here still   285
    And make moues° on° the moon.   *grimaces / at*
SOLDIER 4.   Then may we wend° at will.   *go*
SOLDIER 1.   Nay good sirs, not so soon,

    For certes us needs another note:°   *advantage*
    This kirtle° would I of you crave.   *tunic (i.e., Jesus' tunic)*   290
SOLDIER 2.   Nay, nay sir, we will look by lot°   *lottery, draw*
    Which of us four falls° it to have.   *chances*
SOLDIER 3.   I rede° we draw cut° for this coat.   *counsel / lots, straws*
    Lo, see how soon°—all sides to save.°   *quickly / be fair to*
SOLDIER 4.   The short cut shall win, that well ye wot,°   *know*   295
    Whether it fall to knight or knave.
SOLDIER 1.   Fellows, ye thar° not flyte,°   *need / argue*
    For this mantle is mine.
SOLDIER 2.   Go we then hence tite,°   *quickly*
    This travail° here we tine.°   *labor / lose*   300

---

1   *Pilate* Pontius Pilate, Roman prefect (governor) of Judea (26–36? CE), before whom Jesus
was brought for judgment in all four Gospel accounts and in the plays preceding this one.
According to the Gospel accounts, he evaded responsibility for Jesus' final judgment, but he
would have overseen executions nevertheless, and so the crucifixion is "done and dight" as
"Pilate deemed."

The York Corpus Christi Play: The Death of Christ

The Butchers' *Death of Christ* play has been attributed to the so-called "York Realist" on the basis of its alliteration, although some critics contend that the diction and the use of a three-beat line rather than a longer four-beat alliterative line do not match the Realist's typical style. The stanza form—thirteen lines rhyming ababbcbcdeeed—is also different from the playwright's other forms. What is more, the play shows less interest in psychologically-driven conflicts than do the trial plays. Some similarities remain, however. This play begins with the boasts of an authority figure (as do the trial plays), and Pilate, Annas, and Caiaphas play their usual roles: Pilate contends that Jesus did not deserve his fate and claims that he, Pilate, is not to blame, while the Pharisees continue to insist on the various laws that Jesus has broken, especially in treasonously claiming himself son of God and a king. From there, however, the play moves into more contemplative vignettes. It draws on a lyric mode in presenting the intense emotional experience of one character at a time, from Christ's own death, to Mary's mourning, to the blind soldier Longinus's being forced to pierce Jesus with a spear, only to be cured of his blindness (which miracle then inspires his heartfelt conversion).

The mixed modes of the play may in large part be accounted for by its mixed sources. The basic narrative hews closely to the biblical account, but expands the roles of the faithful. Longinus's story derives from the fourth-century, apocryphal *Gospel of Nicodemus*, which circulated in a Middle English translation. Mary remains silent in the Gospel accounts, but here, her heart-wrenching laments draw on vernacular lyric poetry and Latin liturgical drama and music. Mary's mourning, Longinus's miraculous experience and conversion (followed by the Centurion's conversion), and Joseph's and Nicodemus's care of Christ's body, all draw the audience into the play, with each of these characters potentially serving as figures of the believer's own affective and spiritual relation to Christ's sacrifice.

The Butchers were a relatively prosperous guild, although not necessarily a prestigious one. They occupied a part of the city now called the Shambles (from a word meaning a table, stall, or place to sell meat)—still a well-preserved medieval street and one of York's tourist attractions. A simple image search on the web of "The Shambles York" will turn up hundreds of views of the street.

Pageant 36 of the York Corpus Christi Play: *The Death of Christ*

CHARACTERS

Pilate
Caiaphas
Annas
Jesus
Mary
John
Mary Cleophas[1]
Thief on Left
Thief on Right
Boy
Longinus
Soldier
Centurion
Nicodemus
Joseph (of Arimathea)

[Enter Pilate, Caiaphas, and Annas. Christ and thieves on crosses.]

PILATE. Cease, seigniors,° and see what I say,	*worthy men*
Take tent[2] to my talking entire.°	*entirely*
Devoid° all this din here this day,	*end*
And fall to my friendship in fere.[3]	
Sir Pilate, a prince without peer,	5
My name is full namely° to neven,°	*precisely / utter*
And doomsman,° full dearworth° and dear,	*judge / worthy*
Of gentlest Jewry full even[4]	
Am I.	
Who makes° oppression	*causes* 10
Or does transgression,	
By my discretion	
Shall be deemed° duly to die.	*judged*
To die shall I deem° them, to dead,°	*judge / death*

---

1 *Mary Cleophas* The *Ordo Paginarum* identifies this Mary as "Mary the mother of James" and also lists "Mary Salome" as present, but the latter has no lines in the surviving play text.
2 *Take tent* Pay attention.
3 *in fere* Altogether; i.e., all of you.
4 *full even* Certainly, indeed.

15	Those rebels that rule° them°	*govern, control / themselves*
	unright.°	*badly*
	Who that to yon hill[1] will take heed	
	May see there the sooth° in his sight,	*truth*
	How doleful° to death they are dight°	*cruelly / put*
	That list° not our laws for to lere.°	*care / learn*
20	Lo, thus by my main° and my might	*strength*
	Those churls° shall I chastise and chare,°	*wretches / punish*
	By law.	
	Ilka° felon false	*each*
	Shall hang be the halse.°	*neck*
25	Transgressors als°	*also*
	On the cross shall be knit° for to know.[2]	*bound*
	To know shall I knit them on cross,	
	To shend° them with shame shall I shape.°	*destroy / endeavor*
	Their lives for to leese° is no loss,	*destroy*
30	Such tyrants° with teen° for to trap.	*outlaws / misery*
	Thus leally° the law I unlap°	*faithfully / reveal*
	And punish them piteously.°	*mercilessly*
	Of Jesus I hold° it unhap°	*consider / unlucky*
	That he on yon hill hung so high	
35	For guilt.	
	His blood to spill	
	Took ye you till,[3]	
	Thus was your will	
	Full spitously° to speed he were spilt.[4]	*maliciously*
40	CAIAPHAS. To spill° him we spoke in a speed,°	*destroy / haste*
	For falsehood he followed in fay.[5]	
	With frauds our folk gan° he feed	*did*
	And labored to lere° them his lay.°	*teach / doctrine*

---

1 *yon hill* Yonder hill, i.e., Calvary, where Christ and the two thieves hang on crosses. The repeated references to "yon" suggest that the crosses are situated on the pageant wagon while Pilate, Caiaphas, and Annas enter from the "platea," or ground level, or that Pilate and the Pharisees are at one end of the wagon, while the crosses are at the other. Pilate's opening address to "seigniors," bidding them to listen to him, may be directed at both the Pharisees and the York audience.

2 *knit for to know* I.e., made to understand.

3 *Took ye you till* You took upon yourselves.

4 *to speed he were spilt* To hasten his death.

5 *in fay* In faith, truly.

ANNAS. Sir Pilate, of peace we you pray—
    Our law was full like° to be lorn.°   *likely / destroyed*   45
    He saved° not our dear Sabbath day,   *observed*
    And that—for to scape° it—were a scorn,°   *escape, ignore / scandal*
    By law.
PILATE. Sirs, before your sight,
    With all my might   50
    I examined him right,°   *carefully*
    And cause° none in him could   *i.e., cause for conviction*
       I know.°   *discover*

CAIAPHAS. Ye know well the cause sir, in case;°   *(this) case*
    It touched° treason untrue.°   *concerned / disloyal*
    The tribute to take or to trace°   *seek out*   55
    Forbade he, our bale° for to brew.°   *sorrow / stir up*
ANNAS. Of japes° yet jangled° yon Jew,   *nonsense / babbled*
    And cursedly he called him° a king.   *himself*
    To deem° him to death it is due,   *judge*
    For treason it touches, that thing,   60
    Indeed.
CAIAPHAS. Yet principal,
    And worst of all,
    He gart him call[1]
    God's son—that° foul° mote° him speed.[2]   *for that / foully / may*   65

PILATE. He speeds for to spill in space,[3]
    So wonderly° wrought° is your will.   *astonishingly / performed*
    His blood shall your bodies embrace,[4]
    For that° have ye taken you till.[5]   *that which, i.e., his death*
ANNAS. That foreward° full fain° to fulfill   *promise / eagerly*   70
    Indeed shall we dress us[6] bedene.°   *forthwith*
    Yon losel° him likes full ill,[7]   *wretch*
    For turned is his trants° all to teen,°   *tricks / misery*
    I trow.°   *believe*

---

1 *He gart him call* He caused himself to be called.
2 *foul mote him speed* A curse: foully may he prosper.
3 *He speeds ... space* He will quickly die in a short space of time.
4 *His blood ... embrace* I.e., his blood will be on your heads.
5 *have ye taken you till* You have undertaken.
6 *dress us* Endeavor.
7 *him likes full ill* Is in a miserable state.

75 CAIAPHAS. He called him° king,   *himself*
    Ill joy[1] him wring.°   *torment*
    Yea, let him hang
    Full madly on the moon for to mow.°   *make faces*

    ANNAS. To mow on the moon has he meant.[2]
80   We![3] Fie on thee, faitour,° in fay![4]   *deceiver*
    Who, trows thou,[5] to thy tales took tent?° *heed*
    Thou saggard,° thyself gan° thou say,   *sagging one / did*
    The temple destroy thee today,
    By the third day were done ilka deal
85   To raise it thou should thee array.[6]
    Lo, how° was thy falsehood to feel,°   *so, thus / manifest*
    Foul fall° thee.   *befall*
    For thy presumption
    Thou hast thy warison.°   *reward*
90   Do fast come down,
    And a comely king shall I call thee.

    CAIAPHAS. I call thee a coward to ken,°   *know (i.e., blatant)*
    That marvels and miracles made.
    Thou mustered° among many men;   *showed (your tricks)*
95   But, brothel,° thou bourded° too broad.°   *wretch / jested / broadly*
    Thou saved them from sorrows, they said—
    To save now thyself let us see.
    God's son if thou gradely° be graid,°   *truly / made to be*
    Deliver thee down off that tree°   *i.e., cross*
100 Anon.°   *immediately*
    If thou be found
    To be God's son,
    We shall be bound
    To trow° on thee truly, ilkone.°   *believe / every one (of us)*

105 ANNAS. Sir Pilate, your pleasance° we pray,   *good will*
    Take tent° to our talking this tide,°   *heed / time*

---

1 *Ill joy* I.e., sorrow, suffering.
2 *has he meant* It is appropriate for him.
3 *We!* Interjection expressing derision or contempt (as here), distress, or surprise.
4 *Fie … in fay!* Curse you, deceiver, truly!
5 *trows thou* Do you think.
6 *The temple … array* Were you to destroy the temple today, by the time the third day had passed completely, you would arrange to raise it again.

And wipe ye yon writing[1] away,
It is not best it abide.°   *remain*
It sits° you to set it aside   *behooves*
And set that° he said in his saw,°   *what / teachings* 110
As he° that was prent° full of pride: *one / marked*
'Jews' king am I,' comely to know,
Full plain.

PILATE. *Quod scripsi, scripsi.*[2]
    Yon same wrote I;   115
    I bide thereby,[3]
    What° gadling° will grudge°   *whatever / scoundrel / complain*
       thereagain.°   *against that*

JESUS. Thou man that of miss° here has meant,°   *sin / intended*
    To me tent° entirely thou take.   *heed*
    On rood° am I ragged° and rent,°   *cross / broken / torn* 120
    Thou sinful soul, for thy sake;
    For thy miss,° amends will I make.   *sins*
    My back for to bend here I bide,°   *stay*
    This teen° for thy trespass° I take.   *suffering / offences, sins*
    Who could thee more kindness have kid°   *shown* 125
    Than I?
    Thus for thy good
    I shed my blood.
    Man, mend thy mood,°   *will*
    For full bitter° thy bliss mun° I buy.   *bitterly / must* 130

    [*Enter Mary and John.*]

MARY. Alas for my sweet son I say,
    That dolefully° to death thus is dight.°   *grievously / put*
    Alas, for full lovely he lay
    In my womb, this worthily° wight.°   *beloved / man*
    Alas, that I should see this sight   135
    Of my son so seemly° to see.   *fair*
    Alas, that this blossom so bright
    Untruly° is tugged° to this tree.°   *unnaturally / nailed / i.e., the cross*

---

1   *yon writing*   Refers to what is written above Jesus on the cross. Pilate has written "Jesus of Nazareth, King of the Jews," but the Pharisees want it made plainer that this is only Jesus' claim; see John 19.20–22.

2   *Quod scripsi, scripsi*   Latin: What I have written, I have written (John 19.22).

3   *I bide thereby*   I stand by that.

Alas,

140 My Lord, my lief,°   *dear*
With full great grief
Hangs as a thief.
Alas, he did never trespass.

JESUS. Thou woman, do way of[1] thy weeping,
145 For me may thou nothing amend.°   *change*
My father's will to be working,
For mankind my body I bend.
MARY. Alas, that thou likes° not to lend,°   *wishes / stay (with us)*
How should I but weep for thy woe?
150 To care° now my comfort is kenned.°   *distress / consigned*
Alas, why should we twin° thus in two   *part*
Forever?
JESUS. Woman, instead of me,
Lo, John thy son shall be.
155 John, see to thy mother free,°   *worthy*
For my sake do thou thy dever.°   *duty*

MARY. Alas son, sorrow and site,°   *grief*
That me were closed in clay.[2]
A sword of sorrow me smite,
160 To death I were done this day.[3]
JOHN. Ah, mother, so shall ye not say.
I pray you be peace° in this press,°   *quiet / crowd*
For with all the might that I may
Your comfort I cast° to increase,   *endeavor*
165 Indeed.
Your son am I,
Lo, here ready;
And now forthy°   *therefore*
I pray you hence for to speed.°   *hasten*

170 MARY. My steven° for to stead° or to steer,°   *voice / steady / control*
How should I, such sorrow to see,
My son that is dearworthy° and dear   *beloved*
Thus doleful° a death for to die?   *miserable*

---

1 *do way of* Do away with, cease.
2 *That me ... clay* If only I were buried in the earth; I wish I were buried in the earth.
3 *A sword ... this day* May a sword of sorrow strike me so that I might be put to death this day.

JOHN. Ah, dear mother, blin° of this blee,°   stop / behavior
  Your mourning it may not amend.   175
MARY CLEOPHAS. Ah, Mary, take trist° unto thee,   hope
  For succor° to thee will he send   comfort
  This tide.°   time (i.e., soon)
JOHN. Fair mother, fast
  Hence let us cast.°   go   180
MARY. Till he be passed°   dead
  Will I busk° here bainly° to bide.°   seek / humbly / remain

JESUS. With bitterful° bale° have I bought,°   intense / suffering / paid for
  Thus, man, all thy miss° for to mend.   sin
  On me for to look let° thou not,   cease   185
  How bainly° my body I bend.   willingly
  No wight° in this world would have wend°   person / endured
  What sorrow I suffer for thy sake.
  Man, cast° thee my kindness be kenned,°   endeavor / made known
  True tent° unto me that thou take,   heed   190
  And trest.°   trust
  For foxes their dens have they,
  Birds have their nests to pay,[1]
  But the son of man this day
  Has naught° on his head for to rest.[2]   nothing 195

THIEF ON LEFT. If thou be God's son so free,°   noble
  Why hang thou thus on this hill?
  To save now thyself let us see,
  And us now, that speeds for to spill.[3]
THIEF ON RIGHT. Man, stint° of thy steven° and be still, stop / noise 200
  For doubtless thy God dreads thou not.[4]
  Full well are we worthy theretill,[5]
  Unwisely wrong have we wrought,
  Iwis.°   indeed
  None° ill° did he   no / evil 205
  Thus for to die.

---

1 *to pay* At their liking.
2 *on his head for to rest* To rest his head on. See Matthew 8.20.
3 *that speeds for to spill* Who will soon be killed.
4 *dreads thou not* You do not dread.
5 *Full well ... theretill* We full deserve it (i.e., crucifixion).

Lord, have mind of me[1]
When thou art come to thy bliss.

JESUS. Forsooth° son, to thee shall I say,   *truly*
210   Since thou from thy folly will fall,°   *desist*
With me shall dwell now this day,
In Paradise, place principal.[2]
Eloi, Eloi![3]
My God, my God full free,
215   *Lama sabacthani?*[4]
Whereto° forsook thou me   *why*
In care?°   *misery*
And I did never ill
This deed for to go till,[5]
220   But be it at thy will.
Ah, me thirsts sore.[6]

BOY. A drink shall I dress° thee, indeed,   *prepare (for)*
A draught that is full daintily° dight.°   *carefully / prepared*
Full fast shall I spring for to speed,
225   I hope° I shall hold° that° I have hight.°   *expect / do / as / promised*
CAIAPHAS. Sir Pilate that most is of might,
Hark, 'Elias'° now heard I him cry.   *Elijah*
He weens° that that worthily° wight°   *thinks / good / man*
In haste for to help him in hie[7]
230   In his need.
PILATE. If he do so
He shall have woe.
ANNAS. He were° our foe   *would be*
If he dress him to do us[8] that deed.

---

1 *have mind of me*   Remember me.
2 *place principal*   Best of all places.
3 *Eloi, Eloi!*   Aramaic: My God, my God! See Mark 15.34. Rendered as "Eli, Eli!" in Matthew 27.46.
4 *Lama sabacthani*   Hebrew: Why have you forsaken me? See Mark 15.34 and Matthew 27.46. Quotes Psalm 21.2, as numbered in the Latin Vulgate and Douay-Rheims English bible (22.2 in modern and Protestant bibles).
5 *for to go till*   Thus to undergo.
6 *me thirsts sore*   I am very thirsty.
7 *In haste ... in hie*   (Comes) in haste to help him forthwith.
8 *dress him to do us*   Tries to perform.

BOY. That deed for to dress if he do,   235
    In certes[1] he shall rue° it full sore.   *repent*
    Nevertheless, if he like it not, lo,
    Full soon may he cover° that care.   *be released from*
    Now sweet sir, your will if it were,
    A draught here of drink have I dressed,°   *prepared*   240
    To speed for no spence° that ye spare,[2]   *expense*
    But boldly ye bib° it for the best.   *drink*
    Forwhy°   *because*
    Eisell° and gall   *vinegar*
    Is menged° withal;°   *mingled / with the rest* 245
    Drink it ye shall—
    Your lips I hold° them full dry.   *consider*

JESUS. Thy drink it shall do me no dere,°   *harm*
    Wit° thou well, thereof° will I none.   *understand / of that*
    Now father, that formed all in fere,[3]   250
    To thy most might make I my moan:°   *lament*
    Thy will have I wrought in this wone,°   *place*
    Thus ragged° and rent° on this rood,°   *broken / torn / cross*
    Thus dolefully° to death have they done.   *cruelly*
    Forgive them by grace that is good,   255
    They ne wot° not what it was.[4]   *know*
    My father, hear my boon,°   *request*
    For now all thing is done.
    My spirit to thee right soon
    Commend I, *in manus tuas.*[5]   260

[*Jesus dies.*]

MARY. Now dear son, Jesus so gent,°   *gentle, gracious*
    Since my heart is heavy as lead,
    One word would I wit° ere° thou went.   *know (hear) / before*
    Alas, now my dear son is dead,
    Full ruefully° reft° is my rede.°   *cruelly / taken / support* 265
    Alas for my darling so dear.

---

1   *In certes*   Certainly.
2   *To speed ... spare*   To hasten (things), don't be sparing because of the expense.
3   *in fere*   Together, entirely.
4   *They ne wot ... was*   They did not know what they were doing.
5   *in manus tuas*   Latin: into your hands (Luke 23.46).

JOHN. Ah, mother, ye hold up your head,
  And sigh not with sorrows so sere,°   *many*
  I pray.
270 MARY CLEOPHAS. It does her pine°   *pain*
  To see him tine.°   *die*
  Lead we her hyne,°   *away*
  This mourning help her ne may.[1]

CAIAPHAS. Sir Pilate, perceive, I you pray,
275 Our customs to keep well ye can.
  Tomorn° is our dear Sabbath day,   *tomorrow*
  Of mirth must us move ilka° man.   *every*
  Yon warlocks° now wax° full wan° *scoundrels / grow / pale*
  And needs must they buried be.
280 Deliver° their death sir, and then   *hasten*
  Shall we sue° to our said solemnity°   *proceed / feast*
  Indeed.
PILATE. It shall be done
  In words fone.°   *few*
285 Sir knights, go soon,
  To yon harlots° you hendly° take heed. *reprobates / fittingly*

  Those caitiffs° thou kill with thy knife;   *wretches*
  Deliver,° have done they were dead.[2]   *make haste*
SOLDIER. My Lord, I shall length° so their life *prolong*
290 That those brothels° shall never bite bread. *good-for-nothings*
PILATE. Sir Longinus,[3] step forth in this stead;° *place*
  This spear, lo, have hold in thy hand.
  To Jesus thou rake° forth, I rede,°   *go / advise*
  And stead° not, but stiffly° thou stand *delay / boldly*
295 A stound.°   *while*
  In Jesus' side
  Shove it this tide.°   *time*
  No longer bide,°   *wait*
  But gradely° thou go to the ground.° *promptly / place*

---

1 *help her ne may* Cannot help her.
2 *have done they were dead* See to it that they are killed.
3 *Longinus* The name traditionally given to the soldier who pierces Jesus' side in John 19.34
  (where he is unnamed). He is first named and his story expanded in the apocryphal *Gospel of*
  Nicodemus, a fourth-century text that exerted great influence on medieval art and literature.

[Longinus stabs Jesus' side with a lance, perhaps guided by the Centurion who speaks after him. Blood issues forth. Longinus regains his sight.]

LONGINUS. Oh maker unmade, full of might,   300
  Oh Jesus so gentle° and gent°   *noble / courteous, gracious*
  That suddenly has sent me my sight,
  Lord, lofing° to thee be it lent.°   *praise / given*
  On rood° art thou ragged° and rent,°   *cross / broken / torn*
  Mankind for to mend of his miss.°   *sin*   305
  Full spitously° spilt° is and spent°   *maliciously / spilled / let*
  Thy blood, Lord, to bring us to bliss
  Full free.
  Ah, mercy, my succor,
  Mercy, my treasure,   310
  Mercy, my savior,
  Thy mercy be marked in me.

CENTURION. O wonderful worker iwis,°   *indeed*
  This weather is waxen° full wan.°   *grown / dark*
  True token° I trow° that it is   *sign / believe*   315
  That mercy is meant unto man.
  Full clearly conceive thus I can
  No cause in this corse° could they know,   *man*
  Yet doleful° they deemed° him then   *cruelly / judged*
  To lose thus his life by their law,   320
  No right.[1]
  Truly I say,
  God's son verray°   *true*
  Was he this day,
  That dolefully to death thus is dight.°   *put*   325

JOSEPH.[2] That lord leal,° ay-lasting° in land,   *true / everlasting*
  Sir Pilate, full prest° in this press,°   *bold / crowd, gathering*
  He save thee by sea and by sand,
  And all that is dearworth° on dais.[3]   *worthy*
PILATE. Joseph, this is leally,° no less;   *loyally (spoken)*   330

---

1 *No right* Unjustly.

2 *JOSEPH* This is Joseph of Arimathea, a disciple (not Joseph the carpenter, Jesus' foster-father).

3 *That lord ... on dais* Sir Pilate, (you who are) very bold in this gathering, may that true lord, everlasting, save thee by sea and by sand (i.e., everywhere), as well as all who are worthy on (the) dais. Joseph shows conventional deference to Pilate in flattering him.

To me art thou welcome, iwis.°   *indeed*
Do say me the sooth° ere° thou cease,   *truth / before*
Thy worthily° will, what it is,   *worthy*
Anon.°   *at once*

335 JOSEPH. To thee I pray,
Give me in hie°   *haste*
Jesus' body,
In gree° it for to grave° all alone.   *seemly manner / bury*

PILATE. Joseph sir, I grant thee that gest,°   *action*
340 I grudge not to graith° him in grave.   *bury*
Deliver,° have done he were dressed,°   *hasten / dealt with*
And sue,° sir, our Sabbath to save.°   *proceed / observe*
JOSEPH. With hands and heart that I have
I thank thee in faith for my friend.
345 God keep thee thy comfort to crave,[1]
For wightly° my way will I wend°   *quickly / go*
In hie.°   *haste*
To do that deed
He° be my speed°   *i.e., Jesus / aid*
350 That arms gan° spread,   *did*
Mankind by his blood for to buy.°   *redeem*

NICODEMUS. Well met, sir. In mind gan I move[2]
For Jesus that judged was ungent.°   *unjustly*
Ye labored for license° and leave   *permission*
355 To bury his body on bent?[3]
JOSEPH. Full mildly that matter I meant,
And that for to do will I dress.°   *attend to*
NICODEMUS. Both sam° I would that we went   *together*
And let° not for more nor for less,[4]   *hesitate*
360 · Forwhy°   *because*
Our friend was he,
Faithful and free.°   *noble*
JOSEPH. Therefore go we
To bury that body in hie.°   *haste*

---

1 *God keep ... crave* God grant you the comfort you desire.
2 *In mind gan I move* My mind was moved.
3 *on bent* Afield.
4 *not for more nor for less* Not for anything.

All mankind may mark° in his mind   *ponder*   365
To see here this sorrowful sight.
No falseness in him could they find
That dolefully to death thus is dight.°   *put*
NICODEMUS. He was a full worthy wight,°   *man*
   Now blemished° and bolned° with blood.   *wounded / swollen*   370
JOSEPH. Yea, for° that he mustered° his might,   *because / manifested*
   Full falsely they felled° that food°[1]   *destroyed / person*
   I ween.
   Both back and side
   Has wounds wide,   375
   Forthy° this tide°   *therefore / time*
   Take we him down us between.

NICODEMUS. Between us take we him down
   And lay him on length on this land.
JOSEPH. This reverent° and rich of renown,   *holy one*   380
   Let us hold him and halse° him with hand.   *embrace*
   A grave have I gart here be ordained[2]
   That never was in note,° it is new.   *use*
NICODEMUS. To this corse° it is comely°   *body / properly*
     accordand,°   *suitable*
   To dress him with deeds full due   385
   This stound.°   *moment*
JOSEPH. A sudary,°   *shroud*
   Lo, here have I.
   Wind him forthy,°   *therefore*
   And soon shall we grave° him in ground.   *bury*   390

NICODEMUS. In ground let us grave him and go;
   Do lively° let us lay him alone.   *quickly*
   Now savior of me and of mo,°   *more*
   Thou keep us in cleanness° ilkone.°   *purity / everyone*
JOSEPH. To thy mercy now make I my moan:°   *lament*   395
   As savior by sea and by sand,
   Thou guide me that my grief be all gone,

---

1   *food*   Here this word means "person"—it derives from the sense "one who requires food." But it also serves here as a pun on Christ's body offered at the Last Supper ("Take ye, and eat. This is my body," Matthew 26.26, Douay-Rheims translation), which is then reenacted and commemorated in the sacrament of the Eucharist during every mass, and celebrated in the very day of performance of these plays.
2   *I gart here be ordained*   I caused to be ordered here.

With leal° life to leng° in this land,　　　　　　*righteous / dwell*
　　And ease.
400 NICODEMUS.　Sere° ointments here have I　　　　　*many*
　　Brought for this fair body.
　　I anoint thee forthy
　　With myrrh and aloes.

JOSEPH.　This deed it is done ilka deal,[1]
405　And wrought is this work well, iwis.°　　　　　*indeed*
　　To thee, king, on knees here I kneel,
　　That bainly° thou bield° me in bliss.　　　　*readily / shelter*
　　NICODEMUS.　He hight° me full hendly° to be his　*promised / graciously*
　　A night when I nighed° him full near.　　　　*approached*
410　Have mind,[2] Lord, and mend me of miss,°　　　*sins*
　　For done is our deeds full dear
　　This tide.
　　JOSEPH.　This Lord so good
　　That shed his blood,
415　He mend your mood,
　　And busk° on his bliss for to bide.°　　　　*hasten / remain*

The York Corpus Christi Play:
The Harrowing of Hell

The idea that Christ descended into Hell between his death and resurrection in order to free the righteous souls from eternal torment was doctrinal in the medieval church, but its authority comes from the interpretation of implicit and suggestive lines of the Bible, rather than from any explicit biblical narrative. Nevertheless, the story of the Harrowing was widely depicted in art and literature from the early Middle Ages to the late medieval and early modern periods. The Saddlers' *Harrowing of Hell* play, like other depictions of the event, presents a narrative which comes from a tradition that derives largely from the apocryphal (that is, non-canonical and unofficial) *Gospel of Nicodemus*, a text that became widely influential and popular in the Middle Ages.

1　*ilka deal* Every whit, in every detail.
2　*Have mind* Remember (me).

Following the plays depicting Christ's crucifixion and death, *The Harrowing of Hell* provides the turning point in a narrative arc that at first suggests tragedy but ends in Christ's triumph over death. Likewise, *The Harrowing of Hell* replaces the suffering Christ of affective piety with the knightly, warrior-like Christ often depicted in the early Middle Ages, particularly in Anglo-Saxon literature and art, the latter of which would have still been visible and available to late-medieval audiences. In formal terms, *The Harrowing of Hell* play both echoes the raucous *Crucifixion* and looks forward to the more grave aspects of the *Resurrection*, using its twelve-line stanzas (rhyming abababababcdcd) for both stately speeches and the bickering of the demons. The play also provides great opportunities for spectacle, from the gates of hell as a monstrous Hellmouth, to the frequent figurative references to light, which may suggest occasions for effects using flame and reflection.

Pageant 37 of the York Corpus Christi Play: *The Harrowing of Hell*

CHARACTERS

Jesus
Adam
Eve
Isaiah
Simeon
John the Baptist
Moses
David
Michael, the Archangel
Ribald (a devil)
Beelzebub (a devil)
Belial (a devil)
Satan

[Jesus appears before the gates of Hell.][1]

---

1 *gates of Hell* The gates of Hell are likely depicted as a monstrous Hellmouth, conventional in the visual arts in the late Middle Ages (see the In Context materials). The speeches of the Old and New Testament figures, whom Christ comes to release, refer repeatedly to light, so it is possible that the Saddlers, who produced and performed this play, used medieval special effects—flames and reflective surfaces—to surround the actor playing Jesus with light. But it is equally possible that they left the imagery to the imagination of the audience.

JESUS. Man on mold,° be meek to me,   *earth*
    And have thy maker in thy mind,
    And think how I have tholèd° for thee,   *suffered*
    With peerless pains for to be pined.°   *afflicted, tortured*
5   The foreward° of my father free°   *agreement, contract / noble*
    Have I fulfilled, as folk may find,
    Therefore about now will I be
    That° I have bought for to unbind.[1]   *those that*
    The fiend them won with train°   *treachery*
10   Through fruit of earthly food;
    I have them gotten again
    Through buying with my blood.

    And so I shall that stead° restore   *state, condition*
    From which the fiend fell for sin,
15   There shall mankind wone° evermore   *dwell*
    In bliss that shall never blin.°   *cease*
    All that in world my workmen were,
    Out of their woe I will them win,
    And some sign shall I send before
20   Of grace, to gar° their games° begin.   *make / celebrations*
    A light I will° they have   *desire that*
    To show them I shall come soon.
    My body bides in grave
    Till all these deeds be done.

25   My Father ordained° on° this wise°   *commanded / in / manner*
    After° his will that I should wend,°   *according to / betake myself, behave*
    For to fulfill the prophecies,
    And as I spake,° my solace°   *have spoken / spiritual joy*
      to spend.°   *distribute*
    My friends that in me faith affies,°[2]   *affirm*
30   Now from their foes I shall them fend,°   *defend*
    And on the third day right° uprise,°   *immediately / rise up*
    And so till° heaven I shall ascend.   *to*
    Sithen° shall I come again   *afterwards*
    To deem° both good and ill   *judge*

---

1 *Therefore ... unbind* Therefore right away I will busy myself to release those that I have bought (with my death).

2 *My friends ... affies* My friends who affirm their faith in me.

Till° endless joy or pain;
Thus is my Father's will.

(*Then they shall sing.*)

ADAM.   My brethren, harken° to me here—   *listen*
   Swilk° hope of heal° never ere°   *such / remedy / before*
     we had;°   *have had*
   Four thousand and six hundred year
   Have we been here in this stead.°   *place*   40
   Now see I sign of solace sere,°   *several*
   A glorious gleam to make us glad,
   Wherefore I hope our help is near
   And soon shall cease our sorrows sad.
EVE.   Adam, my husband hend,°   *courteous, gracious*   45
   This means solace certain.°   *certainly*
   Such light gan on us lend[1]
   In Paradise full plain.°   *plainly*

ISAIAH.   Adam, we shall well understand—
   I, Isaiah, as God me kenned,°   *taught*   50
   I preached in Neptalim,[2] that land,
   And Zabulon,[3] even until end.°   *death*
   I spoke of folk in murk° walkand,°   *darkness / walking*
   And said a light should on them lend.°   *be shed*
   This lered° I while I was livand;°   *taught / living*   55
   Now see I God this same hath send.°   *sent*
   This light comes all of° Christ,   *from*
   That seed to save us now.
   Thus is my point published°—   *shown*
   But Simeon, what says thou?   60

SIMEON.   This, my tale of ferlies° fele,°   *wonders / many*
   For in the temple his friends me fand.°   *found*
   I had delight with him to deal

---

1   *gan on us lend*   Has landed on us.
2   *Neptalim*   Napthali, one of the tribes of Israel.
3   *Zabulon*   Zebulun, one of the tribes of Israel.

And halsèd° homely°   *embraced (him) / simply, unpretentiously*
  with my hand.[1]
65 I said, "Lord, let thy servant leal°   *loyal, true*
  Pass now in peace to life lastand,°   *lasting, everlasting*
  For now myself has seen thy heal
  Me list[2] no longer to live in land."
  This light thou hast purveyed°   *provided*
70 To folk that lives in lede,°   *the nation, land*
  The same that I them° said   *to them*
  I see fulfilled indeed.

JOHN THE BAPTIST. As voice crying to folk I kenned° *made known*
  The ways of Christ as I well can.
75 I baptized him with both my hend°   *hands*
  Even in the flood° of flume° Jordan.[3] *water / river*
  The Holy Ghost from heaven descend°   *descended*
  As a white dove down on him then;
  The Father's voice, my mirth to mend,°   *restore*
80 Was made° to me even as man: *revealed*
  "This is my Son," he said,
  "In whom me pays[4] full well."
  His light is on us laid,
  He comes our cares to keel.°   *assuage, lessen*

85 MOSES. Of that same light learning have I:
  To me, Moses, he mustered his might,
  And also unto another, Eli,°   *Elijah*
  Where we were on an hill on height.[5]
  White as snow was his body,
90 And his face like to the sun to sight;

---

1 *This, my tale … with my hand* Simeon refers to meeting Jesus as a newborn in the temple when Mary came for the rights of purification, dramatized in York Pageant 17: *The Purification*, and recounted in Luke 2.22–40. The event is celebrated in the modern Roman Catholic church as the Feast of the Presentation of the Lord, but in the Middle Ages it was known as the Feast of the Purification of Mary, and popularly called Candlemas in England because of its association with the blessing of candles.

2 *Me list* I desire (literally, it is desirable to me).

3 *Jordan* John's baptism of Jesus in the Jordan river is narrated in Matthew 3.13–17, Mark 1.9–11, and Luke 3.21–22.

4 *me pays* I am pleased (literally, it is pleasing to me).

5 *unto another … on an hill on height* Moses refers to the story of the Transfiguration of Jesus, narrated in Matthew 17.1–9, Mark 9.2–8, and Luke 9.28–36, and dramatized in York Pageant 23: *The Transfiguration*.

No man on mold° was so mighty   *earth*
Gradely° to look against that light.   *properly, directly*
That same light see I now
Shining on us certain,°   *certainly*
Wherefore truly I trow°   *trust, believe*   95
We shall soon pass from pain.

RIBALD. Help, Beelzebub, to bind these boys!°   *fellows (used derisively)*
Such harrow[1] was never ere° heard in Hell.   *before*
BEELZEBUB. Why roars thou so, Ribald? Thou roys!°   *raves*
What is betid, can thou aught tell?[2]   100
RIBALD. What, hears thou not this ugly noise?
These lurdans° that in Limbo dwell,   *evildoers, criminals*
They make meaning° of many joys   *mention*
And muster° great mirth them amell.°   *show / among*
BEELZEBUB. Mirth? Nay, nay, that point is past,   105
More Hell shall they never have.
RIBALD. They cry on Christ full fast°   *very strongly*
And say he shall them save.

BEELZEBUB. Yea, if he save[3] them not, we shall,
For they are speared° in special space.   *locked*   110
While I am prince and principal
Shall they never pass out of this place.
Call up Astoreth and Anaball
To give their counsel in this case,
Baal-Berith and Belial,   115
To mar them that swilk°   *such*
    masteries° mase.°   *presumptuous acts / make*
Say to Satan our sire,
And bid them bring also
Lucifer, lovely of lyre.°   *face*
RIBALD. All ready, lord, I go.   120

---

1   *harrow*   Uproar. The word "harrow" is also a pun on the verb *to harrow*, which means to harry, rob, or spoil, which is what Christ is doing to Hell. Hence the conventional title of the play and the traditional English name for Christ's descent into Hell: The Harrowing of Hell.

2   *What is betid … tell?*   What has happened, do you have anything to say?

3   *save*   Beelzebub puns here: "save" in this context means both redeem or rescue (what Jesus does) and keep or preserve (what the devils want to do).

JESUS. *Attollite portas, principes,*[1]
    Open up, ye princes of pains sere,°   *various*
    Et elevamini eternales,[2]
    Your endless° gates that ye have here.   *eternal*
125 SATAN. What page° is there that makes   *servant, underling*
      press°   *commotion*
    And calls him° king of us in fere?°   *himself / company*
DAVID. I lered° living,[3] without lease,°   *taught / lies*
    He is a king of virtues clear,
    A lord mickle° of might   *great*
130 And strong in ilka° stour,°   *every / combat*
    In battles fierce to fight
    And worthy to win honor.

SATAN. Honor? In the devil's way![4] For what deed?
    All earthly men to me are thrall.°   *enslaved*
135 The lad that thou calls lord in lede°   *nation*
    Had never yet harbor,° house, nor hall.   *lodging*
RIBALD. Hark° Beelzebub, I have great dread, *listen*
    For hideously I heard him call.
BELIAL. We,[5] spear° our gates, all ill may thou speed,[6] *fasten*
140 And set forth watches° on the wall;[7] *guards, look-outs*
    And if he call or cry
    To make us more debate,°   *dispute, challenge*
    Lay on him then hardily°   *fiercely*
    And gar° him gang° his gate.°   *make / go / way*

145 SATAN. Tell me what boys dare be so bold
    For dread to make so mickle° deray.° *great / disturbance*
RIBALD. It is the Jew that Judas sold
    For to be dead this other day.

---

1 *Attollite portas, principes* Latin: Lift up (your) gates, princes. Together with the next Latin
  line (*Et elevamini eternales*), this line comes from Psalm 24.7. In the Douay-Rheims translation (where it is Psalm 23, following an older numbering system), the complete verse
  reads: "Lift up your gates, O ye princes, and be ye lifted up, O eternal gates: and the King
  of Glory shall enter in."
2 *Et elevamini eternales* Latin: And be ye lifted up, everlasting (doors).
3 *I lered living* While living, I taught.
4 *In the devil's way!* Expression of disbelief.
5 *We* Interjection expressing distress (as here), derision, or surprise.
6 *all ill … speed* May all bad luck hasten to you.
7 *wall* Hell is imagined as a walled fortress or city. See also *gates* in the previous line.

SATAN. Oh, this tale in time is told,
    This traitor traverses° us always.   *crosses* 150
    He shall be here full hard in hold,°   *held in*
    Look that he pass not,[1] I thee pray.
BEELZEBUB. Nay, nay, he will not wend°   *go*
    Away ere° I be ware,°   *before / aware*
    He shapes him[2] for to shend°   *destroy* 155
    All Hell ere he go far.

SATAN. Nay, faitour,° thereof° shall he fail,   *liar / in that*
    For all his fare° I him defy.   *doings, activity*
    I know his trants° from top to tail,   *methods, strategies*
    He lives with gauds° and with guilery.°   *tricks / deception* 160
    Thereby he brought out of our bail°   *custody*
    Now° late Lazarus of Bethany;[3]   *recently*
    Therefore I gave to the Jews counsel
    That they should always° gar° him die.   *in any way / make*
    I entered in Judas   165
    That foreward° to fulfill,   *promise*
    Therefore his hire° he has   *payment*
    Always to wone° here still.°   *dwell / forever*

BEELZEBUB. Sir Satan, since we hear thee say
    That thou and the Jews were sam° assent,° *together / agreed* 170
    And wot° he won Lazarus away   *know*
    That til° us was ta'en° for to tent,°   *to / given / tend to*
    Trow° thou that thou mar him may,   *think*
    To muster mights what he has meant?[4]
    If he now deprive us of our prey,   175
    We will ye wit° when they are went.[5]   *make known*
SATAN. I bid you be not abashed,°   *afraid*
    But boldly make you boun°   *ready*
    With tools° that ye on traist,[6]   *i.e., weapons*
    And ding° that dastard° down.   *beat / base coward* 180

---

1 *Look that he pass not* See to it that he doesn't get away.
2 *He shapes him* He plans to.
3 *he brought ... Lazarus of Bethany* Jesus' recalling of Lazarus from the dead is narrated in John 11 and dramatized in York Pageant 24.
4 *Trow thou ... he has meant?* Do you think you can harm him, (that you can) muster power equal to his?
5 *We will ... are went* We will inform you when they have gone.
6 *on traist* (Have) confidence in.

JESUS. *Principes, portas tollite,*
    Undo your gates, ye princes of pride,
    Et introibit rex glorie,[1]
    The king of bliss comes in this tide.°   *time*
185 SATAN. Out, harrow!° What   *exclamation of distress*
      harlot° is he   *scoundrel*
    That says his kingdom shall be cried?°   *proclaimed*
    DAVID. That may thou in my Psalter[2] see,
    For that point I prophesied.
    I said that he should break
190 Your bars and bands by name,
    And on your works take wreak°—   *vengeance*
    Now shall ye see the same.

    JESUS. This stead° shall stand no longer stocken:°   *place / locked up*
    Open up, and let my people pass.
195 RIBALD. Out! Behold, our bayle° is broken,   *outer wall of a fortress*
    And burst are all our bands of brass!
    Tell Lucifer all is unlocken.°   *unlocked*
    BEELZEBUB. What then, is Limbo lorn?° Alas,   *lost*
    Gar Satan help that we were wroken;[3]
200 This work is worse than ever it was.
    SATAN. I bad° ye should be boun°   *commanded / ready*
    If he made masteries more.
    Do ding° that dastard° down   *beat / base coward*
    And set° him sad and sore.   *make*

205 BEELZEBUB. Yea, set him sore—that is soon said,[4]
    But come thyself and serve° him so.   *deal with*
    We may not bide° his bitter braid,°   *endure / attack*
    He will us mar and° we were mo.°   *even if / more (in number)*

---

1 *Principes ... glorie* Latin: Lift up (your) gates, princes, and the King of Glory shall enter in. Psalm 24.7. In the Douay-Rheims translation (where it is Psalm 23, following an older numbering system), the complete verse reads: "Lift up your gates, O ye princes, and be ye lifted up, O eternal gates: and the King of Glory shall enter in."

2 *Psalter* Literally, a Psalter is a portable book that contains only the Psalms. Here the word refers to the Psalms themselves, which are traditionally attributed to David.

3 *Gar Satan ... were wroken* Get Satan to help avenge us.

4 *that is soon said* Easy for you to say.

SATAN. What, faitours,° wherefore°   *imposters / why*
    are ye flayed?°   *frightened* 210
  Have ye no force to flit him fro?[1]
  Belive° look that my gear be graithed,°   *quickly / prepared*
  Myself shall to that gadling° go.   *low-born person*
  [*He goes to Jesus and addresses him.*]
  Ho, belamy,°abide,°   *good friend / wait*
  With all thy boast and bere,°   *clamor*
  And tell to me this tide°   *news, tidings* 215
  What masteries make thou here?

JESUS. I make no masteries but for mine,
  Them will I save, I tell thee now.
  Thou had no power them to pine,°   *torment*
  But as my prisons° for their prow°   *prisoners / benefit* 220
  Here have they sojourned, not as thine,
  But in thy ward°—thou wot° well how.   *custody / know*
SATAN. And what devil° hast thou done ay syne[2] *the devil*
  That never would nigh° them near ere° now? *approach / before*
JESUS. Now is the time certain   225
  My father ordained before,
  That they should pass from pain
  And wone° in mirth ever more.   *dwell*

SATAN. Thy father knew I well by sight,
  He was a wright° his meat° to win,   *carpenter / living, sustenance* 230
  And Mary me means° thy mother hight°—   *think / was called*
  The uttermost end of all thy kin.[3]
  Who made thee be so mickle° of might?   *great*
JESUS. Thou wicked fiend, let be thy din.
  My father wones° in heaven on height,   *dwells* 235
  With bliss that shall never blin.°   *end*
  I am his own son,
  His foreward° to fulfill,   *contract, promise*

---

1 *flit him fro* To flee from him.
2 *ay syne* Ever since.
3 *Thy father ... thy kin* I knew your father well by sight, he earned his living as a carpenter, and I think your mother was called Mary—that's the sum total of all your relatives. When Jesus speaks of his father, Satan takes that to mean Joseph, Jesus' earthly foster-father, instead of Jesus' divine father, God.

And sam ay[1] shall we wone
240 And sunder° when we will.°   *part / want*

SATAN. God's son? Than should thou be full glad,
        After no cattle° need thou crave![2]   *chattel, goods*
        But thou has lived ay° like a lad,°   *always / low-born person*
        And in sorrow as a simple° knave.   *humble*
245 JESUS. That was for heartly° love I had   *heartfelt*
        Unto man's soul, it for to save;
        And for to make thee mazed° and mad,°   *confused / insane*
        And by that reason thus duly to have
        My Godhead here, I hid
250   In Mary mother mine,
        For° it should not be kid°   *so that / known*
        To thee nor to none of thine.

SATAN. Ah, this would° I were°   *wish / had been*
           told in ilka° town.   *every*
        So, since thou says God is thy sire,°   *father*
255   I shall thee prove by right reason
        Thou moots° his men into the mire.[3]   *argue*
        To break his bidding were they boun,°   *eager*
        And, for° they did at my desire,   *because*
        From Paradise he put them down
260   In Hell here to have their hire.°   *reward (used ironically)*
        And thyself, day and night,
        Has taught all men among
        To do reason and right,
        And here works thou all wrong.

265 JESUS. I work not wrong, that shall thou wit,°   *understand*
        If I my men from woe will win.
        My prophets plainly preached it,
        All this note° that now begin.   *business*
        They said that I should be obit,°   *dead*
270   To Hell that I should enter in,

---

1 *sam ay* Together forever.
2 *After no cattle need thou crave!* I.e., you'll never want for anything!
3 *Thou moots … the mire* You are arguing his men into a terrible situation. The debate
   between Satan and Jesus takes on a legalistic quality throughout, as they argue the terms of
   the "foreward" or contract God made with his people.

And save my servants from that pit
Where damnèd souls shall sit for sin.
And ilka° true prophet's tale   *every*
Must be fulfilled in me;
I have them bought with bale,°   *suffering* 275
And in bliss shall they be.

SATAN. Now since thee list allege[1] the laws,
 Thou shall be attainted° ere° we twin,°   *convicted / before / separate*
 For those that thou to witness draws
 Full even against thee will begin.[2]   280
 Solomon said in his saws°   *sayings*
 That whoso° enters Hell within   *whosoever*
 Shall never come out, thus clerks° knows—   *learned men*
 And therefore fellow, leave thy din.
 Job, thy servant, also   285
 Thus in his time gan° tell   *did*
 That neither friend nor foe
 Should find release in Hell.

JESUS. He said full soth,° that shall thou see,   *truth*
 That in Hell may be no release,   290
 But of that place then preached he
 Where sinful care shall ever increase.
 And in that bail° ay° shall thou be   *jurisdiction / forever*
 Where sorrows sere° shall never cease,   *diverse, various*
 And for° my folk therefrom were free,   *because* 295
 Now shall they pass to the place of peace.
 They were here with my will,
 And so shall they forth wend,°   *go*
 And thyself shall fulfill
 There woe without end.   300

SATAN. Oh, then see I how thou means among
 Some measure with malice to mell,[3]
 Since thou says all shall not gang,°   *go*

---

1 *thee list allege* You want to choose.
2 *For those ... against thee will begin* Even those that you call as witnesses will be fully against
 you.
3 *Oh, then see I ... malice to mell* Oh, now I see how you mean to mix moderation with
 malice.

But some shall always with us dwell.
305 JESUS. Yea, wit° thou well, else were it wrong,   *understand*
As° cursed Cain that slew Abel,   *such as*
And all that° hasten themselves to hang,   *those who*
As Judas and Achitophel,
Dathan and Abiram,[1]
310 And all of their assent;
Also tyrants every one
That me and mine torment.

And all that° list° not to lere° my law   *who / care / learn*
That I have left in land now new[2]—
315 That is, my coming° for to know,   *second coming*
And to my sacraments pursue,°   *follow, abide by*
My death, my rising, read by row[3]—
Who will not trow,° they are not true.   *believe*
Unto my doom° I shall them draw,   *judgment*
320 And judge them worse than any Jew.[4]
And all that likes to lere
My laws and leve° thereby,   *believe*
Shall never have harms here,
But wealth,° as is worthy.   *happiness*

325 SATAN. Now here° my hand, I hold me paid,[5]   *have here*
This point is plainly for our prow.°[6]   *evidence, testimony*
If this be sooth° that thou hast said   *truth*
We shall have mo° than we have now.   *more (in number)*
This law that thou now late° has laid°   *just / set forth*

---

1 *Judas ... Abiram* Of these four biblical figures, only Judas and Achitophel committed suicide—Judas in Matthew 27.9–10, Achitophel in 2 Samuel 17.1–23. Dathan and Abiram led a revolt against Moses and Aaron in the desert and were swallowed up by the earth in punishment (Numbers 26.9–10). All four figures rebelled against their leaders—Judas against Jesus; Achitophel against King David.

2 *now new* Just recently.

3 *read by row* Understand rightly.

4 *worse than any Jew* As discussed in the introduction to the volume, anti-Semitism is a powerful and disturbing presence in several of the York plays. Here the shocking effect is compounded by being assigned to Jesus' dialogue. Generally the play's writers take little leeway with Jesus' words, hewing close to the Gospel accounts, but in this non-biblical event, the writer found room for present-day bigotries.

5 *I hold me paid* I consider myself satisfied.

6 *This point ... our prow* This point plainly assists our case.

I shall lere° men not to allow;°	*teach / accept* 330
If they it take,° they be betrayed,	*accept*
For I shall turn° them tite,° I trow.	*pervert / quickly*
I shall walk east and west,	
And gar° them work well° war.°	*make / entirely / worse*
JESUS. Nay, fiend, thou shall be fast,°	*fettered, chained* 335
That° thou shall flit° not far.	*so that / go*

SATAN. Fast? That were° a foul reason°—	*would be / intention*
Nay belamy,° thou bus° be smit.°	*good friend / must / struck down*
JESUS. Michael, mine angel, make thee boun°	*ready*
And fast° yon° fiend that he not flit.°	*fetter / yonder / flee* 340
And, Devil, I command thee go down	
Into thy cell where thou shall sit.	
SATAN. Out! Ay harrow! Help, Mahound!¹	
Now wax° I wood° out of my wit.	*grow / deranged*
BEELZEBUB. Satan, this said we ere,°	*before* 345
Now shall thou feel thy fit.²	
SATAN. Alas for dole and care,	
I sink into Hell pit.	

[Satan descends from the pageant wagon, likely by means of a trap door.]

ADAM. Ah, Jesus, Lord, mickle° is thy might,	*great*
That meeks° thyself in this manner,	*humbles* 350
Us for to help as thou has hight,°	*promised*
When both forfeit,° I and my fere.°	*transgressed / spouse*
Here have we lived without light	
Four thousand and six hundred year;	
Now see I by this solemn sight	355
How thy mercy hath made us clear.°	*free from blame*
EVE. Ah, Lord, we were worthy	
More torments for to taste,	
But mend us with mercy	
As thou of might is most.	360

---

1 *Mahound* Muhammad, prophet and founder of Islam (c. 570–632). Medieval English texts often depict demons, as well as non-Christian characters, as worshipping or otherwise calling on Muhammad, as a way of constructing their "otherness," simultaneously demonizing Islam as well.

2 *feel thy fit* Experience your punishment.

JOHN THE BAPTIST. Ah, Lord, I love thee inwardly,°   *deeply*
    That me would make thy messenger
    Thy coming in earth for to cry,
    And teach thy faith to folk in fere;[1]
365   And sithen before thee for to die
    And bring bodeword° to them here,   *tidings*
    How they should have thine help in hie.°   *haste*
    Now see I all thy points° appear   *actions, feats*
    As David, prophet true,
370   Oft-times told unto us;
    Of this coming he knew,
    And said it should be thus.

DAVID. As I have said, yet° say I so,   *still*
    Ne derelinquas, domine,
375   *Animam meam in inferno,*[2]
    Leave not my soul, lord, after thee
    In deep Hell where damned shall go;
    Nor suffer never thy saints to see,
    The sorrow of them that wone° in woe   *dwell*
380   Ay° full of filth, and may not flee.   *forever*
  ADAM. We thank his great goodness
    He fetched us from this place.
    Make joy now, more and less.
  ALL. We laud° God of his grace.   *praise*

(They all sing.)

385 JESUS. Adam, and my friends in fere,°   *company*
    From all your foes come forth with me.
    Ye shall be set in solace sere°   *various*
    Where ye shall never of sorrows see.
    And Michael, mine angel clear,°   *bright*
390   Receive these souls all unto thee
    And lead them as I shall thee lere,°   *instruct*
    To Paradise with play and plenty.

---

1 *in fere* Together, in company.
2 *Ne derelinquas ...: in inferno* Latin: Lord, you do not leave my soul in hell. The first half of
    Psalm 16.10 (15.10 in the Douay-Rheims version): "Because thou wilt not leave my soul in
    hell; nor wilt thou give thy holy one to see corruption."

My grave I will go till,°   *to*
Ready to rise upright,
And so I shall fulfill   395
That I before have hight.°   *promised*

MICHAEL. Lord, wend we shall after thy saw,°   *instruction*
   To solace sere they shall be send.°   *sent*
   But that these devils no draught us draw,[1]
   Lord, bless us with thy holy hend.°   *hands* 400
JESUS. My blessing have ye all on row,[2]
   I shall be with you where ye wend,
   And all that leally° loves my law,   *loyally*
   They shall be blessed without end.
ADAM. To thee, Lord, be lofing,°   *praise* 405
   That us has won from woe.
   For solace will we sing
   Laus tibi cum gloria, etc.[3]

---

1   *no draught us draw* Don't trick us.

2   *on row* In order.

3   *Laus tibi cum gloria, etc.* Latin: Praise to you with glory. The "etc." signifies a cue for a complete liturgical song.

The York Corpus Christi Play: The Resurrection

The *Resurrection*, produced and performed by York's Carpenters' craft, follows directly after the *Harrowing of Hell*. Unlike that play, the *Resurrection* consists of multiple settings and subplots—as do many of the trial plays leading up to the crucifixion—and must have called for the ingenuity of the Carpenters in using the wagon stage and the ground, changes of scenery, and possibly even two wagons. The play opens in Pilate's court, where the Pharisees, Annas and Caiaphas, suggest that Pilate place guards at Christ's tomb, and Pilate gives such orders to two soldiers; on the page, the scene then shifts to the tomb, where Christ's resurrection is signaled by the Angel singing "Christ arising," an anthem associated with the Easter Mass, while the three Marys lament Christ's death and encounter the Angel who shares the good news. However, there must be some stage business in which the soldiers travel to and arrive at the tomb before the moment of resurrection, since they are later shown to be asleep at the tomb (where they are now four soldiers, rather than two), having missed the moment of the resurrection as well as the Marys' encounter with the Angel. The play then returns to Pilate's court when the soldiers leave to report the news to him. In short, what looks simple on the page is a complexly structured juxtaposition of scenes, tones, and dramatic effects.

In poetic and linguistic style, *The Resurrection* shares some of the naturalism of *The Crucifixion* (the common idiom, the flow of dialogue across stanzas) and the mix of tones, pace, and atmosphere of *The Harrowing of Hell*, but it departs from their twelve-line stanza form. Here the rapid six-line stanzas rhyme aaabab, and the b-rhyme lines are shorter than the rest. The effect created is a cacophonous confusion at Pilate's court, both before and after the resurrection, countered by the solemn mourning of the three Marys, and all punctuated by Christ's wordless resurrection accompanied by the harmony of liturgical music. On the page, that moment is easily missed, but in performance it can be truly arresting, drawing an immediate contrast between the busy activity and wordiness of all of the rest of the cycle and the resurrection's speechless, meditative harmony, which marks it as the devotional center of the plays and the theological mysteries they explore.

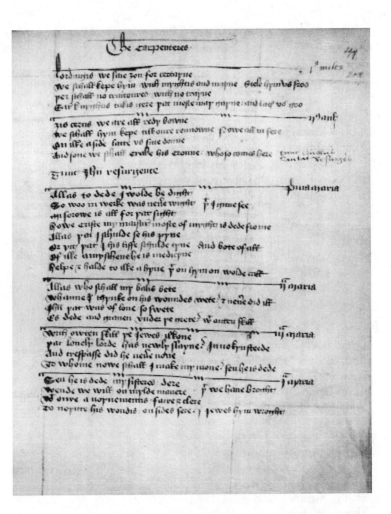

A page from the York Carpenters' *Resurrection* play, from the "Register," or official copy, of the York cycle (York, c. 1463–77), London, British Library MS Add. 35290, f. 202r. The stage directions, *Tunc Jhesu resurgente*, Latin for "then Jesus being risen," appears as part of the main text, following the first two stanzas on the page. Another direction, added later in the right margin by John Clerke, a clerk working for the city from 1530 through the plays' suppression in 1569, reads *tunc angelus cantat Resurgens*, Latin for "then the angel sings 'Resurgens'." Resurgens is a cue for "Christus resurgens," or "Christ is risen," most likely a liturgical song from Easter.

CHARACTERS

Pilate
Caiaphas
Annas
Centurion
Soldier 1
Soldier 2
Soldier 3
Soldier 4
Jesus
Mary Magdalene
Mary Jacobi
Mary Salome
Angel

[*Enter Pilate, Caiaphas, Annas, and all soldiers.*]

PILATE.	Lordings, listen now unto me:	
	I command you in ilka° degree°	*every / status*
	As doomsman° chief in this country,	*judge*
	·For counsel° kenned,°	*wisdom / known*
5	At my bidding you owe° to be	*are obliged*
	And bainly° bend.°	*readily / bow down*
	And sir Caiaphas, chief of clergy,	
	Of your counsel let hear in hie.°	*haste*
	By your assent since we did die°	*execute*
10	Jesus this day,	
	That ye maintain, and stand thereby	
	That work always.[1]	
CAIAPHAS.	Yes sir, that deed shall we maintain,	
	By law it was done all bedene,°	*completely*
15	Ye wot° yourself without ween°	*know / doubt*
	As well as we.	
	His saws° are now upon him seen[2]	*sayings*
	And ay° shall be.	*always*

---

1 *By your assent … work always* Since we put Jesus to death with your assent, you must uphold that and stand by that action always.

2 *upon him seen* Visited upon him.

ANNAS. The people, sir, in this same stead,°   place
    Before you said with a whole-head[1]   20
    That he was worthy to be dead,
    And thereto swore.
    Since all was ruled by right's rede°   counsel, advice
    Neven° it no more.   utter

PILATE. To neven methinketh it needful thing.[2]   25
    Since he was had° to burying   taken
    Heard we neither of° old nor young   from
    Tidings° between.   news
CAIAPHAS. Centurion, sir, will bring tiding
    Of all bedene.°   entirely   30

    We left him there for° man most wise,   as a
    If any rebels would aught° rise   at all
    Our rightwise° doom° for to despise   righteous / judgment
    Or it offend,°   violate
    To seize them till the next assize°   court session   35
    And then make end.[3]

    [*Enter Centurion.*]

CENTURION. Ah, blessed Lord, Adonai,[4]
    What may these marvels[5] signify
    That here was showed so openly
    Unto our sight,   40
    This day when that the man gan ° die   did
    That Jesus hight?°   was called

    It is a misty° thing to mean.°   obscure, unclear / speak of
    So selcouth° a sight was never seen,   strange, marvelous
    That our princes and priests bedene°   all together   45
    Of this affray°   disturbance
    I will go wit,° without ween,   inform
    What they can say.

---

1   *with a whole-head* Unanimously.

2   *To neven ... needful thing* It seems to me necessary to talk about it.

3   *make end* Determine the outcome.

4   *Adonai* Hebrew: God.

5   *these marvels* Refers to the extreme weather and other natural events traditionally associated with the moment of Jesus' death, which he will describe in more detail below.

God save you sirs on ilka° side,   *every*
50 Worship and wealth in worlds wide;[1]
    With mickle° mirth° might ye abide   *great / happiness*
    Both day and night.
    PILATE. Centurion, welcome this tide,°   *time*
    Our comely° knight.   *agreeable*

55 Ye have been missed us here among.[2]
    CENTURION. God give you grace gradely to gang.[3]
    PILATE. Centurion, our friend full long,
        What is your will?
    CENTURION. I dread me that ye have done wrong
60   And wonder° ill.°   *extremely, very / badly*

    CAIAPHAS. Wonder ill? I pray thee, why?
        Declare it to this company.
    CENTURION. So shall I, sirs, tell you truly
        Without train:°   *deceit*
65 The rightwise° man then mean I by[4]   *righteous*
        That ye have slain.

    PILATE. Centurion, cease of such saw,°   *talk*
        Thou art a learned man in the law,
        And if we should any witness draw°   *call*
70   Us to excuse,
        To maintain° us evermore thee owe,°   *uphold / ought*
        And not refuse.

    CENTURION. To maintain truth is well worthy.
        I said you° when I saw him die   *to you*
75   That he was God's son almighty
        That° hangeth there;   *who*
        Yet° say I so, and stand thereby°   *still / by it*
        For evermore.

---

1   *Worship and wealth in worlds wide*   (May you have) reverence and well-being throughout
    the world.
2   *us here among*   Among us here.
3   *gradely to gang*   To go well, i.e., to prosper.
4   *then mean I by*   I mean by this.

CAIAPHAS. Yea sir, such reasons may ye rue.°   *regret*
  Ye should not neven° such note° anew°   *mention / a matter / again*   80
  But° ye couth° any tokenings° true   *unless / know / signs*
  Unto us tell.°   *to tell*
CENTURION. Such wonderful case never yet ye knew
  As now befell.

ANNAS. We pray thee tell us of what thing.   85
CENTURION. All elements, both old and young,
  In their manners they made mourning
  In ilka° stead,°   *each / place*
  And knew by countenance[1] that their king
  Was done° to dead.°   *put / death*   90

  The sun for woe he waxèd° all wan,°   *became / dark*
  The moon and stars of shining blan,°   *ceased*
  The earth trembled and also° man   *like*
  Began to speak;
  The stones that never was stirred ere° then   *before*   95
  Gan° asunder break.   *did*

  And dead men rose, both great and small.
PILATE. Centurion, beware withal,°   *moreover*
  Ye wot° our clerks the eclipses they call   *know*
  Such sudden sight.   100
  Both sun and moon that season° shall   *at that time*
  Lack of their light.

CAIAPHAS. Yea, and if dead men rose bodily
  That might be done through sorcery,
  Therefore we set nothing thereby   105
  To be abashed.°   *worried*
CENTURION. All that I tell for truth shall I
  Evermore trast.°   *believe*

  In this ilka° work that ye did work   *same*
  Not alone the sun was murk,°   *dark*   110
  But how your veil rave° in   *was torn*
    your kirk,°   *church, i.e., temple*

---

1   *knew by countenance*   Showed by their appearance.

That wit I would.[1]
PILATE. Swilk° tales full soon will make us irk°   such / bored
And° they be told.   if

115 ANNAS. Centurion, such speech withdraw,
Of all these words we have none awe.
CENTURION. Now since ye set nought°   nothing
by my saw°   tale
Sirs, have good day.
God grant you grace that ye may know
120 The sooth° alway.°   truth / always

ANNAS. Withdraw thee fast since thou thee dreads,[2]
For we shall well maintain our deeds.
[*Exit Centurion.*]
PILATE. Such wonder reasons as he redes
Was never before.[3]
125 CAIAPHAS. To neven° this note no more us needs,   discuss
Neither even° nor morn.°   evening / morning

Therefore look no man make ill cheer,[4]
All this doing may do no dere.°   harm
But to beware yet of more were°   doubt
130 That folk may feel,
We pray you sirs, of these saws sere°   various
Advise you well.[5]

And to this tale take heed in hie,°   haste
For Jesus said even openly
135 A thing that grieves all this Jewry,
And right so may:[6]
That he should rise up bodily
Within the third day.

And be it so, as mote° I speed,°   may / prosper
140 His latter deed is more to dread

---

1   *That wit I would*   I'd like to know that (i.e., how the veil in the temple was torn).
2   *thou thee dreads*   You are afraid.
3   *Such wonder reasons … never before*   Such marvelous things as he describes have never happened before.
4   *make ill cheer*   Be melancholy.
5   *Advise you well*   Think carefully.
6   *And right so may*   And so it surely should.

Than is the first if we take heed
Or tent° thereto.   *attend*
To neven this note methinks most need°   *necessary*
And best to do.

ANNAS. Yea sir, if all[1] that he said so,   145
He has no might to rise and go
But if his men steal him us fro°   *from*
And bear away.
That were° to us and other mo[2]   *would be*
A foul fray,°   *affront*   150

For then would they say everilkone°   *everyone*
That he rose by himself alone.
Therefore let him be kept° anon°   *guarded / at once*
With knights hend,°   *skilled*
Until three days be come and gone   155
And brought to end.

PILATE. In certain, sirs, right well ye say,
For this ilka° point now to purvey°   *same / pursue*
I shall ordain,° if that I may.   *order*
He shall not rise,   160
Nor none shall win° him thence away   *procure by ingenuity*
On no-kin wise.[3]

Sir knights, that are in deeds doughty,°   *valiant*
Chosen for chief of chivalry,
As we ay° in your force affy°   *ever / place trust*   165
Both day and night,
Wend° and keep° Jesus' body   *go / guard*
With all your might.

And for thing that ever be may[4]
Keep him well to the third day,   170
And let no man take him away
Out of that stead°—   *place*

---

1 *if all* Even though.
2 *other mo* Many others.
3 *On no-kin wise* In no way.
4 *And for … be may* And whatever happens.

For and° they do, soothly° I say   *if / truly*
Ye shall be dead.

175 SOLDIER 1. Lordings, we say you° for certain,   *to you*
    We shall keep him with might° and main.°   *power / force*
    There shall no traitors with no train°   *treachery*
    Steal him us fro.
    Sir knights,[1] take gear that most may gain[2]
180 And let us go.

[*The soldiers travel to the tomb.*]

SOLDIER 2. Yes, certes,° we are all ready boun,°   *indeed / prepared*
    We shall him keep to our renown,
    On ilka° side let us sit down   *every*
    Now all in fere,[3]
185 And soon we shall crack his crown
    Whoso° comes here.   *whoever*

[*The soldiers fall asleep.*]

(*Then Jesus being risen. Then the Angel sings "Resurgens."*)

[*Mary Magdalene, Mary Jacobi, and Mary Salome enter.*][4]

---

1 *Sir knights* Although only two soldiers speak at this time, Soldier 1 addresses "knights," plural, and there are four knights at the tomb later in the play, suggesting that all four are present at this moment.

2 *most may gain* Will be most useful.

3 *in fere* Together.

4 *The soldiers ... Mary Salome enter* The stage directions in square brackets are not original to the medieval text. Since Soldier 1 later admits that they were sleeping, and the soldiers are traditionally depicted this way in the visual arts, that is what logically happens here. The next part of the stage direction, in parentheses, is in the manuscript; *Resurgens* Latin: The first word of a Latin liturgical song from Easter. Note that this is the moment of the resurrection, easily missed on the page since Jesus has no lines in the play, but likely a powerful moment in performance. Whether or not the risen Christ exits the playing area completely or stays visible to the audience during the following scene with the "three Marys" is unknown and up to a director.

MARY MAGDALENE.[1] Alas, to death I would°   *would rather*
    be dight,°   *ordered*
So woe in work was never wight,°[2]   *creature, person*
My sorrow is all for that sight
That I gan° see,   *did* 190
How Christ my master most of might
Is dead from me.

Alas that I should see his pine,°   *suffering*
Or yet that I his life should tine,°   *endure the loss of*
Of ilka° mischief° he was medicine   *every / misfortune* 195
And boot° of all,   *remedy*
Help and hold° to ilka hine°   *support / person*
That on him would call.

MARY JACOBI. Alas, who shall my bales° bete°   *sorrows / comfort*
    When I think on his wounds wet?   200
Jesu, that was of love so sweet
And never did ill,
Is dead and graven° under the grit,°   *buried / earth*
Without skill.°   *reason*

MARY SALOME. Without skill the Jews ilkone°   *every one* 205
    That lovely lord has newly slain,
And trespass did he never none
In no-kin° stead.°   *no such / place*
To whom now shall I make my moan
Since he is dead?   210

MARY MAGDALENE. Since he is dead, my sisters[3] dear,
    Wend° we will in mild manner   *go*
With our anointments fair and clear

---

1   *MARY MAGDALENE* The York text refers to the three women here only as Mary 1, Mary
   2, Mary 3, but the analogous Towneley manuscript play, which is based on the York play,
   identifies them as Mary Magdalene, Mary Jacobi, and Mary Salome. These three women—
   with Mary Cleopas sometimes substituting for Jacobi or Salome—are the traditional "three
   Marys," followers of Jesus who are frequently depicted weeping at the foot of the cross,
   often with the Virgin Mary, and at the empty tomb in both medieval drama and in the
   visual arts. They appear briefly in the Gospels.
2   *So woe ... never wight* No one was ever in such a woeful condition.
3   *sisters* Mary Magdalene speaks metaphorically; none of the women are actually related to
   her.

That we have brought,
215 To anoint his wounds on sides sere°   *various*
That Jews him wrought.

MARY JACOBI. Go we sam° my sisters free,°   *together / noble, worthy*
Full fair us longs his corse° to see.[1]   *body*
But I wot° not how best may be,   *know*
220 Help have we none.
And who shall now here of us three
Remove the stone?

MARY SALOME. That do we not but°   *unless*
  we were mo,°   *more (in number)*
For it is huge and heavy also.
225 MARY MAGDALENE. Sisters, a young child, as we go
Making mourning,
I see it sit where we wend° to,   *go*
In white clothing.

MARY JACOBI. Sisters, certes,° it is not to hide,[2]   *certainly*
230 The heavy stone is put beside.°   *aside*
MARY SALOME. Certes, for thing that may betide[3]
Near will we wend,
To lait° that lovely° and with him bide°   *seek / lovely one / wait*
That was our friend.
235 ANGEL. Ye mourning women in your thought,
Here in this place whom have ye sought?
MARY MAGDALENE. Jesus, that to death is brought,
Our lord so free.
ANGEL. Women, certain here is he not,
240 Come near and see.

He is not here the sooth° to say,   *truth*
The place is void that he in lay,
The sudary° here see ye may   *shroud*
Was on him laid.
245 He is risen and went his way,
As he you said.

---

1 *Full fair … to see* We long greatly to see his body.
2 *it is not to hide* It can't be denied.
3 *for thing that may betide* Whatever happens.

Even° as he said, so done has he,   *just*
He is risen through great poustie,°   *power*
He shall be found in Galilee
In flesh and fell.[1]   250
To his disciples now wend° ye   *go*
And thus them tell.

MARY MAGDALENE. My sisters dear, since it is so
That he is risen death thus fro,°   *from*
As the angel told me and you too—   255
Our lord so free—
Hence will I never go
Ere° I him see.   *before*

MARY JACOBI. Mary, us thar[2] no longer lend,°   *remain*
To Galilee now let us wend.   260
MARY MAGDALENE. Not till I see that faithful friend
My lord and leech,[3]
Therefore all this, my sisters hend,°   *gracious*
That ye forth preach.

MARY SALOME. As we have heard so shall we say.   265
Mary, our sister, have good day.
MARY MAGDALENE. Now very° God as he well may—   *true*
Man most of might—
He wis° you, sisters, well in your way   *guide*
And rule you right.   270

[*Mary Jacobi and Mary Salome exit.*]

Alas, what shall now worth on me?[4]
My caitiff° heart will break in three   *wretched*
When I think on that body free,°   *noble*
How it was spilt.°   *destroyed*
Both feet and hands nailed to a tree,°   *i.e., the cross*   275
Without guilt.

---

1 *In flesh and fell* In bodily form.
2 *us thar* We need.
3 *leech* Healer. Because leeches were used in traditional medicine, the word "leech" became
   a metonymy for the physicians and healers who used them. Here it is also a metaphor for
   Christ's power as spiritual healer.
4 *worth on me* Become of me.

Without guilt the true° was ta'en,°   *true one / taken*
For trespass did he never none,
The wounds he suffered many one
280   Was for my miss.°   *sin*
It was my deed he was for slain
And nothing° his.   *none of*

How might I, but° I loved that sweet,°   *except / sweet one*
That° for my love tholèd° wounds wet,   *who / suffered*
285   And sithen° be° graven° under the grit,   *then / to be / buried*
Such kindness kithe?°   *make known*
There is nothing till that we meet
May make me blithe.°   *happy*

[*Exit Mary Magdalene. The soldiers awaken.*]

SOLDIER 1. What—out alas!—what shall I say?
290   Where is the corse° that herein lay?   *body*
SOLDIER 2. What ails thee, man? Is he away°   *gone*
That we should tent?°   *guard*
SOLDIER 1. Rise up and see.
SOLDIER 2.   Harrow, for ay°   *ever*
I tell us shent.[1]

295   SOLDIER 3. What devil is this, what ails you two,
Such noise and cry thus for to make too?
SOLDIER 1. Why is he gone?
SOLDIER 3. Alas, where is he that here lay?
SOLDIER 4. We,[2] harrow! Devil, where is he away?

300   SOLDIER 3. What, is he thusgates° from us went,   *in this way*
That false traitor that here was lent,°   *placed*
And we truly here for to tent
Had underta'en?°   *undertaken*
Sikerly,° I tell us shent°   *truly / destroyed*
305   Wholly ilkone.°   *each one*

---

1   *Harrow, for ay / I tell us shent* Alas, forever I hold us destroyed. I.e., we're done for;
Harrow Interjection. A cry of distress.
2   *We* Interjection. Expresses distress (as here), derision, or surprise.

SOLDIER 1. Alas, what shall we do this day,
That thus this warlock is went his way?
And safely,° sirs, I dare well say   *by all means, truly*
He rose alone.
SOLDIER 2. Wit° sir Pilate of this affray°   *learn / commotion* 310
We mun° be slone.°[1]   *must / slain*

SOLDIER 3. Why, can° none of us no better rede?°   *knows / advice*
SOLDIER 4. There is not° else but we be dead.   *nothing*
SOLDIER 2. When that he stirred out of this stead°   *place*
None could it ken.°   *perceive* 315
SOLDIER 1. Alas, hard hap° was on my head   *luck*
Among all men.

Fro° sir Pilate wit° of this deed,   *when / learns*
That we were sleeping when he yode,°   *went*
He will forfeit,° without dread,°   *confiscate / doubt* 320
All that we have.
SOLDIER 2. Us must make lies, for that is need,°   *necessary*
Ourselves to save.

SOLDIER 3. Yea, that rede° I well,° as mote I go.[2] *advise / as well*
SOLDIER 4. And I assent thereto also.   325
SOLDIER 2. An hundred shall I say, and mo,
Armed ilkone,
Come and took his corse° us fro   *body*
And us near° slain.   *nearly*

SOLDIER 1. Nay. Certes,° I hold there   *in fact* 330
    none° so good   *no alternative*
As say the sooth° even as it stood,[3]   *truth*
How that he rose with main° and mood°   *strength / will*
And went his way.
To sir Pilate if° he be wood°   *even if / enraged*
This dare I say.   335

---

1   *Wit sir Pilate ... mun be slone*   If Pilate finds out about this disaster, we're dead.
2   *as mote I go*   As I hope to prosper. I.e., for my own benefit, to save myself.
3   *Certes, I hold ... as it stood*   In fact, I think there's no better alternative to telling the truth,
    as it actually happened.

SOLDIER 2. Why, dare thou to sir Pilate go
    With these tidings and say him so?
SOLDIER 1. So rede° I; if he us slo°   *advise / slay, kill*
    We die but once.
340 SOLDIER 3. Now he that wrought us all this woe,
    Woe worth° his bones!   *become, be to*

SOLDIER 4. Go we then, sir knights hend,
    Since that we shall to sir Pilate wend.°   *go*
    I trow° that we shall part no friend   *think*
345   Ere that we pass.
SOLDIER 1. And I shall him say ilka° word till end,   *every*
    Even° as it was.   *just*

Sir Pilate, prince without peer,
Sir Caiaphas and Annas in fere,°   *company*
350 And all ye lordings that are here
    To neven° by name,   *call*
God save you all on sides sere[1]
From sin and shame.

PILATE. Ye are welcome, our knights keen,
355   Of mickle° mirth° now may ye mean,°   *great / joy / speak*
    Therefore some tales tell us between
    How ye have wrought.
SOLDIER 1. Our waking,° lord, without ween,°   *watch / doubt*
    Is worthèd to naught.[2]

360 CAIAPHAS. To naught? Alas, cease of such saw.
SOLDIER 2. The prophet Jesus that ye well know
    Is risen and gone for° all our awe,°   *despite / threat*
    With main and might.
PILATE. Therefore the devil himself thee
    draw,°   *punish by dragging behind a horse*
365   False, recrayed° knight.   *cowardly*

Cumbered° cowards I you call,   *miserable*
Have ye let him go from you all?
SOLDIER 3. Sir, there was none that did but small°   *little*

---

1 *on sides sere* Everywhere.
2 *Is worthèd to naught* Has come to nothing.

When that he yode.°	*went*	
SOLDIER 4. We were so feared° down gan we fall[1]	*afraid*	370
And dared° for dread.[2]	*cowered*	

ANNAS. Had ye no strength him to gainstand?°	*withstand*	
Traitors, ye might have bound in band°	*rope*	
Both him and them that ye there found,		
And ceased° them soon.°	*stopped / immediately*	375
SOLDIER 1. That deed all earthly men livand°	*living*	
Might not have done.		

SOLDIER 2. We were so rad° everilkone°	*frightened / everyone*	
When that he put beside the stone,		
We were so stonied° we durst°	*stunned / dared*	380
stir none,°	*not at all*	
And so abashed.°	*perplexed*	
PILATE. What, rose he by himself alone?		
SOLDIER 1. Yea sir, that be ye trast.°	*sure*	

SOLDIER 4. We heard never since we were born,		
Nor all our fathers us beforn,°	*before*	385
Such melody, midday nor morn,		
As was made there.		
CAIAPHAS. Alas, then is our law lorn°	*destroyed*	
For evermore.		

SOLDIER 2. What time he rose good tent° I took,	*heed, attention*	390
The earth that time trembled and quook,°	*quaked*	
All kindly° force° than me forsook	*natural / strength*	
Till he was gone.		
SOLDIER 3. I was afeared,° I durst not look,	*frightened*	
Nor might° had none,	*strength*	395

I might not stand, so was I stark.°	*stiff, rigid*	
PILATE. Sir Caiaphas, ye are a cunning clerk:		
If we amiss° have ta'en our mark,°	*wrongly / aim*	
I trow sam fail[3]—		

---

1 *gan we fall* We fell.

2 *We were so feared … for dread* This suggests that the soldiers woke up from their slumber during the resurrection itself, but could not move because of their fear and dread.

3 *trow sam fail* I believe we fail together.

400	Therefore what shall worth° now of this work?°	*become / business*
	Say your counsel.	

CAIAPHAS. To say the best forsooth° I shall, *truly*
That shall be profit to us all.
Yon° knights behooves their words *yonder*
   again-call,°[1] *take back, retract*
405 How he is missed.° *missing*
We would,° for thing that might befall,[2] *want*
That no man wist.° *know*

ANNAS. Now sir Pilate, since that it is so
That he is risen dead us fro,° *from*
410 Command your knights to say, where° they go, *wherever*
That he was ta'en
With twenty thousand men and mo,
And them near slain,

And thereto of our treasury
415 Give to them a reward forthy.° *therefore*
PILATE. Now of this purpose° well pleased am I, *plan*
And further thus:
Sir knights, that are in deeds doughty,° *valiant*
Take tent° to us, *heed*

420 And harken° what that ye shall say *listen*
To ilka° man both night and day: *every*
That ten thousand men in good array
Came you until,[3]
With force of arms bore him away
425 Against your will.

Thus shall ye say in ilka land,
And thereto on° that same covenant° *as part of / agreement*
A thousand pounds have in your hand
To° your reward— *as*
430 And friendship sirs, ye understand,
Shall not be spared.

---

1 *Yon knights … again-call* It is required of those knights there to take back their words.
2 *for thing that might befall* Because of what might happen.
3 *Came you until* Came to you (and).

CAIAPHAS. Ilkone° your state°   *each one / status*
    we shall amend,°   *improve*
    And look ye say as we you kenned.°   *instructed*
SOLDIER 1. In what country so ye us send
    By night or day,   435
    Whereso° we come, whereso we wend   *wherever*
    So shall we say.

PILATE. Yea, and whereso ye tarry in ilka country,
    Of our doing in no degree[1]
    Do° that no man the wiser be   *let* 440
    Nor frayne beforn,[2]
    Nor of the sight that ye gan° see   *did*
    Neven° it neither evening nor morn.   *mention*

For we shall maintain you always,
    And to the people shall we say   445
    It is greatly against our lay°   *law*
    To trow° such thing.   *believe*
    So shall they deem both night and day
    All is leasing.°   *lying*

Thus shall the sooth° be bought and sold   *truth* 450
    And treason shall for truth be told,
    Therefore ay° in your hearts ye hold   *always*
    This counsel clean.°   *entirely*
    And fare now well both young and old,
    Wholly bedene.[3]   455

The York Corpus Christi Play: Christ's Appearance to Mary Magdalene

The Winedrawers' pageant of *Christ's Appearance to Mary Magdalene* follows the *Resurrection* pageant and flows narratively from it, but it is written in a quieter register and a simpler verse form (largely eight-line

---

1 *in no degree* In no way, on no account.
2 *Nor frayne beforn* Nor ask questions in front of you.
3 *Wholly bedene* All of you.

stanzas rhyming ababcdcd). Despite having been told by the angel of Jesus' resurrection in the previous play, Mary Magdalene still weeps for the death and loss of her beloved. Weeping is frequently associated with the Magdalene, in large part because of the traditional conflation of her identity with that of the sinful woman who washes Christ's feet with her tears in Luke 7.37–38 (even though that woman is unnamed in the Gospel text). Mary's slowness to understand the nature of the resurrection—in this play, for example, she mistakes the risen Christ for a gardener—together with the traditional association of Mary with sin and sorrow, makes her the perfect figure of the Christian audience member. Each member of the audience could see the resurrection dramatized, but could not get close or touch; each was called to understand and weep for the suffering Jesus had taken on to atone for humanity's own sins. As such a figure of the ordinary Christian, the Magdalene was extremely popular in late medieval English worship, art, and literature. She was also widely seen as the "apostle to the apostles" for being the first of Jesus' followers to spread the news of his resurrection. In that sense, Mary's experience initiates a sequence in the York *Corpus Christi Play* of post-resurrection encounters that all speak to the audience's position as disciples themselves, who may or may not struggle with their belief after Christ's death. But it is Mary Magdalene who has pride of place.

Christ's appearance to Mary is not without its puzzling and troubling aspects, however. Following the account given in John 20.17, here Jesus tells Mary to "touch me not" (*noli me tangere* in the Latin Vulgate Bible). Theologians, scholars, and devotional writers, both past and present, have wondered over the meaning of the injunction not to touch. This play mitigates the harshness of Jesus' command by having Jesus and Mary repeatedly address each other in terms of endearment. The intimacy of this brief but emotionally-charged, two-person pageant, together with Mary's exquisite joy at its end, act to overwhelm any sense of rejection.

More disturbing to a modern reader than any perceived harshness in Jesus' "touch me not" is the anti-Semitism of Mary's repeated charge at the beginning of the play that "the Jews" were responsible for Jesus' death. To be sure, the cycle as a whole depicts a mixed conspiracy of the Pharisees, Judas, Pilate, and the soldiers who do their bidding, and does not depict the actual crucifiers as Jews; the *Crucifixion* play itself, arguably, invites the audience to see themselves in the crucifiers. The difference between the attitudes expressed in that play and the crude anti-Semitism expressed here could hardly be more stark. That difference speaks to the corporate creation of the plays—many hands were involved, and many attitudes find expression in the play as a whole.

CHARACTERS

Mary Magdalene
Jesus

[*Enter Mary Magdalene.*]

MARY MAGDALENE. Alas, in this world was never no wight°   *creature*
   Walking with so mickle° woe.   *great*
   Thou dreadful death, draw hither and dight°   *condemn*
   And mar° me as thou hast done mo.°   *destroy / others*
   In loam° is it locken,° all my light,   *earth / enclosed*   5
   Forthy° on ground unglad I go;   *therefore*
   Jesus of Nazareth he hight,°   *was called*
   The false Jews slew him me fro.°   *from*

   My wit is waste° now in wede.°   *wasted, decayed / madness*
   I wallow, I walk, now woe is me,   10
   For laid now is that lovesome° in lead,°   *lovely one / i.e., a coffin*
   The Jews him nailed until° a tree.   *unto*
   My doleful heart is ever in dread,
   To ground now gone is all my glee.°   *joy, bliss*
   I spurn there° I was wont° to speed,°   *where / accustomed / prosper*   15
   Now help me God in persons three.[1]

   Thou lovesome lede° in ilka° land,   *person (i.e., God) / every*
   As thou shaped both day and night,
   Sun and moon both bright shinand,°   *shining*
   Thou grant me grace to have a sight   20
   Of my Lord, or else his sand.°   *messenger*

[*Enter Jesus.*]

JESUS. Thou willful woman in this way,
   Why weeps thou so as° thou would wede,°   *as if / (go) mad*
   As thou on field would fall down faie?°   *dead*

---

1   *God in persons three*   The Trinity of God the Father, God the Son, and the Holy Spirit.

25   Do way,¹ and do no more that deed.
      Whom seekest thou this long day?
      Say me the sooth,° as Christ thee rede.°   *truth / guides, teaches*
      MARY MAGDALENE. My Lord Jesus and God verray,°   *true*
      That suffered° for sins his sides bleed.   *allowed, endured*

30 JESUS. I shall thee say, will thou me hear,
      The sooth° of him that thou hast sought: *truth*
      Without dread, thou faithful fere,°   *companion*
      He is full near that° mankind bought.°   *who / redeemed*
      MARY MAGDALENE. Sir, I would look both far and near
35   To find my Lord—I see him not.
      JESUS. Woman, weep not, but mend thy cheer,
      I wot° well whither° that he was brought.   *know / where*

      MARY MAGDALENE. Sweet sir, if thou him bore away,
      Say me the sooth and thither me lead
40   Where thou him did; without delay
      I shall him seek again good speed.

      Therefore, good gardener,² say thou me,
      I pray thee for the prophet's sake,
      Of these tidings that I ask thee.
45   For it would do my sorrow to slake
      When God's body found might be,
      That Joseph off the cross gan° take.   *did*
      Might I him fang° unto my fee,°   *take / possession*
      Of all my woe he would me wrake.°   *deliver, rescue (wreak)*

50 JESUS. What would thou do with that body bare
      That buried was with baleful° cheer?°   *miserable / mood*
      Thou may not salve him of his sare,°   *suffering*
      His pains were so sad° and sere.°   *serious / many*
      But he shall cover° mankind of° care,   *deliver / from*
55   That° clouded was he shall make clear,   *that which*
      And the folk well for to fare°   *get on*
      That filed° were all in fere.³   *defiled*

---

1 *Do way* Leave off, cease.
2 *gardener* See John 20.15: "She, thinking it was the gardener, saith to him: Sir, if thou
    hast taken him hence, tell me where thou hast laid him, and I will take him away" (Dou-
    ay-Rheims translation).
3 *all in fere* Altogether.

MARY MAGDALENE. Ah, might I ever with that man meet,
  The which that is so mickle° of might,   *great*
  Dry should I wipe that now is wet;   60
  I am but sorrow of worldly sight.

JESUS. Mary, of° mourning amend thy mood,   *from*
  And behold my wounds wide.
  Thus for man's sins I shed my blood
  And all this bitter bale° gan° bide.°   *suffering / did / endure* 65
  Thus was I raised on the rood°   *cross*
  With spear and nails that were unride.° *severe, causing much suffering*
  Trow° it well, it turns to good   *believe*
  When men in earth their flesh shall hide.[1]

MARY MAGDALENE. Ah, Rabboni,° I have thee sought,   *rabbi (teacher)* 70
  My master dear, full fast this day.
JESUS. Go away, Mary, and touch me not,
  But take good keep what I shall say:
  I am he that all things wrought,
  That thou calls thy Lord and God verray.   75
  With bitter deed I mankind bought,°   *redeemed*
  And I am reason as thou see may.

  And therefore, Mary, speak now with me,
  And let° thou now be[2] thy greet.°   *stop / weeping*
MARY MAGDALENE. My Lord Jesus, I know now thee,   80
  Thy wounds they are now wet.°   *fresh, bleeding*
JESUS. Nigh° me not, my love, let be,   *come near*
  Mary, my daughter sweet;
  To my father in Trinity
  Forth I sty° not yet.   *ascend*   85

MARY MAGDALENE. Ah, mercy, comely conqueror,
  Through thy might thou hast overcome dead.°   *death*
  Mercy, Jesus, man and savior,
  Thy love is sweeter than the mead.°   *drink made from honey*
  Mercy, mighty comforter,   90

---

1 *When ... hide* I.e., when people die and are buried. Christ's death and resurrection will
   then turn to good since humankind will have access to life after death.
2 *let thou now be* Now let be; now stop.

For ere° I was full will of rede.¹   *formerly*
Welcome Lord, all mine honor,
My joy, my love, in ilka° stead.°   *every / place*

JESUS. Mary, in thine heart thou write
95   Mine armor rich and good:
  Mine acton° covered all with white   *a padded jacket under armor*
  As corse° of man behewed,°   *body / colored*
  With stuff° good and parfite°   *quilted padding under armor / perfect*
  Of maiden's flesh and blood;
100 When they gan° thirl° and smite   *did / pierce*
  My head for hauberk° stood.   *mail coat*

  My plates° were spread all on brede,°   *plate armor / breadth*
  That was my body upon a tree;
  Mine helm° covered all with   *helmet*
    manhead,°   *manhood, human nature*
105 The strength thereof may no man see;
  The crown of thorn that gart° me bleed,   *caused*
  It bemeans° my dignity.   *signifies*
  My diadem says,° without dread,   *means*
  That dead shall I never be.²

110 MARY MAGDALENE. Ah, blessed body that bale°   *misery*
    would bete,°   *mend*
  Dear° hast thou bought mankin.°   *dearly, at great cost / mankind*
  Thy wounds hath made thy body wet
  With blood that was thee within.
  Nailed thou was through hand and feet,
115 And all was for our sin.
  Full grisly° must we caitiffs° greet°—   *sorrowfully / wretches / weep*
  Of bale how should I blin?°   *stop*

---

1 *will of rede* At a loss for a plan.
2 *Mine armor rich ... never be* These two stanzas participate in a conceit of the incarnation in which the dual nature of Christ as both God and human is represented as a knight in the arms and armor of humankind and the crown of God, the king. The conceit draws on common medieval literary tropes of knights fighting in disguise (full armor hides their true identities—"The strength thereof may no man see") and of knights fighting with some insignia of those they champion, and turns up elsewhere in late medieval literature, perhaps most famously in Passus 18 of William Langland's *Piers Plowman*. Also relevant is Paul's Letter to the Ephesians, 6.11, where he urges Christians to put on the armor of God; Christ here putting on the armor of humankind reverses Paul's metaphor.

To see this ferly° food°[1]
Thus ruefully dight,°
Rugged° and rent° on a rood,°
This is a rueful° sight;
And all is for our good,
And nothing for his plight.
Spilt thus is his blood,
For ilka° sinful wight.°

wondrous / man
~~dealt with~~
~~pulled~~ / torn / cross   120
pitiful

every / person 125

JESUS. To my God and my father dear,
   To him as-swith° I shall ascend,
   For I shall now not long dwell here;
   I have done as my father me kenned,°
   And therefore look that ilka man lere°
   How that in earth their life may mend.
   All that me loves[2] I shall draw near
   My father's bliss that never shall end.

very swiftly (soon)

made known
learn 130

MARY MAGDALENE. All for joy me likes[3] to sing,
   Mine heart is gladder than the glee,°
   And all for joy of thy rising
   That suffered death upon a tree.°
   Of love now is thou crowned king,
   Is none so true living more free.
   Thy love passes all earthly thing.
   Lord, blessed mot° thou ever be.

joy (i.e., gladder than glad) 135

i.e., the cross

140
must

JESUS. To Galilee shall thou wend°
   Mary, my daughter dear,
   Unto my brethren hend,°
   There they are all in fere.[4]
   Tell them ilka° word to end[5]
   That thou spoke with me here.
   My blessing on thee lend,°
   And all that we leave here.

go

courteous
145

every

light upon

---

1 *food* Man, with pun on "food" as nourishment (suggesting the Eucharist, in which believers consume Christ's body and blood in the form of the communion bread and wine).

2 *me loves* Loves me.

3 *me likes* It is pleasing to me; I like.

4 *in fere* Together.

5 *ilka word to end* I.e., everything. This injunction to Mary to go to Galilee and report to the apostles everything that transpired here is what makes her the "apostle to the apostles" in medieval tradition.

The York Corpus Christ Play: The Death of Mary

The Drapers' *Death of Mary* play may seem straightforward on the page, but it would have been the occasion for awe-inspiring spectacle. The pageant wagon was likely two-tiered—similar to the one described in the Mercers' Indenture—so that it could accommodate Jesus speaking to Mary from on high and the angels descending to her for her assumption into heaven (dramatized in the following pageant). Before that moment, Mary prays that the Apostles will be by her side at her death, and they appear there miraculously, having been whisked away from other locations. Perhaps this was effected on stage with the apostles appearing from behind curtains; we do not know for sure. And at the moment of Mary's death, angels appear, and a devil—or possibly a pair of devils—competes for her soul, in the manner of both visual arts and morality plays depicting a "psychomachia," or battle for the soul. If the presentation followed conventional iconographic depictions of death in other ways, then Mary's soul might have been represented as a miniature version of herself, perhaps in the form of a puppet or doll. The angels and Christ might have been accompanied by light effects using reflectors and fire. Like the Mercers who staged the spectacular *Last Judgment*, the wealthy, mercantile Drapers would have been able to afford such dazzling effects.

The story of Mary's death, along with her assumption into heaven and her coronation as Queen of Heaven, each depicted in its own pageant following this one, is nowhere to be found in the Bible; it comes from a number of apocryphal works from late antiquity. This version of her death ultimately derives from the *Transitus Beatae Mariae* (*The Passing of the Blessed Virgin Mary*). Such narratives were popularized and spread in works such as *The Golden Legend* by Jacobus de Voragine, and then replicated in visual arts, lyric poetry, devotional works, and drama. Because of its non-canonical status and association with Catholic practices, this play and the following plays about her assumption and coronation were suppressed during the reign of Protestant King Edward VI (January 1547–July 1553), only to be revived under the Catholic Queen Mary I (July 1553–November 1558) and suppressed again when Elizabeth I succeeded to the throne in 1558.

The play largely consists of stately eight-line stanzas rhyming abab-cddc, which suit the solemn and dignified spectacle of its content.

Pageant 44 of the York Corpus Christi Play: The Death of Mary

CHARACTERS

Gabriel
Mary
John
Peter
James
Andrew
Maid 1
Maid 2
Jew 1
Jew 2
Jesus
Angel 1
Angel 2
Angel 3
Angel 4

[*Enter Gabriel.*][1]

GABRIEL. Hail, mightful Mary, God's mother so mild,
  Hail be thou, root of all rest, hail be thou, royal.°   *royal one*
  Hail flower and fruit not faded nor filed,°   *defiled*
  Hail, salve° to all sinful.° Now say   *remedy / sinful people*
    thee° I shall,   *to thee*
  Thy son to thyself me has sent,   5
  His sand,° and soothly° he says   *messenger / truly*
  No longer than these three days
  Here left thee this life that is lent.°[2]   *given*

  And therefore he bids thee look that thou blithe° be,   *glad*
  For to that bigly° bliss that   *perfect* 10
    bird° will thee bring,   *child, son (i.e., Jesus)*

---

1 *Enter Gabriel* Presumably Mary is already in place on the pageant wagon when Gabriel comes to her. She may be accompanied by her two Maids throughout the play, or they may enter when she is on her death bed. Clifford Davidson suggests in his edition that she might be seated reading a book, in the conventional iconography of the Annunciation, which Gabriel's message to her here echoes.

2 *No longer ... lent* No more than three days are left to you of this life that has been given (to you). The three days elapse quickly in the play.

There to sit with himself, all solace° to see,   *joy*
And to be crowned for his queen and he himself king
In mirth that ever shall be new.
He sends to thee worthily, iwis,°   *indeed*
15   This palm out of paradise,
In tokening[1] that it shall be true.

[*Gabriel gives Mary a palm frond.*]

MARY. I thank my son seemly° of all his   *worthy*
     sands° sere;°   *messages / many*
Unto him lastingly° be ay° lofing°   *everlastingly / forever / praise*
That me thus worthily would mensk° in this manner,[2]   *honor*
20   And to his bigly bliss my bones° for to bring.   *body*
But good sir, neven° me thy name.   *say*
GABRIEL. Gabriel, that bainly° gan° bring   *gladly / did*
The bodeword° of his bearing—   *message*
Forsooth° lady, I am the same.   *truly*

25 MARY. Now Gabriel that soothly is from my son sent,
I thank thee these tidings thou tells me until,[3]
And lovèd° be that Lord of° the loan°   *praised / for / gift*
     that has me lent°   *given*
….[4]
And dear son, I beseech thee,
Great God, thou grant me thy grace,
30   Thine apostles to have in this place,
That they at my bearing° may be.   *bearing (of the body), i.e., funeral*

GABRIEL. Now food° fairest of face, most faithful   *person*
     and free,°   *gracious*
Thine asking° thy son has granted of his grace,   *request*
And says all sam° in sight ye shall see   *together*
35   All his apostles[5] appear in this place,

---

1 *In tokening* As a sign.
2 *That me … manner* Who would honor me thus in this manner.
3 *thou tells me until* You tell to me.
4 …. A line is missing in the manuscript here.
5 *All his apostles* Only four apostles have speaking parts, but the *Ordo Paginarum* lists eight apostles. This promise, meanwhile, suggests that they were all there; however, traditionally Thomas is not present, being far away in India, and in the next play, he regrets not being by her side.

To work all thy will at thy wending.°   *going, i.e., passing away*
And soon shall thy pains be passed,
And thou to be in life that shall last
Evermore without any ending.

[*Exit Gabriel. Enter John.*]

JOHN. Mary my mother, that° mild is and meek,   *who*   40
    And chief chosen for chaste,° now tell me, what cheer?[1]   *chastity*
MARY. John, son, I say thee forsooth I am sick.
    My sweet son's sand° I hent,° right now it was here,   *message / received*
    And doubtless° he says I shall die.   *without doubt*
    Within three days, iwis,°   *indeed*   45
    I shall be bielded° in bliss   *sheltered*
    And come to his own company.

JOHN. Ah, with thy leave lady, thou neven° it me° not,   *say / to me*
    Nor tell me no tidings to twin° us in two,   *separate*
    For be thou, blissed bird,° unto bier brought,   *noble lady*   50
    Evermore whilst I wone° in this world will me be full woe,   *dwell*
    Therefore let it stint,° and be still.   *cease*
MARY. Nay John, son, myself now I see:
    At God's will must it needs be,
    Therefore be it wrought at his will.   55

JOHN. Ah, worthy,° when thou art   *worthy one*
    went° will me be full woe—   *gone*
    But God give the apostles wist° of   *knowledge*
    thy wending.°   *passing away*
MARY. Yes John, son, for certain shall it be so,
    All shall they hardly° be here at mine ending.   *assuredly*
    The sand° of my son said° me this,   *message / told*   60
    That soon shall my penance° be passed   *pain*
    And I to be in life that ever shall last,
    Then bainly° to bield° in that bliss.   *gladly / dwell*

[*Enter Peter, James, Andrew, and, possibly, seven additional Apostles.*]

---

1   *what cheer?*   How are you? How do you feel?

PETER. Oh God, omnipotent, the giver of all grace,
65   *Benedicite Dominus*,[1] a cloud now full clear
    Umbelapped° me in Judea preaching as I was,   *surrounded*
    And I have mickle° marvel how that I come here.[2]   *great*
JAMES. Ah, cease, of this assembling can I not say
    How and in what wise° that we are here met,   *way*
70   Either mirth° or of mourning mean well it may,   *joy*
    For suddenly in sight here soon was I set.

ANDREW. Ah, brother, by my witting° and   *knowledge*
    iwis° so were we,   *truly*
    In diverse lands leally° I wot° we were lent,°   *truly / know / dwelling*
    And how we are assembled thus can I not see,
75   But as God of his sand° has us sam° sent.   *message / together*
JOHN. Ah, fellows, let be your fare,°   *fuss*
    For as God will it must needs be,
    That peerless is of poustie,°   *power*
    His might is to do mickle° more.   *much*

80   For Mary that worthy shall wend° now I ween,°   *pass away / think*
    Unto that bigly° bliss that high berne°   *perfect / man*
    bainly° us bought;   *willingly*
    That we in her sight all sam° might be seen   *together*
    Ere° she dissever° us from,[3] her son   *before / separates*
    she besought.°   *entreated*
    And thus has he wrought at her will,
85   When she shall be brought on a bier,
    That we may be nighing her near[4]
    This time for to tent her until.[5]

MARY. Jesus, my darling that ding° is and dear,   *worthy*
    I thank thee my dear son of thy great grace
90   That I all this fair fellowship at hand now has here,
    That they me some comfort may kithe° in this case.   *show*
    This sickness it sits° me full sore;°   *affects / painfully*

---

1 *Benedicite Dominus* Latin: God bless.
2 *marvel how … come here* Peter, James, and Andrew have been spirited away from their missions and brought miraculously to Mary's side. How their sudden appearance was effected on stage is unknown.
3 *us from* From us.
4 *nighing her near* Coming near her.
5 *tent her until* Attend to her.

My maidens, take keep now on me
And cast some water upon me—
I faint, so feeble I fare.°   *get on*   95

MAID 1. Alas, for my lady that leamed° so light,°   *shone / brightly*
   That ever I lived in this lede° thus long   *place*
      for to lend,°   *go on living*
   That I on this seemly° should see such a sight.   *beautiful one*
MAID 2. Alas, help, she dies in our hend.°   *hands*
   Ah, Mary, of me have thou mind   100
   ....¹
   Some comfort us two for to kithe,°   *show*
   Thou knows we are come of thy kind.°   *people*

MARY. What ails you women for woe thus winly° to weep?   *excessively*
   Ye do me dere° with your din, for me must needs die.   *harm*
   Ye should, when ye saw me so slip on° sleep,   *into*   105
   Have left all your late° and let me lie.   *noise*
   John, cousin, gar° them stint° and be still.   *make / cease*
JOHN. Ah, Mary that mild is of mood,
   When thy son was raised on a rood°   *cross*
   To tent° thee he took me thee till,²   *attend to*   110

   And therefore at thy bidding full bain° will I be.   *obedient*
   If there be aught,° mother, that I amend may,   *anything*
   I pray thee, mildest of mood, move° thee to me,   *speak*
   And I shall, dearworthy° dame, do it ilka° day.   *noble / this same*
MARY. Ah, John, son, that this pain were   115
   over-passed!°   *passed over, ended*
   With good heart ye all that are here
   Pray for me faithfully in fere,³
   For I mun° wend° from you as fast.   *must / go*

JEW 1. Ah, food° fairest of face, most faithful to find,   *person*
   Thou maiden and mother that mild is and meek,   120
   As thou art courteous and come of our kind°   *people*
   All our sins for to cease, thy son thou beseech,
   With mercy to mend us of miss.°   *sin*
JEW 2. Since thou, lady, come of our kin,

---

1 .... A line is missing from the manuscript here.
2 *thee till* To you.
3 *in fere* Together.

125   Thou help us now, thou verray° virgin,   *true*
        That we may be brought unto bliss.

      MARY. Jesus my son,[1] for my sake beseech I thee this,
        As thou art gracious and great God, thou grant me thy grace.
        They that is come of my kind and amend will their miss,
· 130   Now specially thou them speed° and   *assist*
          spare them a space,°   *i.e., in heaven*
        And be their bield,° if thy will be.   *supporter*
        And dear son, when I shall die,
        I pray thee then for thy mercy—
        The fiend thou let me not see.

135   And also my blessed bairn,° if thy will be,   *child*
        I sadly° beseech thee, my son, for my sake,   *solemnly*
        Men that are stead° stiffly° in storms or in sea   *steadfast / valiantly*
        And are in will[2] witterly° my worship to awake,°   *wisely / cause*
        And then neven° my name in that need,   *call*
140   Thou let them not perish nor spill.°   *be killed*
        Of this boon° my son, at thy will,   *request*
        Thou grant me specially to speed.°   *succeed*

      Also my blessed bairn, thou grant me my boon,°   *prayer*
        All that are in noy° or in need and neven me by name,   *trouble*
145   I pray thee son for my sake thou succor them soon,
        In all their showers° that are sharp,   *suffering*
          thou shield them from shame.
        And women also in their childing,°   *childbirth*
        Now special thou them speed,°   *assist*
        And if so be they die in that dread
150   To thy bliss then bainly° thou them bring.   *readily*

      JESUS. Mary, my mother, through the might now of me
        For to make thee in mind with mirth° to be mending,   *joy*
        Thine asking° all wholly here hight° I now thee.   *request / promise*
        But mother, the fiend must be needs° at thine ending   *necessarily*
155   In figure° full foul for to fear° thee.[3]   *form / frighten*

---

1 *Jesus my son* Jesus may appear at this point—likely on the upper level of the pageant, signifying heaven—but he does not speak until after Mary's prayer.

2 *in will* Willing.

3 *the fiend ... to fear thee* As the penultimate stage direction of the play shows, there will indeed be a devil present at Mary's death.

Mine angels shall then be about thee.
And therefore, dear dame, thou thar°   *need*
   not doubt° thee,°   *worry / yourself*
For doubtless° thy death shall not   *without doubt, certainly*
   dere° thee.   *harm*

And therefore, my mother, come mildly to me,
   For after the Son° my   *i.e., himself as son of God* 160
      sand° will I send,   *messenger*
And to sit with myself all solace° to see   *joy*
In ay-lasting° life in liking° to lend.°   *ever-lasting / bliss / dwell*
In this bliss shall be thy bielding,°   *dwelling*
Of mirth° shall thou never have missing°   *joy / lack*
But evermore abide° in my blessing—   *remain* 165
All this shall thou have at thy wielding.°   *control*

MARY. I thank thee my sweet son, for certes° I am sick;   *certainly*
   I may not now move me for mercy almost.[1]
To thee, son mine that made me, thy maiden so meek,
Here through thy grace, God's son, I give thee my ghost.°   *spirit* 170
My seely° soul I thee send   *innocent*
To heaven that is highest on height,
To thee, son mine that most is of might,
Receive it here into thine hend.°   *hands*

JESUS. Mine angels lovely of late,° lighter than   *aspect* 175
   the levin,°   *lightening*
Into the earth wightly° I will° that ye wend°   *swiftly / want / go*
And bring me my mother to the highest of heaven,
With mirth and with melody her mood for to mend,
For here shall her bliss never be blinning.°   *ceasing*
My mother shall mildly° by me   *meekly* 180
Sit next° the high Trinity,[2]   *next to*
And never in two to be twinning.°   *separated*

ANGEL 1. Lord, at thy bidding full bain° will I be,   *obedient*
   That flower that never was faded full fain° will we fet.°   *gladly / fetch*
ANGEL 2. And at thy will, good Lord, work will we   185

---

1 *I may ... almost* I am almost unable to ask for mercy for myself.
2 *Trinity* The concept that the godhead is one God in three persons: the Father, the Son (Jesus), and the Holy Spirit.

With solace° on ilka° side that seemly°   *joy / every / lovely one*
    umsit.°   *to surround*
ANGEL 3. Let us fond° to her fast, her force° to defend,   *go / strength*
    That bird° for to bring unto this bliss bright.   *lady*
    Body and soul we shall her ascend
190   To reign in this regally be regency° full right.   *dominion*

ANGEL 4. To bliss that bird° for to bring,   *lady*
    Now Gabriel, let us wightly° be wending.°   *swiftly / going*
    This maiden's mirth° to be mending   *joy*
    A seemly° song let us sing.   *beautiful*

(*With one devil.*)[1]

(*And they shall sing an antiphon,*[2] *for example, "Ave regina celorum."*[3])

The York Corpus Christi Play: The Assumption of Mary

The Assumption of Mary—the taking up of her body and soul into heaven—was celebrated on August 15 in England until the Reformation, and continues to be celebrated by the modern Catholic church on that date. As the York dramatization suggests, it is a solemn and significant feast day, and it continues to be a Holy Day of Obligation for Catholics today. The doctrinal basis for belief in the Assumption in the modern church comes from the interpretation of various verses from both the Old and New Testaments; the narrative itself derives from apocryphal and popular sources from late antiquity and the Middle Ages, and was widely represented in art, literature, and drama. Veneration of Mary in general (not to mention the story of the Assumption in particular and the celebration of this feast day) was strongly associated with Catholic doctrine. Consequently this play, along with the *Death of*

---

1   *With one devil* This stage direction and the next are original to the text. Presumably the devil does what Jesus, above, said he would do: attempt to frighten Mary at her death. The *Ordo Paginarum* lists two devils in the play.

2   *antiphon* A hymn.

3   *"Ave regina celorum"* Latin: "Hail, Queen of Heaven." The opening words to a common medieval hymn to Mary.

Mary and *The Coronation of Mary*, was suppressed under the Protestant monarchs Edward VI and Elizabeth I before the cycle as a whole ceased to be performed.

The significance of the Assumption to medieval devotion can be seen in the spectacle and apparent expense that almost certainly went into the Weavers' play. In the fifteenth century, especially, the Weavers were a wealthy craft, fully able to provide the pageant with the splendor it required. The wagon was likely a two-tiered wagon such as the one described in the Mercers' Indenture; some device would have been needed to raise Mary into heaven. Although nothing is specified in the dialogue, the appearance of the angels and Mary must have been lavishly represented, with fabric and other costume elements (perhaps gold masks for the angels—again, see the Mercers' Indenture), and light effects signifying the glory of heaven.

Music plays a very important role in this play, and the musicians and singers needed would have added to the expense; they were likely experienced performers hired from the Minster or a local monastery or parish. Clifford Davidson points out in his edition that this is the York pageant richest in music; it not only provide cues for music in the rubrics of the play, but also provides musical settings in the manuscript of the Register.

It is worth noting that the music which accompanies the appearance of the angels and Mary's assumption would have added time to the performance. On the page, its seems that the apostle Thomas's mourning for Jesus' suffering takes up a third of the play, but his soliloquy would have been ultimately overshadowed by the spectacular vision of the angels and Mary. His opening speech and its focus on Christ's Passion has an important function, nevertheless. It ties Mary's death and assumption to Christ's death, resurrection, and ascension, underscoring the centrality of Mary's story as part of the beliefs of the devout. Thomas's intimate experience of both the risen Jesus and the risen Mary—his touching the wounds of the risen Christ is also dramatized, in Pageant 41—also ties the events together.

Through his uncertainty and mourning (relieved through a special spiritual encounter, which he then recounts to the other apostles), Thomas becomes a male counterpart to Mary Magdalene. As such, especially in his doubt and uncertainty, he also becomes a figure of identification for the ordinary Christian watching the play. He is the witness through whom the audience sees the marvelous spiritual spectacle. Likewise, the mix of emotions in the play—the other apostles' anger at having been abandoned by Thomas, and their subsequent forgiveness and unification—adds psychological realism to the otherwise formal play. Such an emotional arc also figures the struggle of maintaining unity in the Christian community—the body of Christ—that the Corpus Christi cycle celebrates.

The heavily alliterative thirteen-line stanzas, which rhyme ababbcb-cdeeed, are adaptable to both the formal and lyrical speeches of Thomas, Mary, and the angels, and the more worldly dialogue of Thomas with his fellow apostles.

Pageant 45 of the York Corpus Christi Play: *The Assumption of Mary*

CHARACTERS

Thomas
Angel 1
Angel 2
Angel 3
Angel 4
Angel 5
Angel 6
Angel 7
Angel 8
Angel 9
Angel 10
Angel 11
Angel 12
Mary
Peter
James
Andrew
John

THOMAS. In wailing and weeping, in woe am I wapped,°   *enveloped*
  In site° and in sorrow, in sighing full sad.   *grief*
  My Lord° and my love, lo, full low is   *i.e., Jesus*
    he lapped,°   *placed, brought*
  That makes me to mourn now full mate°   *defeated*
    and full mad.°   *distraught*
5   What harling° and what hurling° that   *blows / violence*
    headsman° he had,   *leader*
  What breaking of branches were bursten° about him,   *broken*

What bolning° with beating of°   *swelling / from*
  brothels° full bad;   *scoundrels*
It leres° me full leally° to love° him and   *teaches / faithfully / praise*
  lout° him,   *submit to*
That comely° to ken.°   *gracious one / know*
God's son Jesus,   10
He died for us;
That makes me thus
To mourn among many men.

Among men may I mourn for the malice they meant°   *intended*
To Jesus the gentlest of Jews' generation.°   *lineage*   15
Of wisdom and wit° were the ways that he went   *knowledge*
That drew all those doomsmen's°   *judges'*
  derf° indignation,   *daringly wicked*
For doubtless° full dear° was his   *certainly / costly*
  due domination.°   *sovereignty*
Unkindly they kid° them their king   *declared*
  for to ken°   *make known*
With careful° comfort and cold° recreation,   *grievous / unhappy*   20
For he mustered° his miracles among many men   *showed*
And to the people he preached.
But the Pharisees fierce
All his reasons reverse,
And to their headsmen° rehearse°   *leaders / report*   25
That untrue were the tales that he teached.°   *taught*

He teached full true, but the tyrants were teened.°   *angry*
For° he reproved their pride, they purposed°   *because / planned*
  them pressed°   *quickly*
To mischieve° him, with malice in their mind have   *harm*
  they meaned,°   *intended*
And to accuse him of cursedness° the caitiffs°   *wickedness / scoundrels*   30
  have cast.°   *tried*
Their rancor was raised, no rink° might it rest,°   *man / assuage*
They took him with treason, that turtle° of truth,   *turtledove*
They fed him with flaps,° with fierceness him fast,° *blows / fettered*
To rug° him, to rive° him; there reigned   *pull violently / tear*
  no ruth.°   *pity*
Unduly° they deemed° him: *unjustly / judged*   35
They dushed° him, they dashed° him,   *struck / hit*
They lushed° him, they lashed him,   *beat*

They pushed him, they pashed° him,   *smashed*
All sorrow they said that it seemed° him.   *befitted*

40 It seemed him all sorrow, they said in their saying.
They skipped° and scourged him—   *caused to jump*
   he scaped° not—with scorns;°   *escaped / mockery*
That he was leader and lord in their law, lay no laying,[1]
But throng° on and thrusted a crown of thick thorns. *pushed, pierced*
Ilka° tag° of that turtle° so tattered and torn is *each / shred / turtledove*
45 That that blessed body blo° is and bolned°   *black and blue / swollen*
   for° beating.   *from*
Yet° the headsmen° to hang him with huge   *urged / leaders*
   hideous horns°   *trumpets*
As brothels° or   *scoundrels*
   bribers° were bellowing and bleating: *swindlers*
'Crucify him' they cried.
Soon Pilate in parliament
50 Of Jesus gave judgment—
To hang him the harlots° him hent°—   *rogues / seized*
There was no deed of that doomsman° denied.   *judge*

Denied not that doomsman to deem° him to dead,°   *condemn / death*
That friendly fair food°[2] that never offended.   *person*
55 They hied° them in haste then to hang up their head,° *hurried / leader*
What woe that they wrought him, no wight° would   *person*
   have wend° it.   *thought*
His true title they took them no time for to attend° it,   *consider*
But as a traitor attainted° they   *convicted*
   tolled° him and tugged him,   *pulled*
They shunt° for no shouts his shape° for to   *shied away / figure*
   shend° it,   *destroy*
60 They raised him on rood° as full rasely° they   *cross / fiercely*
   rugged° him.   *pulled*
They pierced him with a spear,
That° the blood royal   *so that*

---

1 *That he … no laying* They pronounced no declaration that he was leader and lord in their
law; i.e., they did not recognize him as leader and lord of their law.

2 *food* The first meaning here is "person" (one who requires food), but the frequent use of
this word for Christ here and in other pageants also puns on the sacrament of the Eucharist,
the rite during mass in which the bread and wine is believed to become Christ's body and
blood. Jesus is also the spiritual food of believers, as conveyed in the next stanza. That sense
will also be applied to Mary in this play.

To the earth gan° fall,   *did*
In redemption of all
That° his leal° laws likes to lere.°   *who / true / learn*   65

To lere he that likes of his law that is leal
May find in our friend here full faithful° feast,   *spiritual*
That would hang thus on height to enhance° us   *improve*
  in heal°   *well-being*
And buy us from bondage by his blood that is best.
Then the comfort of our company in cares were cast,   70
But that Lord so alone would not leave us full long.
On the third day he rose right with his rinks° to rest,°   *men / remain*
Both flesh and fell° fiercely° that figure   *skin / boldly*
  gan° fang°   *did / take*
And to my brethren° gan appear.   *brothers (i.e., the other apostles)*
They told me of this   75
But I leved° amiss;°   *believed / wrongly*
To rise fleshly,° iwis,°   *bodily / indeed*
Methought° that it passed man's power.   *it seemed to me*

But the power of that prince was preciously° proved   *splendidly*
When that sovereign showed himself to my sight.   80
To mean° of his manhood my mind was all moved,   *mourn, lament*
But that reverent°   *one worthy of respect*
  reduced° me by reason and by right.   *restored*
The wounds full wide of that worthy wight°   *person*
He frayned° me to feel them my faith for to fast,°   *asked / secure*
And so I did doubtless,° and down I me dight;¹   *certainly*   85
I bent my back for to bow and obeyed him for best.²
So soon he ascended
My fellows in fere³
Were sundered° sere;°   *parted / severally*
If they were here   90
My mirth° were°   *joy / would be*
  mickle° amended.°   *greatly / repaired, renewed*

Amended were my mirth with that meinie° to meet.   *company*
My fellows in fere for to find will I fond,°   *try*

---

1 *down I me dight*   I put myself down; i.e., I knelt down (in reverence).
2 *for best*   As the best (i.e., most exalted) one.
3 *in fere*   Together.

I shall not stead° in no stead° but in stall and in street¹   *remain / place*
95 Graith° me by guides to get° them on ground.   *make ready / come to*
Oh sovereign, how soon am I set here so sound!°   *safe*
This is the Vale° of Josaphat,² in Jewry so gent.°   *valley / noble*
I will stem of my steven³ and stead° here a stound,°   *remain / time*
For I am weary for walking the ways that I went
100 Full wilsome° and wide.   *lonely and wild*
Therefore I cast°   *decide*
Here for to rest,
I hold it best
To busk° on this bank for to bide.°   *make ready / wait*

[*Thomas rests himself on the "bank." Enter all Angels.*]

ANGELS. [*Singing.*] *Surge proxima, mea columba,*
  *Mea tabernaculum glorie, vasculum vite, templum celeste.*⁴

105 ANGEL 1. Rise Mary, thou maiden and mother so mild.
ANGEL 2. Rise, lily full lusty,° thy love is full liking.° *beautiful / desirable*
ANGEL 3. Rise, chieftain° of chastity in   *chief source*
  cheering° thy child.   *nursing*
ANGEL 4. Rise, rose ripe redolent, in rest to be reigning.
ANGEL 5. Rise, dove of that doomsman° all deeds   *judge*
  is deeming.°   *judging*
110 ANGEL 6. Rise turtle,° tabernacle, and temple full true.   *turtledove*
ANGEL 7. Rise, seemly° in sight, of thy son   *lovely*
  to be seeming.°   *fitting*
ANGEL 8. Rise, graithed° full goodly in grace for to grow.   *equipped*
ANGEL 9. Rise up this stound.°   *time (instant)*
ANGEL 10. Come, chosen child.
115 ANGEL 11. Come, Mary mild.
ANGEL 12. Come, flower unfiled.°   *undefiled*
ANGEL 8. Come up to the king to be crowned.

---

1 *in stall and in street* I.e., everywhere; *stall* Fixed place, position.
2 *Vale of Josaphat* Biblical place mentioned in Joel 3.2 and 3.12, associated with divine judgment.
3 *stem of my steven* Halt my voice, stop talking; *steven* Voice.
4 *Surge ... celeste* Latin: Rise up, my dearest one, my dove, my tabernacle of glory, container of life, heavenly temple. The source of this hymn is unknown; it is unique to the York plays.

ANGELS. [*Singing.*] *Veni de libano sponsa, veni coronaberis.*[1]

THOMAS. Oh glorious God, what gleams are gliding,
   I move° in my mind what may this bemean?°   *turn over / signify*
   I see a bird° borne° in bliss to be biding°   *lady / carried / dwelling* 120
   With angels' company, comely° and clean.°   *lovely / pure*
   Many selcouth° sights in certes° have I seen,   *marvelous / certainty*
   But this mirth° and this melody mings° my mood. *joy / stirs up, cheers*
MARY. Thomas, do way all thy doubts bedene,°   *immediately*
   For I am founding° forth to my fair food°   *going / child* 125
   I tell thee this tide.°   *time, moment*
THOMAS. Who,° my sovereign lady?   *who (are you)*
MARY. Yea, certes° I say thee.°   *truly / to thee*
THOMAS. Whither wends° thou, I pray thee?[2]   *goes*
MARY. To bliss with my bairn° for to bide.°   *child / dwell* 130

THOMAS. To bide with thy bairn in bliss to be bielding?°   *dwelling*
   Hail, gentlest° of° Jesse[3] in   *noblest / (descended) from*
      Jews' generation,°   *lineage*
   Hail, wealth of this world all wealths is wielding,
   Hail, hendest,° enhanced° to high habitation,   *most gracious / raised*
   Hail, dearworth° and dear is thy due domination,° *worthy / dominion* 135
   Hail, flower fresh flourished, thy fruit is
      full fulsome,°   *abounding in grace*
   Hail, seat of our savior and siege° of salvation,   *throne*
   Hail, happy to hield° to, thy help is   *incline*
      full healsome.°   *salutary, wholesome*
   Hail, peerless in pleasance,°   *courtesy*
   Hail, precious and pure,   140
   Hail, salve that is sure,
   Hail, letter° of languor,°   *preventer / suffering*
   Hail, boot° of our bale°   *remedy / misery*
      in obeisance.°   *obedience (i.e., Mary's)*

---

1 *Veni ... coronaberis* Latin: Come from Libanus, my spouse, come forth, thou shall be crowned. The text is a quotation of Song of Songs 4.8. This passage was traditionally interpreted as prefiguring Mary's Assumption.

2 *Whither ... I pray thee?* The fact that Thomas asks a question Mary has already answered (and that he seems to know the answer to) suggests his state of wonder, but also transforms the repetitive exchange into a liturgical-style call and response.

3 *Jesse* In the Bible, father of David and ancestor of Mary and Jesus.

MARY. Go to thy brethren[1] that in bale are abiding,°   *dwelling*
145 And of what wise° to wealth° I am wending°   *way / well-being / going*
Without tarrying thou tell them this tiding,°   *news*
Their mirth° so° be mickle° amending.°   *joy / thus / greatly / renewing*
For Thomas, to me were they tending°   *attending*
When I drew to the death, all but° thou.   *except*
150 THOMAS. But I lady? Whilst in land I am lending°   *remaining*
Obey thee full bainly° my bones will I bow.   *readily*
But I, alas!
Where was I then
When that barrat° began?   *distress*
155 An unhappy° man   *unlucky*
Both now and ever I was.

Unhappy, unhend° am I holden° at home;   *unworthy / held, regarded*
What dreary destiny me drew from
that deed?°   *i.e., being by Mary's side*
MARY. Thomas, cease of thy sorrow for I am soothly° the same.   *truly*
160 THOMAS. That wot° I well, the worthiest that wrapped   *know*
is in weed.°   *garments*
MARY. Then spare not a space now my speech for to speed,[2]
Go say them soothly thou saw me ascending.
THOMAS. Now doubtless,°   *certainly*
dearworthy,° I dare not for dread,   *worthy one*
For to my tales that I tell they are not attending,°   *listening*
165 For no spell° that is spoken.   *word*
MARY. I shall thee show
A token° true: *sign*
Full fresh of hue,
My girdle,° lo, take them this token.   *belt*

170 THOMAS. I thank thee as reverent root of our rest,
I thank thee as steadfast stock for to stand,
I thank thee as trusty tree for to trust,
I thank thee as buxom° bough to   *pliant, obedient*
the band,°   *promise, bond*
I thank thee as leaf the lustiest° in land,   *loveliest*
175 I thank thee as beauteous branch for to bear,

---

1 *thy brethren* Although only five apostles have speaking parts, the *Ordo Paginarum* lists
"eight Apostles" in addition to Thomas.
2 *Then spare ... speed* Then do not delay in carrying out my words.

I thank thee as flower that never is fadand,°   *fading*
I thank thee as fruit that has fed us in fere,[1]
I thank thee forever.
If they reproved° me   *disapproved of*
Now shall they leve° me.   *believe*   180
Thy blessing give me
And doubtless[2] I shall do my dever.°   *duty*

MARY. Thomas, to do then thy dever be dressing,°   *preparing*
He bid thee his blessing that bields° aboven.°   *dwells / above*
And in sight of my son there is sitting   185
Shall I kneel to that comely° with crown,   *beautiful one*
That who despairs by dale or by down[3]
With piteous plaint° in perils will pray me,°   *lament / to me*
If he swink° or sweat, in swelt° or in swoon,   *toil / illness*
I shall sue° to my sovereign son for to say me   *petition*   190
He shall grant them their grace.
Be it man in his mourning
Or woman in childing,°   *childbirth*
All these to be helping
That prince shall I pray in that place.   195

THOMAS. Gramercy,° the goodliest°   *great thanks / noblest*
     grounded in grace,
Gramercy, the loveliest lady of lire,°   *flesh, body*
Gramercy, the fairest in figure and face,
Gramercy, the dearest° to do our desire.   *most worthy*
MARY. Farewell, now I pass to the peerless empire.   200
Farewell, Thomas, I tarry no tide° here.   *time*
THOMAS. Farewell, thou shining shape that shinest so shire,°   *bright*
Farewell, the belle° of all beauties to bide here,   *beauty*
Farewell, thou fair food.°   *dear person*
Farewell, the key of counsel,   205
Farewell, all this world's weal,°   *well-being*
Farewell, our hope and our heal,
Farewell now, both gracious and good.

---

1 *in fere* All together.
2 *doubtless* Certainly; also punning on Thomas's now no longer being in doubt. (This may also be true in other places in the text.)
3 *by dale or by down* By valley or by hill, i.e., anywhere.

ANGELS. [*Singing.*] *Veni electa mea et ponam in te tronum meum*
  Quia concupivit rex speciem tuam.[1]

THOMAS. That I met with this maid here my mirth°　　　　　*joy*
  is amend.°　　　　　*amended, renewed*
210 I will hie° me in haste and hold that° I　　　　　*hurry / that which*
  have hight,°　　　　　*promised*
  To bear my brethren this bodeword° my back shall I bend　　*message*
  And say them in certain the sooth° of this sight.　　　　　*truth*
  By dale and by down shall I dress° me°　　　　　*prepare / myself*
  to dight°　　　　　*make (my) way*
  To° I find of this fellowship faithful in fere,[2]　　　　　*until*
215 I shall run and rest not, to ransack° full right.　　　　　*search*
  Lo, the meinie° I meant° of, I meet them even here　*company / spoke*
  At hand.
  God save you in fere,
  Say brethren, what cheer?[3]
220 PETER. What does thou here?
  Thou may now of thy gates° be gangand.°　　　　　*ways / going*

THOMAS. Why dear brethren, what bale° is begun?　　　　　*distress*
PETER. Thomas, I tell thee that teen° is betid us.[4]　　　　　*sorrow*
THOMAS. Me forthinketh° for my friends that　　　　　*am sorry*
  faithful are found.
225 JAMES. Yea, but in care° little kindness thou kid° us.　　*misery / show*
ANDREW. His brag and his boast is he busy° to bid° us,　*eager / tell*
  But and° there come any cares° he keeps°　　*if / sorrows / stays*
  not to ken.°　　　　　*know*
  We may run till we rave ere° any ruth°　　　　　*before / pity*
  rid° us　　　　　*relieve*
  For the friendship he fetched° us, by frith or by fen.[5]　　*procured*
230 THOMAS. Sirs, me marvels,[6] I say you,
  What moves in your mind.

1　*Veni ... tuam*　Latin: Come, my chosen one, and I will place you on my throne, because
  the king greatly desires your beauty. A responsory chant from the Feast of the Assumption.
  This marks the moment of Mary's assumption into heaven.
2　*in fere*　All together. Again, this suggests all the apostles are represented, even though only
  five speak.
3　*what cheer?*　How are you?
4　*is betid us*　Has happened to us.
5　*by frith or by fen*　By wood or by marsh; i.e., any and everywhere.
6　*me marvels*　It is a wonder to me; I marvel.

JOHN. We can well find
   Thou art unkind.
THOMAS. Now peace then, and prove it I pray you.

PETER. That thou come not to court here, unkindness 235
   thou kid° us,   *show*
  Our truth has off-turned° us to teen° and   *diverted / sorrow*
   to tray.°   *suffering*
  This year hast thou raked,° thy ruth° would not   *gone / pity*
   rid° us,   *relieve*
  For wit° thou well that worthy°   *know / worthy one*
   is went on her way.
  In a deep den° dead is she dolven° this day,   *grave / buried*
  Mary, that maiden and mother so mild.   240
THOMAS. I wot° well, iwis.°   *know / indeed*
JAMES.   Thomas, do way.[1]
ANDREW. It force not[2] to frayne° him, he will not   *question*
  be filed.°   *polite*
THOMAS. Sirs, with her have I spoken
  Later than ye.
JOHN. That may not be.   245
THOMAS. Yes, kneeling on knee.
PETER. Then tite° can thou tell us some token?°   *quickly / sign*

THOMAS. [*Holds up Mary's belt.*] Lo, this token full trusty she took me
  to take you.
JAMES. Ah, Thomas, where got thou that girdle° so good?   *belt*
THOMAS. Sirs, my message is moving° some   *proposing, intending* 250
  mirth° for to make you,   *joy*
  For founding° fleshly° I found her till° her   *going / bodily / within*
  fair food,°   *body*
  And when I met with that maiden it mended my mood.
  Her sand° has she sent you, so seemly to see.   *message*
ANDREW. Yea, Thomas, unsteadfast full staring thou stood,
  That makes thy mind now full mad° for to be.   *insane* 255
  But harken° and hear now;   *listen*
  Let us look where we laid her,
  If any folk have affrayed° her.   *disturbed*

---

1 *do way* Stop, cease.
2 *It force not* It doesn't work; it does no good.

JOHN. Go we grope° where we graved° her,   *search / buried*
260   If we find aught° that fair one, in fere¹ now.   *anything of*

PETER. Behold° now hither,° your   *look / to that place*
       heeds° in haste,   *attention*
This glorious and goodly is gone from this grave.
THOMAS. Lo, to my talking ye took you no tent° for   *heed*
       to traist.°   *trust*
JAMES. Ah, Thomas, untruly now trespassed we have.
265   Mercy full kindly we cry and we crave.
ANDREW. Mercy, for foul have we faulted in fay.²
JOHN. Mercy, we pray thee, we will not deprave.°   *disparage*
PETER. Mercy, for deeds we did thee this day.
THOMAS. Our savior so sweet
270   Forgive you all,
       And so I shall.
       This token tall°   *fair*
Have I brought you, your bales° to bete.°   *sorrows / assuage*

PETER. It is welcome, iwis,° from that worthy wight,°   *indeed / person*
275   For it was wont° for to   *accustomed*
       wap° that worthy virgin.   *wrap about*
JAMES. It is welcome, iwis, from that lady so light,
       For her womb° would she wrap with it and wear it   *abdomen*
       with win.°   *joy*
ANDREW. It is welcome, iwis, from that salver° of sin,   *healer*
       For she bent it about her with blossom so bright.
280 JOHN. It is welcome, iwis, from the key of our kin,°   *people*
       For about that reverent it reached full right.
PETER. Now kneel we ilkone°   *each one*
       Upon our knee.
       [*All kneel.*]
JAMES. To that lady free.
285 ANDREW. Blessèd mot° she be,   *must*
       Yea, for she is lady lofsome° alone.   *praiseworthy*

THOMAS. Now brethren, be busy and busk° to   *hurry*
       be bouning.°   *going*
       [*They rise.*]

---

1   *in fere* All together.
2   *in fay* In faith, truly.

To India will I turn° me and travel to teach.   *return*
PETER. And to Romans so royal the rinks° to   *people*
    be rouning°   *speaking to*
Will I pass from this place my people to preach.   290
JAMES. And I shall Samaria¹ so sadly° ensearch,°   *solemnly / search out*
    To were° them by wisdom they work not in waste.   *assure, support*
ANDREW. And I to Achaea,² full leally° that lede°   *faithfully / people*
    for to leech,°   *heal*
Will hie° me to help them and heal them in haste.   *hurry*
JOHN. This covenant° accords;°   *agreement / is suitable* 295
    Sirs, since ye will° so,   *will (go)*
    Me must needs part you fro,°   *from*
    To Asia will I go.
    He lead you, that Lord of all lords.

THOMAS. The Lord of all lords in land shall he lead you   300
    Whilst ye travel in trouble the truth for to teach.
    With fruit of our faith in firth° shall we feed you,   *woods*
    For that labor is lofsome,° ilka° lede°   *praiseworthy / each / person*
        for to leech.°   *heal*
    Now I pass from your presence the people to preach,
    To lead them and lere° them the law of our Lord.   *teach* 305
    As I said, us must asunder° and   *separate*
        sadly° ensearch°   *solemnly / search out*
    Ilka country to keep clean° and knit in one cord   *pure*
    Of our faith.
        That freely° food°   *noble / person*
        That died on rood°   *cross*   310
        With main° and mood°   *strength / spirit*
    He graith° you be° guides full graith.°   *prepares / to be / ready*

---

1   *Samaria*   Ancient city in the land of Israel.
2   *Achaea*   Region of modern Greece, in the northwestern part of the Peloponnese peninsula;
    at the time of Christ, it was part of the Roman empire.

The York Corpus Christi Play: The Last Judgment

The Last Judgment, produced by the York Mercers as the final York *Corpus Christi Play*, is similar to the *Creation* in its rhetorical and tonal formality. Characters speak in turn in set speeches of eight-line stanzas rhyming ababab, and only on rare occasions are stanzas shared between two characters. Unlike in some of the other York pageants, characters never share metrical lines between them, and the diction draws on law and theology more than everyday idiom. The result is a stately performance, giving a glimpse of the variety of styles and tones in the complete cycle.

Nevertheless, like the York *Corpus Christi Play* as a whole, *The Last Judgment* draws on its contemporary world of York and its guilds for the richness of its social, political, and theological meanings. Like other episodes in the cycle it relies on the lexicon of work; for example, Jesus returns to earth in the second coming to judge people "after their working, wrong or right." As the final pageant in the cycle, *The Last Judgment* not only brings narrative closure to the Christian history of the world but also emphasizes the status of its extremely wealthy and powerful sponsors, the Mercers, a wholly mercantile craft whose membership often produced mayors and council members of York's civic government. As in modern processionals and parades, the last place in a procession in the Middle Ages was an important and anticipated place, and it is no accident that the most powerful guild in York held that place in its most significant annual event. Moreover, every performance of the *Corpus Christi Play* ended, at the last station, in a part of the city called the Pavement, a section of the city occupied mainly by merchants. Thus every pageant, produced by every craft, had to come to rest for its final performance in the Mercers' world, and the play as a whole also arrived at its dramatic end—with doomsday and the sorting of all humans into good and bad—in the Mercers' territory. All the world's history (from a medieval Christian point of view) therefore reaches fruition among the wealthy merchants.

Although the assignment of *The Last Judgment* to the Mercers served ideological functions, it also had practical value, for the Mercers' wealth allowed them to produce a pageant of extraordinary spectacle. A surviving document from 1433 called "The Mercers' Indenture" (see the "In Context" section) gives us some idea of the lavishness of their pageant. It describes a multi-tiered pageant wagon with lifting machinery and other moving scenery, and costumes that include masks and wigs. The details of this pageant also hint at the spectacular potential of the cycle as a whole.

Pageant 47 of the York Corpus Christi Play:
The Last Judgment

CHARACTERS

God the Father
Jesus[1]
Angel 1
Angel 2
Angel 3
Devil 1
Devil 2
Devil 3
Apostle 1
Apostle 2
Good Soul 1
Good Soul 2
Bad Soul 1
Bad Soul 2

GOD. First when I this world had wrought°—   *made*
  Wood and wind and waters wan,°   *dark*
  And all-kin° thing that now is aught°—   *all kind of / anything*
  Full well methought° that I did then.[2]   *it seemed to me*
  When they were made, good me them thought;[3]   5
  Sithen° to my likeness made I man   *then*
  And man to grieve me gave he naught,[4]
  Therefore me rues[5] that I the world began.

  When I had made man at my will,
  I gave him wits himself to wis °   *guide*   10
  And Paradise I put him till°   *into*
  And bade° him hold° it all as his.   *commanded / govern*
  But of the tree of good and ill°   *evil*

---

1   *Jesus*   In keeping with the doctrine of the Trinity—that God is three persons (Father, Son, and Holy Spirit) in one godhead—the manuscript lists all parts for the deity as "Deus," Latin for God. However, it is clear that "Deus" speaks first as God the Father and then, beginning with "This woeful world" and continuing for the rest of the play, as the Son, Jesus.

2   *Full ... then*   It seemed to me that I did (this) very well then.

3   *good ... thought*   They seemed good to me.

4   *And man ... naught*   And man thought nothing of grieving me.

5   *me rues*   I regret.

I said, "What time[1] thou eats of this,
15 Man, thou speeds° thyself to spill°—   hasten / destroy
Thou art° brought out of all bliss."   will be

Belive° broke man my bidding.   quickly
He weened° have° been a god thereby;   thought / to have
He weened have witten° of all-kin thing,   known
20 In world to have been as wise as I.
He ate the apple I bade should hang,
Thus was he beguiled through gluttony;
Sithen both him and his offspring
To pine°I put them all forthy.°   affliction / for that

25 Too long and late methought it good[2]
To catch° those caitiffs° out of care.°   take / wretches / suffering
I sent my son with full blithe°   mild, merciful
   mood°   disposition
Till° earth, to salve° them of their sare.°   to / heal / sorrow
For ruth° of them he rest on rood°   pity / cross
30 And bought° them with his body bare;   redeemed, ransomed
For them he shed his heart-blood.
What kindness might I do them mare?°   more

Sithen afterward he harrowed Hell[3]
And took out those wretches that were therein;
35 There fought that free° with° fiends fell°   noble one / against / many
For them that were sunken° for° sin.   i.e., in Hell / because of
Sithen° in earth then gan° he dwell,   since / did
Ensample° he gave them Heaven to win,°   example / earn, achieve
In temple himself to teach and tell,
40 To buy° them bliss that never may blin.°   procure, obtain / cease

Sithen° have they found me full of mercy,   since then
Full of grace and forgiveness,

---

1   *What time*   Whenever.
2   *Too long ... good*   A very long time later it seemed good to me.
3   *he harrowed Hell*   To "harrow" means to harry, rob, or spoil. The "Harrowing of Hell"
    is a popular legendary narrative in medieval and early modern art, literature, and drama,
    including in the York *Corpus Christi Play*, Pageant 39. Based on the apocryphal *Gospel of
    Nicodemus*, the harrowing narrative takes place between Christ's death and resurrection,
    during which time he is said to have descended into Hell to release the souls of good people
    damned by original sin, thus robbing Hell of its captives.

And they as wretches, witterly,°   *indeed*
Has° led their life in litherness.°   *have / wickedness*
Oft have they grieved me grievously,   45
Thus have they quit° me my kindness;   *repaid*
Therefore no longer, sikerly,°   *truly*
Thole° will I their wickedness.   *tolerate*

Men see the world but vanity,
Yet will no man beware thereby;°   *in accordance with that* 50
Ilka° day their mirror may they see,   *every*
Yet think they not that they shall die.
All that ever I said should be
Is now fulfilled through prophecy;
Therefore now is it time to° me   *for* 55
To make ending of man's folly.

I have tholèd° mankind many a year   *permitted*
In lust° and liking° for to lend,°   *pleasure / delight / remain*
And uneathes° find I far or near   *scarcely*
A man that will his miss° amend.   *sin* 60
In earth I see but sins sere;°   *many*
Therefore mine angels will I send
To blow their bemes,° that all may hear   *trumpets*
The time is come I will make end.

Angels, blow your bemes belive,°   *at once* 65
Ilka° creature° for to call.   *every / created one, person*
Lerèd° and lewd,° both man   *learned / unlearned*
   and wife,°   *woman*
Receive their doom° this day they shall;   *judgment*
Ilka lede° that ever had life—   *person*
Be none forgotten, great ne° small.   *nor* 70
There shall they see the wounds five[1]
That my son suffered for them all.

And sunder° them before my sight,   *divide*
All same in bliss shall they not be.
My blessèd children, as I have hight,°   *promised* 75
On my right hand I shall them see;

---

1   *the wounds five* The five wounds that Christ received during his crucifixion: four holes in
   his hands and feet from the nails and a spear wound to his right side.

Sithen° shall ilka waried° wight°   *then / cursed / person*
On my left side for fearedness° flee.   *terror*
This day their dooms thus have I dight°   *ordained*
80   To ilka man as he hath servèd me.

ANGEL 1. Lovèd be thou, Lord of mights most,
That angel made to° messenger.   *as*
Thy will shall be fulfilled in haste,°   *i.e., immediately*
That Heaven and Earth and Hell shall hear.
[*Angels blow trumpets.*]
85   Good and ill, every-ilka ghost,[1]
Rise and fetch your flesh that was your fere,°   *companion*
For all this world is brought to waste.
Draw to your doom,[2] it nighs° near.   *approaches*

ANGEL 2. Ilka° creature, both old and young,   *every*
90   Belive° I bid you that ye rise;   *quickly*
Body and soul with you ye bring,
And come before the high justice.
For I am sent from Heaven° king   *heaven's*
To call you to this great assize;°   *inquest, sentencing*
95   Therefore rise up and give reckoning
How ye him served upon sere° wise.°   *sundry / ways*

GOOD SOUL 1. Lovèd° be thou Lord, that is so sheen,°   *praised / radiant*
That on this manner made us to rise,
Body and soul together, clean,°   *completely*
100   To come before the high justice.
Of our ill deeds, Lord, thou not mean,[3]
That we have wrought upon sere wise,
But grant us for thy grace bedene°   *at once*
That we may wone° in Paradise.   *dwell*

105 GOOD SOUL 2. Ah, lovèd be thou, Lord of all,
That Heaven and Earth and all has wrought,
That with thine angels would us call

---

1   *every-ilka ghost* Each and every soul.
2   *Draw to your doom* Gather for your judgment.
3   *thou not mean* Do not state as a grievance.

Out of our graves hither to be brought.
Oft have we grieved thee, great and small;
Thereafter,° Lord, thou   *in accordance with that*   110
     deem° us not,   *judge*
Ne° suffer° us never to fiends to be thrall,°   *nor / allow / enslaved*
That oft in earth with sin us sought.°   *persecuted*

[*Angels blow trumpets.*]

BAD SOUL 1. Alas, alas, that we were born,
     So may we sinfull caitiffs° say;   *wretches*
     I hear well by this hideous horn   115
     It draws full near to doomsday.
     Alas, we wretches that are forlorn,°   *lost*
     That never yet served God to pay,[1]
     But oft we have his flesh forsworn°—   *renounced*
     Alas, alas, and welaway![2]   120

What shall we wretches do for dread,
Or whither° for fearedness may we flee,   *to what place*
When we may bring forth no good deed
Before him that our judge shall be?
To ask mercy us° is° no need,   *for us / there is*   125
For well I wot° damnèd be we,   *know*
Alas, that we swilk° life should lead   *such*
That dight° us has this destiny.   *caused*

Our wicked works they will us wry,°   *expose*
That we weened° never should have been witten;°   *believed / known*   130
That° we did oft full privily,°   *what / secretly*
Apertly° may we see them written.   *openly*
Alas, wretches, dear° mun° we buy°—   *dearly / must / pay*
Full smart° with hell fire be we smitten.°   *sharply / struck*
Now mun never soul ne° body die,   *nor*   135
But with wicked pains evermore be bitten.

Alas, for dread sore[3] may we quake,
Our deeds be our damnation.

---

1   *God to pay*   So as to please God.
2   *Alas … welaway!*   A cry of lamentation and woe, conventional in Middle English poetry.
3   *for dead sore*   With great distress.

	For our miss° moaning° mun we make,	sin / lamentation
140	Help may none excusation.°	apology, defense
	We mun be set° for our sins' sake	diverted, divided
	Forever from our salvation,	
	In Hell to dwell with fiends black,	
	Where never shall be redemption.	

145	BAD SOUL 2. As careful° caitiffs° may we rise,	sorrowful / wretches
	Sore may we wring our hands and weep;	
	For cursedness° and for covetise°	wickedness / covetousness
	Damned be we to Hell full deep.	
	Rought° we never of God's service;	took heed
150	His commandments would we not keep,	
	But oft then made we sacrifice	
	To Satan when others sleep.°	slept

	Alas, now wakens all our were!°	distress, fear
	Our wicked works may we not hide,	
155	But on our backs us must them bear—	
	They will us wray° on ilka° side.	betray / every
	I see foul fiends that will us fear,°	frighten
	And all for pomp of wicked pride.	
	Weep we may with many a tear,	
160	Alas, that we this day should bide.	

	Before us plainly be forth brought	
	The deeds that us shall damn bedene;°	completely
	That° ears has heard, or heart has° thought,	i.e., the deeds that / have
	Since any time that we may mean,°	speak of
165	That foot has gone or hand has wrought,	
	That mouth hath spoken or eye has seen—	
	This day full dear then be it bought.[1]	
	Alas, unborn and we had been![2]	

[*Angels sort the redeemed and the damned, directing them to the right and left sides of God, respectively.*]

ANGEL 3. Stand not together, part you in two!
170   All same shall ye not be in bliss;

---

1   *This day ... bought*   Today it shall be paid for dearly.
2   *Alas ... had been*   Alas, if only we had never been born!

Our Father of Heaven will° it be so,   *desires, intends*
For many of you has° wrought amiss.   *have*
The good on his right hand ye go,
The way till° Heaven he will you wis;°   *to / demonstrate*
Ye waried° wights, ye flee him fro[1]   *damned* 175
On his left hand as none of his.[2]

JESUS. This woeful world is brought till° end,   *to*
My Father of Heaven he will it be;
Therefore till earth now will I wend°   *go*
Myself to sit in majesty.   180
To deem my dooms[3] I will descend;
This body will I bear with me—
How it was dight,° man's miss to mend°— *treated / atone for*
All mankind there shall it see.

[*Jesus descends from the upper level of the pageant wagon by means of machinery.*]

My 'postles° and my darlings dear,   *apostles* 185
The dreadful doom this day is dight.°   *destined*
Both Heaven and Earth and Hell shall hear
How I shall hold that° I have hight:°   *what / commanded*
That ye shall sit on seats sere°   *several*
Beside myself to see that sight,   190
And for to deem folk far and near
After° their working,° wrong or right. *according to / doing*

I said also when I you sent
To suffer sorrow for my sake,
All those that would them right° repent   *properly* 195
Should with you wend° and winly°   *go / joyfully*
 wake;°   *remain awake in vigil*
And to your tales° who° took no   *words / those who*
 tent°   *heed, attention*
Should fare° to fire with fiends black.   *go*
Of mercy now may not be meant,°   *spoken*
But, after working, wealth° or wrake.° *bliss / punishment* 200

---

1 *ye flee him fro* You flee from him.
2 *as none of his* As none belonging to him.
3 *To deem my dooms* To hand out my judgments.

My heting° wholly shall I fulfill,   *promises*
Therefore come forth and sit me by
To hear the doom of good and ill.
APOSTLE 1. I love° thee, Lord God almighty,   *praise*
205 Late and early, loud and still;°   *quietly*
To do thy bidding bain° am I.   *willing*
I oblige me to do thy will
With all my might, as is worthy.

APOSTLE 2. Ah, mightful God, here is it seen
210 Thou will fulfill thy foreward° right,° *covenant / justly*
And all thy saws° thou will maintain.° *words / uphold*
I love° thee, Lord, with all my might,   *worship*
That for us that has° earthly° been, *have / on earth*
Swilk dignities° has dressed° and dight.[1] *honors / prepared*
215 JESUS. Come forth, I shall sit you between,
And all fulfill that I have hight.°   *promised*

(*Here he goes to the judgment seat, with songs of angels.*)

DEVIL 1. Fellows, array° us for to fight,   *prepare*
And go we fast our fee° to fang.° *property / seize*
The dreadful doom this day is dight—
220 I dread me that we dwell° full° long. *delay / too*
DEVIL 2. We shall be seen ever in their sight
And warely° wait,° else° work we wrong, *carefully / watch / or else*
For if the doomsman° do us right, *judge (i.e., God)*
Full° great party° with us *very / proportion (of the souls)*
  shall gang.°   *go*

225 DEVIL 3. He shall do right to foe and friend,
For now shall all the sooth° be sought.   *truth*
All waried° wights with us shall wend, *damned*
To pain endless they shall be brought.

JESUS. Ilka° creature, take entent°   *every / heed*
230 What bodeword° I to you bring: *message*
This woeful world away is went,°   *gone*
And I am come as crownèd king.

---

1 *That for us …dight* Who, for those of us who have been on earth, has prepared and
ordeined such honors (in Heaven).

My Father of Heaven, he has me sent
To deem your deeds and make ending.
Come is the Day of Judgment; 235
Of sorrow may ilka sinful° sing.°   *sinful soul / lament*

The day is come of caitifness,°   *wretchedness*
All them to care° that° are unclean,   *afflict / who*
The day of bale° and bitterness—   *sorrow*
Full long abiden° has it been;   *awaited* 240
The day of dread to more and less,
Of ire, of trembling, and of teen,°   *trouble*
That ilka wight that waried° is   *wicked*
May say, "Alas, this day is seen."

Here may ye see my wounds wide,°   *deep* 245
The which I tholed° for your misdeed.   *suffered*
Through heart and head, foot, hand and hide,°   *flesh*
Not for my guilt, but for your need.
Behold both body, back and side,
How dear° I bought your   *dearly, at great cost* 250
  brotherhood.°   *right to be my brothers*
These bitter pains I would abide[1]—
To buy you bliss thus would I[2] bleed.

My body was scourged without skill,°   *reason*
As thief full throly° was I threat;°   *violently / threatened*
On cross they hanged me, on a hill,   255
Bloody and blo,° as I was beat,°   *bruised / beaten*
With crown of thorn thrusten° full ill.°   *pierced / evilly*
This spear unto my side was set°—   *struck*
Mine heart-blood spared not they[3] for to spill;
Man, for thy love would I not let.°   *prevent (this)* 260

The Jews spit° on me spitously,°   *spat / with contempt*
They spared me no more than a thief.
When they me struck I stood full stilly,°   *meekly*
Against them did I nothing grieve.[4]

---

1   *would abide*   Was willing to suffer.
2   *would I*   I was willing.
3   *spared not they*   They did not hesitate.
4   *did I nothing grieve*   I did not get angry.

265　Behold, mankind, this ilk is I,[1]
　　　That for ye suffered swilk° mischief.　　　　　　　　　*such*
　　　Thus was I dight° for thy folly—　　　　　　　　　　*treated*
　　　Man, look, thy life was to me full lief.°　　　　　　　　*dear*

　　　[*Jesus displays his wounds.*]

　　　Thus was I dight thy sorrow to slake;°　　　　　　　　*end*
270　Man, thus behoved thee to borrowed be.[2]
　　　In all my woe took I no wrake,°　　　　　　　　　　*vengeance*
　　　My will it was for the love of thee.
　　　Man, sore ought thee for to quake,[3]
　　　This dreadful day this sight to see.
275　All this I suffered for thy sake—
　　　Say, man, what suffered thou for me?

　　　My blessèd children on my right hand,
　　　Your doom this day ye thar° not dread,　　　　　　　　*need*
　　　For all your comfort is command,°　　　　　　　　　　*coming*
280　Your life in liking° shall ye lead.　　　　　　　　　　*happiness*
　　　Come to the kingdom ay-lastand°　　　　　　　　　　*ever-lasting*
　　　That you° is dight° for your good deed;　　　　　　*for you* / *prepared*
　　　Full blithe may ye be where ye stand,
　　　For mickle° in Heaven shall be your meed.°　　　　*great* / *reward*

285　When I was hungry ye me fed,[4]
　　　To slake my thirst your heart was free;°　　　　　　　*generous*
　　　When I was clotheless ye me clad,°　　　　　　　　　*dressed*
　　　Ye would no sorrow upon me see.
　　　In hard press when I was stead,[5]
290　Of my pains ye had pity;
　　　Full sick when I was brought in° bed,[6]　　　　　　　*to*
　　　Kindly ye come° to comfort me.　　　　　　　　　　*came*

1　*this ilk is I*　I am the same (one).
2　*behoved ... be*　It was necessary for you to be saved.
3　*sore ... quake*　You ought to tremble terribly.
4　*When ... fed*　Cf. Matthew 25.35–46, from which Jesus' and the Good and Bad Souls'
　　remaining speeches derive.
5　*In ... stead*　When I was placed in hardship.
6　*Full ... bed*　When I was bedridden with great sickness.

When I was will° and weariest°   *distraught / wearied*
Ye harbored° me full heartfully;°   *sheltered / generously*
Full glad then were ye of your guest,   295
And plained° my poverty piteously.   *lamented*
Belive° ye brought me of the best   *quickly*
And made my bed full easily,°   *comfortably*
Therefore in Heaven shall be your rest,
In joy and bliss to be me by.[1]   300

GOOD SOUL 1. When had we, Lord that all has wrought,
    Meat° and drink thee with to feed,[2]   *food*
    Since we in earth had never naught
    But through the grace of thy Godhead?
GOOD SOUL 2. When was't° that we thee   *was it* 305
      clothes brought,
    Or visit thee in any need,
    Or in thy sickness we thee sought?°   *helped*
    Lord, when did we thee this deed?

JESUS. My blessèd children, I shall you° say   *to you*
    What time this deed was to me done: 310
    When any that need had, night or day,
    Asked you help and had it soon.°   *readily*
    Your free hearts said them never nay,
    Early ne° late, midday ne none,[3]   *nor*
    But as oft-sithes° as they would pray,°   *often / ask* 315
    Them thurt° but° bid°   *needed / only / ask*
      and have their boon.°   *reward*

Ye cursed caitiffs° of Cain's kin,   *villains*
That never me comfort in my care,°   *sorrow.*
I and ye forever will twin,°   *separate*
In dole° to dwell for evermore.   *woe* 320
Your bitter bales° shall never blin°   *torments / cease*
That ye shall have when ye come there;
Thus have ye served° for your sin,   *deserved*

---

1   *to be me by*   To be by my side.
2   *thee with to feed*   To feed you.
3   *none*   Three p.m., the canonical hour of nones.

For derf° deeds ye have done ere.°   *evil / previously*
325 When I had mister° of meat° and drink,   *need / food*
Caitiffs, ye catched° me from your gate.   *cast*
When ye were set as sirs° on bink,°   *nobles / bench*
I stood there-out,° weary and wet;   *outside*
Was none of you would° on° me think,   *who would / of*
330 Pity to have of my poor state,
Therefore till° Hell I shall you sink—   *to*
Well are ye worthy to go that gate.°   *way, path*

When I was sick and sorriest°   *most wretched*
Ye visited me not, for I was poor;
335 In prison fast° when I was fest°   *firmly / locked up*
Was none of you looked how I fore.°   *fared*
When I wist° never where for to rest,   *knew*
With dints° ye drove me from your door,   *blows*
But ever to pride then were ye prest,°   *inclined*
340 My flesh, my blood, oft ye forswore.

Clotheless when I was oft, and cold,
At° need of you, yode° I full naked;   *in / went*
House ne harbor,° help ne hold°   *shelter / assistance*
Had I none of you, though I quaked.°   *shivered*
345 My mischief° saw ye manifold,°   *misfortune / in many ways*
Was none of you my sorrow slaked,°   *eased*
But ever forsook me, young and old,
Therefore shall ye now be forsaked.°   *forsaken*

BAD SOUL 1. When had thou, Lord that all thing has,
350 Hunger or thirst, since thou God is?
When was that thou in prison was?
When was thou naked or harborless?°   *homeless*
BAD SOUL 2. When was it we saw thee sick, alas?
When kid° we thee° this unkindness?   *showed / to you*
355 Weary or wet to let thee pass,°   *go*
When did we thee this wickedness?

JESUS. Caitiffs,° as oft as it betid°   *villains / happened*
That needful° aught° asked in my name,   *the needy / anything*
Ye heard them not, your ears ye hid,°   *covered*
360 Your help to them was not at home.
To me was that unkindness kid,°   *showed*

Therefore ye bear this bitter blame;
To least or most when ye it did,
To me ye did the self and the same.[1]

My chosen children, come unto me,   365
With me to wone° now shall ye wend.°   *dwell / go*
There joy and bliss shall ever be,
Your life in liking° shall ye lend.°   *a state of happiness / live*
Ye cursed caitiffs, from me ye flee,
In Hell to dwell withouten end,   370
There ye shall never° but sorrow see   *nothing*
And sit by Satan the fiend.

Now is fulfilled all my forethought,°   *plan*
For ended is all earthly thing.
All worldly wights° that I have wrought,   *people* 375
After° their works have now woning.°   *according to / dwelling*
They that would sin and ceased not,
Of sorrows sere° now shall they sing,°   *various / lament*
And they that mended them whilst they might
Shall bield° and bide° in my blessing.   *live / endure* 380

(*And thus he makes an end with the melody of angels crossing from place
to place.*)

---

1   *the self and the same*   The self-same thing; the exact same thing.

In Context

The Ordo Paginarum

The *Ordo Paginarum*, or "Order of the Pageants," was written in Latin, with some English and French, in 1415 by Roger Burton, Common Clerk of the city of York. It lists and describes the 51 pageants that comprised the *Corpus Christi Play* that year in the order of their appearance, along with their sponsoring occupational guilds, or "crafts." Burton describes what he must have perceived as most significant for record-keeping: the number of actors and the names or titles of their characters, the major properties, and the primary actions and gestures of each pageant. The document clearly served practical purposes as an announcement, checklist, and memorandum of responsibility. But as a subjective list of what most stands out in each play, it is also an interpretative document and thus gives us one of the earliest records of the play's reception by a member of its audience. For instance, like much of the surviving manuscript of the *Corpus Christi Play* itself, the *Ordo* does not offer titles for the plays (most of which are modern editorial conventions) but identifies them by sponsoring crafts instead, thus suggesting that in both Burton's time and in the time the play manuscript was copied half a century later, the civic and general craft sponsorship of the play was of primary importance. These crafts are not always same between the two documents, giving us one source of evidence of the changing nature of the play and its practical details. Similarly, the *Ordo* lists 51 pageants, but only 47 are copied in the later surviving manuscript of the play. Like the play text, the *Ordo* provides but one snapshot of the play at a single point in time and, in this case, from the point of view of one civil servant.

The York *Corpus Christi Play*: The *Ordo Paginarum*[1] (1415)

The order of the pageants of the Corpus Christi play at the time of Mayor William Alne, in the third year of the reign of King Henry V after the conquest of England. Compiled in the year of our Lord 1415 by Roger Burton, Common Clerk,[2] who had it registered.

The schedule of pageants must be delivered subsequently in the sub-scribed form to the craftsmen by six of the Mayor's Sergeants of the Mace[3] in the first or second week of Lent,[4] annually—to be written by the Common Clerk.[5]

TANNERS[6] Almighty God, the Father, creating and forming the heavens, the Angels and Archangels, Lucifer and the Angels who fell with him into hell.

PLASTERERS[7] God the Father in his substance[8] creating the earth and every thing in it in the space of five days.

---

1   *Ordo Paginarum*   Latin: Order of the Pageants. The present text has been translated by Christina M. Fitzgerald from the mostly Latin original, which exists in one manuscript, a record book of the city of York known as the "A/Y Memorandum Book," now North York-shire County Library Manuscript E20. An edition of the original, along with an alternative translation, can be found in Alexandra Johnston and Margaret Rogerson, eds., *Records of Early English Drama: York*, 2 vols. (Toronto: University of Toronto Press, 1979).

2   *Common Clerk*   The Common Clerk was the official record-keeper of the city of York.

3   *Sergeants of the Mace*   A Mace-Bearer or Sergeant-at-Arms was a ceremonial position in the civic hierarchy in York, whose duty it was to carry the city's ceremonial mace and sword in processions. The mace and sword represented the monarch's recognition of the dignity of the office of the Lord Mayor. Their role here, in delivering the *Ordo Paginarum* to the crafts, suggests that even this seemingly bureaucratic business was treated in ceremonial fashion.

4   *Lent*   Lent is the season of fasting 40 days before Easter in the Christian liturgical calendar.

5   *The schedule ... by the Common Clerk*   This paragraph appears in the margin of the text, written by someone other than Burton.

6   *TANNERS*   Later called Barkers, the Tanners tanned leather hides. Their work with noxious and odiferous solutions made them an appropriate choice for depicting the descent into hell, which was traditionally said to smell of sulfur. In the original document, the craft names are written in English and sometimes French, while the descriptions are written in Latin. English spelling has been modernized in accordance with the practices of this volume.

7   *PLASTERERS*   The Plasterers were one of the building guilds.

8   *substance*   Presence, his own person.

CARDMAKERS[1] God the Father forming Adam from the lime[2] of the earth and making Eve from Adam's rib and breathing into them the spirit of life.

FULLERS[3] God forbidding Adam and Eve to eat from the Tree of Life.

COOPERS[4] Adam and Eve and the Tree between them, the Serpent deceiving them with fruit. God speaking to them and cursing the Serpent, and the Angel with a sword driving them out of Paradise.

ARMORERS Adam and Eve and the Angel with a spade and a distaff[5] assigning work to them.

GAUNTERS (Glovers)[6] Abel and Cain offering sacrifices.

SHIPWRIGHTS God warning Noah to make an ark out of smoothed boards.

PESSONERS (Fishmongers)[7] & MARINERS[8] Noah, his Wife, the three Sons of Noah with their Wives, in the Ark, with various animals.

PARCHMENTERS,[9] BOOKBINDERS Abraham sacrificing his son, Isaac, upon an altar, a Servant Boy with wood, and the Angel.

---

1 *CARDMAKERS* The Cardmakers made the "cards" or combs for carding wool, which was the process of straightening and separating its fibers so that it could be more easily spun into yarn. The wool trade was an important source of wealth for England in the late Middle Ages.
2 *lime* Mud or clay.
3 *FULLERS* Like the Cardmakers, the Fullers were part of the thriving wool and cloth industry. Using a water mill, fullers cleansed the woven wool cloth of its oils, dirt, and other impurities, and made it thicker in the process.
4 *COOPERS* The Coopers made wooden barrels used for storage.
5 *spade and a distaff* The spade and distaff are the traditional medieval symbols not only for Adam and Eve's labor after the Fall, but also for its gendered division. Thus the distaff—a long wooden tool used to hold unspun wool or flax during the spinning process—becomes also a symbol for women in general, and in modern English the adjective "distaff" means female or maternal (as in "the distaff side of a family").
6 *GAUNTERS (Glovers)* Burton provides the French word, while another scribe has written the English above it. Here and elsewhere in this text, those later additions are provided in parentheses.
7 *PESSONERS (Fishmongers)* Fish-sellers.
8 *MARINERS* Sailors largely involved in cargo shipping.
9 *PARCHMENTERS* Parchment-makers.

HOSIERS[1] Moses raising up the serpent[2] in the desert, King Pharaoh, eight Jews wandering and waiting.

SPICERS[3] A Doctor declaring sayings of the prophets concerning the future birth of Christ. Mary, the Angel greeting her, Mary greeting Elizabeth.

PEWTERERS, FOUNDERS[4] Mary, Joseph wishing to send her away secretly, an Angel speaking to them so that they go to Bethlehem.

TILERS[5] Mary, Joseph, the Midwife, the newborn Child lying in a manger between the ox and the ass. The Angel speaking to the Shepherds, players in the following pageant.

CHANDLERS[6] Shepherds speaking to one another, the star in the East, an Angel announcing to the Shepherds the joy of the new-born Child.

ORFEVERS (Goldsmiths), GOLDBEATERS,[7] MONEYMAKERS The Three Kings coming from the East, Herod interrogating them about the child Jesus. The Son of Herod, the two Counselors, and a Messenger. Mary with the Child and the star above, and the Three Kings offering gifts.

FORMERLY THE HOUSE OF ST. LEONARD,[8] NOW MASONS Mary with the Child, Joseph, Anna, the Midwife with the young doves, Simeon receiving the Child into his arms, and the two Sons of Simeon.

---

1 *HOSIERS* Hosiers made the various kinds of leggings men wore throughout the period.
2 *raising up the serpent* Refers to his miracle of turning his staff into a serpent.
3 *SPICERS* Spice merchants.
4 *FOUNDERS* The Founders cast metal implements, particularly in iron.
5 *TILERS* One of the building trades, Tilers laid bricks and tiles and are distinct from the Tilemakers, below.
6 *CHANDLERS* These artisans made wax candles, which in the Middle Ages were more luxurious and expensive than the more common tallow candles, made of animal fat and available from butchers.
7 *GOLDBEATERS* Related to but distinct from the Goldsmiths' trade, Goldbeaters beat gold into sheets for use as gold leaf in the decorative and bookmaking arts.
8 *HOUSE OF ST. LEONARD* Hospital of St. Leonard. This is the only play that was at one time sponsored solely by a group other than a merchant or artisans' guild, although the Pardoners co-sponsored a play, below, and the Masons were a more loosely organized occupational group than a true guild.

MARSHALS[1] Mary with the Child and Joseph fleeing into Egypt, with the Angel announcing it.

GIRDLERS, NAILERS[2] Herod ordering that the children be killed, four Soldiers with spears, two Counselors of the King, and four Mothers weeping over the slaughter of their children.

SPURRIERS, LORIMERS[3] The boy Jesus sitting in the Temple in the midst of the Doctors, questioning them and answering them. Four Jews, Mary and Joseph looking for him and finding him in the Temple.

BARBERS Jesus, John the Baptist baptizing him, and two Angels attending.

VINTNERS[4] Jesus, Mary, the Bridegroom and Bride, the Steward and his Servant, with six jars of water when the water turns into wine.

FEVERS (Smiths) Jesus on the pinnacle of the Temple, and the Devil tempting him with stones, and two Angels ministering.

CURRIERS[5] Peter, James, and John, Jesus ascending the mountain and transfiguring himself in front of them. Moses and Elijah appearing, and a voice speaking in a cloud.

IRONMONGERS Jesus, Simon the Leper asking Jesus to eat with him. Two Disciples, Mary Magdalene washing the feet of Jesus with her tears and drying them with her hair.

PLUMBERS, PATTENMAKERS[6] Jesus, two Apostles, the Woman taken in adultery, four Jews accusing her.

POUCHMAKERS, BOTTLERS, CAPMAKERS Jesus, four Apostles, Lazarus in the tomb, Mary Magdalene and Martha, and two Jews, marveling.

---

1 *MARSHALS* The Marshals were farriers, dealing with the care of horses and horse-related equipment.
2 *GIRDLERS, NAILERS* Girdlers made belts and other similar items, while nailers made nails of various sizes and uses.
3 *SPURRIERS, LORIMERS* Both of these guilds made equestrian equipment; Spurriers made spurs and Lorimers made bridles.
4 *VINTNERS* Wine merchants.
5 *CURRIERS* Leatherworkers.
6 *PLUMBERS, PATTENMAKERS* Plumbers were lead workers and Pattenmakers made wooden shoes.

SKINNERS,[1] VESTMENTMAKERS Jesus on the ass with its foal, twelve Apostles following Jesus, six Rich Men and six Poor Men, eight Boys with palm branches singing *Benedictus*, etc.,[2] and Zaccheus climbing the sycamore tree.

CUTLERS, BLADESMITHS, SHEATHERS, SCALERS, BUCKLERMAKERS, HORNERS[3] Pilate, Caiaphas, two Soldiers, three Jews, and Judas selling Jesus.

BAKERS The Pascal[4] Lamb, the Lord's Supper, the twelve Apostles, Jesus girded with a linen cloth washing their feet. The institution of the Sacrament of the Body of Christ in the New Law, the Communion of the Apostles.

CORDWAINERS[5] Pilate, Caiaphas, Annas, fourteen armed Soldiers, Malchus, Peter, James, John, Jesus, and Judas kissing Jesus and betraying him.

BOWYERS, FLETCHERS[6] Jesus, Annas, Caiaphas, and four Jews striking and hitting Jesus. Peter, the Woman accusing Peter, and Malchus.

TAPITERS, COUCHERS[7] Jesus, Pilate, Annas, Caiaphas, two Counselors, and four Jews accusing Jesus.

LITSTERS[8] Herod, two Counselors, four Soldiers, Jesus, and three Jews.

---

1 *SKINNERS* Furriers.

2 *Benedictus, etc.* The first word of Luke 1.68–79, meaning "Blessed be." The "etc." suggests that the crowd sings the whole "canticle" or song. In its Gospel context, it is a song of thanksgiving sung by Zechariah on the birth of his son, John the Baptist, and points to John's role in announcing the coming of Christ the Redeemer; it was typically sung in the Middle Ages as part of the liturgy of Lauds, the dawn service, signifying new life in Christ. Here it is the people of Jerusalem who "go before the face of the Lord to prepare his way" (Luke 1.76, Douay-Rheims translation).

3 *SCALERS, BUCKLERMAKERS, HORNERS* Scalers made scales, Bucklermakers made shields (called "bucklers"), and Horners made various objects from deer horn.

4 *Pascal* Of or having to do with Easter, here anachronistically—but purposely so—used to refer to Passover, the Jewish holy day being observed at the Last Supper. As Burton's description continues to note, the *last* supper of Jesus and his Apostles is also traditionally interpreted as the *first* Eucharist of Christ and his Church.

5 *CORDWAINERS* Shoemakers.

6 *BOWYERS, FLETCHERS* Bow makers and arrow makers.

7 *TAPITERS, COUCHERS* Tapestry makers and upholsterers.

8 *LITSTERS* Dyers, makers of dye for fabrics.

Cooks, Waterleaders[1] Pilate, Annas, Caiaphas, two Jews, and Judas returning the thirty pieces of silver to them.

Tilemakers, Millers, Ropers, Servers Jesus, Pilate, Caiaphas, Annas, six Soldiers holding poles with banners, and four others leading Jesus from Herod, asking for Barabas to be released and Jesus to be crucified, and in the same place binding and whipping him, putting the crown of thorns on his head. Three Soldiers casting lots for the clothing of Jesus.

Shearmen, Turners, Hayresters, Bollers[2] Jesus covered with blood carrying the cross to Calvary. Simon of Cyrene, the Jews forcing him to carry the cross. Mary, the mother of Jesus, then John the Apostle first telling her about the condemnation and journey of her son to Calvary. Veronica wiping blood and sweat from the face of Jesus with a veil on which the face of Jesus is imprinted. And other Women lamenting Jesus.

Pinners, Lateners,[3] Painters The cross, Jesus stretched out on it on the ground,[4] four Jews[5] whipping him and dragging him with ropes, and afterwards raising the cross and the body of Jesus nailed to the cross upon the Mount of Calvary.

Butchers, Poulters[6] The cross, two Thieves crucified, Jesus hung on the cross between them. Mary the mother of Jesus, John, Mary the mother of James, and Mary Salome. Longinus with his spear, a Slave with a sponge, Pilate, Annas, Caiaphas, the Centurion. Joseph of Arimathea and Nicodemus taking him down and putting him in the tomb.

---

1 *WATERLEADERS* The Waterleaders carted and delivered water.
2 *TURNERS, HAYRESTERS, BOLLERS* Turners made wooden objects requiring "turning"—for example, turned legs on a table; Hayresters worked with horsehair; and Bollers made wooden bowls.
3 *PINNERS, LATENERS* Pinners made pins, needles, and other small wire implements. Lateners worked in brass.
4 *on the ground* Perhaps this description gives evidence that the action of nailing Jesus to the cross happened on the street level, while the pageant wagon served as the Mount of Calvary.
5 *four Jews* Only here are the crucifiers said to be Jews.
6 *POULTERS* Those who raised, sold, or prepared poultry.

SELLERS (Saddlers), VERROURS (Glaziers), FUSTERS[1] Jesus harrowing Hell, twelve Good and six Evil Spirits.[2]

CARPENTERS, JOINERS, CARTWRIGHTS, CARVERS, SAWYERS The Centurion reporting to Pilate, Caiaphas, and Annas with other Jews concerning the signs accompanying the death of Jesus. Jesus rising from the tomb, four armed Soldiers and the three Maries lamenting. Pilate, Caiaphas, and Annas. A Youth clad in white sitting at the tomb, talking to the women.

WINEDRAWERS Jesus, Mary Magdalene with spices.

BROKERS, WOOLPACKERS, WOADMEN[3] Jesus, Luke and Cleophas dressed as pilgrims.

SCRIVENERS, ILLUMINATORS, QUESTORS (Pardoners), DUBBERS[4] Jesus, Peter, John, James, Phillip, and the other Apostles with a piece of roasted fish and a honeycomb, and Thomas the Apostle touching the wounds of Christ.

TALLIAUNDERS (Tailors) Mary, John the Evangelist, eleven Apostles, two Angels, Jesus ascending from them, and four Angels holding a cloud.

POTTERS Mary, two Angels, eleven Apostles, and the Holy Spirit descending upon them, and four Jews, marveling.

DRAPERS Jesus, Mary, Gabriel with two Angels, two Virgins and three Jews of Mary's family, eight Apostles, and two Devils.

LINENWEAVERS Four Apostles carrying the bier of Mary, and Fergus hanging from the bier with two other Jews and one Angel.

---

1 *FUSTERS* Makers of saddletrees.

2 *twelve Good and six Evil Spirits* Since the play as we have it has fewer good and evil spirits with speaking parts, either the play changed from this 1415 record to the text from 1463–77, or else there were non-speaking parts not accounted for in the play text.

3 *WOADMEN* Harvesters and sellers of woad dye, a blue dye made from the woad plant.

4 *SCRIVENERS, ILLUMINATORS, QUESTORS (Pardoners), DUBBERS* Except for Pardoners, the occupations here are all related to book making. Scriveners are scribes, Illuminators are illustrators, and Dubbers apply gold gilt to the illuminations. Pardoners, one of the few church-related professions in the *Ordo*, are church officials authorized to give pardons for sins in exchange for charitable donations.

WOOLWEAVERS Mary ascending with a crowd of Angels, eight Apostles, and Apostle Thomas of India preaching in the desert.

HOSTLERS[1] Mary, Jesus crowning her, with a crowd of Angels singing.

MERCERS[2] Jesus, Mary, twelve Apostles, four Angels with trumpets and four with a crown, a spear, and two whips. Four Good Spirits and four Evil Spirits, and six Devils.[3]

—1415

The York Mercers' Indenture

The Mercers were the wealthiest and most powerful mercantile craft in medieval York; from their ranks came numerous aldermen and mayors of the city, and with their wealth they were able to contribute lavishly to the York *Corpus Christi Play* in their presentation of *The Last Judgment* pageant. The document known as the Mercers' Indenture, recorded on the feast of Corpus Christi in 1433 (11 June that year) and preserved by the Mercers in their records, was drawn up between the company and its four "pageant masters," men in charge of bringing forth the pageant each year. In this document, the company hands over the pageant (i.e., the wagon) and all of its props, décor, and costumes into the care of the pageant masters, who agree to "deliver forth" the materials to the next pageant masters in subsequent years. The document then itemizes those properties. Since the document was written for readers who already knew what all of these materials were and what their uses were, some of the details are fuzzy. But the Indenture nevertheless gives us significant insight into the lavish production accorded *The Last Judgment* play. It also provides hints of the symbolic practices of costuming and creating the space of the play. It tells us of the wigs ("chevelures") and masks ("viserns") used for characters (from the souls to the Apostles, angels, devils, and God) and reveals that God was costumed with a halo ("diadem"), a gilded mask, and a "sark wounded," or a shirt painted with the wounds of

---

1 *HOSTLERS* Innkeepers.
2 *MERCERS* Merchants.
3 Compare this description with both the text of the Mercers' *Last Judgment* play and also with the more detailed description in the Mercers' Indenture.

Christ, in a representation of both his godhead and his humanity. We also learn that the pageant is multi-tiered with the use of "irons to bear up heaven," where mechanical angels "run about." Also among the pageant's special effects is a lifting device on which "God shall sit" when he ascends to that higher tiered heaven, after having judged the souls on earth. The Indenture further tells us that Hell was depicted, as in the visual arts, as a great bestial mouth. Where it was placed we do not know for sure, since the Indenture only tells us that there was a "hell mouth"; however, the use of the wagon base for earth and the second tier for heaven suggests that the hell mouth was placed on the ground in a visual hierarchy common in iconography. Along with the details of the rich cloths and painted sets, these details of the Indenture provide a picture of a spectacular display of wealth, power, and piety.

The York Mercers' Indenture[1] (11 June 1433)

This indenture, made in the feast of Corpus Christi in the year of our Lord God ml. CCCC xxxiii[2] between Richard Louth, Master of the Company of Mercers of the City of York, & Nicholas Useflete & William Yarom, Constables of the said Company, on the to side,[3] and William Bedale, William Holbek, Henry Market, & Thomas Curtays, the Pageant Masters, on the tother side,[4] bears witness that the said Master & Constables has delivered to the said Pageant Masters all their parcels underwritten longing[5] to their pageant, safely to keep & to govern for their time; and those same parcels to deliver forth again in reasonable time to the next Pageant Masters that shall occupy in the next year after; and so all Pageant Masters to deliver forth by this indenture to other Pageant Masters that shall occupy for the year while the Pageant gear lasts: first a

---

1   *The York Mercers' Indenture*   The present text has been edited by Christina M. Fitzgerald. Spelling and punctuation of this text have been modernized in accordance with the practices of this volume. The text is based on the edition found in *Records of Early English Drama: York*, vol. 1, eds. Alexandra F. Johnston and Margaret Rogerson (University of Toronto Press, 1976), 55–56.

2   *ml. CCCC xxxiii*   1433 in medieval-style Roman numerals. Note that unlike classical Latin usage, *ml.* is used for *mille* (one thousand) instead of a simple M, and CCCC is acceptable for 400, instead of the classical CD, or 100 (C) subtracted from 500 (D). Also, spaces are used between the units for ease of reading, and not all numerals are capitalized.

3   *on the to side*   On the one side.

4   *on the tother side*   On the other side.

5   *longing*   Belonging.

pageant[1] with iiii[2] wheels; hell mouth; iii garments for iii devils; vi devils'
faces in iii viserns;[3] array[4] for ii evil souls, that is to say, ii sarks,[5] ii pair
hoses,[6] ii viserns, & ii chevelures;[7] array for ii good souls, that is to say,
ii sarks, ii pair hoses, ii viserns, & ii chevelures; ii pair angel wings with
iron in the ends; ii trumps[8] of white plate, and ii reeds;[9] iiii albs[10] for iiii
Apostles; iii diadems[11] with iii viserns for iii Apostles; iiii diadems with
iiii chevelures of yellow for iiii Apostles; a cloud & ii pieces of rainbow
of timber; array for God, that is to say, a sark wounded,[12] a diadem with
a visern gilded;[13] a great coster[14] of red damask painted[15] for the back
side of the pageant; ii other less[16] costers for ii sides of the pageant; iii
other costers of lewyn brede[17] for the sides of the pageant; a little coster
iiii squared to hang at the back of God; iiii irons to bear up[18] heaven;
iiii small coterelles[19] & a iron pin; a brandreth[20] of iron that God shall
sit upon when he shall sty[21] up to heaven, with iiii ropes at iiii corners;
a heaven of iron with a nave[22] of tree;[23] ii pieces of red clouds & stars of
gold longing to heaven; ii pieces of blue clouds painted on both sides;
iii pieces of red clouds with sun beams of gold and stars for the highest[24]

---

1 *pageant* Pageant wagon.
2 *iiii* 4 in medieval-style Roman numerals. Note that *iiii* is allowable, in contrast to the
classical Latin practice of representing 4 as IV, or one (I) less than five (V).
3 *viserns* Masks. Six faces in three masks suggests that each mask had two faces.
4 *array* Costumes.
5 *sarks* Shirts, tunics.
6 *hoses* Hose (for men), tights.
7 *chevelures* Wigs.
8 *trumps* Trumpets.
9 *reeds* Reed pipes.
10 *albs* Tunics of white cloth reaching to the feet, worn by clerics in religious ceremonies.
11 *diadems* Halos.
12 *sark wounded* Shirt depicting the wounds of Christ, perhaps in particular the wound in
his side.
13 *visern gilded* Mask gilded with gold.
14 *coster* Cloth hanging.
15 *red damask painted* Damask, a rich silk fabric woven with elaborate designs and figures,
that has been painted red.
16 *less* Smaller.
17 *lewyn brede* Breadth of lewyn, a kind of linen cloth; breadth is a unit of cloth meas-
urement.
18 *bear up* Support.
19 *coterelles* Iron brackets, most often used for hangings pots over fires.
20 *brandreth* Iron grate, gridiron.
21 *sty* Ascend.
22 *nave* Hub.
23 *tree* Wood.
24 *highest* Highest part.

of heaven, with a long, small[1] border of the same work;[2] vii great angels holding the Passion of God[3]—one of them has a vane of latten[4] & a cross of iron in his head,[5] gilded; iiii smaller angels, gilded, holding the Passion; ix smaller angels painted red to run about in the heaven; a long, small cord to gar[6] the angels run about; ii short rolls of tree[7] to put forth the pageant. Item[8] i banner of red buckram[9] beat with gold,[10] with the Trinity[11] & with ostrich feathers & with i long streamer; item iiii small banners with Trinity in them & russet.[12]

—1433

Four Middle English Crucifixion Poems

C. 1340–1400

Medieval lyric poetry had a close relationship to drama and often had quasi-dramatic qualities itself, while drama frequently displayed lyrical moments of intense emotion focused on the experience of one character. All of this is especially true with regard to the large body of poems about the crucifixion; three of the four poems selected here show strong similarities with moments in the York *Corpus Christi Play*. Each of these fourteenth-century poems pre-dates the York play, so they, or poems like them, might have influenced the play's writers. The

---

1 *small* Narrow, thin.
2 *work* Workmanship, material.
3 *Passion of God* Instruments of the Passion of Christ (i.e., the hammer, nails, and crown of thorns) which Jesus recounts in *The Last Judgment* play.
4 *vane of latten* Plate made of latten (a metal similar to brass) in the form of flag or banner, usually bearing a coat of arms.
5 *in his head* On his head.
6 *gar* Make.
7 *rolls of tree* Wooden rollers.
8 *Item* Latin: Also.
9 *buckram* Fine linen cloth.
10 *beat with gold* Embroidered or woven with gold thread.
11 *Trinity* Symbol or figural representation of the Trinity, the three persons of the Godhead in Christian doctrine (Father, Son, and Holy Spirit).
12 *russet* Serviceable woolen cloth; or the color russet, a red brown.

fourth poem here has few dramatic qualities; it too, however, suggests some intersections between the lyric and the dramatic modes.

The first poem reproduced here, "Ye that passen by the way," comes from the commonplace book made in 1372 by John Grimestone, a fourteenth-century Franciscan friar. Commonplace books were books in which the user copied texts or excerpts from texts that he or she wanted to have to read, re-read, or remember. Grimestone's book is organized by topic—this poem appears in a large section on the Passion of Christ—and consists of Latin sermon material as well as related lyric poetry in English. "Ye that passen by the way" is spoken by Jesus from the cross to the passer-by (or, likewise, to the reader) and bears a strong resemblance to Christ's words from the cross in the York *Crucifixion* pageant, where those "that walk by way or street" (in York Jesus's words) are also simultaneously the audience in York's streets. The similarity likely stems from their shared source and inspiration, Lamentations 1.12, which reads "O all ye that pass by the way, attend, and see if there be any sorrow like to my sorrow: for he hath made a vintage of me, as the Lord spoke in the day of his fierce anger" (Douay-Rheims translation). In lyric and dramatic form, however, the two poetic texts share a more direct engagement with the reader or audience.

The next poem presented, "Men rent me on rood," comes from a Dominican preaching manuscript from the second half of the fourteenth century. It, too, is voiced by Jesus and addresses readers directly, asking them to meditate on his suffering on the cross. In asking the reader to "behold," the poem engages the reader's visual imagination in a quasi-dramatic way. The poem also enlists a conceit in which Christ's crucifixion and suffering for the sake of humankind is compared to a knight fighting for the one whom he champions. A more complex rendering of this metaphor occurs in York Pageant 39: *Christ's Appearance to Mary Magdalene*.

The next two poems come from the Harley 2253 manuscript, a miscellaneous, multi-lingual manuscript especially known for its large collection of Middle English poetry—a collection now known as "The Harley Lyrics." The first of these two, "Stand well, mother, under rood," presents a quasi-dramatic dialogue between Jesus and Mary as he dies on the cross and she laments his death at its foot. The subject of Mary's suffering on behalf of her son was a very common one in religious lyrics and often served the functions it serves here: to engage the reader's emotion through Mary's very human and understandable pain, but also to teach them—as Jesus teaches Mary—that the crucifixion and Christ's death are paradoxically things to be glad for, since they are the means of the redemption of humankind. There are echoes of this poem's dialogue in York Pageant 36: *The Death of Christ*, although the dialogue is much expanded here, and both Mary's initial suffering and ultimate joy are more fully emphasized.

In "I sike when I sing," the speaker is an ordinary Christian who laments the suffering Christ underwent for the sake of people like the speaker. A lyric of this sort is potentially a more intimate emotional experience for readers than drama; they can easily project themselves into the subject position of the speaker and thus become the "I" who speaks, sighs ("sike"), and sings. That is not something drama can do, even when it presents characters with whom the audience might identify. The poem thus more fully engages in "affective piety"—devotional piety stirred first by intense feeling—than the drama might do. But the lyric is not without its dramatic qualities, since it puts the speaker—and thus the reader—in the present moment of the crucifixion, as witness to it. Likewise, the York play turns its audience into cross-temporal witnesses to the crucifixion.

Ye that passen by the way[1]

Ye that passen° by the way	*pass*
Abideth° a little stound!°	*stay / while, time*
Beholdeth, all my fellows,	
If any me like[2] is found.	
5 To the tree° with nails three	*cross*
Well° fast° I hang bound;	*very / firmly*
With a spear all through my side,	
To mine heart is made a wound.	

—1372

---

1   *Ye that passen by the way*   The present text, edited for this volume by Christina M. Fitzgerald, is based on the text as it appears in *Middle English Lyrics*, edited by Maxwell S. Luria and Richard L. Hoffman (Norton, 1974). Spelling and punctuation have been modernized in accordance with the practices of this volume. The poem is found in John Grimestone's book of sermon material and related poetry, created in 1372, now the National Library of Scotland's manuscript Advocates 18.7.21, fol. 125v. The poem appears in one other manuscript, there written as four long lines.

2   *If any me like*   If any like me.

Men rent me on rood[1]

Men rent° me on rood°   *tore / cross*
With wounds wolly° wood,°   *woefully / savage*
All bled my blood.
Think, man, all it is ye to good.[2]

Think who ye first wrought,[3]   5
For what work° hell you sought;   *deed*
Think who ye again bought:°   *redeemed*
Work warely,° fail me not.   *prudently*

Behold my side,
My wounds spread so wide;   10
Restless I ride:[4]
Look upon me! Put from ye pride.[5]

My palfrey° is of tree,°   *a type of horse / wood*
With nails nailed through me.
Ne° is more sorrow to see: *nor*   15
Certes° none more no° may be.[6]   *certainly / not*

Under my gore°   *clothing*
Been° wounds selcouth° sore.   *are / wondrously*
Lere,° man, my lore:°   *learn / teaching*
For my love, sin no more!   20

Fall not for° fonding;°   *because of / temptations*
That shall ye most turn to good;
Make stiff° withstanding;°   *strong / resistance*
Think well who me rent on the rood!

—c. 1350–1400

---

1   *Men rent me on rood*   The present text, edited for this volume by Christina M. Fitzgerald, is based on the text as it appears in *Middle English Lyrics*, edited by Luria and Hoffman. Spelling and punctuation have been modernized in accordance with the practices of this volume. The poem is found only in the British Library manuscript Harley 2316, fol. 25, a miscellaneous collection of Latin and English prose and verse.

2   *all it is ye to good*   It is all for your good.

3   *who ye first wrought*   Who first created you.

4   *Restless I ride*   I.e., on the cross. At this point begins a conceit in which Christ is a knight on his horse (the cross) fighting as humankind's champion. A more complex version of this conceit, again spoken by Jesus, can be found in York Pageant 39: *Christ's Appearance to Mary Magdalene.*

5   *Put from ye pride*   Put pride from you; turn from pride.

6   *none ... be*   No more may be. Double, triple, and even quadruple negatives are common and allowable in Middle English. They reinforce the negative sense.

Stand well, mother, under rood![1]

"Stand well, mother, under rood!°   *cross*
Behold thy son with glad mood;°   *mind*
Blithe,° mother, might° thou be."   *joyful / must*
"Son, how should I blithe° stand?   *joyfully*
5 I see thine feet, I see thine hand°   *hands*
Nailed to the hard tree."°   *cross*

"Mother, do way° thy weeping.   *away with*
I thole° death for mankind;   *suffer*
For my guilt thole I none."
10 "Son, I feel the deadstound,°   *time of death*
The sword is at mine heart's ground°   *bottom*
That me bihet° Simeon."[2]   *promised*

"Mother, mercy! Let me die,
For° Adam out of hell buy°   *in order to / redeem*
15 And his kin that is forlore."°   *damned*
"Son, what shall me to rede?[3]
My pain pineth° me to dead.°   *torments / death*
Let me die thee before."[4]

"Mother, thou rue° all° of thy bairn,°[5]   *have pity / completely / son*
20 Thou wash away the bloody tearn;°   *tears*
It doth° me worse than my dead."°   *does / death*
"Son, how may I tears warn?°   *restrain*
I see the bloody streams earn°   *run*
From thine heart to my feet."

---

1 *Stand well, mother, under rood* The present text has been edited for this volume by Christina M. Fitzgerald, based on the text as it appears in *Middle English Lyrics*, edited by Luria and Hoffman. Spelling and punctuation have been modernized in accordance with the practices of this volume. The poem is found in the British Library manuscript Harley 2253, fol. 79r–79v, a multilingual, miscellaneous collection, as well as in five other manuscripts, in whole or in part. This poem and the next are part of the famous "Harley Lyrics" collection within Harley 2253, the largest single collection of Middle English lyric poetry.

2 *The sword ... bihet Simeon* The sword that Simeon promised (i.e., prophesied) is piercing my heart. The reference is to Luke 2.35: "And thy own soul a sword shall pierce, that, out of many hearts, thoughts may be revealed." (Douay-Rheims translation).

3 *what shall me to rede?* What shall come to me as counsel; what counsel shall I take?

4 *thee before* Before you.

5 *thou rue ... bairn* Have pity fully on your son.

"Mother, now I may thee° say: *to you* 25
Better is that I one° die   *alone*
Than all mankind to hell go."
"Son, I see thy body beswongen,°   *scourged*
Feet and hands throughout stungen°   *pierced*
No wonder though me be woe!"   30

"Mother, now I shall thee tell
If I ne° die, thou gost° to hell;   *not / will go*
I thole° dead° for thine sake."   *suffer / death*
"Son, thou art so meek and mind;°   *kind*
Ne wit° me not—it is my kind°   *blame / nature* 35
That I for thee this sorrow make."

"Mother, now thou might well leren°   *teach*
What sorrow haveth that children bearen,[1]
What sorrow it is with child gone."°   *to go*
"Sorrow, iwis,° I can thee tell;   *indeed* 40
But° it be the pine° of hell,   *unless / torment*
More sorrow wot° I none!"   *know*

"Mother, rue of mother care,[2]
For now thou wost° of mother fare[3]   *know*
Though thou be clean° maiden-man."° *pure (without sin) / virgin person* 45
"Son, help at all need,
All those that to me grede,°   *cry out*
Maiden, wife, and foul° woman."   *sinful*

"Mother, may I no longer dwell:
The time is come, I shall° to hell;[4]   *shall go* 50
The third day I rise upon."
"Son, I will with thee founden;°   *go*
I die, iwis,° for thine wounden.°   *certainly / wounds*
So sorrowful dead° nas° never none!"   *death / was not*

When he rose, tho° fell° her sorrow;   *then / abated* 55
Her bliss sprung the third morrow:°   *morning*

---

1 *What ... bearen* What sorrow have they who bear children.
2 *Mother ... care* Mother, have pity on mothers' sorrow.
3 *mother fare* A mother's plight.
4 *to hell* Refers to the Harrowing of Hell. See Pageant 37.

Blithe° mother were thou tho!°   *joyful / then*
Levedy,° for that ilka° bliss,   *lady / same*
Beseech thy son of° sin's liss;°   *for / remission*
60 Thou be our shield again° our foe.   *against*

Blessed be thou, full of bliss!
Let us never heaven miss
Through thy sweet son's might.
Lord, for that ilka blood
65 That thou sheddest on the rood,
Thou bring us into heaven° light!   *heaven's*

                    —c. 1340

I sike when I sing[1]

I sike° when I sing   *sigh*
For sorrow that I see,
When I with weeping
Behold upon the tree
5 And see Jesu the sweet—
His heart's blood forlet°   *lost*
For the love of me;
His wounds waxen° wet;   *grow*
They weepen° still° and meet.°   *weep / continually / fittingly*
10 Mary, rueth° thee.   *it grieves*

High upon a down°   *hill*
There° all folk it see may,   *where*
A mile from each° town,   *any*
About the midday,
15 The rood° is up areared;°   *cross / raised*
His friends are afeared°   *afraid*
And clingeth° so° the clay.   *shrink in fear / as*
The rood stand° in stone;   *stands*
Mary stand her one°   *alone*
20 And saith,° "Wellaway."[2]   *says*

---

1 *I sike when I sing* The present text, edited for this volume by Christina M. Fitzgerald, is based on the text as it appears in *Middle English Lyrics*, edited by Luria and Hoffman. Spelling and punctuation have been modernized in accordance with the practices of this volume. Like the previous poem, this lyric is also found in British Library manuscript Harley 2253, fol. 80, and is part of the "Harley Lyrics" sequence in that manuscript; it appears in one other manuscript, as well.

2 *Wellaway* Exclamation of sorrow or lamentation.

When I thee behold
With eyen° bright bo,°   *eyes / both*
And thy body cold—
Thy blee° waxeth° blo,°   *complexion / grows / leaden-colored*
Thou hangest all of blood,[1]   25
So high upon the rood
Between thieves two—
Who may sike° more?   *sigh*
Mary weepeth sore
And sight° all this woe.   *sees*   30

The nails beth° too strong,   *are*
The smiths are too sly;°   *skillful*
Thou bleedest all too long,
The tree° is all too high;   *cross*
The stones beth° all wet.   *are*   35
Alas, Jesu the sweet,
For now friend hast thou none
But° Saint Johan° mourning,   *except / John (Latin)*
And Mary weeping,
For pine° that thee is on.[2]   *suffering*   40

Often when I sike°   *sigh*
And make my moan,°   *lament*
Well ill though me like,[3]
Wonder is it none,
When I see hang high,   45
And bitter pines° dreigh,°   *torments / endure*
Jesu, my leman!°   *beloved*
His wounds sore smart;
The spear all to his heart
And through his sides gone.   50

Often when I sike,°   *sigh*
With care I am throughsought;°   *pierced through*
When I wake, I wick;°   *fail, flag*
Of sorrow is all my thought.
Alas, men beth° wood°   *are / insane*   55

---

1   *of blood*   Bloody.
2   *For pine ... on*   For the suffering that is upon you.
3   *Well ... like*   Though I am much distressed by it.

That sweareth by the rood,°   *cross*
And selleth him for naught!°[1]   *nothing*
That° bought° us out of sin,   *he who / redeemed*
He bring us to win,°   *joy*
60 That hath us dear° bought.   *dearly, at a great cost*

—c. 1340

Select Civic and Guild Records

York has a wealth of surviving records from the city and from some individual guilds, or "crafts" in York's terminology. Together these records tell us much about the organization, planning, and implementation of the York *Corpus Christi Play*, beginning with the first cycle-related record from 1376, the rent paid for a building to house three pageants. Even with this bounty, the records often raise more questions than they answer, and not everything scholars would like to know has been recorded or has survived. The following brief selection, along with the *Ordo Paginarum* and the Mercers' Indenture, give but a taste of what one might find in the archives. These records and many more pertaining to drama and performance in York have been collected, edited, and translated in *The Records of Early English Drama: York*, edited by Alexandra F. Johnston and Margaret Rogerson.

from the Mercers' Pageant Accounts (1462)

The following account, recorded twenty-nine years after the Mercers' Indenture, demonstrates the upkeep needed for a pageant wagon, particularly one with complex moving parts and plentiful props and costumes. It also attests to the amount of human labor that a pageant requires—work by the actors; by the laborers who created the wagon, the scenery, the costumes, and the props; by those who brought the pageant and its accoutrements in and out of storage; by those who provided the security; and by the guildsmen themselves, whose work

---

1   *That sweareth ... naught*   The sense of "swear" here is the modern "curse"—that is, swearing in vain, using "by the cross" as an expletive. Those who do so cheapen the crucifixion and "selleth him for naught." The economic diction continues in the following lines, playing on terms deeply embedded in the concept of redemption.

was needed to organize and raise funds for all this activity. All of these people needed to be paid for their expenses, time, and work—as well as fed and hydrated.

Records such as this one that note payment to "players" raise the question of whether actors outside of the guild were hired and, if so, for which parts. It is a question, however, with no definite answer.

These be the parcels° of expenses made about the pageant of the Mercers[1]	*particulars*

In primis[2] paid to the players for playing	xviii s ii d[3]	
Item[4] paid for the cloth of god's sark° & the hose making & painting	ii s iiii d[5]	*shirt*
Item paid for a pair of new wheels	iii s viii d	

---

1 *Mercers* The present text has been edited for this volume by Christina M. Fitzgerald. Spelling and punctuation have been modernized in accordance with the practices of this volume. The original document can be found in Box D63 of the Merchant Adventurers' Archives, York. The present text is based on the version found in *Records of Early English Drama: York*, Vol. 1, eds. Alexandra F. Johnston and Margaret Rogerson (University of Toronto Press, 1976), 95.

2 *In primis* Latin: First.

3 *xviii s ii d* Latin: 18 shillings 2 pence (abbreviated). The *s* and *d* are abbreviations deriving from the Latin *solidus* and *denarius*, standard Roman coins, but here stand for shillings and pence. Medieval record keepers routinely used Roman numerals, often in lower case. (See note 5 for an explanation of Roman numerals.) 12 pence made up a shilling; 20 shillings equaled a pound (abbreviated *l* or *li*). According to the calculator on the web site of The National Archives in the United Kingdom (http://www.nationalarchives.gov.uk/currency/), 18 s 2 d in 1460 would be worth approximately £426 (or roughly $750–780 US) in 2005 money (the last year for which the National Archives updated this tool). These numbers are merely approximations; suffice it to say that the financial outlay for a play was significant.

4 *Item* Latin: Also. From the use of this word in documents such as this, we get the modern sense as a noun meaning an article or unit in an enumeration.

5 *iiii d* In the medieval use of Roman numerals, iiii was allowable for 4, rather than the classical iv, and was often used in accounting documents. If you are not familiar with Roman numerals, i = 1, v = 5, x = 10, l = 50, c = 100. For this record and the following one, reading the numerals requires simply adding the individual numerals. So, for example, xviii = 18, or 10+5+1+1+1. In other cases here, and in the classical system, subtraction was involved, denoted by placing the lower numeral before the higher one from which it is subtracted. For example, in the next record, King Edward the Fourth is Edward IV, or 5 (V) minus 1 (I). And in the Tanners' Ordinance below, a craftsman who marries into the craft owes 40 shillings, or xl s; 50 (l) minus 10 (x) equals 40.

Item paid for the putting forth of the pageant[1]	ii d	
Item paid for mending of the pageant	x d	
Item paid to a wright°	ii d	*carpenter*
Item paid for a new rope	ii d	
Item paid for mending of the angels	ii d	
Item paid for mending of the trumps°	i d	*trumpets*
Item paid for iiii angels' wings' hire°[2]	iiii d	*rent*
Item paid for putting home[3] of the pageant	v d	
Item paid for the pageant gear bearing to and fro[4]	iii d	
Item paid for costs when we went about pageant silver[5]	vi d	
Item in expenses for drink upon Corpus Christi Day by the way°	vi d	*route*
Item for players' supper & ours	ii s	
Item paid to a Sergeant that went with us at diverse° times	iii d	*different*
Item paid for ink, paper, & for writing	ii d	

Summa[6] xxx s ii d

Richard Yorke
William Thelle
John Lightlamp
Richard Sawer[7]

---

1 *putting forth of the pageant* This item and the one regarding the pageant's "putting home" (seven lines below) refer to taking the pageant wagon out of and returning it to its place of storage.

2 *wings' hire* Apparently the Mercers did not own their angels' wings outright, but rented them, perhaps from the Minster or some other ecclesiastical body.

3 *putting home* Returning it to storage.

4 *pageant gear bearing to and fro* Carting all of the things belonging to the wagon to and from storage.

5 *went about pageant silver* I.e., collected money for the costs of the pageant.

6 *Summa* Latin: Total.

7 *Richard ... Sawer* Ranking members of the Mercers' guild. Richard Yorke later twice became Mayor of York, in 1469 and in 1482.

from the City Chamberlains' Rolls: Account of Receipts for Station Placement (1462)

Another financial account from 1462 demonstrates other kinds of economic costs and benefits of the *Corpus Christi Play*. This itemized list, originally in Latin and here translated, gives the amounts collected from various bodies of people who paid for the stations of the play route to be located where they each desired. The city clearly made money from such rents, but there were also benefits to the renters. Presumably, the renter of the station had choice viewing spots—perhaps from their own place of business or residence—and businesses located nearby, particularly those selling refreshments, might benefit from the placement. Cultural prestige, too, was gained from being able to associate a station with your institution, home, or occupation. Piety may have also motivated these renters to want the very best viewing location. Note that in this year, only ten stations were used, rather than the common twelve, as represented on the map at the beginning of this volume.

Receipts for the Corpus Christi plays to be held this year at established stations[1]

...[2]

And of xiii s iiii d[3] from Nicholas Halliday and Adam Hudson for license of the Corpus Christi plays[4] to be held opposite the building on the holding at the gate of Holy Trinity in Micklegate this year.

And of vi s viii d from Thomas Scauceby, lord Thomas Wright, Thomas Kilburn, and others for the second station.

---

1 *established stations* The present text, edited for this volume by Christina M. Fitzgerald, is based on that found in *Records of Early English Drama: York*, 2 vols., eds. Alexandra F. Johnston and Margaret Rogerson (University of Toronto Press, 1976), vol. 1, 93 and vol. 2, 768–69. The original document is in the C3:3 roll, membrane 1, in the North Yorkshire County Library collection of Chamberlains' Account Rolls in York.
2 ... Only the parts of the record relating to the stations are presented here.
3 *xiii s iiii d* 13 shillings, 4 pence. See previous entry for explanations of the monetary system and of Roman numerals.
4 *plays* Although in English the York cycle was generally referred to as the "Corpus Christi Play" (singular), in the Latin from which this is translated, it is designated in the plural.

And of xi s from John Fulford and others for the third station this year.

And of xiii s viii d from John Beese, Richard Sawer,[1] Thomas Barbour, and others opposite the church of St. John the Baptist, namely, for the fourth station.

And of x s from Laurence Marshall, John Wath, and others in Coney Street for the fifth station.

And of vii s from Robert Butler, Thomas Hodgson, and others for the sixth station in Coney Street.

And of x s from John Sherwood and Robert Walker and others for the seventh station.

And of vi s vi d from Richard Key and others in Stonegate for the eighth station.

And of ii s iiii d from Peter Parrot, John Stalby, and others in the market-place for the ninth station.

And of ii s from Thomas Wrangwish[2] and others on the Pavement, for the tenth station.

Total iiii li. ii s. vi d.[3]

An Ordinance of the Tanners (1476)

The following ordinance from the Tanners—who tanned hide into leather—reveals some of the rules regulating the craft. This English ordinance supplements two earlier Latin ordinances from 1416 and 1428; later English ordinances were added in the sixteenth century. This particular ordinance demonstrates the ways in which the *Corpus Christi Play* and a craft's particular pageant were often intertwined with occupational duties. Almost every fee and fine mentioned here was to be

---

1   *Richard Sawer*   Sawer is one of the Master Mercers who signed the previous document.

2   *Thomas Wrangwish*   Wrangwish, another Master Mercer, would serve as Mayor in 1476 and in 1484.

3   *iiii li. ii s. vi d.*   £4 2s 6d. The abbreviation *li* for pounds comes from the Latin *librae*; the libra was a basic Roman unit of weight.

divided between the civic council (the "chamber" in this document) and the craft's financial upkeep, including the support of their pageant. The document also gives a sense of the general purpose of a guild: to train apprentices in the craft, to license new masters, and to oversee the quality of goods made and sold by the licensed members. This ordinance, like so many other similar documents, also shows the ways guilds levied fines on those outside their craft, again partly to support their pageant. Each guild designated "searchers" who searched out those who were not authorized to practice the craft or those from other towns and cities selling their wares in York (and therefore "foreign" to York); if these individuals were found to be producing the craft's goods, they were fined. Note, too, that even marrying a widow of a member of the guild requires paying a fee before being admitted to the occupation.

An Ordinance of the Tanners[1]
31 December 1476

Final day of December, 16 Edward IV.[2] Thomas Wrangwish,[3] Mayor of this city of York; aldermen[4] Thomas Nelson, John Gilliot, John Marshall, William Snawshill,[5] Christopher Marshall, John Glasyn, John

---

1   *Tanners*   The present text has been edited for this volume by Christina M. Fitzgerald. Spelling and punctuation have been modernized in accordance with the practices of this volume. The original document can be found in the A/Y Memorandum Book, York, North Yorkshire County Library MS E20, fol. 281v–282r. This present text is based on the version found in *York Memorandum Book Part II (1388–1493)*, Surtees Society vol. 125, ed. Maud Sellers (London: Andrews and Co., 1915), 166–67.

2   *16 Edward IV*   The sixteenth year of the reign of Edward IV (Edward the Fourth); i.e., 1476.

3   *Wrangwish*   Note that Wrangwish is one of the renters of a station in the previous document from 1462.

4   *aldermen*   Aldermen were the highest ranking members of the civic council. Although only eight are listed here, they numbered twelve in total and were therefore sometimes referred to as "The Twelve." Aldermen were generally part of the mercantile elite, and potential mayors were chosen from among their ranks. All but one of the eight listed here (John Glasyn) served as Mayor for at least one term.

5   *William Snawshill*   Snawshill was a master Goldsmith, a Sheriff in 1465, and Mayor of York in 1468. His former residence on a narrow lane off of Stonegate—part of the play route—has been restored to its fifteenth-century state by the York Archaeological Trust and operates as a tourist attraction called Barley Hall. You can view pictures and learn more about it on the Barley Hall website: http://barleyhall.co.uk.

Tonge, Robert Amyas; [members of] the Twenty-Four,[1] Richard Clay-broke, Thomas Catour, John Leathley, Thomas Alleyn, Thomas Marriot, William Chimney, Allen Wilberforce.

At which day in the council chamber of this City of York, by the instance[2] and full humble supplication of the whole craft of the Tanners of the said city, it was enacted, ordained, and established by the assent of all the council of the chamber from henceforth perpetually to be observed and keeped.[3] First, if there be any manner man that is not of the Tanner craft, and shall happen to wed and take to wife a widow of the same craft, then that man shall pay ere[4] he occupy [the craft], and by the searchers[5] of the said craft [be] admitted thereunto, xl s,[6] the one half unto the chamber of the city, and the other half to the supportation[7] of the pageant and charges of the said craft.

Item,[8] if there be any Tanner of the country that hath not been apprentice within this city, and will set up the craft and occupy as a master within this city, that then he shall pay at his upset[9] xiii s iiii d,[10] to the chamber and craft as is aforesaid.[11]

Item, whosoever of the said craft that is duly warned by his searchers to appear afore[12] them, for any matter concerning the honor of the city and the well[13] of his said craft, and willfully absent him and come not, to lose and pay at every time ii d, in manner and form above said.

---

1   *Twenty-Four*   The Twenty-Four were next in rank after the aldermen. In the fifteenth and early sixteenth centuries the Mayor, the Twelve, and the Twenty-Four were the effective members of government, together running its day-to-day business. Members of the Twenty-Four could rise to appointment to the Twelve, and from there to Mayor, as did William Chimney, who served as Mayor in 1486.

2   *instance*   Insistence.

3   *keeped*   Kept.

4   *ere*   Before.

5   *searchers*   The searchers were officials of the guild charged with seeing to it that regulations were followed by members; that no non-members were practicing the craft; and that new members were duly trained and admitted.

6   *xl s*   40 shillings. In Roman numerals *x* equals 10 and *l* equals 50. Placing the lower numeral before the higher one signifies subtraction; hence 50 (*l*) minus 10 (*x*) equals 40.

7   *supportation*   Support.

8   *Item*   Latin: Also.

9   *upset*   Setting up.

10   *xiii s iiii d*   13 shillings, 4 pence. See the first record here and its notes for detailed explanations of the monetary system and Roman numerals.

11   *aforesaid*   Stated before, aforementioned.

12   *afore*   Before.

13   *well*   Well-being.

Item, if there be any man of the said craft that after the searchers have made due search of his leather, and find it not sufficiently barked,[1] and warn him to amend it, and then the said man take upon him to sell any of the said leather not sufficiently barked, to pay and lose iiii s, in like manner and form as is aforesaid.

Item, if there be any man, master, or servant in the said occupation that taketh upon him to teach any other person that is not of the said craft, in any point belonging to the said craft, or to make leather hungry[2] within his own house, he to pay vi s viii d, to be divided in manner and form aforesaid.

Item, that the searchers of the said craft shall yearly have and receive of every foreign[3] barker[4] that cometh to this city and accustomably[5] selleth red leather or buyeth rough[6] within this said city, that they pay unto the sustentation[7] of the pageant of the said craft yearly, iiii d.

from the City Council Minutes: Two Judgments Concerning Pageant Costs (1517)

The two brief records excerpted here from the "House Books"—minutes of the York civic government—demonstrate the problems that the expense of the *Corpus Christi Play* could cause, despite the piety and civic pride that they might otherwise have engendered. When crafts fell on hard times, they petitioned the civic authorities for help to support their pageant, as the first record shows. But sharing sponsorship of a pageant could also cause tensions between crafts. As these records show, only six months after the City required the Vestmentmakers to share responsibility for the *Entry into Jerusalem* pageant with the Skinners, the City had to make peace between the two crafts by mediating the cost-sharing through the City Chamberlains, the civic financial officers. These two records are only one small glimpse of the stress and tensions that could arise from the *Corpus Christi Play*.

---

1   *barked*   Tanned.
2   *hungry*   Greedily.
3   *foreign*   I.e., from outside of York.
4   *barker*   Tanner.
5   *accustomably*   Customarily, habitually.
6   *rough*   Unworked leather.
7   *sustentation*   Maintenance, cost for upkeep.

27 May 1517[1]

...

Skinners & Vestmentmakers

At which day was put in a bill by the body of the craft of Skinners which then was considered by the said presence[2] that they were of little substance & was not able to bring forth their pageant. Wherefore the said day by the said presence it was ordered that the Vestmentmakers of this City shall be contributory to the bringing forth of their said pageant & to pay as the Skinners now does to the same. Provided always that & they cannot agree[3] what every man shall pay that then they to be ordered by the Mayor[4] for the time being, etc.

...

21 November 1517[5]

Skinners & Vestmentmakers

At which day it was agreed that for a peace to be had betwixt the Skinners and the Vestmentmakers, that from henceforth the Vestmentmakers shall pay yearly to the bringing forth of the Skinners' pageant—

---

1 *27 May 1517*   The present text has been edited for this volume by Christina M. Fitzgerald. Spelling and punctuation have been modernized in accordance with the practices of this volume. The original document can be found in minute books of the York council, known as the House Books, now York, North Yorkshire County Library MS B9, fol. 91v. The present text is based on the version found in *Records of Early English Drama: York*, vol. 1, eds. Alexandra F. Johnston and Margaret Rogerson (University of Toronto Press, 1976), 214.

2 *the said presence*   I.e., the civic council members present at the time.

3 *Provided always ... agree*   With the provision always that if they cannot agree.

4 *they to be ordered by the Mayor*   That they would be ordered to pay (a certain amount) by the Mayor.

5 *21 November 1517*   The present text has been edited for this volume by Christina M. Fitzgerald. Spelling and punctuation have been modernized in accordance with the practices of this volume. The original document can be found in minute books of the York council, known as the House Books, now York, North Yorkshire County Library MS B9, fol. 93v. The present text is based on the version found in *Records of Early English Drama: York*, vol. 1, eds. Alexandra F. Johnston and Margaret Rogerson (University of Toronto Press, 1976), 215.

every Master: viii d, & every Journeyman:[1] iiii d, & no more, to be paid without deny[2] over yearly to the Chamberlains' hands afore the feast of Whitsunday.[3] And then the Skinners to receive it at Chamberlains' hands and they[4] not to be charged with the reparations[5] of their pageant.

…

---

1 *Master … Journeyman* Master and Journeyman were the two highest ranks in a craft. An Apprentice, the lowest of three ranks, was still in training. A Journeyman had completed training but likely still worked for a Master craftsman. A Master had obtained or purchased the "freedom"—the right to trade free of tolls and fees—and generally ran his own shop or place of business.
2 *deny* Refusal, contradiction.
3 *Whitsunday* Another name for Pentecost, the seventh Sunday after Easter and ten days before Corpus Christi.
4 *they* Grammatically this seems to refer to the Skinners, but it is likely meant to refer to the Vestmentmakers, since they are the ones being charged a fixed fee.
5 *reparations* Repairs.

Selected Images

London, British Library MS Additional 35290, *The York Corpus Christi Play*, f. 236r (*The Assumption of Mary*), the "Register," or official copy of the cycle. The surviving text of this pageant is unique within the manuscript for its inclusion of musical notation. While a number of plays in the York cycle call for the performance of familiar melodies borrowed from the Church's liturgy, the six pieces from this pageant—three separate texts in two different musical settings each—appear to be original compositions created specifically for the Weavers. The scribe adds the notation on f. 236r at the moment when the angels attending the Virgin are to begin singing their second song. The text reads, "Veni de Libano, sponsa. Veni coronaberis" (Latin: Come from Libanus, wife. Come, you will be crowned. Song of Songs 4:8). All six songs are of a type known as the *gymel* (from *cantus gemellus*, Latin: twin song) and are in two voice parts written in alternating lines. The gymel, described by some late-medieval music theorists as a distinctively English form of song, is so called because the two parts begin and end on the same note but cross in between, with the two voices taking turns singing the higher pitches. Following the conclusion of the play in the manuscript, melodically more complex and rhythmically denser versions of each of the three songs appear, one following immediately after the other. In these settings, a greater number of notes accompanies each syllable of the Latin text, which remains the same. These longer runs, called *melismas*, tend to obscure the meaning of the text, even for audiences who understood Latin, by extending the space between the individual segments of words. Why the scribe would have included both a simple and a more complex musical version of each of the three sung texts remains one of the unresolved cruxes of the York cycle.[1] (Weavers' *Assumption*, from York Register. BL Additional MS 35290, fol. 236r. Copyright © British Library Board. All rights reserved/Bridgeman Images.)

---

[1] The present caption has been written by John T. Sebastian. The image also appears in color on the cover of this volume.

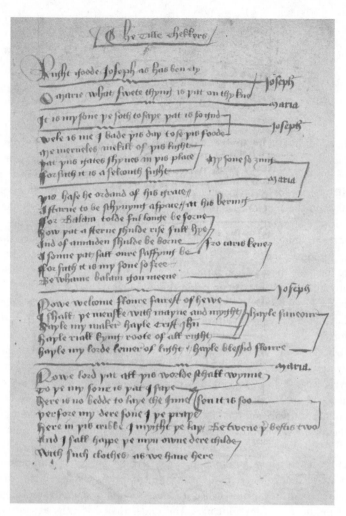

A page from the York Tile Thatchers' *Nativity* play, from the "Register," or official copy, of the York cycle (York, c. 1463–77), London, British Library MS Add. 35290, f. 54r. Like all the plays in the manuscript, this one is identified not by the play's name or subject matter, but by the producing guild—"The Tille Thekkers" in the original spelling—in the running heads at the top of each page. Speech headings are written in red to the right, not the left, and the beginning of a character's speech is signalled by a red line. The brackets indicate the rhyme scheme, and short lines are written to the right of the longer lines they follow.

A page from the York Girdlers and Nailers' *Slaughter of the Innocents* play, from the "Register," or official copy, of the York cycle (York, c. 1463–77), London, British Library MS Add. 35290, f. 79r. Like the page from the Tile Thatchers' *Nativity*, this page shows the guilds' names at the top ("The Girdillers and Nayle[r]s"). The brackets indicate rhyme scheme and stanza structure, and speech headings appear on the right. Character names are in Latin (mil and miles for "soldier," and mulier for "woman"), as they typically are throughout the manuscript, with the numbers in medieval-style Roman numerals, as well: i° for 1st, ij° for 2nd.

A page from the York Pinners' *Crucifixion* play, from the "Register," or official copy, of the York cycle (York, c. 1463–77), London, British Library MS Add. 35290, f. 184r. In this selection the soldiers (identified by an abbreviated form of *miles*, Latin for soldier) are making their first attempt to raise the cross. The soldiers are numbered in medieval-style Roman numerals: i°, ij°, iij°, and iiij° for 1st, 2nd, 3rd, and 4th. One of the main scribes of the manuscript has added some lines that he apparently had forgotten when first copying the play.

Adam and Eve tempted by the serpent in Paradise, and their expulsion from Eden, from the Holkham Bible (England, c. 1325–35), London, British Library MS Add. 47682, f. 4r. The image provides two episodes which are given separate pageants in the York *Corpus Christi Play*. The serpent appears with a woman's face, a common convention in medieval art and literature, suggesting that the serpent fooled Eve through familiarity. York does not explicitly follow this convention, although in the Chester *Adam and Eve* play, the Devil assumes the form of an adder with "a maiden's face."

Coment ue leng comenda a noel fauir bue airle et p metteir bue pauir de couf lefires pourle deinge.

Noah Building the Ark, from the Bedford Hours (Paris, c. 1423), British Library MS Add. 18850, f. 15v, a manuscript made for John, Duke of Bedford, and his wife, Anne of Burgundy, on the occasion of their marriage. Noah builds an ark that looks like a structure made more for land than for sea, dresses like a wealthy fifteenth-century citizen, and commands a large company of men who use late medieval tools and building methods. Like the plays, illustrations of Biblical episodes often symbolically brought the ancient, sacred world into the contemporary world of viewers and readers.

Scenes from the Infancy of Christ, leaf from an English Psalter (Canterbury, middle of the twelfth century), London, British Library MS Add. 37472, f. 1r. Many of the events from Jesus' nativity and infancy illustrated here mirror pageants in the York *Corpus Christi Play*. Top row: the angel appears to the shepherds; the Magi follow the star; the Magi arrive at Herod's court. Second row: Herod consults his counselors; the Magi leave Herod's court; the Magi present their gifts to the infant Jesus. Third row: the angel warns the Magi not to return to Herod's court; Mary presents Jesus in the temple; the angel warns Joseph to flee Herod's rage. Bottom row: the flight into Egypt; the slaughter of the innocents; the death of Herod.

Crucifixion scene from the Holkham Bible (England, c. 1325–35), London, British Library MS Add. 47682, f. 32r. As in the York *Crucifixion*, the soldiers struggle to erect the cross because the hole has been dug too wide. Unlike the York plays, multiple episodes are here presented simultaneously; much of what is represented here is depicted in the York *Death of Christ* pageant in addition to the *Crucifixion* pageant. York is unusual in separating the crucifixion from the death, and in isolating the crucifixion from those who mourn Christ's death, especially the "three Marys," depicted on the left of this image. (Holkham Bible Crucifixion. BL Additional 47682, f.32r. Copyright © British Library Board. All rights reserved/Bridgeman Images.)

The Harrowing of Hell, from the Gough Psalter (England, c. 1300–10), Oxford, Bodleian Library MS Gough liturg.8, f. 62v. Christ rescues Adam and Eve from the gaping jaws of a giant monster representing the entrance to Hell. A "hell mouth" is specified in the York Mercers' Indenture for their *Last Judgment* play, and the craft possibly had something like this image in mind. Such a "hell mouth" would likely also have been part of the Saddlers' *Harrowing of Hell* play.

The York Minster rising above the city, with a portion of the city walls in the foreground (2009, photo by Sam Nelson). Built in the late thirteenth and fourteenth centuries, York Minster remains one of Britain's finest and most important cathedrals and the seat of the Archbishop of York, and signifies the importance of the city in the Middle Ages. York has been defended by walls since Roman settlement, but they were altered and rebuilt over the centuries. The majority of the surviving walls date from the twelfth through fourteenth centuries. York has more miles of intact wall than any other city in England.

Micklegate Bar from outside the city wall (2009, photo by Sam Nelson). Micklegate Bar is one of York's four main gatehouses, or "bars" (i.e., barriers), which controlled entry into the city, allowed the collection of tolls—including from "foreign" merchants from outside of York—and provided a defensive position during war. Rebuilt in the fourteenth century from a twelfth century original, Micklegate Bar was the traditional entry for visiting monarchs, and was also used to display the heads of those executed for treason. Micklegate is the street which the gatehouse traverses—its name means "Great Street"—and just within the wall was the location of Station 1 of the play, in front of Holy Trinity Priory.

From the Publisher

A name never says it all, but the word "Broadview" expresses a good deal of the philosophy behind our company. We are open to a broad range of academic approaches and political viewpoints. We pay attention to the broad impact book publishing and book printing has in the wider world; for some years now we have used 100% recycled paper for most titles. Our publishing program is internationally oriented and broad-ranging. Our individual titles often appeal to a broad readership too; many are of interest as much to general readers as to academics and students.

Founded in 1985, Broadview remains a fully independent company owned by its shareholders—not an imprint or subsidiary of a larger multinational.

For the most accurate information on our books (including information on pricing, editions, and formats) please visit our website at www.broadviewpress.com. Our print books and ebooks are also available for sale on our site.

broadview press
www.broadviewpress.com

The interior of this book is printed on 100% recycled paper.